....

FOOD · WINE · BUDAPEST

....

FOOD

WINE

BUDAPEST

{ BY }

CAROLYN BÁNFALVI
PHOTOGRAPHS BY GEORGE KONKOLY-THEGE

A Terroir Guide

THE LITTLE BOOKROOM

© 2007 Carolyn Bánfalvi
Photographs © 2007 George Konkoly-Thege

Book design: Louise Fili Ltd

Library of Congress Cataloging-in-Publication Data
Bánfalvi, Carolyn.
Food wine Budapest / by Carolyn Bánfalvi
photography by George Konkoly-Thege
p. cm. — (Terroir guides)
ISBN 1-892145-56-1 (alk. paper)
1. Cookery, Hungarian
2. Cookery—Hungary—Budapest
3. Wine and wine making—Hungary—Budapest
4. Restaurants—Hungary—Budapest
I. Konkoly-Thege, George. II. Title.
TX723.5.H8B28 2007
641.59439--dc22
2007040932

Published by The Little Bookroom
435 Hudson Street, 3rd floor • New York NY 10014
editorial@littlebookroom.com • littlebookroom.com
Distributed by Random House.

Printed in China

Because two Hungarian letters have accents that are not available
in English type fonts (the "o" and the "u" with accents above
them that look like two long lines), those characters have been
replaced with "o's" and "u's" minus the Hungarian accents.

CREDITS:

The quotation on Page 17 from "The Cookery Book and the Toy Shop" from
The Knight of Dreams: The Journeys of Sindbad and Other Stories by Gyúla
Krudy, published by Noran Books, Budapest. Translated by Eszter Milnar.

The quotation on page 51 from "Sumach Trees in Blossom " from The Adven-
tures of Sindbad by Gyúla Krudy, published by Central European University
(CEU) Press, 1998. Translated by George Szirtes.

Page 113 from "Sunflower" by Gyúla Krudy, published by New York Review
Classics. Translated by John Batki.

The quotation on Page 265 from "Spring" from The Knight of Dreams: The
Journeys of Sindbad and Other Stories by Gyula Krúdy, published by Noran
Books, Budapest. Translated by Eszter Milnar.

All other Krúdy translations courtesy of Gabor Bánfalvi.

This book is dedicated to Gábor,

because it wouldn't exist without him,

and to Anna and Róza, because they

have been such good eaters right

from the beginning.

TABLE OF CONTENTS

· ·

INTRODUCTION

....

I T IS THEIR VITALITY AND LOVE OF LIFE THAT GIVES THE HUNGARIANS THEIR SPECIAL QUALITY... AND their food and cooking are as integral to their lives as they were in olden times. In Hungary the meal of the day is a ritual, not just a matter of filling the stomach. Sometimes Hungarians talk about the way things have changed. They are not at all sure that change means progress, but it has to be accepted. What else can you do? But however they may talk and shrug their shoulders, in their hearts the stubborn pride in an old and steadfast nation endures.

— *The Cooking of Vienna's Empire*,
JOSEPH WECHSBERG, 1968

Hungary is the right place to be for good eating and drinking. Hungarians are often passionate about food and wine—from the old ladies on the tram comparing cake recipes and the price of tomatoes to the young winemakers successfully resurrecting the country's long and proud wine tradition. There are radio programs devoted to cooking, and it's not surprising that Central Europe's first television channel devoted entirely to food is a Hungarian one (Paprika TV). On Sunday evenings buses and trains are filled with young people returning to Budapest with bags full of carefully wrapped containers of their mothers' food to last them through the week. There are beautiful ingredients, talented chefs and winemakers, and a long tradition of recipes and cooking techniques. While Hungarians tend to take the quality and variety of their produce for granted, the country has all of the raw materials necessary for great eating. In fact, Hungary's natural resources—rivers, valleys, volcanic hills with slopes facing the sun, plains, thermal springs, and a continental climate suitable for growing countless varieties of fruits and vegetables—are some of its best assets.

Despite its vast repertoire and variety, Hungarian cuisine is possibly one of the most under-appreciated and unknown European cuisines. There are few Hungarian restaurants outside of the country itself and there are few good Hungarian cookbooks available to the international market. Most people already know about paprika and "goulash" (although when they come to Hungary, they'll learn that their goulash is actually *pörkölt*). But goulash (*gulyás* in Hungarian) is just one of the many world-class dishes that define Hungarian cuisine. And despite what you may have heard, Hungarian food isn't all about paprika. Since Hungarian cuisine is so under-represented abroad, those who are interested in discovering Hungarian cuisine (and any epicurean should be!) must go to Hungary to sample everything firsthand, prepared with real Hungarian ingredients.

This book is for anyone who loves to eat and drink, and wants to discover the best that Hungary has to offer. This applies whether you have just a few days in Budapest and want to make the most of them by sampling the right foods at the right places, or you'll be here for a few years and want to seek out the best shops, markets, and restaurants to add to your routine. This book also provides a few starting points for wine trips in Hungary, some of which are easy day trips from Budapest. The Hungarian wine industry is young, dynamic, and relatively undiscovered outside of the country, which makes sampling Hungary's wines and visiting its wineries deliciously adventurous.

One obstacle to discovering Hungarian food and wine is the difficult Magyar language. Many good things tend to hide behind hard-to-decipher Hungarian names, and can easily remain that way. This book is a practical guide, which contains the vocabulary you'll need to dig deeper into Hungarian cuisine; restaurant, café, and shop reviews; and descriptions of Hungarian foods and wines. But it also goes into history and traditions, which will make it useful to Hungarian food lovers even when they're not traveling in Hungary. This book is also for anyone interested in Hungarian culture. Exploring Hungary's cuisine is one of the best routes into the country's culture, and you will quickly learn that food is extremely important to most Hungarians.

Budapest is a fantastic city, once nicknamed the "Paris of the East." It has wide boulevards, smoky bars, beautiful buildings, fancy restaurants, green parks, bustling markets, rocky hills, and the wide Danube running between Buda and Pest. There's a lot to do, see, eat, and drink here, and there's a reason so many expats suddenly realize that they've stayed years longer than they planned. They may like to complain about Budapest, but so many of them find it hard to pack up and leave.

Despite the fancy cars, the shopping malls, and the international chains of shops that are increasingly prevalent, it's important to remember that the Communist era is not such a distant memory in Hungary, especially for people working in the industries that were nearly destroyed during that period. Throughout my research for this book, nearly everyone I talked to, from winemakers and *pálinka* distillers to butchers and chefs, told me how difficult it has been, and still is, to undo the effects of Communism (which favored mass production without any regard for quality) and rebuild their industries and businesses. They complain about a lack of resources, bureaucratic difficulties, and getting little or no help from governmental organizations. "Our biggest disadvantage is that all of our traditions disappeared during the forty years of Communism. And worse, we don't have anyone to ask about our past traditions. We didn't just have to start from the beginning [in 1989], but from below the beginning," said Zoltán Radics, a butcher who specializes in Mangalica pigs and Hungarian Grey cattle, two indigenous animals that nearly died out during the Communist era. "I have visited farms in Tuscany and they have notebooks of all of their records for every year going back 150 years. We don't have any of that. We have had to learn everything by ourselves."

Radics was only one of the many people who expressed similar frustrations. But they're not giving up, and Hungarians seem to be hungry (and thirsty) for quality traditional products. It's hard to imagine how things must have been back then, before the country was nationalized. And it's heartbreaking to think of the traditions, skills, products, and resources that were lost. During the process of writing this book I've met enough passionate people to make me confident that things will continue to significantly improve every year.

Budapest was a thriving restaurant and café town before World War I. Half of the city's coffeehouses closed between the two world wars, and the scene never fully recovered. Bombs, guns, and looters destroyed renowned restaurants, cafés, and hotels during World War II, but even worse, the culture of eating and drinking was also greatly damaged. Following the war, whatever businesses had survived became nationalized and more or less uniform. "Hungarians don't even know what Hungarian food is," a winemaker's wife once told me. "During Communism we lost our cooking traditions." That may be true to a certain extent, but in my opinion, Hungary still has one of the great culinary traditions of Europe, and many old customs and recipes have been (or hopefully will be) resurrected. There are many who would agree, but Hungarians are also notorious for not really realizing just how special some of their traditions and products are. Perhaps what best characterizes good Hungarian cuisine is its use of everyday ingredients, prepared simply, but resulting in deeply flavorful dishes.

Although the restaurant scene got off to a slow start when Communism ended in 1989, since then it has changed dramatically for the better and there has been somewhat of a small business revolution. What hasn't changed is that Hungarians still love eating, and sometimes in surprisingly big quantities. While it will be a long time before Budapest's restaurants are as sophisticated as those in New York or Paris, there are many fine eateries in the capital and to a lesser extent in the countryside. Hungarian hospitality is justly legendary (though more so in the countryside than in busy Budapest), and in the right hands, you'll eat extremely well here. But like anywhere else, even the good restaurants can be inconsistent.

This is the book that I wish I had when I first moved to Budapest and didn't know where to shop, where to eat, or what kind of wine to drink. I had a shelf full of guidebooks, but none revealed the best place to buy good cheese, to get wine advice, or to sample the Mangalica pork.

During my years discovering Hungarian food, I've had some amazing eating and drinking experiences, and some I'd rather forget. It's always disappointing to have expectations of a good dinner then to get a meal cooked by a lazy kitchen, served by an indifferent waiter. For travelers with limited time to discover Hungarian cuisine, this is especially true. When I travel, every meal counts. Although museums and monuments are always important stops, it's sampling the food in a new country that makes traveling memorable.

Since my first trip to Hungary, I've been lucky to be surrounded by people who share my passion for good food, whether it was eating walnuts picked fresh from the tree or a drinking a glass of wine lovingly drawn from the barrel by a winemaker in his musty cellar. In this book I have concentrated on the many good things that Hungary has to offer and I hope it will help you discover everything that's delightful about Hungarian cuisine, guide you in navigating Budapest's restaurant scene, and inspire you to venture beyond the city to a winery or a food festival.

Jó étvágyat! Egészségedre!

Enjoy your meal, and cheers!

CHAPTER 1:

HUNGARIAN FOOD

Evés közben jön meg az étvágy.
Appetite comes while eating.

Ha már lúd, legyen kövér.
If it is a goose, it should be a fat one.

—HUNGARIAN PROVERBS

HUNGARY IS SO FAR FROM HERE!" SHE SAID AT LAST, STIFLING A SIGH. "IT IS HERE IN MY POCKET," Sindbad the Elder unexpectedly replied. "Since I find it impossible to eat the local fare, I carry a Hungarian cookery book about with me, and satisfy my appetite by browsing through it every day. It is true that it is not a work by anyone of note, it's written by everyone's Auntie Rézi, but from this book I can lunch and dine to my liking. Tonight I shall read the chapter on the various ways of preparing bean soup. For there a great difference in the preparation of French beans and kidney beans. And as I read, I hear the wind rummaging in the attic back home, where the beans are always spread out to dry. A cookery book such as this is your best friend abroad."

A smile flitted across Viola's face. "So the local fare does not suit your taste then?"

—*The Cookery Book and the Toy Shop,*
GYULA KRÚDY

HUNGARIAN CUISINE, PAST & PRESENT

....

THE STORY OF HUNGARY'S CUISINE IS INEXTRIC-ABLY LINKED TO THE COUNTRY'S DRAMATIC, complicated thousand-year history, in which food and wine show up at every twist and turn. Hungarian cuisine is the result of the mix of Hungary's indigenous recipes and cooking methods and the influence of those introduced by invaders, foreign royalty, and foreign chefs. Along the way, new ingredients appeared and were adopted by both peasants and nobility alike. Despite the tragedy that has punctuated much of Hungary's history, the country's kitchens have benefited from centuries of mingling with foreigners and their flavors. Long before the term "fusion cooking" was coined, techniques, ingredients, and ideas were borrowed and blended with Hungarian ones so seamlessly that the resulting dishes are now considered wholly Hungarian. But while Hungarians seem to have always been willing to experiment in the kitchen, their cuisine has retained its own characteristics through the ages.

Things have certainly changed since the thirteenth century when peacock was considered a great delicacy. *Gulyás* (better known internationally as goulash) and *pörkölt* (a slow-cooked stew seasoned with paprika) are probably the two dishes that define today's Hungarian cuisine more than any other. Even they have evolved over the years to incorporate paprika, tomatoes, and potatoes, which are New World ingredients that arrived in Hungary only a few hundred years ago. Though Hungary is now widely exposed to international culinary influences, its food is far from transforming itself into something modern or fusion. There seems to be an ethnic restaurant opening every week in Budapest, but many of the great chefs working in Hungary are now returning to the old ways of sourcing and preparing ingredients. Hungarian cuisine was once considered one of the world's greatest and most sophisticated, but the lack of ingredients, money, opportunities, and easy access to the outside world during the Communist era was extraordinarily detrimental to attitudes about food and cooking in Hungary, and to the food itself. These days there's a small—and hopefully growing

—resurgence of the old Hungarian ways of doing things and a return to old ingredients.

During the Middle Ages there was rigid class separation and a system of strictly regulated guilds. The butcher's guilds had a self-inspection system; the pharmacists made the pastries; and the bakers' guild even regulated what types of bread each baker could bake. "At the marketplace you could buy three kinds of bread, each one sold by bakers of three different ranks. The master baker baked the white bread and rolls. The 'middle' baker baked the everyday bread, and the black-bread baker the cheapest, unrefined loaves," wrote George Lang in *The Cuisine of Hungary*. "Anyone who didn't bake good bread was punished—the first time with a fine and the second time by a dunking in the Danube."

For more than two centuries royal cooks and chefs came from a village south of Lake Balaton called Nagyszakácsi, where young generations of chefs were trained by their elders and the favored were granted noble status. There's an annual festival today where chefs recreate both the medieval atmosphere and some of the actual dishes that were cooked back then. Hungarian cuisine really started to take shape during the reign of King Mátyás, who ruled from 1458 to 1490 and was just eighteen years old when he took power. The court chronicler recorded extensive details of the feasts and day-to-day eating habits of Mátyás and his Italian wife Beatrice of Aragon, who were perhaps the first Hungarian foodies. Some of the earliest documents relating to Hungarian food come from this era, and they elaborately describe the palace banquets and the workings of the kitchen. Beatrice brought Italian chefs and pastry chefs with her when she arrived in Hungary. She introduced garlic and onions, as well as pastas, certain herbs, chestnuts, and figs. Mátyás brought turkeys and turkey breeders from Italy; Hungarian turkeys today are among the best in Europe. Italian-style cooking spread beyond the palace to the upper classes, and with the new imported Italian techniques and ingredients, Hungarian cuisine became more refined. This was a time when chefs were highly respected and gastronomy was considered a hobby. Hungarian kings and aristocrats were (and have always been) devoted game hunters, especially in the Pilis and the Bükk hills where game is plentiful. Hungary was rich and powerful, and Mátyás brought Hungarian cuisine to a level matching the stature of the country.

The battle of Mohács in 1526 was another turning point for the country, which soon after split in three: the middle fell under Turkish rule, the northern and western regions were dominated by the Habsburgs, and Transylvania remained relatively independent. The Turkish occupation was devastating, but Hungarian customs and recipes changed little in many of the poorest and most isolated areas. Besides cabbage leaves, it now became common to stuff peppers, grape leaves, kohlrabi, and other vegetables with meat. *Rétes*, strudel originally made from filo, stemmed from Turkish baklava. The names of two beloved Hungarian snacks—*lángos* and *pogácsa*—are of Turkish origin and Hungarians probably learned honey-cake making from the Turks. Tomatoes, corn, and cherries were all introduced by the Turks. Most importantly, coffee and paprika arrived during this period. Though there are different theories about how paprika arrived in Hungary, it was most likely first grown by the Turks. The wealthier classes didn't adopt paprika until a few hundred years later (in the Ottoman Empire, paprika was used as a substitute for expensive black pepper), and it wasn't mentioned in cookbooks until the early nineteenth century.

The Turks were defeated in 1686 at the siege of Buda. The Habsburgs then took over and there were several peasant revolts against their harsh policies. When a Transylvanian prince, Ferenc Rákóczi, attempted to stage a war of independence, he sent Louis XIV barrels of Tokaj wine to woo him as an ally. The war didn't succeed, but in appreciation, Louis sent one of his own French chefs, who introduced French cooking methods and refined the Transylvanian cooking style. The first Hungarian-language cookbook appeared in 1695, and by this time the typical Hungarian use of sour cream and vinegar as flavorings was already commonplace.

During the time of the Austro-Hungarian Empire, the Habsburg court was based in Vienna and its cuisine was mainly French, which not only influenced the cooking of the individual aristocrats who came from throughout the empire to work there, but also the cooking habits of their home countries. There were a dozen countries that spoke sixteen different languages in the empire. "Each section influenced the others—to the point where it is often impossible to tell which dish originated where," wrote Lang in *The Cooking of Vienna's Empire*.

The Habsburgs attempted to Germanize everything, but Hungarian cuisine held its ground and a national revival movement and a strong sense of patriotism emerged. Writers and politicians traveled throughout the countryside in an attempt to document the folk customs and food there. Those travelers needed places to sleep and eat, and inns (known as *csárda*), pubs, and restaurants became widespread. Throughout the eighteenth century the Habsburgs used Hungary primarily for agriculture, which gave the Hungarians fantastic access to fresh ingredients. It became known as the "food basket" of Central Europe, and the quality and variety of Hungarian wine vastly improved since more attention was paid to the vineyards.

From the early eighteenth century, cookbooks and restaurants in Pest emphasized French dishes like pâtés, consommés, ragouts, and braised meats. But there was a stark difference between the way the upper and the lower classes ate, and the aristocracy saw the heavily spiced Hungarian dishes as peasant food. Despite the French influences in restaurants, home cooking didn't change much, though by the beginning of the nineteenth century even middle-class cooking had become more complex. After the failed 1848 revolution, potatoes became a staple in the Hungarian diet.

Joseph Marchal, known in Hungary as Marchal József, is the French chef credited with modernizing Hungarian cuisine into pretty much what it is today. From the early nineteenth century several chefs who were either French or trained in France worked in Hungary, but Marchal had the most lasting influence. Before arriving in the 1860s to cook at the restaurant of the Nemzeti Kaszinó in Pest (which was an exclusive club), he was Napoleon III's chef and had spent time working for the Russian czar. When he first arrived in Hungary he continued to cook the French way, but as he settled into life here, he experimented with mixing French techniques and Hungarian ingredients. Paprika and other spices were used more cautiously, and his food became generally lighter and more refined.

Marchal prepared the coronation dinner in 1867 for Franz Joseph in Budapest and he opened the luxurious Angol Királyno (Queen of England) hotel and restaurant in Budapest. There he trained the next generation of great Hungarian chefs, including József Dobos and Rezso Görög. Dobos went on to own a specialty food shop where he created the *Dobos torta*, which remains a popular Hungarian cake. Görög went on to work with Escoffier in France and was responsible for suggesting that chicken *paprikás* and *gulyás* be included on a menu in 1879, introducing the spice to the French. Hungarian writers and artists took a great interest in the culinary scene during the nineteenth century, spending their spare time in cafés and restaurants, and contributing a wealth of writings involving food and the city's illustrious coffeehouses.

János Gundel and then his son Károly were the next major influences in the Hungarian kitchen. János ran the luxurious István Foherceg (Archduke Stephen) hotel and restaurant, which was said to be one of the finest in Hungary at the time. His son, Károly, got his start here as a busboy. In 1910 Károly took over the run-down Wampetics restaurant in Budapest's City Park and in its place opened the Gundel Restaurant, which became known as one of the best restaurants in the world. Károly Gundel is credited with being Hungary's greatest restaurateur, also opening a Gundel Restaurant in the Gellért Hotel. János, Károly, and the kitchens at Gundel created dishes that became essential parts of the Hungarian repertoire, like *palócleves* and *Gundel palacsinta.* Like everything else in the country, Gundel was nationalized in 1949. Hungarian-American restaurateur and author George Lang renovated and reopened the place in 1992.

The golden age of Budapest's legendary coffeehouses was from the end of the 1800s to 1940. They were centers of intellectual and social life, and by 1900 there were nearly 600 in Budapest. "This was, of course, the peak of the coffeehouse culture in continental Europe, certainly in such cities as Vienna and Paris, but the coffeehouses of Budapest were different," wrote Hungarian-American historian John Lukacs in *Budapest 1900.* "To begin with, their history was longer. Whereas the Turkish habit of coffee drinking came suddenly to Vienna and Paris at the end of the seventeenth century, in Hungary it had come more than a century before." Coffeehouses were affordable and some were open twenty-four hours a day, which made them second homes for many people. Writers and journalists had their favorite tables and often wrote through the day at the noisy cafés on paper supplied for free by the waiters. By the turn of the century coffeehouses were becoming increasingly elegant. The New York Kávéház, which opened in 1894 and has recently been renovated, was considered to be the most stunning.

Hungary's punishment for being aligned with Germany and Austria during World War I was the Treaty of Trianon (1920), which was signed after the Treaty of Versailles and stripped the country of more than two-thirds of its territory. One-third of its citizens found themselves suddenly living outside of the new borders. These shifting borders have further increased the mingling of cuisines in the region, and ethnic Hungarians living in the countries bordering Hungary still cook the Hungarian way, with a touch of Romania, Slovakia, Serbia, Austria, Ukraine, Slovenia, or Croatia thrown in.

Coffeehouses remained popular between the wars (although their numbers decreased dramatically). World War II saw an immense amount of destruction in Hungary, particularly in Budapest, where the Germans and Soviets fought for two months in the 1944 Battle of Budapest. The Soviets stayed and the Communist era that would last for the next four-and-a-half decades began. Everything was nationalized and Hungarian cuisine, as well as life in general, suffered greatly. There were food shortages in the 1950s, standards were poor, and the emphasis was on mass production rather than quality. In many ways, things still haven't fully recovered.

Hungary's transition to democracy was smooth; the first free parliamentary elections were held in 1990. Budapest has rapidly modernized since then. New construction is constant, and many of the old buildings have been renovated and restored. Restaurants and bars are also booming once again, and so are cafés. Budapest could once again be called a city of cafés, only these days customers are typing on laptops instead of penning novels on paper. Either way, Hungary has come a long way since the days when peacock was a prized delicacy.

SEASONAL EATING

I N HUNGARY THE FOOD THAT COMES WITH THE CHANGING SEASONS IS AS EAGERLY ANTICIPATED AS THE SUN, the falling leaves, or the first snow. Holidays are closely associated with traditional foods, and the food can be more important than the holiday itself. In Budapest, holiday traditions and customs are generally less elaborate than in the countryside, but customs differ with every family. Consider yourself lucky if you're invited to a Hungarian home for a holiday feast. Bring an empty stomach and a bottle of wine for the host. Season by season, this is how Hungarians eat. (For further explanations of dishes and ingredients, see separate sections later in this chapter.)

WINTER (*Tél*)

Winters in Hungary seem never-ending. This is the season for heavy Hungarian dishes like *pörkölt*, *gulyás*, and fatty cuts of roasted pork. Cabbage and sauerkraut dishes like stuffed cabbage, *székelygulyás* (sauerkraut and pork stew), and roasted goose or duck with braised red cabbage are also best appreciated now. A shot of strong *pálinka* (fruit brandy) really does warm you up, and Hungarians swear by it to cure a winter cold. Another cure for the bitter cold is a mug of spicy mulled wine (*forralt bor*), which is sold on the street, in bars, and in restaurants. Colorful dried beans (*tarkabab*; borlotti beans) are available year-round, but are perfect for winter dishes like *Jókai bableves*. Nursing coffee along with a fancy piece of cake inside a warm café is another winter perk. The Christmas (*karácsony*) season kicks off in Hungary with Mikulás nap (St. Nicholas Day) on December 6 when children polish their shoes and set them out for Mikulás (St. Nick) to fill with goodies like chocolate and toys. If you've been bad, Mikulás' helper, Krampusz, will leave twigs instead. Between now and Christmas, bakeries and home cooks are busy baking roulade cakes filled with walnuts or poppy seeds (*bejgli*), which are a crucial part of the holiday season. December 24 is the big day, when the children are banished from the living room and the angels and Jézuska (baby Jesus) bring the presents and decorate the tree.

No Hungarian Christmas tree is complete without shiny pieces of *szaloncukor* (candies wrapped in colorful foil wrappers) decorating it. In the weeks running up to Christmas it's sold everywhere, by the kilogram from street vendors and at fancier shops and bakeries. It's customary to abstain from meat on Christmas Eve, so dinner revolves around fish. The meal most often starts with *halászlé* (fisherman's soup), followed by whole roasted fish or breaded carp and potato salad with tartar sauce. Christmas Day dinner was traditionally turkey, but these days seems to be anything from stuffed cabbage to roasted duck. *Borleves*, white wine soup thickened with egg yolks, is common at this time of year. Dessert is, of course, the *bejgli*, but *mákos guba* (bread pudding flavored with honey and poppy seeds) can also be served.

Like the rest of the world, Hungarians greet the New Year (called Szilveszter, because it falls on St. Szilveszter's feast day) with sparkling wine, and lots of it. Traditionally, roast suckling pig with horseradish and braised red cabbage was eaten on New Year's Day. These days the most significant food to consume is some form of lentils, which are said to bring money in the coming year. *Korhelyleves*—a tangy sauerkraut and sausage soup with sour cream—and sausages (more commonly frankfurters) are also eaten in the early morning hours. At midnight everyone gathers around to sing the rather solemn Hungarian national anthem.

SPRING (*Tavasz*)

Spring can take an agonizingly long time to make its first appearance, and the best places to await its arrival are the markets. You'll know the season has finally arrived when little bright red radishes, spring onions, pale green kohlrabies, and fresh green-stemmed garlic are piled on the market tables. A simple market meal this time of year would include bread, fresh butter (farm-made tastes even better now), new onions and garlic for eating raw, fresh cheese, and dried sausages (*kolbász*). Wash it down with a glass of rosé and a bowl of sweet strawberries. Later in the season, green peas and spinach arrive, and green and white asparagus makes appearances in soups and under sauces.

Easter (*húsvét*) is imminent when you see buckets of pussy willows for sale at the markets and on the street corners. The Easter meal is one of the biggest of the year with boiled smoked ham, freshly grated horseradish, boiled eggs, deviled eggs in homemade tartar sauce, light and fluffy Easter bread (*tejes kalács*, similar to challah bread), potato salad in tartar sauce, pickled vegetables, and walnut and poppy-seed rolls (*bejgli*).

SUMMER (*Nyár*)

When the perfumey elderflowers start blooming, summer has nearly arrived. When three-liter glass jars of small, warty cucumbers (*kovászos uborka*) begin popping up on doorsteps, windowsills, and terraces, fermenting in the sun, then summer has really arrived. There will be vast fields of pretty sunflowers (used to make sunflower oil) in the countryside and the markets in Budapest will be at their finest. Now is the time to order a juicy tomato salad or a cold fruit soup with your meal. Hungarians spend a lot of time canning summer fruits and vegetables for the rest of the year. Huge quantities of peppers and ripe tomatoes are made into *lecsó* (pepper and tomato stew). *Lekvár* (jam) and *pálinka* are made from apricots from Kecskemét and plums from Szatmár. Peaches are plentiful and several varieties of cherries begin showing up in June and July. From July to September juicy red watermelons, cantaloupes, and honeydews are sold at roadside stands and in the markets.

Landlocked Hungary has plenty of freshwater fish. At Lake Balaton and Rómaifürdo, there's nothing better than a plate of fried fish with fries and pickles during the summer. Now's the best time for drinking a *fröccs* (or a spritzer, see Chapter 3). Or go the non-alcoholic route and have a soda water with a splash of raspberry syrup or a homemade elderflower juice. Hungarians love to grill and to cook soups over open fires, and the *szalonnasütés*, or bacon roasting, is a favorite summer event. Boiled corn-on-the-cob is sold by street vendors everywhere.

AUTUMN (*Ősz*)

Vineyards are now bursting with the delicate grapes that will be harvested and soon turned into wine. Harvest festivals and processions are held throughout the country during September and October, but the harvest in Tokaj for the sweet wine only begins at the end of October, so the grapes have a chance to turn into sweet, shrively raisins for the *aszú* wine (see Chapter 2). The paprika that was harvested at the end of the summer was strung together and hangs in bundles several feet long in the regions around Szeged and Kalocsa. Chestnuts ripen in early autumn and roasted chestnuts are hawked on the streets. Rum-flavored chestnut purée, a favorite Hungarian dessert, is sold year round, but is best this time of year if it's freshly made.

Autumn, when restaurant menus are full of game, is the best time to sample things like venison, quail, partridge, wild boar, pheasant, wild duck, and rabbit. Hungarians take celebrating "name days" as seriously as birthdays. November 11 is the feast day of Saint Martin (*Szent Márton nap*), who was born in what is now Hungary, but what was then the Roman province of Pannonia. Legend has it that Martin was a devout hermit when he was asked to become the Bishop of Tours. He refused, hid in a goose pen, and then killed and ate one of the geese after their squawking gave away his hiding place. Ever since, it has been a Hungarian tradition to mark the day by eating goose (*liba*) and drinking the season's first wine (*újbor*). "He who doesn't eat goose on St. Márton's Day will go hungry all year," goes one Hungarian proverb. "St. Márton is the judge of new wine," goes another. It's more of a mystery how the day became associated with wine, since Márton was a modest holy man. No doubt, it's because the season's new wine is always released around this day.

GYULA KRÚDY:

HUNGARY'S GOURMET WRITER

....

HUNGARY'S FOOD IS CLOSELY ASSOCIATED WITH ITS LITERATURE, AND PERHAPS NO OTHER WRITER captures the romance of early-twentieth-century Budapest café society and the magic of Hungarian food better than Gyula Krúdy. Born in 1878 in eastern Hungary, he started writing for his local newspaper at the age of thirteen. Krúdy's move to Budapest in 1896 coincided with the beginning of the coffeehouse golden age, which deeply colored his writing and his life. Krúdy's Budapest was cosmopolitan and burgeoning. He loved good food, lots of wine, and women. He was prolific—writing more than fifty novels, 3,000 short stories, 1,000 articles, and seven plays—but chronically short of money. "He wrote because he had to. He never cared for his reputation. Some of his companions and admirers were writers, but he would never—absolutely never—talk literature with them. The topics that interested him were the preparation of certain standard Magyar dishes, the odd habits of attractive men and women, stories of the turf, and the fascinating legerdemain of certain people able to lay their hands on money whenever they had to," wrote Hungarian-American historian John Lukacs in a profile of Krúdy for the *New Yorker*. "He would tuck his sixteen pages into his pockets, hail a carriage or walk to an editorial office, and request his honorarium. Then came a long midday dinner…in a half-empty restaurant, where he would be surrounded by the silent, respectful service of the owner and the waiters. Then the turf, the gaming table, and the night life. By midnight, he would have little or no money left."

Krúdy wrote about both the Hungarian countryside and life in Budapest. His Sindbad (Szindbád) stories—surrealistic tales weaving fantasy with reality and death with life, published between 1911 and 1917—were his most famous. "By 1919 Sindbad's Hungary was dead," wrote poet and translator George Szirtes in an introduction to a Sindbad collection. World War I, followed by the Treaty of Versailles (which divided the country), forever changed Hungary. The country Krúdy wrote about was the Hungary of the past, even in his own time. Krúdy's contribution to Hungarian literature wasn't fully realized until years after he died—in debt and threatened with eviction. A very few of Krúdy's books have been translated into English. The rest most likely will never be since he is notoriously difficult to translate. "His prose is poetic, and profoundly national, soaked with history, with images, with associations, including not only words, but rhythms recognizable only to Hungarians," wrote Lukacs, who also referred to him as "a Magyar-writing Homer" and "the magician of the Magyar language."

Because he captures so much of the romance that I associate with the Hungary of the past, I've quoted him throughout this book. (While hard to find, film buffs may be interested in the 1971 Hungarian film *Sinbad*, which was based on Krúdy's life and his Sinbad stories.)

STAPLES &
SPECIALTIES

BREAD AND BAKED GOODS
(*Kenyér* and *Péksütemény*)

BREAD IS TAKEN SO SERIOUSLY IN HUNGARY THAT SOME PEOPLE WAVE A SIGN OF THE CROSS OVER a loaf before cutting into it. Bread is a necessity when eating the all-important bacon, salami, and *kolbász*, and it's also used to sop up the sauce when eating dishes like *pörkölt* and *székelykáposzta*. In Hungary the standard bread is thick crusted, golden colored, soft in the inside and crispy on the outside, and comes in distinctive oval-shaped loaves which have been slashed across the top and typically weigh one kilogram. Bread in Hungary is usually *fehér kenyér* (white bread) or *fél barna kenyér* (bread made with half white and half rye flour). In decent-sized shops there will be a bigger variety like *rozsos kenyér* (rye), *kalács* (challah), *korpás kenyér* (made with graham flour, wheat bran, and oat bran), *magos kenyér* (with added seeds), *diós kenyér* (with walnut), *olajbogyós kenyér* (with olives), *tönkölyös kenyér* (made with spelt), *kukoricás kenyér* (made with wheat flour and a small amount of corn flour), and *krumplis kenyér* (made with a small amount of potato added to the dough). The most common types of bread rolls are the airy *zsemle* (a round roll) and *kifli* (a crescent-shaped roll). For a country that loves its bread so much, there are surprisingly few quality specialized bakeries in Budapest. On the bright side, good bread can be found everywhere, even in the smallest convenience store.

Pogácsa is the most ubiquitous Hungarian baked snack, and it is thought to have developed during the Ottoman occupation. These little biscuits (often translated as "scones") come in many flavors, often in small almost bite-sized pieces. *Pogácsa* is almost always savory, and is often served at wine tastings, eaten on the way to work as a rushed breakfast, or as an anytime snack. Traditional varieties include: *tepertos pogácsa* (with cracklings), *sajtos pogácsa* (cheese), *túrós pogácsa* (curd cheese), and *káposztás pogácsa* (cabbage).

Lángos is the most Hungarian of street food. Back in the days when families baked their own bread, a little piece of dough was snipped from the end to make *lángos* for snacking. Today, the dough (which is best when it has potatoes mixed in with the flour) is shaped into wide, flat disks and deep-fried in oil. Sample *lángos* at the market, where it's almost always served. It's best when it's spread with sour cream and grated cheese and sprinkled with garlic. But it can be eaten plain, spread with jam, or topped with variety of other things. When you order *lángos*, make sure it's being fried to order, and not just sitting around and grabbed from a pile. A relative of the *lángos* is the *töki pompos*, a thick piece of bread (baked, not fried) spread with sour cream, cheese, onions, and chunks of bacon—almost like a pizza. Another common snack at festivals and in wine cellars is *zsíros kenyér*, or "fatty bread," which is a slice of bread spread with a thin layer of lard (goose and duck are the best, but it can also be pork), and then sprinkled with sweet paprika and thin slices of red onions.

CHEESE (*sajt*)

Hungary isn't known for its cheese culture, but cheese is an important part of the Hungarian diet, and is essential to many Hungarian recipes. The most common type of Hungarian cheese is fresh, young, unripened and meant to be eaten quickly. Generally, the markets (though not the Central Market Hall) are great places to buy fresh, homemade cheese, and a host of other dairy products like raw milk, whey, fresh butter, sour cream, and cream. Some of the cheeses you can expect to find at any well-stocked supermarket, specialty cheese shop, or market include: *Túró*, a lumpy curd cheese made with cow's or sheep's milk, and which accounts for half of all cheese consumed in Hungary. You will find it used in dishes such as *túrós csusza* (pasta with *túró* and sour cream) and *túrós gombóc* (dumplings made of *túró*). *Trappista*, a semi-soft cheese made from pasteurized cow's milk, is Hungary's other popular cheese. *Trappista* is a distant, milder cousin to France's Port Salut cheese, said to have arrived in Hungary through monks living in Bosnia at the end of the nineteenth century. *Gomolya* has been made for centuries by shepherds in the Alföld and Transylvania. Even today, you can see wooden huts set up on the Great Plain where cheesemakers sell big round balls of their homemade *gomolya*. Originally made from raw sheep's milk, today *gomolya* is also made from pasteurized cow's milk, and the rind is often rubbed with herbs or spices. It's also delicious when it's smoked. *Márványsajt* (which translates as "marble cheese") is Hungary's blue-veined cheese made from pasteurized cow's milk and aged for three to four months in humid cellars (now the fashion is to call this cheese *kéksajt*, or "blue cheese"). *Orda* is a whey cheese similar to ricotta (some Hungarian companies even label their *orda* as ricotta). It's sold pressed in white chunks (very similar to the Italian *ricotta salata*) and also in the more common creamy version, either plain, sweetened, or flavored with herbs. *Pálpusztai* is by far the stinkiest Hungarian cheese. It is a soft-ripened cheese created in Mosonmagyaróvár in the beginning of the twentieth century. It has an orange-colored rind and a creamy interior (similar to Limburger) and is sold in small foil-wrapped pieces. *Pannónia* is similar to Swiss Emmental and Gruyère. It is a semi-hard cow's milk cheese and has the characteristic big holes that Swiss cheese has, and a mild nutty flavor. It's one of Hungary's best commercially available cheeses. *Körözött* is a spread made from sheep's cheese (or curd cheese) spiced with paprika, caraway seeds, and garlic. Served as an appetizer, it's also known as *Liptauer* outside of Hungary.

SOUPS AND STEWS
(leves and pörkölt)

To most Hungarians a meal just wouldn't be complete if it didn't begin with a bowl of soup. A typical weekend home-cooked lunch starts with a big pot of *húsleves*, which is simple to prepare, but almost always turns out better at home than in restaurants. To me, *húsleves* is the most Hungarian of all soups. It is essentially a full-bodied, flavorful consommé made by slowly simmering beef and marrow bones (and other types of meat if they're on hand), and then adding carrots, parsnips, celery root, or other vegetables about halfway through. It's often served with very thin egg noodles. But the soup is just the beginning. After the soup, eat the tender boiled beef with mustard and horseradish. For the finale, spread the bone marrow over toast and sprinkle with salt, pepper, and paprika. A good *húsleves* is what many homesick Hungarians living abroad say they miss most. *Csontleves*, or "bone soup," is similar to *húsleves*, but is not as rich. It is broth made from bones and root vegetables, thickened with a little flour, with pasta or dumplings added. *Eroleves*, or "strength soup," is another similar consommé, but usually served with tiny quail eggs or matzo balls.

Some soups—particularly *halászlé* (fish soup), *Jókai bableves* (bean soup with sausage or smoked pork), and *gulyás*—are also hearty enough to be meals. And then there are the light herb and vegetable soups, which can be made from whatever is in season—asparagus, mushrooms, green beans, squash, dill—and thickened with sour cream. Chilled fruit soup (*hideg gyümölcsleves*) is a common way to start a meal when it's too hot for warm soup (and during the colder months, is often made from the supply of fruit that was canned at its peak; sour cherry soup being the most common).

GULYÁS VS. PÖRKÖLT

Gulyás is a soup. It's not a stew, as is commonly believed outside of Hungary. What people generally, mistakenly, think of as *gulyás* is actually *pörkölt* in Hungary. "Outside Hungary it has become usual to label all the dishes seasoned with paprika by the name of *gulyás* (goulash)," wrote Károly Gundel. "But by *gulyás* foreigners usually understand something vastly different than what we mean by it, and, without wishing to offend my colleagues abroad, I feel obliged to state that with few exceptions they ruin this excellent dish." *Gulyás* is so simple to prepare that it's surprising so many foreign chefs get it wrong. You start by sautéing onions in lard or smoked bacon fat (or these days, sunflower oil). Next, add cubed beef and sauté, followed by sweet paprika and garlic. Add water, simmer until the meat is tender, throw in a chopped tomato if you'd like, add cubed potatoes, and season with salt and pepper. *Gulyás* is usually served with *csipetke*, a tiny pinched pasta made from flour and eggs that's cooked directly in the soup.

While families and restaurants may have their own versions of *gulyás*, there are a few things that never vary: it should always be made from beef (if it's made from mutton, it's called *birkagulyás*) and wine or flour are never added. Many people add carrots and parsnips, but those aren't used in the strictly traditional recipes. A few linguistic notes: the word *gulyás* means cowboy (or herdsman), after those who invented the dish. *Bográcsgulyás* is simply *gulyás* cooked in a *bogrács* (cauldron). *Gulyás* is also a fairly common last name in Hungary.

Pörkölt is *gulyás* without the broth (or potatoes or *csipetke*). *Pörkölt* is a slow-cooked meat stew made with meat diced slightly larger that would be in a *gulyás*. It can be made from any kind of meat, and even fish. Essentially, *pörkölt* and *gulyás* start out the same way, but water is added to make the *gulyás* a soup. With *pörkölt*, the meat cooks beautifully in its own juices, which are thickened by lots of minced onions. *Pörkölt* is usually eaten with boiled potatoes, *galuska* (flour dumplings), or fresh bread.

If you're learning to cook the Hungarian way, the best place to start is with *gulyás* and *pörkölt*. Using these two dishes as a base, you can create countless others by making additions or substitutions. Use mutton instead of beef in *gulyás* and add green beans and sour cream and you'll have *palócleves*. Make a *pörkölt* and add sauerkraut and sour cream and you'll have *székelygulyás*. *Pörkölt* cooked in red wine is called *pincepörkölt* (cellar stew) and is often made at wine festivals. There are many more.

On restaurant menus the words *gulyás* and *gulyásleves* (*gulyás* soup) seem to be used interchangeably. But the whole idea of what a *gulyás* is and what a *pörkölt* is can be made even more mystifying by well-meaning Hungarian waiters (and even recipe writers and reference books) who confuse the already misunderstood term by calling what is clearly a *pörkölt* a *gulyás*. It may be an attempt to make things simpler for what they think are clueless foreigners, but this mislabeling just deepens the misunderstanding. There have been many occasions when waiters have described dishes to me by saying that it's a *gulyás*, when it clearly says on the Hungarian version of the menu that it is a *pörkölt*. Despite the fact that *gulyás* is one of the few internationally known (or mis-known) dishes, it's not a cliché. Hungarians adore *gulyás*, and *pörkölt* too, and eat them regularly.

Paprikás is considered to be an entirely different type of stew, and with *tokány* (a lesser-known stew), *gulyás*, and *pörkölt*, it makes up the four basic Hungarian cooking methods. "These names were not adopted from popular usage but were rather the result of a gentleman's agreement among restaurateurs to give uniform names to the different ways of preparation," wrote Károly Gundel. "It may happen therefore that these names do not always exactly coincide with the corresponding dishes in the different regions of the country." It seems as if regional differences are less pronounced these days, but for sure there are still a few regional specialties that are hardly found anywhere outside of their locality.

Paprikás dishes are made by slowly braising meat in a mixture of smoked bacon fat, onions, tomato, and paprika, and then served with a sauce made from the cooking juices mixed with sour cream. *Paprikás csirke* (chicken *paprikás*) is the best known, but *paprikás* can also be made with veal, lamb, or fish.

Tokány is similar to *pörkölt*, but the meat (usually beef or lamb) is cut into longer strips and is cooked in its own juices, with added vegetables or herbs (mushrooms, green peas, or peppers are most common), and often mixed with sour cream at the end to make a thick, creamy sauce.

At the end of the summer when tomatoes and sweet green peppers are at their peak (and are ridiculously cheap), Hungarians

PAPRIKA

....

APRIKA IS THE POWDER THAT RESULTS WHEN WHOLE DRIED PEPPERS ARE GROUND, AND IT'S true, Hungarians do love their paprika. According to the growers' association, each Hungarian consumes more than a pound of it annually. Elsewhere it seems to have never quite caught on. But in Hungary, paprika plays an essential role—adding heat, flavor, depth, and color—in many of the country's most beloved dishes. *Halászlé*, *gulyás*, *pörkölt*, chicken *paprikás*, and many others wouldn't be the same without it.

You can see the peppers in whole or ground form everywhere—hanging in strings at the markets; hanging from houses to dry in the sun; in tins, tubes, and jars; in souvenir cloth bags; embroidered onto tablecloths; and even in *pálinka*. In the paprika-producing regions of Szeged and Kalocsa, on the southern Great Plain (known as the Alföld), thousands of strings of deep red peppers hang from houses, fences, and windows, to dry before they're ground (traditionally ground as grapes were once pressed, by stomping on the pods in bare feet, commercial paprika-making today is done entirely by machine in modern plants). While in the rest of the world it may be sprinkled in pinches, here it's scooped by the tablespoon. "Paprika is to the Hungarian cuisine as wit is to its conversation—not just a superficial garnish, but an integral element, a very special and unique flavor instantly recognizable," wrote George Lang. Most Hungarian kitchens have several jars of paprika, ranging from *édes* (sweet) to *eros* (hot), and everything in between. Little bowls or shakers of paprika sit next to the salt and pepper in restaurants and in homes. Considering its abundance, it's not surprising that it was a Hungarian, Albert Szent-Györgyi, who won a Nobel Prize for science in 1937 for discovering that dried paprika is a rich source of vitamin C, even more so than citrus fruit.

Paprika hasn't always been synonymous with Hungarian food. Peppers were unknown to Europe until after Columbus reached America. It's known that they arrived in Europe in the sixteenth century and became widespread in Hungary in the seventeenth century. By the mid-eighteenth century, paprika had become a wholly Hungarian spice. But there are several theories about how the pepper plants got to Hungary. One claims they were brought by the occupying Turks. Another that they were brought from the Balkans by people fleeing from the Turks. Paul Kovi, author of *Transylvanian Cuisine*, theorized that the peppers were from China, rather than the Americas. Yet another theory holds that paprika seeds were brought to Hungary by Bulgarian farmers. Since seasoning with ground paprika was cheaper than using fresh peppers it was used mainly in peasant cooking in the beginning and wasn't adopted by the aristocracy until much later. Once the spice caught on, it conquered Hungarian cuisine.

While vital to Hungarian food, there are countless dishes that *don't* call for it. Before it became an essential element of the Hungarian kitchen, paprika was primarily used for medicinal purposes (and before that it served only decorative purposes). It was prescribed as a cure for malaria, and it was commonly applied to wounds for its healing effects. Paprika was also once said to be a home remedy for ailments ranging from diabetes and rheumatism to colds and stomach aches. Some Hungarians even credit their glowing skin to paprika, also known as "red gold" in the southern cities of Szeged and Kalocsa, where most of it is grown.

Paprika peppers are harvested by hand in stages, since they ripen at different times. They're then strung together and hung out to dry in the autumn sun (or are oven-dried at the commercial manufacturers). While they dry, the peppers further ripen, turning shades of brown and rich red. They're then ground to different degrees of coarseness, the seeds releasing oils essential to the grinding process, as well as heat. For sweet and mild varieties, the seeds are removed and washed to dull the hotness, and the insides of the peppers are scraped. Before 1859 there was no such thing as sweet paprika (that is, paprika that's not hot). The technique for removing the veins and seeds (which contain the hot capsaicin) was invented in Szeged, and since the sweeter version was more palatable to more people than the hot, this helped paprika gain popularity. Today dozens of different paprika strains are grown. See page 280 for advice on choosing paprika at the market.

buy bags of them to make *lecsó*, which is canned to last through the winter. *Lecsó* is peppers and tomatoes, cooked with onions and a little oil or lard (but mostly in their own juices), almost like a stew. It's often called a Hungarian ratatouille. It's an all-purpose dish that can be eaten on its own, with *túrós csusza* (pasta with curd cheese), eggs, bread, or sausage. It's also frequently added to recipes as a substitution for fresh peppers or tomatoes.

PICKLES (*savanyúság*)

Savanyúság (pickled vegetables and fruit) play a hugely important role in Hungarian cuisine. Pickling was originally a way to process surplus produce during the summer, preserving it for the lean winter months. Despite being practical, pickled vegetables are also the ideal accompaniment to heavy, meaty Hungarian meals. All of the markets have stalls selling nothing but pickled fruits and vegetables. Hungarian sauerkraut—*savanyú káposzta* or *Vecsési káposzta* (named for the town that specializes in producing it)—is generally crispier than its counterparts abroad, and is sold by the kilogram, straight from the barrel. Melons, plums, beets, tomatoes, peppers, and cauliflower are pickled, and, of course, so are cucumbers. Colorful peppers are stuffed with sauerkraut and dyed red with beet juice. *Csalamádé* is a mix of shredded pickled vegetables, most often cabbage, peppers, carrots, and onion. In the summer when there are more ripe cucumbers than anyone knows what to do with, *kovászos uborka* (fermented cucumbers) are made from the small, warty, unwaxed gherkin cucumbers. They're stuffed into a big jar with a sprig of dill, covered with water, sprinkled with a little salt, and topped with a slice of bread (to promote the fermentation). After a few days in the sun, they're ready to eat. In Hungary, where nothing is wasted, even the cloudy pickle juice is drunk, sometimes mixed with soda water.

FOIE GRAS (*Libamáj or Kacsamáj*)

Order foie gras in Hungary and you'll be presented with thick slabs so tender they melt in your mouth. Most foie gras lovers would be surprised to learn that their pâtés, terrines, and mousses, (which were likely imported from France) actually originated in Hungary. Hungary is the biggest foie gras producer in the world, producing sixty percent of the world's supply and exporting more than 1,900 tons of it annually. Most of it ends up in France (where seventy percent of the world's foie gras is consumed), where it arrives raw and is then processed and spiced according to French recipes. Foie gras is a fixture on restaurant menus in Hungary with nearly every one offering at least one variation, and sometimes half a dozen. Hungarians tend to prefer their foie gras simply prepared. It's often seared, roasted, or grilled whole with little else but salt added. Purists will say that there's no better way to cook foie gras than in its own fat, just long enough so it's still a little rare in the middle. It can then be eaten hot, or chilled and served with toast and red onion slices. But foie gras is prepared in a variety of ways, and a glass of sweet Tokaji *aszú* is the traditional match.

Foie gras can be the liver of a duck or goose which has been grossly fattened from the force-feeding of corn several times daily for up to six weeks. Duck liver (*kacsamáj*) has become increasingly common because it's cheaper to produce than fattened goose liver. Goose liver (*libamáj*) is generally thought to be superior, with a more subtle flavor, and it's significantly larger. Goose was traditionally important to the diets of European Jews, who ate the prized livers before Hanukkah and Passover. They made the fat into schmaltz, which was added to cholent, and used for cooking and baking. The goose meat was reserved for the holiday meal. It's thought that the Hungarian Jews brought their knowledge of goose farming with them when they migrated from Alsace and the Rhineland to Hungary between the eleventh and fifteenth centuries. Jewish goose farms became plentiful in eastern Hungary, where most of the country's goose farming is still done today. As it is nearly everywhere else, the future of the Hungarian foie gras industry is uncertain, as the EU is considering banning its production. Until then, Hungarian researchers are exploring more humane ways of producing foie gras.

FISH (*hal*)

Hungary has no sea, but it does have an abundance of freshwater fish from the lakes Balaton and Tisza and the rivers Danube and Tisza. Still, Hungarian cuisine is obviously limited in the fish and seafood departments, and also in the cooking methods used to prepare the fish that it does have. In ancient times, Hungary had a greater variety of fish, and the swampy areas of the Great Plain were said to hold varieties no longer found today. Crayfish, too, were once abundant, but are practically non-existent today. Old Hungarian cookbooks describe recipes for freshwater crayfish soups, stews, sauces, and crepes.

Hungary's most common fish is the *ponty*, a variety of carp native to the Danube river system. These days, however, most *ponty* comes from farms. While it's eaten year-round, it comprises one of the main dishes typically eaten on Christmas Eve. *Ponty* has soft, brownish flesh, and is very boney and fatty. *Fogas* is pike perch from Balaton. It's silver skinned and lean. Young pike perch is called *süllo* or *fogas süllo*. Zander is the German name for *fogas*, and it's also often translated that way in English on menus. *Fogas*—with its delicate, firm, white meat—is excellent when simply fried or grilled. Another commonly found fish in Hungary's rivers and lakes is *harcsa*, or catfish. This flavorful scaleless freshwater fish can reach 150 kilograms in weight and is best when made into *pörkölt* or *paprikás*.

When it comes to seafood, linguistics can confuse things. The word *rák* can refer to any type of crustacean (with the exception of lobster, which is *homár*), including crayfish, crab, and shrimp—which means that menus will often mistranslate into English what sort of *rák* they are serving. Blame it on the lack of a sea, but most Hungarians don't seem to know the difference between a shrimp and a crab. Other fish found in Hungary are *csuka* (pike), the long-nosed *kecsege* (sterlet, a relative of the sturgeon), *pisztráng* (trout), *busa* (silver carp), and *keszeg* (rudd, which is a small boney fish).

MEAT, SAUSAGE, SALAMI, AND BACON
(*hús, kolbász, szalámi, and szalonna*)

In Hungary, butcher shops thrive and the neighborhood markets are full of meat counters. Either because they're economical, waste averse, or just plain practical, Hungarian cooks embrace every part of the animal—even the ugly parts—and work wonders with them.

Cattle was the largest Hungarian export for centuries, and in the past much of the food here was prepared from beef. These days, however, pork is the meat of choice and Hungarians live by the philosophy that a little bacon makes everything better. Pork is not only more prevalent in Hungary, but it also wins out over beef in terms of taste. Hungarian pork is flavorful and tender, where beef tends to be tough and often flavorless. "After World War II there was collectivization and there wasn't much food for fifteen years. The government wanted to feed people and decided that its policy would be to raise cheap chicken and pork, which they did well. But that was to the detriment of cattle and beef," said Zoltán Radics, a butcher. "Before then we did have a big beef culture, but during the Communist era, cows were basically used just for milk." Hungarian beef is too dry, said Radics, and

HUNGARIAN
HERITAGE BREEDS

....

T HE DOZENS OF BREEDS OF ANIMALS NATIVE
TO HUNGARY ARE AN IMPORTANT PART OF THE
country's history and its cultural heritage. Hungarians
are proud of their Hungarian specialties (which they like
to call *Hungaricums*, see page 295), but would be hard
pressed to name any indigenous animal other than the
Mangalica pig, Hungarian Grey cattle, and possibly the
Racka sheep. Despite the fact that protected indigenous
breeds are considered to be national treasures (and their
breeding is partially state subsidized), many began to
severely decline after World War II and others were threatened with extinction until conservation programs were
developed in the early 1990s. Today, these native animals
live primarily on the Great Plain in Hungary's two largest
national parks, Hortobágy and Kiskunság (both UNESCO
world heritage sites). In culinary terms, Mangalica pork
and Hungarian Grey beef products are becoming increasingly available, though Racka mutton is harder to find.

The Racka sheep (*Racka juh*), also called the Hortobágyi Racka, has distinctive long horns that twist straight up
like corkscrews and can reach a length of two feet. Once
plentiful in the Great Plain, with the introduction of the
Merino sheep in the eighteenth century, the population
declined and never recovered. Meat from Racka lamb and
sheep is darker than other lamb and mutton, but it's tender
and very flavorful. Though it was once sold in the markets
all over Europe, it's now still unusual to find it in Hungarian markets and restaurants (try the MOM Park organic
market on Saturday morning; see page 285).

THE MANGALICA PIG (*Mangalica disznó*)

Curly haired Mangalica pigs came frighteningly close to
extinction, only to be revived in the early 1990s. The breed
was developed in the 1830s when the market demanded an
animal with tastier, fattier meat. It was the biggest success
of nineteenth-century Hungarian animal breeding, and

Mangalica sausage and salami were popular throughout Europe. After World War II, the demand for leaner meat and the widespread use of sunflower oil for cooking hurt the Mangalica and its breeders. "Older people are very familiar with Mangalica because it was home raised until the 1960s," said Zoltán Radics, a butcher who owns two shops specializing in Mangalica pork and Hungarian Grey beef (in the Fény utca piac; see page 282). "In the 1960s and 1970s, the government wanted to feed people with cheap mass-produced meat and these modern breeds of pork, which were easier to raise, pushed the Mangalica farmers out. It was probably a general phenomenon around the world, but here it really affected the Mangalica breed."

Mangalica pigs traditionally spent much of their lives roaming the woods, which is why they were so poorly suited to the Communist-era industrialized pig farms. The Black Mangalica died out in the 1970s and by 1993 the Red Mangalica and the Swallow-Bellied Mangalica were down to just a few dozen registered sows. The Blonde Mangalica (the most common variety) went from being nearly the only kind of pig in Hungary at the beginning of the twentieth century to reaching the edge of extinction. The entire breed would have died out by the early 1990s if it weren't for the gene banks that had preserved a small number of Mangalicas on cooperative farms and in the national parks.

Meanwhile, a Spanish company called Jamones Segovia saw the Mangalica (with its high-fat content) as an ideal breed for its premium dry cured jamón Serrano and jamón Ibérico. The company, along with a Hungarian agricultural engineer, started reviving the breed, which was long prized for sausage and salami making. Their Mangalicas are born, bred, and butchered in Hungary and spend their days freely foraging for food. The ham, shoulder, and loins are sent to Spain to be cured and aged. The thick layer of fat (meant to insulate the Mangalica from cold Hungarian winters) turned out to be ideal for preventing the meat from drying out in the Spanish cellars. The remaining parts are turned into various types of *szalonna*, *kolbász*, and *szalámi*, and are sold in Hungary.

Today the number of registered Mangalicas is at more

than 5,000 and breeding has become more intensified and organized. Slow Food has recognized Mangalica sausage and made it the first Slow Food presidium in Hungary (a designation meant to promote artisanal products). Despite the greater interest in Mangalica products, it's still not widely available in Hungary. Luckily, Hungarian restaurants have also rediscovered how extraordinarily flavorful Mangalica pork is and it's increasingly appearing on menus. Since Mangalica is still relatively rare, prices are considerably higher than for regular pork. It's more tender than regular pork and because it's fattier, with marbling that looks like a good steak, it's more flavorful too. Mangalicas yield up to sixty percent lard and bacon, but the meat is said to be healthier than regular pork, as it's higher in unsaturated fat. "It's the best meat for grilling in the world," said Radics. You'd be missing out if you left Hungary without sampling it.

HUNGARIAN GREY CATTLE
(szürkemarha)

Hungarian Grey cattle are cherished national icons, and after being threatened with extinction just a few decades ago, they are lucky to exist. Until the beginning of the twentieth century, Hungarian Grey cattle—which have silvery hair and exotic-looking long black and white horns—were the most important breed in the country. In 1870 they made up ninety-nine percent of Hungary's cattle population, but by the end of the 1960s they comprised less than one percent of it. The entire breed consisted of just three herds with a total of 200 cattle.

Theories differ about the origin of the Grey cattle, but it is know that they were the dominant breed by the fifteenth century. Until the eighteenth century their tasty beef was sought after throughout Europe. Things started to decline in the seventeenth century when they began to be used primarily as draught oxen, but after World War I tractors began to replace them. The situation briefly improved when the 1929 economic crisis brought an increased role for the Grey cattle in agriculture. But since Grey cattle mature more slowly and produce substantially less milk than other breeds, they didn't fit into the Communist-era economic model, which valued quantity over quality. By 1966 a few elderly farmers, who had kept their Grey cattle out of attachment, were practically the only ones who owned them. By this time only three state farms had small herds, from which all of today's Grey cattle originate. It was illegal to mate Grey cattle, and the breed only survived because a few breeders at the state farms consciously broke the law and bred them anyway. Because of their devotion, there has been a steady increase in the population of Grey cattle since the 1970s and the breed is no longer considered endangered. Breeding Hungarian Grey cattle isn't profitable, but it's done because the breed is an important part of Hungary's heritage.

Relatives of the Hungarian Grey cattle include the Italian Chianina (best known for its *bistecca Fiorentina*) and the Texas longhorn (another breed saved from extinction). Most Grey cattle are raised under natural conditions and spend their days grazing. Cuts of Grey beef can also be difficult to find in Hungary, but salami and dried sausages are more common. Despite their tasty meat, which is far superior to the rest of Hungary's beef, the Grey cattle are considered no more than a curiosity by most people. It is, after all, considerably more expensive than ordinary Hungarian beef. "Grey beef is a big fashion these days," said Radics. "It has a deeper flavor, maybe because of genetic differences, but probably because of the way they're raised."

doesn't have enough marbling or fat to make it tasty. "Farmers lost their know-how for raising good beef cattle," he said.

Today Hungarian cooking depends on pork and it's added to practically everything. It's stewed, breaded, fried, roasted, braised, eaten in big steaks, and seasoned and stuffed into sausage casings. Pork fat (or goose or duck fat) is made into *teperto* (cracklings). *Kocsonya*, generally a winter dish, is pork jelly with a mix of pig parts like feet, ears, and snouts, and extras like hard boiled eggs, which are set into gelatinous aspic made from rich meat consommé. Ground pork is used for stuffing vegetables like cabbages (*töltött káposzta*), peppers (*töltött paprika*), and kohlrabi (*töltött karalábé*).

Hungary has been long known for the quality of its turkey, much of which is exported to Britain. Chicken is also popular in Hungarian cooking, and gorgeous, small, farm fresh chickens can be found at the markets. Most restaurants offer a few different duck dishes, and Hungarian chefs are generally talented at cooking duck. Most of the geese farms are on the Great Plain and in the eastern part of the country, and crispy goose leg served with red cabbage is a Hungarian classic. Game is popular in Hungary, and Hungarian chefs are also generally talented at preparing it. Hunting is a big business here, and big game (*oz*) like Red deer, Fallow deer, Roe deer, and *vaddisznó* (wild boar) are common, and so is small game like *vadkacsa* (wild duck), *fácán* (pheasant), *nyúl* (hare), pigeon (*galamb*), and partridge (*fogoly*). Generally, game is sold frozen at the markets and at some butchers.

In Hungary, the importance of *kolbász* (sausage), *szalámi* (salami), and *szalonna* (bacon) is evident at the markets. Sausage and salami making are essential parts of Hungary's culinary culture and sausages are eaten for breakfast, lunch, and dinner. At the butcher—above the stacks of bacon and between the dangling white salamis—hang row after row of pairs of dried sausages in different shades of red and orange, each slightly different. Sausage making is also an important element of the traditional village pig slaughter, and every family has its own preferred method. Fresh sausage (*friss kolbász*; which needs to be cooked) comes in three basic varieties: *kolbász* (purely meat and seasonings), *véres hurka* (blood sausage), and *májas hurka* (liver sausage). Cured and dried sausages (*száraz kolbász*) are made almost exclusively from pork, with the biggest difference between them being how heavily seasoned with paprika they are, how hot they are, and how dry they are. These are a few commonly found types: *csabai* (named for the town of

Békescsaba, these are firm, smoked, pork sausages seasoned with hot and sweet paprika), *csípos kolbász* (seasoned with hot paprika), *házi kolbász* ("homemade sausage"), *paraszt kolbász* ("peasant sausage"), *gyulai* (firm, medium-spicy, smoked sausage made from pork and bacon with a distinctive paprika and garlic taste), and *vastag kolbász* ("thick sausage"). *Disznósajt* is head cheese, shaped like a sausage and eaten in slices. There's a great variety of bacon at the markets, and it comes in the form of thick slabs, with the rind still on. It's smoked, boiled, salted, or raw, and there's a great difference in the ratio of fat and meat between the different varieties. Bacon fat is rendered and used for cooking and smoked bacon is sliced and eaten raw with bread. A little bit of smoked bacon is a wonderful way to give a boost of flavor to just about any Hungarian dish.

When Hungarians speak of salami, they are almost always referring to *téli szalámi* ("winter salami"), the most ubiquitous kind. *Téli szalámi*—a firm, mildly spiced salami made with finely chopped pork—has a vibrant pinkish red interior, with an exterior coated with grayish white mould. It's smoked for a few weeks, matured for two to three months, and made from pigs specially bred for salami. Today, the salami is still primarily made by the two companies who first produced the stuff: Pick Szeged (founded in 1869 in Szeged) and Herz (founded in 1882 in Budapest). It's not a coincidence that both factories are located next to rivers. "*Téli szalámi* is ripened just like cheese. In the old days the salami master always kept the salamis in certain places in the ripening room and he knew which windows to leave open so the breezes from the Danube would hit them the right way," said Levente Zelenák, a bioengineer at the Hungarian Meat Research Institute, speaking of Herz salami. "The air from the Danube has a microbiological bacteria that helps with the ripening effect.

MEAT TRANSLATOR

bárány: lamb	*csülök:* knuckle
birka: mutton; also called *juh*	*hús:* meat
borda: cutlet	*jérce:* pullet
borjú: veal	*kacsa:* duck
borjúláb: veal foot	*kakas:* rooster
borjúmirigy: veal sweetbreads	*liba:* goose
csirke: chicken	*máj:* liver

malac: suckling pig

marha: beef

nyelv: tongue

oz: venison

pacal: tripe

pulyka: turkey

sertés: pork; also called *disznóhús*

sonka: ham

szalontüdo: lungs (or lights); or *tüdo*

tyúk: hen

vadhús: game

vaddisznó: wild boar

velo: marrow or brains

velorózsa: brains

veloscsont: bone marrow

COOKING STYLES

angolosan: rare

egész: whole

fott: boiled

füstölt: smoked

grillezett: grilled

jól átsütve: well done

kemencés: cooked in a brick oven

közepesen átsütve: medium

párolt: braised or steamed

rántott, rántva: breaded and fried

rostélyos: braised steak

serpenyos: cooked in a skillet

sült: roasted; also *roston sült*

szelet: slice

töltött: stuffed

MEAT MAIN COURSES & PREPARATION STYLES

THERE ARE AS MANY MEAT DISHES AS THERE ARE COOKS IN HUNGARY, AND THIS IS BY NO MEANS A comprehensive list. This list includes some of the most common dishes, as well as some traditional ones which aren't as widely available. Be aware that recipes for these dishes can vary from restaurant to restaurant, although the idea behind them should be generally the same. A wide variety of starchy *köret* (side dishes) could be served with meat in Hungary like boiled potatoes, potato croquettes, rice, bread dumplings, or french fries.

Bakonyi módra: Meat served with mushrooms in sour cream sauce.

Bécsi szelet: Wiener schnitzel in Hungary is generally breaded pork, rather than the traditional veal. If it's veal, it's often referred to as *borjú bécsi.*

Brassói aprópecsenye: Traditionally this dish is bite-sized pieces of sautéed pork, mixed with deep-fried cubes of potatoes, and seasoned with lots of sweet paprika, dried marjoram, garlic, salt, and pepper. In restaurants, the meat is sometimes served in a whole piece, rather than small pieces.

Budapest bélszín: Steak served with a rich sauce made from chopped peppers, tomatoes, sliced mushrooms, peas, and chunks of goose liver.

Cigánypecsenye: "Gypsy roast" is a pork cutlet sprinkled with paprika and topped with raw crushed garlic and a chunk of roasted *szalonna*.

Cordon Bleu: A breaded and fried chicken breast stuffed with ham and cheese. This dish didn't originate in Hungary (and is often misspelled) but is widely served here.

Csáki rostélyos: Created in honor of Sándor Csáki, a famous 20th-century chef, this dish is a sirloin steak cooked with *lecsó*, eggs, and sour cream.

Csülök pékné módra: Pork knuckle cooked "baker's wife" style is roasted with chunks of potatoes and onions.

Disznótoros: "Pig killing" platter is usually a wooden platter piled high with pork sausages, bacon, and other variations on pork.

Esterházy rostélyos: This steak is named for Prince Pál Antal Esterházy, who was known as an extravagant gourmet. It's served with a puréed sauce made from carrots, parsnips, white wine, cream, and capers.

Fatányéros: A wooden platter with a mix of grilled and fried meats (it could also be called *Erdélyi fatányéros*, or "Transylvanian wooden plate").

Flekken: Barbecued meat, usually pork.

Fott marhahús: Boiled beef, usually served with horseradish.

Fott sonka: Boiled ham, usually served with horseradish; a traditional Easter dish.

Hagymás rostélyos: A thin sautéed steak topped with a pile of onions that have been dredged in flour and deep-fried, and served with mustard.

Hentes módra: "Butcher's style" signifies meat that is cooked with sausage or bacon.

Jóasszony módra: Meat prepared in the style of the "good wife" is braised and served with a mixture of bacon, potatoes, and mushrooms.

Kacsasült: Roasted duck, which is traditionally served with red cabbage and potatoes but can be prepared in any other style.

Kedvessy bélszín: Created by nineteenth-century chef Nándor Kedvessy, this elaborate dish consists of a piece of butter-fried bread topped with sautéed mushrooms, a piece of steak, and a slice of goose liver. It's served with sauce made from onions, paprika, tomatoes, peppers, cream, and dill.

Kolozsvári káposzta (or Rakott káposzta): A dish consisting of layers of sauerkraut, rice, sausage, bacon, and sour cream, which is baked and served with fried pork chops.

Libasült: Roasted goose, typically served with red cabbage and potatoes.

Magyarosan: "Hungarian style" signifies meat served with a sauce made from tomatoes, peppers, onions, and spiced with paprika.

Marhasült: Roast beef.

Mátrai borzaska: Breaded pork cutlet topped with sour cream, cheese, and garlic.

Natúr: This style refers to meat simply dredged in flour and fried, and usually served with potatoes.

Ozgerinc: Saddle of venison (not to be confused with the chocolate cake of the same name).

Párizsi borjúszelet: Veal scallops dredged in flour and eggs, fried, and served with rice or potatoes.

Rablóhús: "Robber's meat" is meat and vegetables cooked on skewers; saslik is similar.

Rántott borjúlab: Breaded calf foot, served with tartar sauce and lemon.

Rántott csirke: Fried chicken.

Ropogós malacsült: Crispy roasted suckling pig.

Serpenyosrostélyos: Steak cooked in a skillet (frying pan).

Sült csülök: Roasted knuckle of pork.

Vadász módra: Not only game is prepared "hunter's style," any meat can be prepared this way. It signifies that it's served with game sauce or brown sauce, and is often served with bread dumplings.

Vasi pecsenye: Pork cutlets that have been tenderized and soaked in milk and garlic before being dredged in paprika-laced flour and sautéed.

PASTA & DUMPLINGS

(tészta and galuska)

....

HUNGARY'S NO ITALY, BUT IT DOES HAVE A CONSID-
ERABLE VARIETY OF PASTA IN DIFFERENT SHAPES
and sizes. The commercially made, dried product is sold
in every grocery store, and old ladies sell their packages
of homemade egg pasta at the markets. Most Hungarian pasta is
made with eggs, and it's labeled according to the number of eggs
used per kilogram of flour. Unlike Italy, Hungarian cuisine doesn't
have a battery of sauces to accompany the pasta. An even bigger
difference is that traditional Hungarian menus list pasta, both
savory and sweet, with the desserts. Probably the most common
pasta dish is *túrós csusza* (see below), which can be eaten on its
own, with *lecsó*, or to accompany some stews. Different kinds of
pasta are often added to soups, and dumplings are important sides
with many savory Hungarian dishes. Additionally, sweet dumplings made with plums, apricots, or curd cheese are eaten for
dessert (see page 192).

PASTA DISHES

Káposztás kocka: Pasta squares mixed with shredded cabbage and
sautéed in a bit of bacon fat.

Mákos tészta: Pasta mixed with poppy seeds, powdered sugar, and
melted butter. It's usually eaten as a light main course, following a
hearty soup, but it could be a dessert.

Túrós csusza: Pasta mixed with *túró* (curd cheese) and browned in
bacon fat. It's topped with sour cream, and often with diced bacon.
It's excellent with a little nutmeg grated over it.

Juhtúrós sztrapacska: Potato dumplings tossed in bacon drippings
and smothered in sheep's curd cheese and bacon.

Gránátoskocka: A simple dish of potatoes and pasta seasoned with
paprika.

DUMPLINGS

Zsemlegombóc: Dumplings made from bread rolls, often served with game.

Nokedli or Galuska: Dumplings made with flour and eggs that are
often served with *pörkölt* or added to soups, and are better known
as *spaetzle* in Germany. Several desserts are also called *galuska*, but
these are something entirely different.

Gombóc: This covers many possibilities. These dumplings are larger than
galuska and usually filled, boiled, and then rolled and sautéed in bread
crumbs. *Gombóc* can also refer to the dumplings served in a soup.

CHAPTER 2:

....

A HUNGARIAN WINE PRIMER

Borban az igazság.
In wine there is truth.

Borban a boldogság.
In wine there is happiness.

Borban a vigasz.
In wine there is solace.

—HUNGARIAN PROVERBS

THE HAPPIEST TIMES, THOUGH, WERE THOSE SPENT IN THE DISTRICT THROUGH WHICH THE WATER USED TO BE drawn up to the castle from the river below, the place still known as Víziváros or Water Town, where the goldsmith's wife had herself been born in a Renaissance-style house. There was a restaurant there which opened in the summer, with sumach trees in the courtyard. These trees changed into a most beautiful red colour as autumn advanced and a red-combed cockerel stood and mused on the unused tables. Red was the wine which the apronned waiter placed before them on the mild end-of-October afternoon when the wild vine was no longer fruiting on the nitrous walls.

—*Sumach Trees in Blossom*, GYULA KRÚDY

HUNGARIAN WINE, PAST AND PRESENT

· ·

H
UNGARY IS A WINE DRINKING COUNTRY, AND HUNGAR-
IANS ARE PROUD OF THAT. WINE WAS MADE HERE
when the Romans lived here, and when the nomadic
Magyars arrived at the end of the ninth century, they too
were already making wine. Throughout Hungary's entire turbu-
lent history—the wars, the occupations, the chopping up of the
country—the winemaking has never stopped. Wine has flavored
Hungary's history, right from the beginning. When the Pannonhalma Abbey, which was the first Christian community in
Hungary, was consecrated in 1002 by King István, grapes were
mentioned as one of the crops which was to be handed over as a
tithe. Tokaj wine is even mentioned in Hungary's solemn National
Anthem, the *Himnusz*. Hungarian wine culture is strong enough
to survive even the setbacks. First there was the 150 years of
Ottoman occupation and then the devastating phylloxera
epidemic at the end of the nineteenth century, which destroyed
sixty percent of the country's grape vines. The most recent blow,
and perhaps the worst, was the five decades of Communist rule
and the bureaucratic policies that favored quantity over quality.
Hungarian winemakers are still struggling to recover from the
destruction and complete transformation of their wine industry
caused by Communism. One of the biggest issues in the Hungarian wine industry right now is the attempt to recreate an international image for Hungarian wine, and restore its good reputation
in the world, but there seems to be a constant lack of money for
marketing and promotion, and the government agency in charge
of promoting the country's wine doesn't do much to help. Winemakers will tell you that they didn't just start from the beginning
after the end of Communism, they started with a handicap.

To begin, everything was nationalized and large vineyards
owned by those considered "enemies of the state" were seized
and broken up into tiny plots. There were severe limits on the
amount of vineyard acreage people could own (which varied from
region to region, and from year to year). There were winemaking
cooperatives and there were state farms, which were essentially
wine factories that took their direction from the government's
notorious five-year plans. Often the people in charge knew nothing about wine. Some winemakers continued to make good wine

to keep for themselves, and many winemakers still have some of these bottles hoarded away. Hungary has dozens of native grape varieties and many of the vineyards planted with these grapes were torn out and replaced by varieties that were easy to grow, yielded large quantities, and were generally more suitable for mass production. These days, some winemakers are replanting the native varieties and remembering and relearning the traditions that were once associated with them. Winemakers and wine drinkers are often fiercely proud of wine that's made from the indigenous Hungarian grapes.

Things have changed significantly since the Iron Curtain fell in 1989. What Hungarians dub their "new generation" of winemakers has brought back the passion in Hungary for drinking wine, learning about it, and, of course, making it. As soon as they could, winemakers—some whose families had vineyards taken away, and some who never had the chance to work for themselves—started buying up vineyards, piece by piece, and building modern wineries. If this were an international wine region with more marketing savvy, most wineries would be called "boutique" or "artisanal." In fact, much of the best wine in Hungary is by definition artisanal: it's made by the grower in the place that it was grown, and it has a personal touch. This is true for even the wine made by most of Hungary's biggest name winemakers. These are people who are involved hands-on in every step of the winemaking process, from planting the grapes and harvesting them, to making the wine and selling it to the tourists who show up at their cellar doors.

Hungary produces about 600 million bottles of wine annually. That's less than South Africa and Chile, and for those who appreciate odd statistics, it's about the same as Austria, Switzerland, and New Zealand combined. Almost without exception, you won't find Hungary's most interesting wines outside of Hungary's borders, the quantities are just too small. Many small-scale winemakers make wine that doesn't even reach the shops in Budapest, let alone the rest of the world. Still, Hungary's wines are increasingly being recognized at wine competitions around the world, and by wine writers in Britain and the United States. Hungarians drink more than thirty-two liters of wine per capita annually, and they almost exclusively prefer Hungarian wine (you'll notice on restaurant wine lists that there are few foreign wines available). Some winemakers would like to grow more grapes and make bigger quantities but can't afford to (financing is a constant problem). Others have no desire to work more than a few hectares of vines because they want to maintain control, remain a family business, and stay connected to both the earth and the wine.

Wine lovers who complain about the world being flooded with wines that taste the same will be happy to know that in Hungary that's not the case. Try wine made from one of Hungary's indigenous grapes like *furmint* or *hárslevelu*, and you'll see how local wine can still be. Of course, it's not all good. In Hungary, like everywhere else, there are industrial-sized wineries and you'll still find floods of wine that tastes like it has nothing to do with grapes. It can be hard shopping for wine in a country with unpronounceable names and unrecognizable grapes, but go to any decent wine store and they'll guide you to the best bottles. Better yet, head to Hungary's wine country and sample the wine firsthand, among the hills patched with neat rows of vineyards where the grapes were grown and the wine was lovingly made. Often, the winemaker himself will be the one pouring it—what can be better? (*See Chapter 8 for a listing of wine shops in Budapest.*)

THE WINE REGIONS

T HERE ARE MORE THAN 140 VARIETIES OF WINE GRAPES GROWN IN HUNGARY, WHICH IS AN ASTOUNDing number for a country approximately the size of Illinois. Hungary's twenty-two wine-growing regions—which produce the full spectrum of reds, whites, rosés, and sparkling wines—cover much of the country. Their unique microclimates, types of soil, and winemaking traditions combine to produce wines with immensely different tastes and styles from region to region. A *furmint* from Somló will be different than one from Tokaj, and a *kékfrankos* from the Great Plain will be nothing like a *kékfrankos* from Szekszárd. The regions vary greatly in size, with the smallest just 1,730 acres and the largest forty times that size. Hungary produces more white wine than red, but there are a few regions that produce almost exclusively red. Remember that both good and bad wine can be found in even the top regions. The most important thing to pay attention to is the reputation of the winery.

AROUND BUDAPEST

Etyek-Buda

Buda was an important wine-growing area until the combination of phylloxera and intensive urbanization in the late nineteenth century hit Budapest and largely ended its days as a winemaking city. These days Buda and the area west of Budapest together make up the Etyek-Buda wine region, which is one of Hungary's mid-sized regions and stretches south from Budapest to Lake Velence. The area is best known for the sparkling wine cellars in Budafok—which calls itself the "city of sparkling wine" and makes more than seventy percent of Hungary's sparkling wine. Most of the winemaking in Budafok today is dominated by the large sparkling wine companies, a few of which are connected to each other (Hungarovin, for example, owns Törley, Hungária, and François, and in turn, Hungarovin is owned by the German Henkell & Söhnlein wine house). White wine dominates here, and in the surrounding areas much of what is produced is the basis for sparkling wine. The most common varieties grown here are chardonnay, *irsai olivér*, *olaszrizling*, and sauvignon blanc. West of Budapest, Tök and Etyek are the main wine-producing areas in the region. Wineries to watch out for are Nyakas Pince and Etyeki Kúria.

Mór

Mór is located between Budapest and Gyor, between the Vértes and the Bakony hills. It's one of the smaller regions, and it produces exclusively white wines. The flagship variety here, and the most widely planted grape, is the indigenous *ezerjó*—a dry wine with both high alcohol and acid contents. Other varieties include *leányka*, *tramini*, *rizlingszilváni*, *zöldveltelini*, and chardonnay. Mór was once well known for making a sweet *aszú*-like dessert wine from good vintages of *ezerjó*, but you're unlikely to find a bottle of this these days unless you actually visit the region. Wines from Mór are mainly local, hard to find even in Budapest. Many winemakers do it purely as a hobby, keeping their product for themselves or selling it in plastic bottles from their homes. The bigger winegrowers usually sell their grapes to larger wineries. The wine route in Mór is small, but well organized. Winemakers to watch out for are Endre Bognár and Bozóky Pincészet.

Balatonboglár, Badacsony, Balatonfüred-Csopak, Balaton-felvidék, and Balatonmelléke

The area around the seventy-eight-kilometer-long Lake Balaton is officially five separate regions. Badacsony, Balatonfelvidék, and Balatonfüred-Csopak are on the northern shore, Balatonmelléke is to the west and south, and Balatonboglár spreads along the southern shore. Overall, the northern shore is hilly, the southern is flat, and both have some of the prettiest wine regions in the country. While the separate regions are not extraordinarily distinctive from each other, there are slight differences. Balaton's wines (particularly those from Badacsony) were among the first to be mentioned in Hungarian historical records, and were often mentioned along with Tokaj wine as the country's best. Reds were traditionally dominant in Balatonboglár, but during the Communist-era the region's state wine farm shifted vineyard plantings from red to white. These days some winemakers, most notably János Konyári, are attempting to get the region back into reds. (Confusingly, Balatonboglár [better known as BB] is also the name of the company that descended from that former state farm, and is known for its sparkling wines.) *Olaszrizling, muskotály*, and *szürkebarát* dominate in Balatonboglár, and chardonnay, *tramini, rajnai rizling*, and an increasing number of very nice reds are there in smaller amounts. Badacsony is certainly one of Hungary's most scenic wine regions, with big vineyard-clad hills, old cellars built into the rocks, and fantastic views of the lake from all angles. Badacsony almost exclusively produces full-bodied whites like *olaszrizling* and *szürkebarát*. It's also just about the only place in the country that grows *kéknyelu*, an indigenous grape that is difficult to grow and nearly disappeared, but is being resurrected by a few dedicated winemakers.

The Balatonfüred-Csopak region stretches from the northeast corner of Balaton to Zánka, and includes the Tihany peninsula and the spa town Balatonfüred. It, too, is an overwhelmingly white wine region, though Tihany is becoming known for its reds. The region produces two distinct types of wine: more full-bodied ones from the Balatonfüred side, and lighter, more acidic ones from the Csopak side. Balaton-felvidék (the Balaton highlands), another region once known for its reds, now also produces predominantly white wines. Though the region is small, it covers a big area (it even encloses Badacsony), with many types of soil. *Olaszrizling* and *szürkebarát* are the stars here. No part of the

Balatonmelléke region actually borders the lake, though one section does sit next to the Kis ("small") Balaton lake. Wineries and winemakers around Lake Balaton to watch out for include Nyári Pince, Huba Szeremley (Elso Magyar Borház), Mihály Figula (Fine Wine), Jásdi Pince, János Konyári, Ottó Légli, László Bussay, Lajos Feind, Zoltán Kovács (Biovitis Pince), and Vencel Garamvári (St. Donatus).

THE NORTHWEST

Somló

Despite being Hungary's smallest wine region—or perhaps because of it—Somló is talked about in a reverent, almost mythological way. It's frequently praised in Hungarian literature, and Maria Theresa and Queen Victoria were said to have especially admired the wines from this pretty hill. *Juhfark* (which is the favored grape here, and translates as "sheep's tail") is called the "wedding night wine." If it's drunk on your wedding night, legend has it that a baby boy will soon be born. Most of the great wines made in Somló—which is located to the north of the Balaton wine regions—are made in such small quantities that it's almost a badge of honor to possess one. Overall, Somló wines tend to be high in alcohol and very acidic. They are meant to be aged for several years. Winemakers to watch out for include Béla Fekete, Imre Györgykovács, Kreinbacher Birtok, and István Inhauser.

Pannonhalma-Sokoróalja

The Pannonhalma wine region is the second smallest in Hungary and is also a predominantly white wine region. Most of the grapes grown here are *olaszrizling*, followed by *rajnai rizling*. It's also probably the wine region with the lowest profile. In fact, most of the small-scale winemakers around here make wine solely for their own use, or to sell to neighbors and local restaurants. If it weren't for the Pannonhalma Abbey Winery, which only harvested its first crop in 2003 and has been making some excellent wines since then, most Hungarians would hardly know a thing about this region.

Sopron

On a map, the Sopron region looks like a little peninsula jutting into neighboring Austria's Burgenland province. Lake Ferto (called the Neusiedlersee in Austria) borders the region in the north and the warm and humid hillsides around it are Sopron's most prized vineyards. The region has several different microclimates—sub-alpine, continental, and sub-Mediterranean. Wines in Sopron are mostly red, and the region is increasingly producing some of Hungary's best. *Kékfrankos* is the king here. Zweigelt, cabernet sauvignon, syrah, merlot, and pinot noir are also made, and so are whites like *zöldveltelini* (which is best known as Austria's most widely planted grape, grüner veltliner), chardonnay, *tramini*, and sauvignon blanc. Many of the wine cellars are located below the houses in the pretty town of Sopron itself. Sopron was the capital of Burgenland during the Austro-Hungarian Empire and its Austrian connection is still strong. Franz Weninger, Sopron's top winemaker, is Austrian and has wineries on both sides of the border (and also a partnership in Villány with Attila Gere). Franz Pfneiszl is another Austrian who works in both countries. Winemakers to watch include: Franz Weninger, Luka Pincészet, Kálmán Jandl, Franz Pfneiszl, and Ráspi.

Ászár-Neszmély

Though wine has been made there since the Roman times, the Ászár-Neszmély region is best known today for the Hilltop winery, which is one of the country's largest. It dominates winemaking in this mid-sized region between Budapest and Gyor and it has also put Hungary on the British wine radar, as most of its wine ends up in British supermarkets. Much of the region lies on slopes overlooking the Danube (Slovakia is visible on the other side), and other vineyards lie on the slopes of the Gerecse Hills. The Danube is important to the micro-climate of the area, which is on the cool and wet side. Ászár-Neszmély produces almost exclusively white wines like sauvignon blanc, *szürkebarát*, *irsai olivér*, *cserszegi fuszeres*, *rajnai rizling*, and *olaszrizling*. Most winegrowers sell their grapes to Hilltop, and much of the rest of the wine is sold as jug wine. With the exception of Hilltop and winemaker Mihály Szöllosi down the road, the region's wines are unremarkable.

THE NORTHEAST

Tokaj-Hegyalja

Tokaj-Hegyalja is justly Hungary's most famous wine region and one of the most beautiful parts of the country. Traditions here are stronger and deeper than anywhere else, in part because this area retained more independence way back during the Ottoman occupation. The region is framed by natural borders: the town of Tokaj in the southwest corner where the Bodrog and the Tisza rivers meet, the Bodrog river to the southeast, and the Zemplén hills to the northwest (*hegyalja* means foothills in Hungarian). Everything about Tokaj—from its mixture of loess and volcanic clay soils and its microclimate (ideal for bringing on the mythical noble rot) to its indigenous grape varieties and its subterranean labyrinth of mold-covered cellars—contributes to the distinctive personality of its wines. Tokaj is a white wine region best known for its sweet *aszú* wines, which are made from botrytized grapes, but more than half of the wine it produces is dry. The majority of grapes grown here are the indigenous varieties of *furmint*, *hárslevelu*, *sárgamuskotály*, and *zéta* (a relatively new variety created by crossing *furmint* and *bouvier*). While tradition rules in Tokaj, winemakers here are also among the country's most innovative. They're allowed to grow small amounts of other grapes for experimental purposes, and they're beginning to produce small quantities of wines that have nothing to do with Tokaj's traditional image: János Árvay makes small batches of sauvignon blanc (it's sold as a Zemplén sauvignon blanc), Dobogó has a small plot of pinot noir, and Chateau Dereszla is experimenting with a new grape variety called the *kabar*. In Tokaj there are numerous small winemakers worthy of seeking out and discovering. Here are some to look for: István Szepsy, Degenfeld, Chateau Dereszla, Dobogó, Füleky, Göncöl, Királyudvar, Oremus, János Árvay, Béres Szolobirtok, Chateau Pajzos and Megyer, Hétszolo, Majoros Pince, Royal Tokaji Wine Company, Zoltán Demeter, Disznókó, Bott Pince, and István Kiss.

Eger

Eger's best known wine—the blend called *Egri Bikavér*, "Bull's Blood from Eger"—is both the pride of the region, and a problem. If there's any wine other than Tokaji *aszú* that's widely known abroad, it's *Egri Bikavér*, Hungary's most famous cuvée. *Bikavér* is essentially a blend of three or more grapes that must meet certain requirements during harvesting and production. The grapes are picked and processed separately and then matured in oak for at least a year. Both Eger and Szekszárd use the name *Bikavér* and winemakers in both regions have slightly different preferences for their blends. The ingredients in a *Bikavér* can vary but always contains some combination of *kékfrankos*,

Portugieser, cabernet sauvignon, cabernet franc, merlot, or *kadarka*. The problem is that when *Egri Bikavér* made its name abroad in the 1970s (during the days of Communist-enforced mass production) it had become a rough wine whose biggest fans liked it for its price rather than its taste. It was made from grapes that didn't make the cut for varietal wines, and it ended up on the bottom shelves of American and British supermarkets. This *Bikavér* has caused many to associate Hungarian wine with cheap plonk.

Things have changed. Although you will still find plenty of bad *Bikavér* around, it can be a great wine, and much of today's *Bikavér* is exceptionally different than those that sullied its reputation in the past. Some of Hungary's best winemakers in Eger (and Szekszárd, too)—like Tibor Gál (who died in 2005, but his family still makes wine under his name) and Vilmos Thummerer—are making top-notch *Bikavérs*. Some Eger winemakers make blends which could just as well be called *Bikavér*, but rather than risk the image problems associated with the name, they choose different names. Before World War II *kadarka* was the dominant red grape variety in Eger (and in the *Bikavér* blend), but it's now *kékfrankos* that's most associated with the region. Eger is best known for its strong full-bodied reds, but it also produces good white wines like *leányka, olaszrizling, királyleányka*, and chardonnay. Winemakers to watch include: Vilmos Thummerer, Tibor Gál (also sold under the Nagygombos and GIA labels), István Tóth, Béla Vincze, Csaba Demeter, Monarchia (winemaker Tamás Pók), Gróf Buttler, and St. Andrea (winemaker György Lorincz).

Bükkalja and Mátra

Eger's neighbors, Bükkalja directly to the east and Mátra directly west, can't compete with Eger's fame, and nowhere near as much quality wine comes from these two regions. Mátra, which lies in the Mátra foothills, is the country's second largest wine region, and it produces better whites than reds. It's widespread whites include *olaszrizling, muskotály, rizlingszilváni, tramini*, and chardonnay. Red varietals are increasingly being planted. Bükkalja, which is sheltered by the Bükk mountains and goes as far east as Miskolc, is one of the country's least known regions. The majority of wine here isn't even bottled, and is said to range from mediocre to terrible. It does have a pretty cellar row, but doesn't offer much else. In Mátra, by far the best winemaker to seek out is Mátyás Szoke, who is a former mechanical engineer who now makes delicious wines. József Ludányi is another one to look for.

THE SOUTH

Villány-Siklós

. . . .

The Villány-Siklós region lies near the Croatian border and because it's the warmest of Hungary's wine regions, it's often called the "Mediterranean of Hungary." Because it produces big reds that demand premium prices, it's also called the "Bordeaux of Hungary." There are eleven villages in the region, but most of the action is in the village of Villány itself, where some of Hungary's top winemakers have their cellars and attached small hotels (*panzió*). Villány's wine is usually identified with quality (though there are bad wines made here, too). In the mid-1990s, when winemakers were busy building modern wineries, replanting vines—and essentially starting to build the Hungarian wine industry—Villány was in the spotlight. Tourists flocked here to taste what winemakers like József Bock, Attila Gere, and Ede Tiffán were creating. Along with Tokaj, Villány has remained one of Hungary's most successful wine regions, and also one of the most tourist-friendly. In Villány mostly reds are made, while Siklós (which lies on the west side of the Villányhegy, or the Villány hill) makes whites. Villány's most prized vineyards are the Jammertal and Kopár vineyards on the slopes of the Szársomlyó hill, and the best known wine from the Kopár vineyard is Gere's cuvée of the same name.

Villány's signature grape is Portugieser (still commonly referred to as *kékoportó*), and *kékfrankos* is also widely planted. Some Villány winemakers have been replanting *kadarka*—a native variety that was the most widely planted red grape in nineteenth-century Hungary, but wasn't suitable to mass production during the Communist era. Much of Villány's wine is made with internationally known grapes like cabernet sauvignon, merlot, and pinot noir. Cabernet franc does particularly well in Villány, and wines produced from it have received raves. It's understandable that native Hungarian varieties have fallen out of favor here. First, there were the five decades of state-enforced mass production when many native varieties were either banned or discouraged. Then when the markets opened, Hungary found itself competing with wineries around the world. "After Communism we had to change the way we did everything," said Andrea Gere, winemaker Attila Gere's daughter. "And a cabernet sauvignon was easier to sell than a *bakator*, for example, so those kind of grapes began to die out." Winemakers in Villány work hard to keep quality high, and with the 2006 vintage they initiated an appellation system that's significantly tougher than what's required by law. Winemakers and wineries to watch for include: József Bock, Attila Gere, Gere and Weninger, Ede and Zsolt Tiffán, Zoltán Günzer, Márton Mayer, Csányi Pince (Chateau Teleki line), Béla Jekl, Csaba Malatinszky, Zoltán Polgár, Szalontai-Bartholy Pince, Vylyan Pincészet, Tamás and Zsolt Gere, and Alajos Wunderlich.

Szekszárd

Szekszárd is another of Hungary's top wine regions, and it's known for its big spicy reds. Along with Eger, Szekszárd is also the homeland of the *Bikavér* cuvée. In fact, the first time the name *Bikavér* was mentioned was in an 1846 poem in connection with Szekszárd. Though Eger's Bikavér gets most of the fame, there's no record of it being written about until a few years later.

Just as in Eger, some of Szekszárd's winemakers (most notably Ferenc Takler and Ferenc Vesztergombi) are also trying to restore the tarnished image of this traditional wine, which has such a beloved name in Hungary. There's some great *Bikavér* coming from Szekszárd, with *kadarka* being more heavily accented in the blend. *Kadarka*, once the favored variety in Szekszárd, is known for being a difficult grape to grow. Though much of it disappeared during Communism, winemakers here are starting to appreciate it again. In Szekszárd they say it goes well with food heavily spiced with paprika, and that a *Bikavér* just isn't a *Bikavér* without some *kadarka* in it. In many ways, Szekszárd is one of Hungary's most exciting wine regions, and it gets better every year as more and more winemakers expand and modernize their facilities. It isn't as tourist friendly (or popular) as Villány and Eger, and in a way it almost feels like Villány's modest, intro-verted sister. In fact, Szekszárd is larger than Villány, but it lacks the compact town center and convenient row of wine cellars open for tastings that has made Villány so popular with wine tourists. Regardless, Szekszárd should be considered in its own right for its fine red wines. After *kadarka*, *kékfrankos* is the other signature grape in Szekszárd. Merlot, cabernet sauvignon, *kékoportó*, and pinot noir are grown here, and so are chardonnay and *olaszrizling*. Tamás Dúzsi's rosé has been often called the best in Hungary. Winemakers to watch for include: Ferenc Takler, Ferenc Veszter-gombi, Tamás Dúzsi, Zoltán Heimann, Csaba Sebestyén, Péter Vida, Pál Mészáros, and Sárosdi Pince.

Mecsekalja and Tolna

Mecsekalja lies between Villány and Szekszárd, but here the flagship wine is the white *cirfandli* (which needs aging to reach its full potential). Despite the success of it's neighbors, Mecsekalja's wines are little known, mainly local, and hardly make it into bottles or stores in Budapest. The region gets its name from the Mecsek hills, which are north of the pretty town of Pécs. Another native grape, *juhfark*, is also widely planted in some parts of the region, and so is chardonnay and *olaszrizling*. There's a well-organized wine route in Bóly and Mohács (famous also for its Carnival tradition), though the wine you'll taste in the cellars seldom reaches beyond the cellar doors. Like other low-profile, small regions, many of the winemakers here are hobby family wineries. Tolna is located just north of Szekszárd and Mecsekalja, and produces both red and whites, which are nothing exceptional, for the most part. One of the region's biggest attractions is the cellar village of Györköny, which is west of Paks. The winery to look out for here is Eurobor in Bátaapáti, which was started as a partnership between Péter Zwack and Piero Antinori (the godfather of Tuscan wine), and Tibor Gál later worked as the director of winemaking. Their wines are sold under two labels: Bátaapáti Estate and Mocsényi Kastélybor.

THE GREAT PLAIN (ALFÖLD)

Csongrád, Hajós-Baja, and Kunság

The Great Plain wine regions of Csongrád, Hajós-Baja, and Kunság occupy much of the space between the Danube and the Tisza rivers in the central and southern part of the country. Although Kunság is the country's largest region (with more than 28,000 hectares), it's hard to say anything nice about the wine produced in the sandy soil here. Mostly, it's just the kind of simple cheap table wine that's sold in convenience stores and musty cellar pubs. During the phylloxera epidemic, the vines in the Great Plain helped save the country's wine industry, since the sandy soil prevented them from being destroyed. The Alföld wine regions were important for the Communist-era strategy of producing massive quantities of cheap wine to export to the Soviet Union and the rest of the Eastern Bloc. Here too, reds once dominated, but for the most part were switched to whites in the 1960s for export reasons. The eighteenth-century cellar village of Hajós is one of the more interesting parts of the region, with its rows of more than 1,300 whitewashed cellars and old press houses. There's a vintage festival in September and a St. Orbán day festival on the last weekend of May. Some of the cellars are open for tastings, typically between May and October.

NATIVE GRAPE VARIETIES

T HERE ARE ALMOST A HUNDRED GRAPE VARIETIES THAT ARE EITHER NATIVE TO HUNGARY, ARE HYBRID varieties created in Hungary, or are varieties that have been growing here for so long that they're now considered to be acclimatized. As wine around the world becomes increasingly similar, it's nice to sample distinctively Hungarian wines like *furmint* or *leányka*. Many native varieties that once thrived have died out due to phylloxera, Communist-era policies, or simply because their growers decided that merlot or chardonnay might be more profitable than unpronounceable and unknown Hungarian varieties. Other varieties came close to dying out, but remain around because of the dedication of a few winemakers. While some winemakers attempt to save these native grape varieties, others see them as too hard to sell on the international market. Regardless, the Hungarian wine varieties still account for more than half of the total grape production. This list isn't comprehensive, but it includes the best-known varieties.

WHITES

Budai zöld: This is the variety that pollinates *kéknyelu*. It makes fresh, acidic wines, and is often used in blends.

Cirfandli: This acclimatized grape variety is mostly grown in the Pécs region. It ages well and develops an apricot flavor after a few years.

Cserszegi fuszeres: This hybrid variety—a mix of *tramini* and *irsai olivér*—was developed at Balaton and was considered un-sellable abroad until Hilltop began labeling it "Woodcutter's White," and it became a supermarket success in Britain. It makes aromatic, vigorous wine, and is best drunk young.

Ezerjó: Ezerjó means "a thousand good things." It was widely planted before phylloxera, but is now most successful in Mór. It also grows in Pannonhalma, the Great Plain, and Ászár-Neszmély. It makes a tart, acidic wine, and in good years, dessert wine can be made from it.

Furmint: Associated with Tokaj, and in a lesser amount, with Somló, *furmint*, when it develops noble rot, is one of the ingredients in *aszú* wine. Furmint's dry wines are distinctive, fragrant, fiery, and tart. Its scent is often associated with ripe apples. Hungarians have a special place in their hearts for *furmint*.

Hárslevelu: Mostly grown in Somló and Tokaj, where it's used in *aszú* wines, *hárslevelu*, or "linden leaf," is usually considered to be more elegant than *furmint*. Its bouquet is floral, fruity, and honey-scented. In Tokaj, dry and semi-sweet wines are made from *hárslevelu*. Somló is known for its dry *hárslevelu*, while in Siklós the semi-sweet and sweet versions are popular.

Irsai olivér: This Hungarian hybrid variety is grown in many white wine regions and generally makes light, fresh, fruity wines with soft acids and Muscat flavors. It ages fast, and makes an ideal aperitif.

Juhfark: Juhfark, which means sheep's tail, is so named because of the shape of the grape cluster. *Juhfark* is the flagship grape in Somló and is high in acid. It's also found on the north shore of Balaton.

Kéknyelu: Badacsony is the only place where this grape is grown. It's a difficult grape to grow because it's entirely female and requires fertilization, so it nearly disappeared. It is now being resurrected by a few wine growers, but it's still a rarity. Its name means "blue stem."

Királyleányka: A Transylvanian hybrid variety which was introduced here after World War II, it makes rich, lively, muscat-flavored wine. It's grown in many regions, including Eger, Mátraalja, and Balaton. The name means "little princess."

Kövidinka: This variety grows best in the sandy soil of the Great Plain, but is hardly found elsewhere. It makes a highly acidic wine.

Leányka: This variety of Transylvanian origin does best in Eger and Mátraalja. It's generally drunk young, and is fresh with soft acids and a floral bouquet. It can also be semi-sweet.

Olaszrizling: This acclimatized grape variety—which translates as "Italian riesling"—bears no relation to Rhine riesling. It accounts for nearly ten percent of the white grapes grown in Hungary and is found in almost every region. This soft wine is especially successful on the northern shore of Balaton, and it has an aftertaste often associated with bitter almonds. *Olaszrizling* varies widely depending on the soil and the region where it's grown. It can be dry, sweet, or semi-sweet.

Zenit: This variety is a cross between *ezerjó* and *bouvier*, created in the 1950s by a Hungarian viticulturist. Zenit makes wines that are light, and slightly sweet.

Zeusz: This hybrid variety is mostly grown around Lake Balaton. It has a high acid content and is often used for making sweet and late harvest wines.

Zéta: This variety is a cross between *furmint* and *bouvier* and has recently been authorized to be planted in Tokaj. It was originally called Oremus, but was changed to avoid confusing it with the Oremus winery. It's becoming increasingly widespread in Tokaj, where it's usually used in Tokaji *aszú* blends.

REDS

Bakator: Bakator very nearly died out, and now there are just a very few acres of it planted. Huba Szeremley in Badacsony is one of the few winemakers who grows it.

Kadarka: This acclimatized grape variety possibly originated in the Balkans and spread to Hungary during the Ottoman period in the sixteenth and seventeenth centuries. It once accounted for two-thirds of Hungary's red grapes, but wasn't suited to mass production and was replaced by *kékfrankos*. Today it's mainly found in Szekszárd and is one of the ingredients in *Bikavér*. Some Villány producers have also been replanting *kadarka*.

Kékfrankos: The Communist goal to manufacture as much wine as possible was good for *kékfrankos*, which became the most widely planted red variety. It still accounts for almost ten percent of red grapes. The origin of this grape is unknown, but it's planted throughout the country. When made well, it can be a complex, peppery wine. When poorly made, it can be highly acidic, thin, lightly colored, and flavorless. It's often harsh when it's young. *Kékfrankos* is best in Eger and Szekszárd. It's often the main ingredient in rosé, and it's an important part of the *Bikavér* blend.

Portugieser: This acclimatized Hungarian grape variety was formerly known as *kékoportó* until the EU ordered its name to be changed to avoid any confusion with the famed fortified sweet Port wine (which it has nothing to do with). This grape needs warmth, and it's the signature grape in Villány. It's best drunk young, when it has nice tannins and light acids. Although the name was officially changed, many in Hungary still refer to this grape as *kékoportó*.

WINE VARIETAL DECODER

....

C HARDONNAY IS STILL CHARDONNAY AND MERLOT IS STILL MERLOT IN *MAGYAR*, BUT SOME INTERNATIONAL wine varietals are masked by Hungarian names. Here's a decoder:

Kékfrankos: blaufränkisch or lemberger (red)

Kisburgundi: the rarely used Hungarian name for pinot noir (red)

Muskotály: muscat ottonel (white)

Olaszrizling: Welschriesling or Italian riesling (white)

Pezsgo: sparkling wine

Portugieser: blauer portugieser, formerly known as *kékoportó* in Hungary (red)

Rajnai rizling: Rhine riesling (white)

Rizlingszilváni: müller-thurgau (white)

Sárgamuskotály: yellow muscat, or muscat lunel (white)

Szürkebarát: pinot gris (white)

Tramini: gewürztraminer (white)

Zöldszilváni: sylvaner (white)

Zöldveltelini: grüner veltliner (white)

Zweigelt: a cross between the *kékfrankos* and St. Laurent. One of the most widely planted varieties in Austria, it's also present in Hungary (red)

WINE TRANSLATOR

W HETHER YOU'RE HEADING OUT OF BUDAPEST INTO THE WINE COUNTRY—OR JUST BUYING WINE AT the wine store—knowing some Hungarian vocabulary will get you a long way toward understanding wine labels or finding your way around the wineries. Tokaj wine requires an entirely different vocabulary (see the separate Tokaj Terminology on page 74).

asztali bor: "table wine"

Bikavér: Bull's Blood cuvée

birtok: estate

bor: wine

borász: winemaker

borászat: winery

borkereskedo: wine merchant

borkorcsolya: snacks to eat with wine

(boros) pohár: (wine) glass

borkóstoló: wine tasting

borpárlat: a drink made from distilled wine; essentially brandy

borvidék: wine region

classicus: The second highest category in the Villány appellation.

családi: family-run

csúcsbor: top wine; this designation is given annually

by the *Pannon Bormíves Céh* (Guild of Pannonian Wines) at the *Pannon Bormustra* competition, Hungary's most prestigious. Five Bikavérs, 20 dry whites, 10 sweet whites, and 25 dry reds receive the designation and their bottles are then stamped with the gold *Pannon Bormustra* seal.

DHC Villány: Districtus Hungaricus Controllatus, Villány's appellation system.

dugó: cork

dugóhúzó: corkscrew

dulo: slope

édes: sweet

évjárat: vintage

fajbor: varietal wine

fehér: white

félédes: semi-sweet

félszáraz: semi-dry

folyóbor: bulk wine (literally "running wine")

gyöngyözo bor: lightly sparkling, or frizzante wine

hegy: hill

hordó: barrel

jégbor: ice wine

késoi szüretelésu: late harvested

kimért bor: "measured wine"; wine by the glass

különleges minoségu bor: "finest quality wine"

küvé: cuvée, blend

minoségi bor: "quality wine"

muzeális: wine that's at least five years old

palackozta: bottled by

palackozott bor: bottled wine

pince: cellar

pincesor: cellar row

prémium: the uppermost category in the Villány appellation

primor: another word for *újbor*, the first wine released from the new harvest

rozé: rosé

siller: A wine that's lighter than red, but darker than rosé.

száraz: dry

szolo: grape

szuretlen: unfiltered

tájbor: "country wine" from a designated region which is slightly higher grade than "table wine" but still not high quality

termeloi bor: wine made by the wine grower

termelte: produced by

tölgy: oak

törköly pálinka: pálinka distilled from the grape residue left after pressing (pomace)

újbor: new wine; the first wine from the harvest, generally released in November

üveg: bottle

válogatás: selection

Villány Védett Eredetu bor: origin protected wine from Villány

vörös: red

TOKAJ WINE: OLD TRADITIONS & NEW TECHNOLOGY

GENERALLY, THE WAY WINE IS MADE IN HUNGARY IS SIMILAR TO THE WAY IT'S MADE THROUGHOUT THE rest of the winemaking world. But Tokaj is a special case that needs some explanation. Long before the Tokaj-Hegyalja region was declared a protected UNESCO World Heritage Site in 2002, it was recognized as a first-class wine region. It's also said to be the first region to produce wine from botrytized grapes. If we believe the legend, then we have the invading seventeenth-century Ottomans to thank for the discovery of the noble rot in Tokaj, which led to the creation of Tokaji *aszú*. Zsuzsanna Lórántffy, the wife of Prince György Rákóczi I, decided to postpone the harvest on the family's extensive vineyards in Tokaj when the Turkish invasion was imminent, the story goes. By the time they got around to harvesting the grapes, they had turned into shriveled little botrytized raisins. The winemakers decided to use them anyway, and Tokaji *aszú* was born. It's also likely that many of the cave-like cellars in the region, which were built with entrances that could be hidden, were meant to hide the wine from invaders like the Turks.

Regardless whether that story is true or not, it's a fact that in 1630 a Calvinist priest named Máté Sepsy Laczkó was the first to describe the *aszú*-making method. "Like Dom Perignon in Champagne, he was the first one to make the delimitation of Tokaj," said Laszló Mészáros of Tokaj's Disznókő winery. "He was the first to write about the method of producing Tokaji aszú which we still follow today." In 1737 the winegrowing area in Tokaj was delimited by royal decree and in 1772 the world's first vineyard-classification system was developed with Tokaj-Hegyalja as the first classified vineyard. Tokaj wine was known and praised around the world. Then came war and nationalization. It was during this period, however, when many of today's winemakers got their training by working for the state-owned wine factories. "Not only bad things happened during those years," pointed out Angelika Árvay (her father, winemaker János Árvay, worked for the state-run winery). "But when the French started bringing in money and investments, winemaking became a different thing here."

Aszú wines have been made essentially the same way for

hundreds of years, although now they are made with modern technology and equipment. When the Iron Curtain fell and the market opened, foreign investors began pouring money into the region and partnering with Hungarians to establish wineries or opening state-of-the-art wineries themselves. Disznókő, Oremus, Dereszla, Királyudvar, the Royal Tokaji Wine Company, Chateau Megyer, and Chateau Pajzos are some of the most prominent foreign-backed companies.

THE TOKAJ WINEMAKING PROCESS

Forget everything you know about traditional winemaking. When it comes to making Tokaji *aszú*, the process is entirely different. In Tokaj the harvest is a long, labor-intensive process that begins at the end of September and usually ends in November.

There are essentially three harvests in Tokaj: the dry wine harvest, the aszú harvest, and the late harvest. First comes the standard dry wine harvest when grapes are picked still firm and pale green. Tokaj dry wine production is straightforward: after the harvest the grapes are pressed, the mixture is fermented, and then it's matured. Dry *furmint*, *hárslevelu*, and *sárgamuskotály* are made from this first harvest, as well as the base wine for Tokaji *aszú*. Despite the fact that Tokaj is best known for its sweet wines, between forty and sixty percent of the wines produced here annually are dry.

More dry wines will be produced in years when the weather conditions aren't good for producing the noble rot that turns grapes into what are called *aszú* berries. The second harvest in Tokaj is the *aszú* harvest at the end of October when the grapes—which have now hopefully acquired the noble rot (or *Botrytis cinerea*) that is essential for making Tokaji *aszú*—start to look like dark, little, shriveled raisins. In good years—when humidity comes from the meeting of the rivers Bodrog and Tisza with the plain and there's lots of autumn morning dew mixed with drying breezes—there will be more *aszú* wine produced and it will be richer and more concentrated. In a bad year, especially when there's a wet fall, there will be a short *aszú* harvest because there will be little or no noble rot. The *aszú* berries are selected by hand, one by one, by experienced pickers in a process that's repeated several times; an average picker can pick only six to eight kilograms of *aszú* berries per day.

After the harvest, the *aszú* grapes are macerated in base wine or fermenting must (which was made from the first harvest) for between twelve and sixty hours. Next, the *aszú* grape mixture that was saturated in the base wine (sometimes called the *aszú* dough) is pressed and the resulting juice is fermented. The wine is then stored in oak barrels—often made from oak from the nearby Zemplén forest—and aged for several years in the underground stone cellar system that's unique to the Tokaj region. The sweetness of Tokaji *aszú* is measured by *puttony,* a 25-liter wooden tub, traditionally used for collecting the *aszú* grapes. Tokaji *aszú* can be between three and six *puttonyos*, which means that the equivalent of between three and six tubs of botrytized grapes have been added to each 136-liter *Gönc* cask (a traditional cask for making *aszú* wines) of must or base wine. The higher the *puttony* number, the sweeter, more golden colored, and more expensive the wine will be. (For a more concrete idea of the sweetness level, a three *puttonyos aszú* has from sixty to ninety grams of residual sugar per liter, a four *puttonyos* has from ninety to 120, a five *puttonyos* from 120 to 150, a six *puttonyos* from 150 to 180, and an *aszú eszencia* from 180 to 260.)

PRECIOUS ESZENCIA

Eszencia—the rarest form of Tokaj wine—is made from the *aszú* berries that are hand picked during the second harvest. "From one hectare of vineyards we can make two bottles of *eszencia*," said Oremus winemaker András Bacsó. "It takes about ten days to make it, and from 150 kilograms of grapes, we will yield about one percent of that as *eszencia*." To make *eszencia*, a vat is filled with *aszú* berries and the pressure of the grapes weighing down on each other pushes out the *eszencia*, which is a thick, honey-like syrup. The sugar content of *eszencia* is so high (between 500 and 700 grams per liter) that it ferments very slowly and resembles a liquidy honey rather than a prized wine. Even after several years of fermentation the alcohol content rarely exceeds five percent. Not much *eszencia* is bottled (and on bad years none is produced). But when it is bottled, it can cost up to $600 for a half-liter bottle and is mostly sold as a novelty for collectors. Despite its price, winemakers don't make *eszencia* for the money. "At least one hundred times more grapes are needed for *eszencia* than for a bottle of table wine," wrote British wine writer Hugh Johnson of a bottle of his own Royal Tokaji Wine Company's *eszencia* (Johnson is a part-owner of the company). "*Eszencia* is the purest expression of a terroir and its vintage known to man."

When it looks as if the grapes will not dry out and botrytize any further, it's time for the final harvest. Bunches which contain a mixture of both botrytized grapes and intact grapes are now picked whole, without the grape-by-grape selection, and used for late-harvest and *szamorodni* wines. The grape clusters are macerated, pressed, and the must is then fermented. After fermentation the *szamorodni* and the late-harvest winemaking processes differ slightly. *Szamorodni* is aged in oak barrels, often for several years, and the resulting wine can be either dry or sweet depending on the amount of botrytized grapes that were in the bunch. Dry *szamorodni* is often compared to good sherry, and both sweet and dry *szamorodni* make ideal aperitifs. Late-harvest wines, on the other hand, are not aged for more than a few months. The idea behind these sweet wines is to capture the freshness, fruitiness, and aroma of the grapes.

A labyrinth of barrel-lined cellars, some of which are several kilometers long, has been dug in the volcanic rock below the ground throughout the entire Tokaj region. Like the soil and the climate, the special character of these dark, narrow passages plays an important role in the winemaking process, according to many winemakers in Tokaj. "There are fifty kilometers of cellars in Tolcsva which were built between the fourteenth and seventeenth centuries," said Bacsó as he led me through Oremus' own four-kilometer-long cellar system. As in all of the subterranean cellars, Oremus' arched tunnel-like cellars (and nearly everything inside of them) are covered in a fuzzy black "noble mold."

"The noble mold forms from the combination of the high humidity and the alcohol, and it purifies the air, keeping it clean," said Bacsó. "This cellar is difficult to use because it's so old fashioned, but the conditions are ideal, so we continue to use it." Cellar temperatures remain at a constant ten or eleven degrees Celsius throughout the year. "In the summer we keep the cellar doors closed to keep it cool," explained Gábor Rakaczki of Degenfeld, which has a 500-meter cellar system. "But in the winter we keep the doors open to collect the cold air that will keep the cellar cool during the summer."

TOKAJ TERMINOLOGY

....

WINE FROM TOKAJ HAS ITS OWN SPECIALIZED VOCABULARY, WHICH CAN MAKE BUYING A BOTTLE of it overwhelming unless you're a little informed. Here's a decoder:

DRY AND SEMI-SWEET

The winemaking process for Tokaj dry wines is straightforward. The grapes are harvested, pressed, fermented, matured, and bottled.

Tokaji furmint: **Furmint** is the most important grape in Tokaj (it makes up about sixty percent of the grapes grown there). *Furmint* wines are full bodied, often matured in oak, and can be *száraz* (dry) or *félédes* (semi-sweet). Dry *furmint* wines are a classically Hungarian flavor.

Tokaji hárslevelu: *Hárslevelu* is the second most important variety grown in Tokaj (about thirty percent). *Hárslevelu* wines can be dry, but are more often semi-dry or sweet.

Tokaji sárgamuskotály: Known internationally as muscat lunel, this grape can also produce floral dry wines, but is most often added to *aszú* wines.

TOKAJI ASZÚ AND ESZENCIA

Tokaji *aszú* and *eszencia* are what have made Tokaj famous.

Tokaji aszú: The wine is made from late-harvested, raisin-like, botrytized grapes, with concentrated levels of sugar and aroma (also known as "noble rot"). The grapes are selectively harvested one at a time and the wine is measured in terms of sweetness from three *puttonyos* to six *puttonyos*. *Aszú* wines are aged in oak for several years and are primarily dessert wines.

Tokaji aszú eszencia: Even sweeter than *aszú*, this is made by adding *eszencia* syrup (see below) to the *aszú* wine. It would be the equivalent of a seven or eight *puttonyos* wine.

Tokaji eszencia: *Eszencia* is not strictly a wine because its high sugar content causes it to ferment extremely slowly. To make *eszencia*, a vat is filled with *aszú* berries and the pressure of the grapes pushing down on each other pushes out the eszencia, which is a thick, honey-like syrup. It's not really meant to be drunk straight, but more to be used as a component in *aszú* blends. It's definitely worth seeking out to taste if you have the opportunity to go to Tokaj.

LATE HARVEST AND SZAMORODNI:

These wines are made from the final harvest in Tokaj. The wine-making process differs from the dry wine process in that the grapes are macerated in base wine before they are pressed.

Tokaji szamorodni: After the *aszú* grapes are harvested by hand, berry by berry, whatever clusters are left are then picked whole during the *szamorodni* harvest. *Szamorodni* is aged in barrels for one or two years and can be either dry or sweet (depending on the amount of botrytized grapes left in the clusters). It's high in alcohol, is similar to Spanish sherry, and makes an excellent aperitif. Up until the eighteenth century, Poland was a major market for Tokaj wine, and this wine was one of the bestsellers. The name *szamorodni* is derived from a Polish word, meaning "as it was born."

Late harvest: These wines first began appearing in the mid-1990s, and are similar to *szamorodni* wines, but with a shorter aging period of just a few months.

TOKAJI FORDITÁS AND MÁSLÁS

These wines aren't as popular as they once were. They have been described as "*aszú*'s of the second try."

Tokaji Fordítás: Fordítás was once popular in Tokaj, but is now made in very small quantities. *Fordítás* means "turning over" and the wine is made by macerating the residue left after pressing the berries the first time for *aszú*. Since it still contains plenty of sweetness, it's soaked in fresh must for a second time, which results in *fordítás. Fordítás* can be as sweet as a three, four, or five *puttonyos aszú* wine, but not as full bodied and with more tannins. Chateau Dereszla, however, has created a dry version.

Tokaji Máslás: Máslás, which means "copy," is made by pouring must on the *aszú* lees (the sediment that has accumulated during fermentation and aging) and then fermenting it again.

THE "KING OF WINE"

For almost as long as they have been being made, Tokaj wines have had a fan club that has included royalty, artists, and popes. Tokaji *aszú* made its way to the capitals and palaces of Europe long before there were advertising campaigns and marketing slogans to spread the word. "The seventeenth to the nineteenth century was the glorious period of Tokaj wines," said Mészáros. "They were drunk by royalty and celebrities." The wine was treated as a symbol of Hungary and was often used as a diplomatic tool. After receiving a shipment of Tokaj wine as a gift from Prince Rákóczi II, Louis XIV famously called it the "wine of kings, the king of wine." Peter the Great is said to have ordered 600 barrels of it every year and subsequent czars spent significant proportions of their court budgets on keeping their supply of Tokaj wine stocked. Pope Pius X was a great fan and enthused: "such wine is what is worthy of the Holy Father." When Empress Maria Theresa sent Pope Benedict XIV a gift of Tokaj wine, he exclaimed: "Blessed be the soil that hath grown thee, blessed

THE TOKAJ NAME DISPUTE

....

FRANCE HAS ITS TOKAY D'ALSACE (WHICH IS ACTU-
ALLY PINOT GRIS). ITALY HAS ITS TOCAI (WHICH IS
also called *tocai friulano* or *tokai*). And in Australia
the muscadelle grape is used to make dessert wines called
Tokay. To confuse matters even further, in English the
spelling "Tokay" (with a "y") is often mistakenly used to
refer to wines from Hungary's Tokaj (with a "j") region.
None of these other "Tokaj" wines are in any way related
to the Tokaj wines made in Hungary. Tokay d'Alsace is a
light, dry white wine, while the Italian *tocai friulano* is an
aromatic dry white. Hungarians hope that like other geo-
graphically protected products—like Champagne and
Prosciutto di Parma—the name Tokaj (and its variations)
will be solely used to refer to wines originating in this
region. During the negotiations for Hungary's accession to
the European Union, the Italian and French governments
agreed to rename their wines by 2007 to appease Hungary.
Alsatian winemakers agreed to change their labels to read
"Tokay-Pinot Gris d'Alsace." Italy's Friuli-Venezia Giulia
region, however, appealed to the European Court of Justice

in Luxembourg, which ruled that the name must be changed. *Friulano bianco* is now the brand new name for the former Italian tocai.

The only other region that produces wines related to the true Tokaj is a small section of Slovakia. When Hungary was broken up in 1920 with the Treaty of Trianon, a few villages that were part of the Tokaj wine region went to Czechoslovakia, in the area which is now Slovakia. There has been a long-standing dispute between Tokaj winemakers and winemakers in Slovakia over Slovakia's right to call its wines "Tokaj." Hungarians argue that quality is lower in Slovakia, and they don't like the fact that Slovakian winemakers produce a two *puttonyos aszú*. The Slovak and Hungarian agriculture ministers eventually signed an agreement in 2004 with the European Commission to coordinate production procedures and quality control. Under this agreement, wine produced on a 565-hectare area in Slovakia will be allowed to continue to use the Tokaj name. On another confusing note, on wine bottles you will see the word "Tokaji" (with an "I" tacked on the end), which refers to a wine from the Tokaj region.

be the woman who sent thee, and blessed am I who drink thee." Catherine the Great, Frederick II of Prussia, Napoleon III, Goethe, Schubert, Beethoven, and Liszt all loved Tokaj wine. Emperor Franz Joseph sent Queen Victoria Tokaji *aszú* as a birthday gift every year. It was also dubbed the greatest sweet wine in the world in an 1866 vineyard reference book. Voltaire praised his favorite wine by saying: "Tokaj brings vigor to the smallest fiber of my brain and revives the enchanting sparkle of wit and good humor." Luckily, we ordinary people can also enjoy the golden sweet nectar that is Tokaji *aszú*.

TOKAJ FOOD PAIRINGS

Similar to Spanish sherry, dry or sweet *szamorodni* makes the perfect aperitif. Drinking sweet Tokaj wine with goose liver or blue cheese is one of the most deliciously classic combinations. Although Tokaji *aszú* is a dessert wine, I prefer to drink it on its own as a liquid dessert. But nobody knows the ideal accompaniments for Tokaj wine better than the people who create them. Here's what some winemakers recommend: "Dry unoaked *furmint* is perfect with seafood, fish, or oysters," said Disznoko's Mészáros. Bacsó from Oremus recommends his *Mandolás* (dry *furmint*) with grilled meats, lamb, or Camembert cheese. In line with the company's Spanish background, he also said his *szamorodni* is great with jamón Ibérico and melon. Füleky's Tamás Majoros drinks semi-dry *furmint* with smoked fish or salads. Degenfeld's semi-dry muscat lunel is nice with desserts that incorporate fruit, caramel, or white chocolate, said Gábor Rakaczki. Angelika Árvay suggests drinking their dry Vulcanus Cuvée with sushi, spicy food, or roasted pork.

These winemakers confirm that sweet Tokaj wines are not just for dessert. "Tokaji *aszú* is nice with Asian food like Chinese sweet and sour or spicy Indian food," said Mészáros. Attila Domokos from Dobogó likes to drink Dobogó's late-harvest wine (called Mylitta) with pumpkin soup or scampi. "We asked chefs like Alain Ducasse and Paul Bocuse to come up with food pairings for our wines without using foie gras, blue cheese, or dessert," said Edit Bai from Dereszla. "They suggested scallops as the ideal food." Bacsó recommends his five *puttonyos aszú* with fruity desserts and those that aren't too sweet. "But six *puttonyos aszú* is better with heavier desserts with hazelnut and chocolate in them," he said. János Árvay's *Édes Élet* (Sweet Life) cuvée (which was created for his business partner's wedding) could be matched with citrus-flavored desserts, said Angelika Árvay. As for *eszencia*? "It can be kept in the refrigerator for years," said Angelika Árvay. "It's good to drip it over goose liver or mix it with olive oil and put it on an arugula salad."

WINE TOURING IN HUNGARY

B UDAPEST UNDOUBTEDLY HOLDS MOST OF THE COUNTRY'S TOP RESTAURANTS, BUT THE REST OF THE COUNTRY is guardian to Hungary's food and wine traditions. If you have the time, head out of Budapest and pay a visit to some of Hungary's wineries. Wine tourism is becoming increasingly popular in Hungary, and it's better organized every year. Most winemakers are eager to give tours and tastings. Still, even in Villány and Tokaj—the two most important (and best-organized) wine regions—things are not always tourist-friendly. In less-visited regions, it can even be downright difficult to visit wineries. It pays to organize your trip at least a few weeks in advance to minimize wasted time, and having a flexible attitude is invaluable. No matter what a winery's official opening hours are (if they even have any), they tend to be flexible. Although I always recommend calling ahead for an appointment, it can't hurt to pop in if you happen to be there. "We won't throw you out if you show up without an appointment, but we would prefer some advance notice," is what many wineries told me.

Part of the pleasure of visiting Hungarian wineries is their sheer variety. One day a winemaker himself may give you a casual tour, drawing wine straight from the casks. The next day you could be part of a group being led on an organized tour of an entire estate—from the vineyards and the fermentation rooms to the bottling plant and the cellar. Many of the smaller wineries don't have dedicated tasting rooms, and often a member of the winemaker's family will be your guide. If a winery has its own kitchen or restaurant, I highly recommend you pre-arrange a meal there. When wineries do serve food, it's usually traditional Hungarian, served family-style. Many wineries also offer accommodation at their guesthouses (*panzió*). Most have at least one person who speaks English. Unless you're interested in very specific details, you'll probably find that it doesn't much matter if your host speaks your language. Here is a short list of wineries within reach of Budapest, and further afield, that should be enough to get you started.

DAY TRIPS FROM BUDAPEST

ETYEKI KÚRIA

ETYEK, ÖREGHEGY ✦ TEL: (22) 708-130, 06-30/922-5261

WWW.ETYEKIKURIA.HU

HILLTOP NESZMÉLY

NESZMÉLY, MELEGESHEGY ✦ TEL: (34) 550-450

WWW.HILLTOP.HU

NYAKAS PINCE

TÖK, KÖZPONTI MAJOR ✦ TEL: (23) 341-129

WWW.NYAKAS.HU

THE TOKAJ-HEGYALJA WINE REGION

ÁRVAY ÉS TÁRSA PINCÉSZET (HÉTFÜRTÖS)

TOKAJ, JÓZSEF ATTILA UTCA 2 ✦ TEL: (47) 552-155

WWW.ARVAYBOR.HU

CHATEAU DERESZLA

BODROGKERESZTÚR, FELSO UTCA 2 ✦ TEL: (47) 396-004

WWW.DERESZLA.COM

DISZNÓKO SZOLOBIRTOK

MEZOZOMBOR, DISZNÓKO-DULO ✦ TEL: (47) 569-410

WWW.DISZNOKO.HU

DOBOGÓ PINCÉSZET

TOKAJ, DÓZSA GYÖRGY UTCA 1 ✦ TEL: (47) 552-147

WWW.DOBOGO.HU

FÜLEKY

BODROGKERESZTÚR, ISKOLA UTCA 15 ✦ TEL: (47) 396-478

WWW.FULEKY-TOKAJ.COM

GRÓF DEGENFELD SZOLOBIRTOK

TARCAL, TERÉZIA KERT 9 ✦ TEL: (47) 380-173

WWW.DEGENFELD.HU

TOKAJ OREMUS

TOLCSVA, BAJCSY-ZSILINSZKY UTCA 45 ✦ TEL: (47) 384-505

WWW.TOKAJOREMUS.COM

THE VILLÁNY-SIKLÓS WINE REGION

ATTILA GERE WINERY AND GERE & WENINGER WINERY

VILLÁNY, ERKEL FERENC UTCA 2/A ✦ TEL: (72) 492-839

WWW.GERE.HU

BÉLA JEKL

VILLÁNY, PETOFI SÁNDOR UTCA 46 ✦ TEL: (72) 492-729

WWW.JEKL.HU

BOCK PINCE

VILLÁNY, BATTHYÁNY UTCA 15 ✦ TEL: (72) 492-919

WWW.BOCK.HU

MALATINSZKY KÚRIA

VILLÁNY, BATTHYÁNY UTCA 27 ✦ TEL: (72) 493-042

WWW.MALATINSZKY.HU

POLGÁR PINCÉSZET

VILLÁNY, HUNYADI JÁNOS UTCA 19 (*winery & panzió*)

VILLÁNY, ARANY JÁNOS UTCA 7 (*cellar*)

TEL: (72) 492-053 ✦ WWW.POLGARPINCE.HU

VYLYAN PINCÉSZET

KISHARSÁNY, FEKETE-HEGY ✦ TEL: (72) 579-725

WWW.VYLYAN.HU

WUNDERLICH PINCÉSZET

VILLÁNY, BAROSS GÁBOR ÚT 108

TEL: (72) 592-970 ✦ 06-30/249-7507

WWW.WUNDERLICH.HU

CHAPTER 3

....

WHAT ELSE TO DRINK

Pálinkás jó reggelt!
Have a good morning with pálinka!

Sörre bor mindenkor, borra sör meggyötör.
Beer before wine anytime, wine before
beer makes a bad rider.

—HUNGARIAN PROVERBS

"Tomorrow we're going to the Kobánya club where the best
royal beer in the entire world is served."

—*Seven Owls*, GYULA KRÚDY

FROM ROUGH TO SMOOTH

O F COURSE THERE'S MORE TO DRINK IN HUNGARY THAN WINE. IN A HUNGARIAN HOME YOU MAY BE offered a shot of rough *házi pálinka* (homemade fruit brandy). Maybe it wasn't made in that very home, perhaps it was even made by relatives in Transylvania. All the same, particularly in the countryside, it's customary to greet guests with a drink. Stick around long enough and you're sure to come across *pálinka* so harsh it feels like gasoline sliding through your insides. But it's not all like that. Just as wine is increasingly being taken seriously in Hungary, so is *pálinka*, and there has been a proliferation of premium *pálinka* over the last few years to prove it. Then there's Unicum, that other very Hungarian drink, which has been a bitter favorite for more than 200 years. Hungary has dozens of types of domestically brewed beer, and the country is virtually spitting out mineral water from its thermal springs. Non-alcoholic drinks like concentrated and sugary fruit syrups (*szörp*) are made from a variety of seasonal fruit at home (and also commercially). They are served diluted with soda water. Another popular homemade drink in the spring is elderflower juice, which is made by soaking elderflowers and lemon slices in sugary water.

PÁLINKA

P ÁLINKA, WHICH IS HUNGARIAN FRUIT BRANDY, IS QUICKLY DOWNED WITH BRAVADO IN SOME CIRCLES, with glasses dramatically slammed down afterwards. The stronger and harsher it is, the better. "*Pálinka* gives strength," goes the old folk saying, which must be why people in rural areas have traditionally sipped a little of it with breakfast to prepare them for a day of work in the fields or factories. It's a necessity in the pre-dawn hours at traditional village pig slaughters, when the cold is biting and you've got hours to go until the feast reaches the table. *Pálinka* is practically essential at family celebrations and holidays wouldn't be complete without a pre-meal round of *pálinka*. It's an aperitif on special occasions or in anticipation of a big meal. It's part of a welcome ritual that hospitable Hungarians go through when guests show up. When there are guests, the more bottles on the table, the better.

Pálinka was first used for medicinal purposes, rather than pleasurable ones. Advertisements no longer boast of its healing properties, but you'll still hear people recommend it for stomach-aches, colds, fever, or even high blood pressure. Despite the craze over high-end *pálinka*, the *házi* stuff still has its following, and in the countryside there are distilling houses where small-scale growers take their own fruit to be processed into *pálinka*.

For most people *pálinka* isn't an everyday indulgence, and for a small but increasing number of people it's a hobby, almost like wine tasting. "It is clear that a much richer, variable distillate culture used to flourish. This colorful culture receded in the twentieth century," wrote Géza Balázs, author of *Pálinka, Hungaricum: The Hungarian Specialty*. But *pálinka* culture has been coming back over the past five years or so. A revival of Hungarian distilleries in the 1990s has resulted in the re-emergence of some nearly forgotten types of *pálinka*. Once made with old or half-rotten fruit that couldn't be used for anything else, today's premium *pálinka* is often made in small batches, and always with the best quality fruit. A selection of premium *pálinka* is usually added to wine lists in the nicer restaurants, and they're not cheap. "The price difference between the different varieties of *pálinka* isn't always reflective of quality," pointed out Ákos Szokolics, the marketing director at the Agárdi distillery. Often, the most expensive *pálinka* is that made from rare, hard-to-pick fruit.

Perhaps the most famous *pálinka* is the *szatmári szilvapálinka* (plum *pálinka* from Szabolcs-Szatmár county in northeastern Hungary). It, along with plum *pálinka* from Békés in the southeast, apricot *pálinka* from the Great Plain around Kecskemét, and apple *pálinka* (also from Szabolcs-Szatmár county) are products with protected designation of origin in Hungary. Another exciting change has been the revival of *törköly pálinka*, the Hungarian version of grappa. This *pálinka* is distilled from pomace (the residue left from grapes after pressing them for wine; mostly stalks, skins, and seeds). In the grape-growing regions *törköly pálinka* was once commonly produced, but during the Communist era of mass produced wines, the tradition suffered. Now, both *pálinka* distilleries and winemakers have returned to making *törköly pálinka*, and they're making excellent varietal *pálinka* from the pomace of grapes like cabernet franc, merlot, *irsai olivér*, *sárgamuskotály*, *olaszrizling*, and chardonnay. Like wine, some of this *törköly pálinka* is also labeled with the vintage year and the best is aged in oak barrels. Also look out for the *aszú törköly pálinka* which is being made by a few distillers and for *törköly pálinka* by wineries like Attila Gere and Ede and Zsolt Tiffán in Villány, Göncöl in Tokaj, Hilltop in Neszmély, Thummerer in Eger, Zoltán Heimann in Szekszárd, and Ottó Légli in Balatonboglár.

Just as it's best to buy your wine at specialized wine shops, if you're looking for premium *pálinka* you're better off going to a *pálinka* shop (there are several in Budapest; see Chapter 8) and some wine shops also sell good *pálinka*. High quality labels to watch out for include: Zwack Nemes, Agárdi, Zimek (also called Treffpunkt GAR 2000), Tarpa, Vitalis, Brill Market, Miskolci Likörgyár, Rézüsti, Zsindelyes, Szicsek, Rézangyal, and Békési.

PÁLINKA TRANSLATOR

P ÁLINKA IS INCREASINGLY BEING MADE WITH MORE UNUSUAL AND LESSER-KNOWN VARIETIES OF FRUIT. Since some of these fruits aren't even available outside of Central Europe, this list should help when you're shopping for *pálinka.*

ágyas pálinka: *pálinka* with fruit or herbs at the bottom of the bottle ("bedded" *pálinka*)

borpárlat: a drink made from distilled wine; it's essentially brandy

erdei or vad: wild

készült: made

kisüsti: small batches of *pálinka* made by using the traditional method of double batch distillation

pálinka: brandy distilled from fruit with no added sugar or alcohol

pálinkafozde: *pálinka* distillery

párlat: any kind of distilled drink

szeszesital: a distilled spirit of lower quality than a true *pálinka*

szilvórium: a high-quality plum *pálinka*

törköly pálinka: *pálinka* distilled from pomace

alma: apple

barack, sárgabarack, or kajszibarack: apricot

bodza: elderberry

birs: quince; it's often called *birsalma* in years when it's shaped like an apple and *birskörte* in years when it's shaped like a pear

cigánymeggy: a collective name for any type of small cherries

cseresznye: cherry

csipkebogyó: rosehip

dió: walnut

eper: strawberry

erdei vadmálna: wild raspberry

fehér eper: mulberry

feketeribizli: black currant

gesztenye: chestnut

kökény: sloe

málna: raspberry

meggy: sour cherry

mézes: honey flavored

oszibarack: peach

ringló: greengage plum

sárgadinnye: cantaloupe or honeydew melon

som: European Cornel (a species of dogwood that produces fruit)

szamóca: wild strawberry

szeder: blackberry

szilva: plum

szolo: grape

vadalma: a type of crabapple native to Central Europe

Vilmoskörte: Williams or Bartlett pear

UNICUM

....

I DISCOVERED UNICUM ON MY FIRST TRIP TO HUNGARY. IT TOOK ME AWHILE TO ACTUALLY LIKE IT, BUT I DID acquire a fascination for it because it's a national institution here. The round, green bottles stamped with a golden cross on a red label are ubiquitous in Hungary. There's hardly a Hungarian home which doesn't have a bottle stashed away, ceremoniously pulled out when visitors arrive. Unicum has such a hold over Hungarian drinkers that they tend not to drink any other brands of bitters, unlike in Italy (which is another bitters-loving nation), where it's common to see up to half a dozen types of bitters (plus Unicum) on bar shelves. In Hungary, Unicum sits alone.

Unicum has a long history that in some ways mirrors the history of modern Hungary itself. The story of Unicum is the story of the Zwack family, which has owned the company since the end of the eighteenth century, with the exception of the forty-year period when it was nationalized by the Communists. Dr. Zwack, a physician for the Imperial Court of the Austro-Hungarian Dual Monarchy, is credited with creating the drink to alleviate the royal family's digestion problems. It wasn't produced for the general public until 1840 when József Zwack founded the company. It was one of the first commercial distilleries to use all natural ingredients, and it eventually became the sole liquor purveyor to the Imperial Court.

The factory was destroyed during World War II. It was then rebuilt, only to be confiscated and nationalized by the Communist government in 1948. Most of the family left the country, ending up in America and Italy. The Zwacks had smuggled the original recipe out of the country, but the factory continued to produce a fake version of Unicum. Péter Zwack returned to Hungary in 1989 to rebuild the family business, and he was among the first in Hungary to buy back a business from the government.

So, what is Unicum? It's a thick black concoction, made from more than forty herbs and spices. The exact composition is a carefully guarded family secret which was stored in a safe deposit box in New York during the Communist era. Zwack won't reveal the formula of herbs and spices, but he will explain the rest of the process. Part of the secret mixture is macerated for thirty days in water, while the other part is distilled. Then, in a process that has remained almost unchanged for more than 200 years, both are blended and aged in oak casks for six months. The distillation gives Unicum its distinctive aroma and bitter bouquet, according to Zwack, and the process of aging adds mellowness and body. The family is serious when they say that the recipe is a secret: only the immediate family members know the exact proportions of herbs that go into a bottle. "In case of an emergency," said former Zwack Communications Director, Péter Kerényi, "the Archbishop of Esztergom safeguards the recipe."

Old Unicum advertisements from the early 1900s are classic, and are among the most famous examples of Hungarian graphic design. The most popular is a poster of a crazed man in the water, on the verge of drowning, who sees a bottle of Unicum floating in front of him, implying that the Unicum has saved him. Even today, said Kerényi, people mail the company photos of themselves trying to recreate this classic poster. "What they don't realize," he said, "is that when the poster was created, there was a contest in Budapest for 'the ugliest man' to appear in the poster."

The trick to drinking Unicum, according to Péter Zwack, is to get people to drink it twice, since he claims that it becomes addictive after the second try. The Unicum marketing campaign in America even used the slogan "Force Yourself." Hungarians are adamant that the drink also has proven medicinal qualities, but that may be just an excuse to drink more of it.

Visit the Unicum Museum, located at the Unicum factory, to learn more about the drink and the family. [IX. Soroksári út 26; Tel: 476-2379; www.zwack.hu; Open Monday through Saturday 10am to 6pm; Tram 2 (to Haller utca), Tram 24 (to Soroksári út)]

PÁLINKA TASTING

In the pub, pálinka is drunk more for the effect than for the taste. But because the growing number of *pálinka* connoisseurs appreciate the craft and raw materials that went into making good *pálinka*, they pay more attention to how they drink it. In restaurants and bars *pálinka* is normally served in portions of two or four centiliters.

+ *Pálinka* is usually served in unflattering shot glasses filled to the rim. But, like wine, the right type of glassware makes a difference. So the alcohol scent won't overwhelm, the ideal glass is long stemmed, round at the bottom, and straight and narrow at the top.

+ Don't swirl your *pálinka*. Rather than smelling the fruit aroma, you'll just smell the alcohol.

+ Don't chill *pálinka*. It will dull both the flavor and the bouquet (sixteen to eighteen degrees Celsius, or sixty-one to sixty-four degrees Fahrenheit, is the recommended serving temperature).

+ Generally, the older the *pálinka*, the better it will be.

+ Distillers talk about the "dry test": if ten minutes after drinking your *pálinka* the empty glass smells like fruit rather than alcohol, then the *pálinka* was good quality.

BEER (SÖR)

Hungary is better known as a wine-drinking country, but Magyars also like to drink beer. They drink more than seventy-five liters of it per capita annually. The history of beer brewing in Hungary goes back to the nomadic Magyars, who likely learned how to use hops, barley, and malt to brew beer from the Slavs. A will from 1152 requesting a beer burial feast is the earliest Hungarian document mentioning beer. In ancient times beer wasn't drunk for its taste or alcohol content. Like *pálinka*, it was drunk for its health benefits and healing properties. Until the fourteenth century beer was only made at home, but then monasteries began producing it and breweries with attached beer halls opened. Guilds were developed around this time in Hungary. But until the sixteenth century, when brewers organized their own guilds, everyone still had the right to brew their own beer at home.

The beer industry really started to develop in the 1840s when a law made it again possible for anyone to brew, sell, and import beer. In 1845 the first commercial brewery was built in Pest by a brewer named Peter Schmidt and he stored his beer in the Kőbánya neighborhood, which today is Budapest's tenth district.

Historically, Kobánya was a vast limestone quarry (which is what its name means) that supplied the stone used to build many of Budapest's buildings. "The heyday of the Austro-Hungarian Empire, and the expansion of Budapest, set the scene for the growth of lager brewing," wrote beer journalist Michael Jackson. "In Kobánya, six breweries rose." It turned out that the massive underground caverns in the neighborhood were ideal for fermenting and storing beer because of their steady cool temperatures. Brewers also discovered high-quality water under the old quarries, and Kobánya soon became known as "beer city."

THE HUNGARIAN BEER SPECTRUM

Dreher:

Dreher Classic is Dreher's flagship pilsner-style lager, with a 5.2 alcohol percentage, in a green bottle. Dreher Bak is a double bock with a 7.3 alcohol percentage. Dreher introduced Arany Ászok, which is a popular pilsner-style lager with 4.5 percent alcohol content, in 1989. Kobányai Világos is an inexpensive lager that was one of the most popular drinks during the Communist era.

Borsodi:

The Borsodi Brewery's slogan is "the foamy side of life" and its flagship beer is Borsodi Sör. With its green and yellow label, this pilsner-type beer has 4.6 percent alcohol and is one of Hungary's best sellers. The Borsodi Bivaly (Bosodi Buffalo) is a lager and is the brewery's newest beer, with 6.5 percent alcohol. Borostyán, which is the brewery's premium beer, is made from roasted malt and has an amber color with 5.2 percent alcohol.

Heineken Hungaria Breweries (formerly Brau Union Hungária):

Brau Union Hungária Breweries is part of the Heineken Group and in addition to the more than a dozen beers it produces under license, its homegrown brands include its flagship lager, Soproni (4.5 percent alcohol). It also produces Sárkány Sör (Dragon Beer, a lager with 4.5 percent alcohol), Talléros, Arany Hordó (Golden Barrel), and Soproni Kinizsi.

Pécsi:

The Pécsi Brewery created Szalon Sör in 1907 and the lager with 4.6 percent alcohol has been the company's flagship ever since. Its other beers include Szalon Félbarna (a semi-dark beer with 5.5 percent alcohol), Szalon Barna (a dark German-style beer with 5.8 percent alcohol), and Szalon Búzasör (an unfiltered wheat beer with 5.2 percent alcohol). The Három Királyok, "the Three Kings", is a seasonal beer with 6.6 percent alcohol produced from around Christmas until New Year's Eve.

DRINKING BEER IN HUNGARY

In bars you'll find many of the world's big-name beers available, but in restaurants the only draft beer available is often Dreher. Hungary's four major breweries produce a wide variety of beer, which is significantly cheaper than the imported kind. All of Hungary's big breweries—Dreher, Borsodi, Heineken Hungaria, and Pécsi—are majority foreign-owned. The microbrewery movement hasn't really caught on yet. The Ilzer Brewery, south of Budapest in Monor, is a joint German-Hungarian operation which started brewing in 1997. It's the best-known small brewery and produces a range of wheat beer (unfiltered, filtered, and semi-dark), a rye beer (called Roggen), and a low calorie beer (called Diet). Ilzer also claims to be the only Hungarian brewery to brew all of its beer following the Bavarian Purity Law of 1516.

Hungarian beer usually has an alcohol content between 4.5 and 6.7 percent and is most often sold in half-liter bottles and cans. Draft beer, or *csapolt sör*, comes in a few different sizes: a *korsó* is a half-liter mug, a pohár is a 300-milliliter glass, and a *pikoló* is a 200-milliliter glass (though this small measurement is hardly used anymore).

In Budapest there are a few places worth visiting for their beer selections:

HAXEN KIRÁLY ÉTTEREM

VI. KIRÁLY UTCA 100 ✦ TEL: 351-6793 ✦ WWW.HAXEN.HU

CC ✦ OPEN MONDAY *through* FRIDAY NOON *to* MIDNIGHT

SATURDAY NOON *to* 1:30AM ✦ M1 *(to Vörösmarty utca)*

TRAM 4, 6 *(to Oktogon)*

PAULANER BRAUHAUS

XII. ALKOTÁS ÚT 53 *(inside the MOM Park shopping center)*

TEL: 224-2020 ✦ WWW.PAULANERSORHAZ.HU ✦ CC

OPEN DAILY 11AM *to* 1AM ✦ TRAM 61 *(to Csörsz utca)*

KOLBÁSZDA BAJOR SÖRÖZO

I. GYORSKOCSI UTCA 6 ✦ TEL: 225-3674 ✦ CC

OPEN DAILY 11AM *to* 11PM ✦ M2 BUS 11, 39, 60, 86

TRAM 19 *(to Batthyány tér)*

ILZER SÖRGYÁRI SÖRÖZO

The Ilzer Brewery (35 kilometers south of Budapest in Monor) doesn't offer organized brewery tours. But there is a beer hall (and a hotel) attached, which offers Ilzer's brews and decent food (and a two-lane bowling alley and squash courts for entertainment). Ilzer got its start as a *pálinka* distillery, and its Ecker line of *pálinka* is also produced in Monor and sold at the restaurant. In addition to the unusual beer *pálinka* (*sör pálinka*), there are flavors like raspberry, melon, apple, and plum. The spacious hall is filled with wooden tables and chairs, with walls covered in beer-themed paintings: coopers making barrels, a horse-drawn beer wagon, and a fermentation cellar. A back room takes a stab at more formal dining, with bubblegum-pink walls and tablecloths and a mural of barmaids holding out their beer mugs. There's also an outdoor beer garden, open during the warm months. The menu here is full of simple Hungarian and Bavarian food, with lots of breaded and fried dishes. The place has a few house specialties, which include dishes made with beer, such as the "Ilzer steak," which is cooked in wheat beer, "beer cheese," and "beer sorbet." In addition to the local guys smoking and drinking beer, the place is popular with families. There's little English spoken here, and there are no English menus.

MONOR, GÉP UTCA 1 ✦ TEL: (29) 611-666

WWW.ILZER.HU ✦ CC ✦ OPEN 24 HOURS

By car from Budapest take Ülloi út towards the airport. Soon before the airport (near Vecsés) there will be signs for Monor and Road 4. Take Road 4 to Monor and turn left at the Ezüst Kanál Étterem. Cross the train tracks and follow the signs towards Gomba, and the brewery and restaurant will be outside of the village on the left-hand side of the road.

BEER TRANSLATOR

....

alkalmi sörkülönlegesség: seasonal beer

alkoholmentes: alcohol free

ászok: lager

bak: bock beer (a strong lager which originated in Munich, and can be dark, amber, or pale in color)

barna sör: dark German-style beer

búzasör: wheat beer

csapolt sör: draft beer

erjesztett: bottle fermented

félbarna: semi-dark beer

korsó: a 500-ml (16.9 ounce) mug of beer

maláta: malt

pikoló: a 200-ml (6.7 ounce) glass of beer

pilzeni or pils: pilsner

pohár: a 300-ml (10.1 ounce) glass of beer

rozs sör: rye beer

sörözo: beer pub

sörfozde, sörgyár, or serfozde: brewery

szuretlen: unfiltered

szurt: filtered

üveges sör: bottled beer

világos sör: pale ale

MINERAL WATER (ÁSVÁNYVÍZ)

....

HUNGARY'S LOCATION IN THE CARPATHIAN BASIN MEANS THAT MOST OF HUNGARY'S MINERAL WATER comes from thermal springs (the same ones that supply the bathhouses). The high temperatures cause more minerals to be dissolved in the water, which is why Hungarian water has a high mineral content (Hungarian waters tend to be high in calcium, magnesium, hydrogen-carbonate, chlorine, and fluorine). True mineral water will always be labeled as *természetes ásványvíz* (natural mineral water). If a bottle is labeled *ásványi anyaggal dúsított víz*, it's essentially tap water with added minerals. Mineral water can be *szénsavas* or *buborékos* (carbonated, which most Hungarians tend to prefer), or *szénsavmentes* (still). The carbonation speeds up the absorption of alcohol into the bloodstream, which may explain why the *fröccs* (wine spritzer) is such a popular drink in Hungary.

IVÓCSARNOK:
DRINKING STRAIGHT FROM THE SOURCE

M INERAL WATER IS A NATIONAL OBSESSION IN HUNGARY, BUT IT DOESN'T ONLY COME BOTTLED. For an all-natural pick-me-up, drink mineral-rich water straight from the springs at the *ivócsarnok*— drinking hall—connected to the Rudas, Lukács, and Széchenyi bathhouses in Budapest. Order a *pohár* and a white-coated attendant will fill a thick glass mug with lukewarm, metallic-smelling water for you to drink on the spot. The regulars bring their own plastic bottles and fill bags with liters of the mineral-rich, sulfur-scented water to drink at home. The mineral content varies from spring to spring and there are signs posting the exact amounts. Compared with most of Hungary's leading brands of bottled water, spring water has a significantly higher mineral content.

Different springs are recommended for healing different ailments. The water from the Széchenyi and the Lukács is particularly recommended for ulcers, intestinal problems, gallbladder problems, and calcium deficiency. Drinking at the Rudas *ivócsarnok* (under the Buda side of the Erzsébet híd) is a more serious matter. You have a choice between three springs—the Attila spring pours out the most mineral-rich water, the Juventus is said to help with high blood pressure and premature aging, and the Hungária supposedly heals stomach and kidney problems. This water is a bargain at 20 HUF for a glass or 35 HUF for a liter. Don't forget to bring a bottle!

Note: these opening hours are for the drinking halls only, the bathhouses keep different hours. See www.spasbudapest.com for more information.

RUDAS GYÓGYFÜRDŐ
I. DÖBRENTEI TÉR 9 ✦ TEL: 356-1322
OPEN MONDAY, WEDNESDAY, *and* FRIDAY 11AM *to* 6PM
TUESDAY *and* THURSDAY 7AM *to* 2PM ✦ BUS 7, 86 (*to Rudas fürdo*)
BUS 8 (*to Erzsébet híd, Budai hídfo*), BUS 5 (*to Szarvas tér*)
TRAM 18, 19 (*to Döbrentei tér*)

LUKÁCS GYÓGYFÜRDŐ

II. FRANKEL LEÓ UTCA 25-29 ✦ TEL: 326-1695

OPEN MONDAY *through* FRIDAY 6AM *to* 6PM, SATURDAY *and*
SUNDAY 6AM *to* 4PM ✦ BUS 6, 60, 86, TRAM 4, 6
HÉV (*to Margit híd*) TRAM 17 (*to Szent Lukács Gyógyfürdő*)

SZÉCHENYI GYÓGYFÜRDŐ

XIV. ÁLLATKERTI KÖRÚT 11 (*in Városliget*) ✦ TEL: 363-3210

OPEN MONDAY *through* FRIDAY 6AM *to* 6PM, SATURDAY
and SUNDAY 6AM *to* 6PM ✦ M1 (*to Széchenyi fürdő*)
TROLLEY 72 (*to Állatkert*)

Spring water gushes from the dome-covered turquoise fountain on the Buda side of the Szabadság bridge in front of the
Hotel Gellért [XI. Kelenhegyi út 4; Tram 18, 19, 47, 49, bus 7,
7A, 86 (to Szent Gellért tér)]. And free spring water flows from
the mouth of a gargoyle outside of the Dagály Gyógyfürdő [XIII.
Népfürdo utca 36; M3 (to Árpád híd), Tram 1, Bus 133 (to Népfürdo utca)].

THE OLD SCHOOL FRÖCCS

D ESPITE THE ABUNDANCE OF BARS IN BUDAPEST,
MOST HUNGARIANS AREN'T BIG COCKTAIL drinkers.
When they do mix alcohol, it's often white wine with soda
to make a *fröccs*, or spritzer (*spriccer*). They aren't as
popular as they once were, no doubt because local wine has gotten so good that it doesn't need to be diluted. You can still order a
fröccs practically anywhere, and they're great to drink when the hot
weather calls for something light and thirst quenching. Nowadays
spritzers come mainly in two varieties: *Kisfröccs* (small; equal parts
wine and soda) and Nagyfröccs (large; twice as much wine as soda).
And, today they are usually made with sparkling mineral water
rather than traditional soda water. Don't expect your *fröccs* to be
served in a stemmed wine glass, or with a twist of lemon. In Hungary they are served in tall, functional water glasses. *Note: 1 deciliter
(dl) equals approximately 3.4 ounces.*

KISFRÖCCS *(or Rövidlépés)*
"small fröccs" (or "small step")
1 DL WINE + 1 DL SODA

NAGYFRÖCCS *(or Hajtás)*
"big fröcc" (or "rush")
2 DL WINE + 1 DL SODA

HOSSZÚLÉPÉS
"big step"
1 DL WINE + 2 DL SODA

NAGY HÁZMESTER *(or Háziúr)*
"head janitor" (or "landlord")
4 DL WINE + 1 DL SODA

HÁZMESTER
"janitor"
3 DL WINE + 2 DL SODA

VICEHÁZMESTER *(or Fordítottja)*
"assistant janitor" (or "his reverse")
2 DL WINE + 3 DL SODA

KIS HÁZMESTER *(or Lakófröccs)*
"little janitor" (or "tenant fröccs")
1 DL WINE + 4 DL SODA

MAFLA
"klutz"
5 DL WINE + 5 DL SODA

SÓHERFRÖCCS
"stingy fröccs"
1 DL WINE + 9 DL SODA

KRÚDYFRÖCCS
"Krúdy fröccs" (named for Gyúla Krúdy)
9 DL WINE + 1 DL SODA

PISZKOS VÍZ
"dirty water"
A GLASS IN WHICH WINE HAS BEEN SERVED
+ WATER, FOR WHEN FUNDS ARE LOW

TRAUBISODA

....

THEY'VE GOT COKE AND PEPSI HERE TOO, BUT THERE'S NO SODA LIKE HUNGARIAN TRAUBISODA. MADE since 1971 at a factory on the shores of Lake Balaton, it's a deliciously light, white grape soda with just the right amount of sweetness, and the perfect amount of fizz. Traubi is made from sweet *saszla* grapes grown around Balaton and water that's rich in minerals, especially magnesium. It was the leading brand during Communism when western brands were hard to come by, and it then faded in popularity for a few years after the fall of the Iron Curtain. In 1991 the company was bought and revived by a Hungarian-American businessman (who had extensive legal problems for years since there were other companies selling soda under the Traubi name). Traubi is seen as a retro brand, and it now also comes in a kosher version. The company also revived another old Hungarian brand, the Márka soft drinks (which come in cherry, raspberry, grape, and orange flavors). But nothing beats the original Traubi. Much has been made of people drinking Traubi as a nostalgic link to the bygone days. I say, just drink it because it's a good local soda.

CHAPTER 4:

RESTAURANT BASICS

Edd meg, amit foztél.
What you have cooked, you should eat as well.

Üres hasnak nem elég a szép szó.
Fair words are not enough to an empty belly.

—HUNGARIAN PROVERBS

AND AT THE SAME TIME THEY ASKED FOR SOME WILD BOAR COOKED IN BULL'S BLOOD FROM EGER, sautéed saddle of venison, and for some fieldfare as well— dishes that at home in Szabolcs were difficult to get.

— *The Last Hungarian Soldier from 1848,*
GYULA KRÚDY

WHERE TO DINE & DRINK

....

RESTAURANTS IN HUNGARY GO BY THE NAMES *ÉTKEZDE*, *ÉTTEREM*, *VENDÉGLO*, OR *CSÁRDA*. TO GO OUT FOR A drink, take your pick from a *sörözo*, a *borozó*, or a *kert*. The Hungarian language is complicated enough for visitors, but don't let the different words for restaurant, café, and bar bog you down. These days the lines between the many types of eateries have been blurred. Restaurants might even call themselves by more than one name, like an *étterem-kávéház*. Or they might just call themselves whatever they please.

Étterem is the most common word for restaurant and can mean anything from a fancy white-tablecloth place to a fast-food eatery. Originally it referred to a more upscale restaurant, but these days *étterem* has taken on a more all-encompassing meaning. Historically a *vendéglo* was a step down from an *étterem*, in terms of both price and décor. It was the kind of place that served hearty portions of classic Hungarian food. Now the two terms are practically interchangeable, though a *vendéglo* might still be decorated with folksy knick-knacks and have red-and-white-checked tablecloths. A *kisvendéglo* is a small version of a *vendéglo*.

An *étkezde* or a *kifozde* is a simple no-frills place that usually serves lunch on weekdays, and sometimes Saturdays. They're usually one-room places with little decoration, and they can be horrible (think school cafeteria), or they can serve welcome portions of home-style comfort food. Regular customers are loyal and table-sharing is the norm. There's rarely coffee or alcohol since the idea is to eat quickly and surrender your table to someone else. There will barely be a word of English spoken, even at the better ones. An *étkezde* serves the kind of simple Hungarian dishes that people prepare at home. The short menu usually changes daily, offering a few soups, ready-made dishes like stew or roasted meat, freshly prepared dishes like big slabs of fried meat, pickled salads, *fozelék* (creamed vegetables), a pasta or two, and one or two desserts. There's often a pitcher of tap water on the table for sharing. When it comes time to pay, you're supposed to list off what you had while the waiter tallies up the bill (they'll be nice and do it for you if you don't speak Hungarian). There are generally two kinds of *étkezde*—those that scoop out their food straight from the chafing dishes under heat lamps, and those that prepare everything to order. Obviously the latter is preferred, and those are the ones I've listed in the next chapter.

Büfé generally refers to a snack counter serving basic things like cold sandwiches, drinks, and sweets. Some, like the ubiquitous Chinese fast-food joints (*kínai büfé*) have hot food. The *büfé* is often standing-room only, with counters for quickly devouring your meal. A *gyors étterem* is a fast food restaurant and a *gyors büfé* is a fast-food *büfé*. Carnivores on the go can pop into a *hús-hentesáru*, or a butcher shop, for a quick stand-up lunch of sausage and bread, and possibly roasted chicken or bacon. (See Chapter 5 for a list of these.)

A *kávéház* (coffeehouse, or café) can be a trendy place serving breakfast, lunch, and dinner along with an extensive wine list. Or it can be a classic *kávéház* where coffee is served on silver trays with tiny glasses of mineral water and the décor is lavish with gold gilt, fancy plasterwork, and crystal chandeliers. These are the places that were plentiful at the end of the nineteenth century and the beginning of the twentieth century, popular with writers, artists, and revolutionaries. During the 1930s the elegant *kávéház* was replaced by the simpler *eszpresszó* (also called *presszó*), which was (and still is) a smoky, unattractive place, serving cheap alcohol and strong coffee. Coffee can also be had at a *kávézó*, which generally refers to a small and simple place that serves coffee, and maybe some alcoholic drinks. A *cukrászda* is a pastry shop. It can be similar to a *kávéház* with an extensive coffee and drink menu, but it's usually a small place with a few tiny tables just big enough for a cup of coffee and a piece of cake. A *pékség* is a bakery, but unfortunately there are few dedicated bakeries left since most people buy their bread in the supermarkets. The upside is that good bread is cheap and plentiful.

A *sörözo* or a *kocsma* is a beer hall or a pub, that will sometimes have a full menu; a *borozó* is a wine bar that rarely serves food. The *borozó*, however, is far from a stylish place to sip a glass of good wine. It's usually a dark, dingy hole-in-the-wall (or ground, as they're often cellars) that pours cheap wine from plastic bottles. You'll be lucky to find anything drinkable here. This breed of seedy place generally opens long before daylight, with working men popping in for quick shots of *pálinka*, beer, or wine before starting their day. A *bár* in Hungarian is still a bar. But for a more unconventional drinking experience, do what Budapest's hipsters do and go to a *kert*. A *kert* is open-air, warm-weather-only bar (though a few are covered and open year-round), which is often behind unmarked doors in the courtyard of a crumbling, abandoned inner-city building. Entrepreneurs take advantage of the time between an old building being bought and the beginning of construction to transform an unused space into a whimsical bar, most of which are extraordinarily popular. Many are located in the old seventh-district Jewish quarter, others are on Margit Island or in green areas of Buda. Locations generally change from year to year. Some are around only for a fleeting summer. (To learn how to find them, see page 256.)

WHEN TO EAT

Eating habits differ widely between Budapest and the small towns and villages in the rest of the country. In the countryside breakfast is an important meal and a filling one, and is typically a variety of cold cuts, raw vegetables (like peppers, tomatoes, or whatever is in season), cheese, and lots of fresh bread. Coffee is essential. Like most cities where mornings are a blur of metro rides and traffic jams, Budapesters tend to eat light in the morning, often grabbing a *pogácsa* or a pastry on the way to work. Coffee is still essential. Though Hungarians prefer to take their coffee sitting down instead of in Styrofoam cups, there are an increasing amount of coffee-to-go shops in the city. Cafés generally offer breakfast, which can range from butter and rolls to ham and eggs. Few restaurants are open for breakfast in Hungary, and the concept of weekend brunch is still limited to hotel restaurants.

Hungarians often have a mid-morning snack, or *tízórai* (ten o'clock snack). Traditionally lunch has always been the main meal of the day, eaten anytime between noon and 2pm. On weekends it's an important family meal, complete with soup and dessert. In the countryside people tend to head home for lunch. In Budapest they're more likely to order food from a delivery service or go to a restaurant for a quick, cheap meal. Dinner, too, can mean different things depending on lifestyle. In the countryside, people tend to eat light dinners. In Hungary, "light" usually means something cold (rather than something low in calories), like a *hidegtál* (cold plate), similar to the traditional breakfast. For most people who spend their days working while their children are at school, dinner is now the main family meal that lunch once was considered.

THE MENU

Restaurant menus are notoriously long in Hungary. Many restaurants have not yet realized that quality is more important than quantity, and it's common for a menu to be the size of a three-ring binder, with several pages listing pork dishes alone. One Budapest restaurant proudly advertises its 192-page menu. To add to the mass of paper, it's typical for every type of liquor, soft drink, juice, and water that the place sells to be listed on the menu. The price of wine by the glass is generally listed by the deciliter, and if you order a glass of wine you will usually be brought a two-deciliter portion (unless you specify otherwise; one deciliter is equivalent to 100 millilters or approximately 3.4 ounces).

Almost without exception, menus in Hungary are the same at lunch and dinner. But many restaurants add inexpensive two or three courses fixed price lunch menus in the afternoon. In many restaurants the price of the main course often doesn't include anything but the meat. What Hungarians refer to as the garnish (*köret*) must be ordered separately. Choices usually include several types of potatoes (croquettes, fried, mashed, boiled, or parsley potatoes), rice, or *túrós csusza* (pasta with curd cheese and sour cream). To add to the stress of combing through long lists of too many choices, servers tend to arrive to take your order before you've had time to read through the appetizers (called *eloételek*, but often translated into English as *entrées*). If the server doesn't give you a wine list, ask for a *borlap*.

THE MEAL

The typical Hungarian meal consists of a starter or soup, followed by a main course, which is eaten with a salad, then coffee and dessert. Soup is an essential element, be it a chilled fruit soup in the summer or a thick bean soup in the winter. Often, a bowl (or cup) of consommé (*húsleves*) is the best way to go. Appetizers, on the other hand, play minor roles in the Hungarian kitchen, neglected by both customers and chefs. For purely practical reasons, it makes sense to skip the appetizer course in a restaurant. They tend to come in main-course portions, and given that main courses themselves are typically huge, the two courses together can be too much. Some typical Hungarian appetizers include: *Hortobágyi palacsinta* (thin pancakes stuffed with thick *pörkölt* [usually veal] and topped with sour cream and paprika sauce), *Tatár beefsteak* (beef tartare), *libamáj* or *kacsamáj* (foie gras, which can be prepared a number of ways), or *rántott sajt* (breaded and fried cheese). These days, however, as dining in Hungary becomes increasingly international, the variety of appetizers is increasing. Bread generally isn't served unless you order soup, and you'll usually have to request butter. Traditionally, when eating in family homes, wine isn't poured until after the soup course.

Vegetarianism does exist here, but most Hungarians are

unabashed meat eaters. Despite Hungary's rich variety of agriculture, at old-school restaurants pickles are the vegetable of choice and potatoes are often complemented by rice. Boiled, steamed, or grilled vegetables are unheard of in traditional Hungarian restaurants. Rather, they are stuffed, stewed, or made into *fozelék*: a classic Hungarian vegetable preparation in which sour cream and roux are added to thicken cooked vegetables. Traditionally, salads are some form of pickled vegetables or vegetables soaked in the typically Hungarian briny salad dressing. They are usually brought to the table before the main course arrives, but they're only eaten alongside the main course. It might seem unusual to order a plate of pickles or pickled peppers at a restaurant, but with a big plate of fatty stew or fried meat, they really do serve their purpose, which is to cut the fat and help everything go down a little smoother. There are so many international restaurants here now that it's no longer impossible to order a proper salad (the kind with lettuce and dressing), and to eat it before your meal (or afterwards, if you please), but main-course salads are still rare in traditional Hungarian restaurants.

Soups like *halászlé* (fisherman's soup), *gulyás* (goulash), and *Jókai bableves* (bean soup) can also be substituted for a main course. As a holdover from the days when baking was strictly regulated by the guilds, you won't find fancy cakes in restaurants. Coffeehouses and pastry shops are the places to go for those, while traditional Hungarian restaurants will serve sweets like *rétes* (strudel), *palacsinta* (crepes), *Somlói galuska* (chunks of chocolate and vanilla sponge cake, with vanilla custard, raisins, walnuts, rum syrup, and chocolate sauce), *gesztenyepüré* (chestnut purée), and *mákos guba* (bread pudding with poppy seed sauce). Or, forego dessert and have a glass of sweet Tokaj dessert wine or a taste of *pálinka* instead.

SERVICE

In ordinary Hungarian restaurants the server will set a plate holding silverware and paper napkins on your table. After your food has been delivered, don't expect much more attention. With the exception of higher-end restaurants, you'll usually have to take the initiative if you want more drinks and food, or if there is any sort of problem with your food. Consider yourself lucky if your server comes around to ask if everything is alright after you've started your meal. This isn't to say that the service is bad here (though it can be very bad), it's just different than the often overly attentive style in America.

It used to be that the extent of most wine lists was red or white and sweet or dry. As Hungarians have developed a new passion for drinking wine, service and selection have also improved. It still happens, however, that red wine is served chilled or white wine is served at room temperature. All but a few restaurants have dedicated sommeliers or wine stewards. Many restaurants place *foglalt* (reserved) signs on all of their tables. But don't let that deter you from trying to get a table—they'll usually just remove the sign and tell you to take a seat. Making reservations, however, is a good idea, especially on weekend nights and at the better restaurants. Reservations are hardly ever needed for lunch, and very few restaurants in Hungary close between lunch and dinner.

THE BILL

Paying the bill at a Hungarian restaurant can be a confusing process to the uninitiated. Even simply getting your bill can be difficult. You could be sitting for what seems like hours with empty glasses and still have to hail down your waiter to ask for the check, but neither will they rush you to turn the table like they do in many other big cities.

Service is not generally included on Hungarian restaurant bills unless you're with a large group (though there are exceptions, in which case it should be clearly marked). In the lower-end restaurants Hungarians tend to round up their bill to include a tip for the waiter. But if you were satisfied with the service, a ten percent gratuity is the norm. Tips are never left on the table in Hungary. Instead, when you're paying the bill, you work out how much you will leave for the gratuity, mentally add it to the bill, and tell your server the total amount (i.e. the amount of the meal plus the tip). Servers usually carry money belts for making change and they'll usually hover and wait for you to pay immediately after dropping the bill. Even if you are paying by credit card, it's courteous to leave the tip in cash (and servers will often request this).

ETIQUETTE

Before eating anything, whether it's a piece of cake or a five-course meal, it's polite to do as the Hungarians do and wish everyone *jó étvágyat* (a good appetite). If you're dining in someone's home, tell your host that the meal was *nagyon finom* (really delicious). A few key phrases like these will take you far in Hungary.

JEWISH AND KOSHER FOOD

Since the fall of Communism there has been a significant revival of Jewish life in Hungary. Estimates of the number of Hungarian Jews today vary, but Bálint Nógrádi, who is a consultant at the Budapest Chabad-Lubavitch, estimates the number to be 100,000, with approximately eighty percent living in Budapest (these households eat exclusively kosher, he said). The city's Jewish life isn't confined to the old seventh-district Jewish quarter—which lies roughly between Erzsébet körút to the east, Károly körút to the west, Dohány utca to the south, and Király utca to the north—but the majority of the kosher food in the city is found here, including kosher restaurants where meals can be ordered and paid for in advance for the Sabbath. There are also several other non-kosher Jewish eateries (sometimes called kosher-style) in this area, most notably the Kádár Étkezde and the Frohlich Cukrászda, which should be towards the top of any Budapest to-do list.

The amount of kosher food and the availability of products is still limited in Hungary, according to Nógrádi. "People here need more products to keep a kosher kitchen," he said, and it is particularly difficult to find kosher dairy products. One of the main problems is the lack of qualified supervisors to oversee restaurant kitchens. Kosher chicken and beef are currently slaughtered here in Hungary, but most other products are imported from Israel or other EU countries, particularly Austria. "We are working on developing the local kosher food industry to serve the domestic market," said Nógrádi. Hungary's own most famous kosher product is the Zwack plum brandy (Slivovitz), and several wine-makers bottle kosher wine.

Mainstream Hungarian cuisine has long been influenced by traditional Jewish cooking. "Jews have lived in Hungary for many centuries, and now everything is mixed. Dishes are mixed, and people are mixed in this part of the world," said András Singer, owner of the Fülemüle Étterem in Budapest's eighth district, which specializes in Hungarian Jewish cuisine. "Traditional Jewish foods—like cholent, matzo balls, and goose soup—have become popular in Hungarian cuisine, and many Hungarians don't even know that they originated as Jewish foods." Cholent (*sólet* in Hungarian) is a slow-cooked bean stew with additions like hard-boiled eggs, goose legs, or other types of meat. "Jewish cuisine is different in every country," noted Singer. "Here we have a Hungarian touch. We always make the cholent with smoked meat and a little paprika." Another Jewish item that's now a *cukrászda* (pastry shop) staple is the *flódni*, a delicious pastry layered with ground walnut paste, poppy seeds, and apples.

The availability of kosher food in Budapest changes often, and the number of products is expected to increase. For the most up-to-date information about kosher products and certified venues (including a list of all products available in Hungary), contact the Chabad-Lubavitch (V. Károly körút 18-20; Tel: 268-0183; www.zsido.com; info@zsido.com). Also see Chapter 8 for kosher specialty shops.

RESTAURANT TRANSLATOR

I N BUDAPEST THERE'S USUALLY AT LEAST ONE PER-
SON WHO SPEAKS ENGLISH AT RESTAURANTS, BUT
there are always times when it helps to speak a few words of
kitchen Hungarian. See the Wine Translator on page 68 for
more detailed wine terminology, and the Culinary Dictionary
that begins on page 344 for more food vocabulary. Meanwhile,
these words will help get you through a meal:

Jó reggelt/napot/estét kívánok:
good morning/afternoon/evening

Szabad ez az asztal? Is this
table free?

igen/nem: yes/no

foglalt: reserved

dohányzó/nem dohányzó:
smoking/non-smoking

pincér: waiter

Mit ajánl? What do you
recommend?

Vegetáriánus vagyok: I am a
vegetarian

Van benne hús? Does it have
meat in it?

Allergiás vagyok és nem ehetek...
I'm allergic, I can't eat...

Kérek egy... Can I have a...

Jó étvágyat! Bon appétit!

Egészségedre! Cheers! (literally,
"to your health")

Hogy ízlik... How do you
like...?

nagyon finom: really delicious

Szervusz/Szia: hello or goodbye
(familiar)

Viszontlátásra: goodbye (polite)

köszönöm: thank you

szívesen: you're welcome

Fizetnék, legyen szíves. Can I
pay?

borravaló: tip (literally, "for the
wine")

Hitelkártyát elfogadnak? Do
you take credit cards?

napi menü: daily menu

étlap: menu

itallap: drink list

borlap: wine list

előétel: appetizer

saláta: salad

leves: soup

főétel: main course

köret: side dish

kávé/tea: coffee/tea

édesség/desszert: dessert

kenyér: bread

pohár bor: glass of wine

üveg bor: bottle of wine

CHAPTER 5:

....

THE RESTAURANTS

Nem töltött káposzta, hogy föl lehessen melegíteni.

It's not stuffed cabbage, you can't reheat it.

(No second chances.)

Több nap, mint kolbász.

There are more days than sausages.

(You can't have delicacies every day.)

—HUNGARIAN PROVERBS

O UR ANCESTORS GUZZLED ENOUGH WINE FOR GENERATIONS TO COME. FOR CENTURIES EVERYBODY'S BEEN wine-drunk in Hungary, for our hills have always been richly blessed. Why, at times wine had to be poured into pits for lack of barrels. Wine was drunk in the early morning and late at night. In the light of the foggy, red-bellied winter sun, rowdy or resigned, life went on. No one ever considered suicide, because wine was a compensation for everything. We'll have to see many a sober generation come and go, before all heads are properly aired out, and the last remnants of a race of drunkards die out… How could a nation accomplish anything when everyone was on a permanent drunk, even on their wedding night?"

—*Sunflower*, GYULA KRÚDY

THE RANGE OF CHOICES

Budapest's Hungarian restaurants can be elegant places with hovering waiters who carve meat tableside, smoky dives serving slabs of meat the size of a plate, and everything in between. This list of restaurants provides options for everybody, whether you're splurging or on a budget. Restaurants in the "traditional Hungarian" category serve classic Hungarian cuisine. Many of them also have traditional folk-style ambience, and a few even have live nightly music. "Upscale Hungarian" restaurants are higher priced, and have both fancier food and décor. "Hungarian wine restaurants" have serious wine programs, heavy wine lists, and many wines by the glass. By "eclectic Hungarian" I don't mean that these restaurants are doing anything crazy like redefining *gulyás*, but rather that they are somewhat difficult to categorize. They could just as well be called continental or international restaurants with a Hungarian accent. Though the menus at these places are not fully Hungarian, they have enough Hungarian specialties or Hungarian influence to make great Hungarian meals entirely possible. The "cheap lunch spots" (or *étkezde*) are simple rooms serving quick, home-style lunches.

RESTAURANT PRICES

I've indicated a general price range for each restaurant in this chapter, based on the scale below, which reflects only the price of the main courses, as appetizers aren't necessities in traditional restaurants (if you're on a budget a good way to cut costs is to skip appetizers altogether, as they often cost nearly as much as, and sometimes more than, main courses) and the price of wine can be so variable that it's difficult to give an accurate range that reflects both the price of the food and the wine. Menu prices are always the same for lunch and dinner. Keep in mind that in Hungary, price does not determine quality. There are just as many bad restaurants as good ones, and they are not afraid of charging top prices for their mediocre food. Knowing the price range for main courses should be enough to direct you towards the right restaurant for your budget. Please note that prices may change, and tend to rise every year in line with Hungary's inflation. In general, it's hard to categorize restaurant pricing so simply. Even the most expensive places will often have a few reasonably priced entrees mixed in with the pricier ones. If a venue accepts major credit cards, and many still do not, this is indicated by *CC* (although American Express isn't always accepted).

❖   *Inexpensive* ~ Main courses cost around 1,000 HUF

❖ ❖   *Moderate* ~ Main courses cost around 2,000 HUF

❖❖❖   *Expensive* ~ Main courses cost between 3,000-4,000 HUF

❖❖❖❖   *Very expensive* ~ Main courses cost 4,000 HUF and up

WINE RATINGS

In order for the reader to quickly and easily know the extent of a restaurant's wine offerings, I have given each restaurant a wine rating. These are very basic ratings, intended only to give a general idea of how much importance a restaurant places on wine and the quality of their offerings. These ratings themselves do not take price into account. Also, wine varieties are generally referred to by their Hungarian names throughout the listings, since that's what you'll see when you look at the wine list and the bottle.

★   *These restaurants don't emphasize wine.* While wine is available, it may be just a single wine by the glass, or no wine by the bottle.

★★   *These restaurants offer a few wines* by the glass and the bottle, but the overall list is short and unmemorable.

★★★   *Wine is of some importance* at these restaurants. They serve wine by the glass made by well-respected producers, and there's a satisfactory selection by the bottle.

★★★★   *These restaurants take wine seriously,* offering long and well-rounded lists with most of Hungary's wine regions represented. There's also a good variety of wine by the glass and knowledgeable servers or wine stewards.

★★★★★   These restaurants have the same standards as above, but *add a selection of foreign wine.*

Note: Metro lines are abbreviated as M1 for the number one (yellow) line, M2 for the number two (red) line, and M3 for the number three (blue) line.

TRADITIONAL

À LA CARTE ÉTTEREM

OWN-TO-EARTH, REASONABLY PRICED RESTAURANTS SEEM INCREASINGLY HARDER TO FIND AMONG THE swanky, high-priced places. À la Carte is a welcome exception. The main attempt at décor here is the wood paneling, the artificial flowers, and the cartoon-like pictures of German men and beer. The straightforward Hungarian menu features well-prepared classics like beef *pörkölt* in red wine with potato dumplings and sheep cheese (*sztrapacska*), *gulyás*, and *halászlé*. Appetizers, like fried cauliflower and breaded mushrooms, aren't the high point here. Perhaps because of its location in the neighborhood known as "water town," fish features heavily on the menu. Two pages of fish specialties include lots of catfish and delicate pike perch, which is best prepared simply—try it here grilled, breaded, or with almond sauce. Many of the fish dishes show some creativity: the catfish stuffed with pike perch and spinach, for example, or the catfish *Brassói* style (seasoned with paprika and marjoram, usually a preparation reserved for pork). The carp stew in red wine sauce is excellent, and my favorite fish dish is one that's often offered as a special. It's what the servers call the catfish "goulash," but is actually a catfish *paprikás* served with *túrós csusza*. There's more than fish; pork tenderloin with *lecsó*, for example, and a specials board often holds the best dishes. (Note that sides aren't included in the price of an entree.) The friendly waiters here have the bad habit of calling just about everything "goulash" to non-Hungarian speakers, which can be confusing if you do want a true *gulyás*. The wine list could use some beefing up, as there's just one house white and red, and six by the bottle. À la Carte makes a perfect spot for unwinding after heading down from the castle.

I. ISKOLA UTCA 29 ✦ TEL: 202-0580 ✦ CC ✦ MAINS ◇-◇◇
WINE ★ ✦ OPEN DAILY NOON *to* 11PM ✦ M2, HÉV, BUS 60, 86
TRAM 19, 41 *(to Batthyány tér)*

BAGOLYVÁR

G EORGE LANG AND RONALD LAUDER FOUNDED BAGOLY-
VÁR ("OWL'S CASTLE") SOON AFTER GUNDEL REOPENED
(see page 144). The restaurant is staffed entirely by women,
the idea being that the food should be prepared and served as
grandma would have done. The place is a great value (especially
considering Gundel's prices), and the Transylvanian country-
house atmosphere is the opposite of formal Gundel. A meal at
Bagolyvár is not, as many claim, a taste of Gundel for a cheaper
price. While the food at Bagolyvár is top-notch, the two kitchens
are at different ends of the spectrum of Hungarian cuisine.
Bagolyvár doesn't claim to be a substitute for Gundel, only to
serve casual, good old-fashioned food. Bagolyvár has a brief menu
of home-style comfort food with starters like goose liver cooked
in its own fat served cold and *Hortobágyi palacsinta*. Complimentary little bowls of *körözött* are served with bread. Main
courses include classics like stuffed cabbage, roasted duck with

braised cabbage and mashed potatoes, and both chicken and veal *paprikás*. But they also feature dishes that are a bit more inventive than what the average grandmother would prepare, like grilled pike perch fillet (with garlic sauce and spinach and potato soufflé) and catfish roulade (with porcini mushrooms and wine sauce served over zucchini with a rice soufflé). They do a nice job with grilled dishes: highlights are *pljeskavica* (Serbian-style grilled ground beef) and a wooden platter of grilled beef, pork, and turkey. Dessert should be Gundel *palacsinta* (which was invented in Gundel's kitchen). Try the house-made green walnut liquor, a drink usually made at home. The wine is reasonably priced and is from the Gundel cellars in Eger and Tokaj. Do sit in the garden if the weather is warm.

XIV. ÁLLATKERTI ÚT 2 ✦ TEL: 468-3110 ✦ WWW.GUNDEL.HU
CC ✦ MAINS ◇◇-◇◇◇ ✦ WINE ★★ ✦ OPEN DAILY NOON *to* 11PM
✦ M1, BUS 30, TROLLEY 75, 79 *(to Hősök tere)*

CENTRÁL KÁVÉHÁZ

THIS GORGEOUSLY RENOVATED CAFÉ, ONCE THE FAVORITE HAUNT OF HUNGARY'S MOST FAMOUS twentieth-century writers, also has restaurant seating in an upstairs gallery called the *Újhold* (New Moon). Like all of the other rooms at Centrál, it's named for the publication that was once edited there. While I generally prefer sitting downstairs where it's always bustling, the wooden tables upstairs draped with white tablecloths can be more pleasant if you're settling in for a full meal. Centrál's menu is solidly Hungarian, the portions are huge, and the food is consistently good. Naturally, *gulyás* is on the menu, but why not try the less ubiquitous *palócleves*, a hearty lamb and green bean soup flavored with sour cream. The grilled goose liver with leeks on toast is fantastic, and grilled or roasted goose liver is often featured in other forms on the list of monthly specials. The appetizer list also includes beef tartare and *Hortobágyi palacsinta*. I tend to skip straight to the list of specials, often more tempting than the compact selection of main courses on the menu which includes Hungarian staples like chicken *paprikás*, veal *paprikás* (called goulash in the English version of the menu), grilled duck breast served with cabbage noodles, and catfish *paprikás* with *túrós csusza*. The short wine list, of about twenty choices, is all Hungarian and reasonably priced, with a few poured by the glass. Centrál is also one of the more pleasant places in town for breakfast, which is served until noon and features ham and eggs, French toast, and an English breakfast, among other choices. Whether you're upstairs or downstairs, the service can be forgetful, and is really the only downside to eating here. (See Chapter 6 for more on Centrál Kávéház's history.)

V. KÁROLYI MIHÁLY UTCA 9 ✦ TEL: 266-2110
WWW.CENTRALKAVEHAZ.HU ✦ CC ✦ BREAKFAST ◇-◇◇
MAINS ◇◇-◇◇◇ ✦ WINE ★★ ✦ OPEN DAILY 8AM *to* MIDNIGHT
M3, BUS 5, 7, 7A, 8, 15, 78, 78É, 112, 173 (*to Ferenciek tere*)

EZÜSTPONTY VENDÉGLO

I N BUDAPEST IT TAKES JUST MINUTES TO GET FROM CROWDED DOWNTOWN TO THE COOL BUDA HILLS WHERE you have your choice of leafy wooded parks crossed with hiking paths or streets lined with grand villas. The shaded patio at Ezüstponty is just a tram ride from *Moszkva tér*, but feels miles away. It's a favorite among expats, who often outnumber Hungarians here. The patio has tables covered in red checked cloths, live gypsy music at night, a gurgling fountain, and a sandy playground. The place looks like a stone cottage, and the dining room is just as charming with white tablecloths and exposed beams. Though the waiters can be disinterested, the good un-fussy Hungarian fare makes up for it. At Ezüstponty (silver carp), fish is the specialty. Start with one of the four varieties of fisherman's soup. Move on to the *rácponty*, Serbian-style carp baked in paprika sauce with potatoes, peppers, tomatoes, and bacon, which is nicely done here. *Orly* style fish (fried in beer batter) can easily be soggy and flavorless, or it can be light and crispy like it is here. Other good fish options include classic breaded carp served with tartar sauce and catfish *paprikás* (called "wels goulash" on the menu). Can't decide? Go for the enormous fish plate for two. Meaty options include the several goose and duck dishes, breaded turkey breast stuffed with prunes, Wiener schnitzel (made with the traditional veal), or veal *paprikás* (called "veal goulash" on the menu). When the patio is open, the aroma of grilling meat wafting from the grill may make your choice clear for you. The wine list could use some work. To avoid the one type of wine by the glass, you'll have to shell out for an overpriced bottle from the short list.

XII. NÉMETVÖLGYI ÚT 96 ✦ TEL: 319-1632 ✦ CC

MAINS ◇ - ◇◇◇ ✦ WINE ★ ✦ OPEN DAILY 9AM *to* 11PM

TRAM 59 (*to Vas Gereben utca*)

FÉSZEK MUVÉSZKLUB ÉTTEREM

WALK INTO THE NEARLY-HIDDEN COURTYARDS OF BUDAPEST'S OLD BUILDINGS FOR A PEEK AT EVERYDAY life. Some are rundown cement squares with hanging laundry and sad-looking plants in tin cans, while others are like secret gardens. One of the nicest of all is the courtyard in the old Artist's Club building which houses the Fészek Étterem. When the seventh district's dusty streets swelter in the summer heat, walk through the lobby of this turn-of-the-century building full of fancy woodwork, mirrors, and stale smoke, and head to the serene courtyard where you'll arrive at a place that feels far from the inner city. The colonnaded yard is shaded by chestnut trees. Rose-colored walls are lined with ceramic sculptures of historic Hungarian artists and musicians (like Ferenc Liszt, Béla Bartók, and Zoltán Kodály) who were club members in its heyday.

Well-known Hungarian artists and performers still frequent the place. Both the courtyard and the inside dining room were restored a few years ago, and the dining room oozes Old World elegance with thick, velvety curtains, dark wood paneling, crystal chandeliers, and delicate stuccowork. And the food? It seems they've forgotten to update the menu. The surroundings, both inside and out, really outshine the food, which is Hungarian with some random international dishes mixed in. While the park-like courtyard will be memorable, the food will most likely be quickly forgotten. But if you stick to basic Hungarian dishes—like the crispy leg of goose or the fried goose liver—you'll be alright. Avoid the dishes that sound like they're trying too hard or straying too far from Hungarian cuisine, like gazpacho and crème brûlée. The wine list also leaves lots to be desired, especially the by-the-glass selection. Despite all that, Fészek's courtyard is still one of the finest places in Budapest to be on a hot summer day.

VII.KERTÉSZ UTCA 36 ✦ TEL: 322-6043
WWW.FESZEK-MUVESZKLUB.HU, WWW.FESZEKETTEREM.HU
✦ CASH ONLY ✦ MAINS ◇-◇◇ ✦ WINE ★ ✦ OPEN DAILY NOON
to MIDNIGHT ✦ M2 (*to Blaha Lujza tér*), TRAM 4, 6 (*to Király utca*)

FIRKÁSZ KÁVÉHÁZ-ÉTTEREM

FIRKÁSZ TRANSLATES AS "HACK" AND THIS JOURNALISM-THEMED RESTAURANT IS FULL OF OLD-TIME DÉCOR. The walls are plastered with yellowing old newspapers, antique cameras, eyeglasses, and even an old record player. Little silver trays full of silverware, coffee cups, and cigarettes are attached to the walls as if they were frozen in time, and old type-writers, pencils, and erasers are nostalgic reminders of how journalists used to work. The walls are lined with wine bottles (another favorite pastime of journalists?), and the fantastic wine selection here is complemented by lots of high-end *pálinka* and a long list of Tokaj dessert wine. The food is pretty good, too, although it is a bit pricey for the standard (though well-made) Hungarian fare that it is. Expect dishes like *Hortobágyi palacsinta*, goose-liver pâté with stewed pears, and a Hungarian cold plate (salami, sausage, goose cracklings, and cheese) for starters. This is as good a place as any to sample veal *paprikás*. Or try crispy roast pork with red cabbage and mashed potatoes, venison fillet with wild mushroom sauce, or a simple Wiener schnitzel. There are several types of grilled goose liver, and in true Hungarian fashion, there are pickled salads to accompany it all. Although the atmosphere at Firkász is meant to evoke the coffeehouse era, it has only been open for a few years. But even though Firkász calls itself a *kávéház*, it doesn't open until lunch-time. Where is a hack to go in the morning to get his morning coffee after stumbling out of bed?

XIII. TÁTRA UTCA 18 ✦ TEL: 450-1118
WWW.FIRKASZETTEREM.HU ✦ CC ✦ MAINS ◇-◇◇◇
WINE ★★★ ✦ OPEN MONDAY *through* SATURDAY NOON *to*
MIDNIGHT, SUNDAY NOON *to* 4PM ✦ TRAM 4,6 (*to Jászai Mari tér*)
TROLLEY 76, 79 (*to Radnóti Miklós utca*)

FÜLEMÜLE ÉTTEREM

WHEN ANDRÁS SINGER BOUGHT THIS PLACE IN 2000 IT TOOK A YEAR OF RENOVATING TO TURN IT INTO A cozy restaurant. The space was first a café in the 1920s and then a state-owned pub. Now the restaurant serves the kind of honest home-style Jewish accented food that keeps neighbor-hood locals coming back, as well as Prime Minister Ferenc

Gyurcsány, Nobel Prize-winning author Imre Kertész, and the Cardinal of Esztergom. The décor is homey, with walls lined with everything from family photos to needlework to Monet prints. Fülemüle specializes in Jewish dishes like goose soup with matzo balls. Indeed, goose of all types, including stuffed goose neck, features heavily. There are five different kinds of cholent, and it might be the best in town. If this place were my neighborhood restaurant, I wouldn't be able to resist the temptation of regularly stopping by for the crispy goose leg with potato latkes and Serbian cabbage (green cabbage flecked with pepper). The goose combo includes a crispy goose leg, a goose breast with wild mushrooms, and fried goose liver. Jewish cuisine and Hungarian cuisine have become intertwined, each influencing the other, and the menu here typifies this with its blend of Jewish dishes and very Hungarian dishes like deer *pörkölt* with bread dumplings and veal *paprikás*. For a different take on matzo, try the tasty dessert that is fried layers of matzo stuffed with walnut paste. Served with chocolate sauce with a hint of rum, it gives plain old matzo a world of new possibilities. The wine list offers nearly two dozen bottles, some by big names such as Thummerer and Vylyan, as well as smaller producers, kosher wine, and kosher beer. Service is casual and friendly, and Fülemüle (which means nightingale) has become one of the restaurants that I most often recommend.

VIII. KOFARAGÓ UTCA 5 ✦ TEL: 266-7947
WWW.FULEMULE.HU ✦ CASH ONLY ✦ MAINS ◇-◇◇◇
WINE ★★★ ✦ OPEN SUNDAY *through* THURSDAY NOON *to* 10PM
FRIDAY *through* SATURDAY NOON *to* 11PM ✦ M2 (*to Blaha Lujza tér*)
TRAM 4, 6 (*to Rákóczi tér*)

HORGÁSZTANYA

STREETS WITH NAMES LIKE ARANYHAL ("GOLDEN FISH") AND PONTY ("CARP") ARE REMINDERS THAT THE VÍZIVÁROS or "water town" was once a neighborhood full of fishermen. Horgásztanya ("angler's farm") is another reminder. The fishing-themed restaurant has dangling fish nets, stuffed fish heads, and a wooden boat hanging from the ceiling. The dark wood paneling further dims the slightly grungy restaurant, which is the type of place where ashtrays sit on tables next to "no smoking" signs. When the weather is nice, there are tables outdoors on Halász utca ("fisherman" street), a more cheerful place to eat. Though there are things other than fish here, I always order one of the thirty-four fish dishes on the menu. *Töpörtyo*, or pork cracklings with red onions and fresh bread, are a common countryside snack. Here there's fish *töpörtyo* served the same way, but made with either carp or catfish. Naturally, there's fisherman's soup, and lots of it, which is served in mini-cauldrons. There's *korhely halászlé*, *halászlé* with plucks (fish innards), *Tiszai halászlé* made from three types of fish, and *halászlé* made from just carp or catfish. In addition to the several dishes each made from carp, catfish, and pike perch (the most popular Hungarian fish varieties), there's trout, salmon, and *keszeg* (rudd, though it's translated as whiting). There's also a fish plate for two. For meatier fare, there are all of the typical mid-range Hungarian restaurant offerings, including chicken *paprikás*, fried calf's feet with tartar sauce, and a few venison dishes. The drink of choice here is beer. There's not even a wine list, but there is a simple house wine by the glass, which is most often drunk as a spritzer.

I. FO UTCA 27 ◆ TEL: 212-3780 ◆ CASH ONLY ◆ MAINS ◇◇
WINE ★ ◆ OPEN DAILY 11AM *to* MIDNIGHT
M2, HÉV, BUS 60, 86, TRAM 19, 41 (*to Batthyány tér*)

KÉHLI VENDÉGLO

HUNGARIAN WRITER GYULA KRÚDY FAMOUSLY WROTE ABOUT KÉHLI (ONE OF HIS FAVORITE HANGOUTS) AND BRIEFLY lived nearby. Being immortalized in Hungarian literature is a lot to live up to, and Kéhli just about does. The restaurant has several different rooms decorated in folk themes, a stone cellar, a shaded garden, and a covered garden—this hundred-plus-year-old restaurant is still as popular as ever. It's also one of Budapest's best traditional Hungarian restaurants, with a menu full of charming quotes. This is the place to try traditional dishes, which come in old-fashioned oversized portions. Kéhli's signature dish is bone marrow. If you're going to try this very Hungarian dish anywhere, do it here. There are more tame starters like pheasant soup with saffron, "Eduard's bean soup" with smoked pork knuckle, or cold goose liver in its own fat. There are almost too many good choices—catfish slices fried in breadcrumbs served with mayonnaise, pike perch *Orly* style, turkey breast stuffed with dried plums and Camembert. The stuffed cabbage, the menu tells us, is prepared from the recipe perfected by the owner's mother. There are lots of stews (many are called "goulash" on the English menu). The "Transylvanian goulash peasant's style"

is actually sauerkraut stew made with pork knuckle, one of Hungary's best winter dishes. The veal fillet stuffed with goose liver and fried in walnuts is also excellent. It's likely that you won't want dessert after all of this. But if you do, there's *Somlói galuska* or sour cherry and walnut strudel. The wine list is exclusively Hungarian, with mostly mid-priced wines, and about a dozen by the glass. There's live gypsy music nightly from 8pm. Reservations are recommended.

III. MÓKUS UTCA 22 ✦ TEL: 368-0613 ✦ WWW.KEHLI.HU

CC ✦ MAINS ◇◇-◇◇◇◇ ✦ WINE ★★★★

OPEN DAILY NOON *to* MIDNIGHT ✦ BUS 86, 6 (*to Kiscelli utca*)

KISKAKUKK ÉTTEREM

W HEN A RESTAURANT HAS ITS OWN HOUSE-LABEL WINE MADE BY CSABA MALATINSZKY, IT'S A SURE SIGN OF more good things to come. Kiskakukk opened in 1913; it has the same worn-in atmosphere as the old coffee houses, inviting you to stay and linger over your meal. With their ankle-length aprons, the waiters have a charming old-school sincerity and the place exudes informal elegance. Kiskakukk ("little cuckoo bird") has a book-filled shelf that gives the dining room a literary touch, high ceilings, and hanging tapestries. I like the semi-private table

in the corner next to the wine rack, surrounded by mirrors and wine paraphernalia. The food here is Hungarian and includes classics like beef tartare, goose consommé with matzo balls, and game soup with tarragon. There are also more sinful things like a goose-liver terrine (with a mixed salad) and grilled goose liver in Tokaj sauce with baked apple rounds. For main courses there are standard Magyar dishes like crispy goose leg with cabbage

and onion mashed potatoes, catfish *paprikás*, and venison *pörkölt* cooked with red wine. While those familiar dishes are always good choices, there are also more sophisticated options like goose-liver cream soup (served with toast spread with goose-liver purée), plaited pork with Calvados sauce, veal tenderloin stuffed with goose liver in Cognac sauce served

with potato croquettes, or beef tenderloin stuffed with goat cheese served with baked potatoes. Salads are the typical pickles and cucumbers. For dessert, *Somlói galuska* (called "light sponge cake with whipped cream and chocolate sauce" on the English menu) and the chocolate soufflé with orange sauce are the clear stars. While the wine list offers nearly four dozen differentent Hungarian wines, they are nearly all from the big-name wineries like Bock and Vylyan, which are great, but it would be nice to see more wines from smaller wineries. Reservations are recommended.

XIII. POZSONYI ÚT 12 ✦ TEL: 450-0829
WWW.KISKAKUKK.HU ✦ CC ✦ MAINS ◇◇-◇◇◇
WINE ★★★ ✦ OPEN DAILY NOON *to* MIDNIGHT
TRAM 4, 6 (*to Jászai Mari tér*)

MENZA ÉTTEREM ÉS KÁVÉZÓ

RETRO CAN IMPLY SECONDHAND KITSCH, BUT IMMENSELY POPULAR MENZA IS SLEEK AND STYLISH, WITH WALLS covered in chrome, grey foam squares, and copper. "Menza" means canteen, and the idea here was to serve traditional dishes in an atmosphere reminiscent of 1970s cafeterias. Menza's design is brilliant—down to the last vase holding a single orange Gerber daisy and the diner-style specials board with stick-on lettering—and the food is simply prepared and reasonably priced, considering its central location. Luckily, the recipes don't taste like they came from a cafeteria. They've been slightly updated with more vegetables than at most traditional restaurants (and also comprise more vegetarian dishes). The simple two-course daily lunch menu is a bargain. There's the occasional pasta or other internationally influenced dish, but you can always choose

from Menza classics like garlic cream soup with sour cream and cheese *lángos* or potato cream soup with bacon and walnuts. There's bone marrow served with toast and red onions, or its polar opposite—grilled vegetables with baked cheese. The brief list of main courses includes the classic *hagymás rostélyos* (a thin steak topped with light, crispy fried onions, served with mustard) and the not-so-classic chicken breast with bananas and apples with plum dumplings. The whole roasted trout, an occasional special, is excellent. The pink-cooked tuna with wasabi mashed potatoes is another not particularly Hungarian dish, but classics like veal paprikás and roasted duck breast with pasta and cabbage add balance. There's a selection of pickled vegetables to accompany it all. Desserts—like the *mákos guba* or the *túrós gombóc*—are worth trying. The wine list is all Hungarian and offers a few reasonably priced house wines by the glass, and mostly mid-range wines by the bottle. Or go the retro route and order a Traubisoda. The sidewalk tables on Liszt Ferenc tér are the place to be when the weather is warm.

VI. LISZT FERENC TÉR 2 ✦ TEL: 413-1482
WWW.MENZA.CO.HU ✦ CC ✦ MAINS ◇◇-◇◇◇ ✦ WINE ★★
OPEN DAILY 10AM *to* MIDNIGHT ✦ M1, TRAM 4, 6 (*to Oktogon*)

NÁNCSI NÉNI VENDÉGLOJE

"AUNT NANCY'S" IS A DELIGHTFUL PLACE IN THE BUDA HILLS, THOUGH IT'S QUITE A TREK BY PUBLIC TRANSPORT. The place is named for the owner's grandmother, and it has an elegant farmhouse feel to it. There are a few different dining rooms and a central "larder" table surrounded by jars of pickled vegetables, fruits, and jams. Old copper pots and strings of paprika hang from above, and wooden spoons, cake pans, and old kitchen utensils sit on the top shelf. The whole place is charming, from the menus to the décor, that it's worth the effort to get here. More importantly, the food is good. Everything is done in a big way and many dishes are served in old-fashioned little red pots. To start, there's a "raiding the larder" platter with smoked ham and horseradish, paprika salami, spicy sausage, goose-liver pâté, goat cheese, smoked quail eggs, peppers, tomatoes, onions, and bread. There's also homemade foie gras pâté marinated in Cognac with pistachios, raisins, and Port wine jelly, with apple and celery salad

and toasted challah bread. There's nothing light here, including the sirloin *gulyás* or the bean soup with smoked pork knuckle. Main course highlights include "quick fried ribs" of pork coated in grated potatoes and garlic and served with sour cream and grated cheese and a smoked pork knuckle slathered with sour cream, garlic, and paprika before it's baked. The weekly special list holds equally gluttonous dishes. Náncsi Néni serves a few desserts of the sort typically only prepared at home, like *fánk* (donuts) with apricot jam and *aranygaluska*, a yeast-risen cake sprinkled with ground walnuts and vanilla sauce. The wine list is exclusively Hungarian and most of the approximately forty bottles can also be poured by the glass. The owner also serves his own Badacsony *olaszrizling*. Reservations are recommended.

II. ÖRDÖGÁROK UTCA 80 ✦ TEL: 398-7127

WWW.NANCSINENI.HU ✦ CC ✦ MAINS ◊◊-◊◊◊

WINE ★★★ ✦ OPEN DAILY NOON-11PM

BUS 63, 157 (TO SZÉCHENYI UTCA) *From the bus stop, take Nagyrét utca, which will lead to Ördögárok utca.*

PAPRIKA VENDÉGLO

THERE'S NO MISTAKING THAT PAPRIKA IS A HUNGAR-
IAN RESTAURANT. THE FURNITURE IS MADE OF LOGS,
and there's so much wood that the place could be a hunting
lodge. The bar is lined with red and green lanterns, candle holders are covered in red wax drippings, and bread comes in little
wooden baskets with wheels. It wouldn't hurt to improve the
music (the radio is usually blasting hits from the 1980s), but the
place is so over-the-top that it works. Located across from City
Park, Paprika is one of the few restaurants in the neighborhood.
There's no need to order appetizers here. Instead, go for a soup.
The *halászlé* is great (and is served in mini cauldrons big enough
for a meal), but there's also Jókai bean soup, *gulyás*, garlic cream
soup with croutons, and Újházy chicken soup. Every other dish is
labeled as being served in some style or another, so you're not
really sure what you'll end up eating. But do make sure you come
hungry. Wiener schnitzel practically hangs over the edges of the
plate, with a pile of fries hidden underneath. It's nice and crispy,
even though it's made the Hungarian way (with pork rather than
with veal). There are a few game dishes (try the game ragout
with croquettes); more pork dishes than anything else; a good
variety of poultry dishes (try the chicken breast with plums and
croquettes, or the grilled goose liver with steamed apples and
mashed potatoes); beef dishes (try the sirloin *gulyás*); and the
typical vegetarian offerings of fried mushrooms or cheese. There
are mixed grill plates for two heaving with meat and potatoes.
The wine list is small with mostly well-priced mid-ranged wines,
and a few top wines mixed in. To drink something decent,
however, you'll have to buy a bottle.

VII. DÓZSA GYÖRGY ÚT 72 ✦ TEL: 06-70/574-6508
CASH ONLY ✦ MAINS ◇◇-◇◇◇ ✦ WINE ★★ ✦ OPEN DAILY
NOON *to* 10:30PM ✦ TROLLEY 70, 74, 79 (*to Dózsa György út*)
BUS 30 (*to Damjanich utca*)

POZSONYI KISVENDÉGLO

THIS LITTLE SMOKE-FILLED RESTAURANT IS THE TYPE OF
PLACE MORE FREQUENTLY FOUND IN SMALL COUNTRYSIDE
towns than in cosmopolitan Budapest, where stylish, expensive restaurants are the fashion. The food is basic and hearty. It

certainly couldn't rank with Budapest's finest, but it's a pleasant enough place to come for some good, simple food. Come when you have a hankering for the kind of typically Hungarian dishes that make vegetarians and health food fanatics shudder—*gulyás* with sweetbreads, bone marrow and toast, breaded pork cutlet stuffed with sweetbreads, lungs in a spicy sauce, fried liver, and breaded veal knuckle. I was never a big tripe fan, but I warmed to it after tasting the tripe *pörkölt* here. Of course, there are tamer choices, from soups like matzo ball and Jókai bean to main courses like fried duck with red cabbage and stuffed cabbage. Don't expect any fancy flourishes or ingredients. Plates come heaping with the kind of food a Hungarian grandmother might serve for Sunday lunch, which is exactly why the locals like this place so much. Some dishes are disappointing, like the beef stroganoff, which is strips of beef and pickles in a heavy cream sauce served with soggy fries. Besides the abundance of wood paneling, the dusty wicker lamps hanging above booths seem to be the only other attempt at decorating. The name of the place means "little Bratislavan restaurant," but the food here is definitely home-style Hungarian. Just don't come here if secondhand smoke is a problem for you; there's really no way to avoid it unless you're sitting at one of the sidewalk tables. Reservations are a good idea.

XIII. RADNÓTI MIKLÓS UTCA 38 ✦ TEL: 787-4877
OPEN MONDAY *through* FRIDAY 8AM *to* MIDNIGHT, SATURDAY
and SUNDAY 9AM *to* MIDNIGHT ✦ CASH ONLY ✦ MAINS ◇-◇◇◇
WINE ★ ✦ TRAM 4, 6 (*to Jászai Mari tér*)

RÉGI SIPOS HALÁSZKERT

IT FEELS AS IF LITTLE HAS EVER CHANGED AT THIS OLD-SCHOOL RESTAURANT IN ÓBUDA. IT'S NAMED FOR THE man, Sipos, who bought the place in 1930, and who was already famous for his boneless fish soup. The waiters are a bit distant, red wine is served colder than white, and the gypsy band is a bit kitschy. You won't be surprised by any creative flourishes or flavors, but the kitchen turns out well-prepared dishes. True to its name (*halászkert* means "fish garden"), there's an impressive selection of fish dishes, including six different types of fisherman's soup. Other starters include goose-liver risotto, breaded mushrooms stuffed with sheep's cheese with dill and paprika sauce, and smoked trout with pearl onions. For main courses, the usual suspects—catfish, carp, pike perch, and trout—are abundant among the dozens of fish dishes, as well as others like sea bass, lobster, and swordfish. The carp *pörkölt* cooked with red wine and served with *túrós csusza* topped with crispy pieces of bacon is excellent, and there's also *pörkölt* made with *kecsege* (sterlet) and served with sheep's cheese dumplings. There's whole roasted trout, roasted calamari with garlic, and even lobster. Like many older Hungarian restaurants, it's wise to stick with the familiar preparations made with local fish, rather than saltwater fish. Carnivores also have plenty of choices. There are three different goose liver main courses, and unusually for a Hungarian restaurant, there's hardly any pork. It's a nice touch that every dish is accompanied by a wine recommendation on the menu, and the list contains mostly small producers. The patio is the best place for eating fish and guzzling white wine on a hot summer day. But the main dining room—with its soothing green walls and a colorful goldfish tank in the corner—seems to attract politicians and businessmen, as well as families.

III. LAJOS UTCA 46 ✦ TEL: 250-8082 ✦ WWW.REGISIPOS.HU
CC ✦ MAINS ◇-◇◇◇ ✦ WINE ★★★ ✦ OPEN MONDAY *through*
SATURDAY NOON *to* 10PM, SUNDAY NOON *to* 9PM ✦ BUS 6, 60, 86
(*to Kolosy tér*), HÉV (*to Szépvölgyi út*)

SCHIESZL VENDÉGLO

BUDAPEST'S EATING STYLE IS VERY DIFFERENT FROM RURAL HUNGARY'S. BUT YOU DON'T HAVE TO HEAD TO the countryside to get Hungarian comfort food at prices that will also keep your wallet comfortable. In the case of the Schieszl Vendéglo, you just need to take the HÉV a few stops. Located in Budakalász, a cute little village with a Swabian and Jewish heritage, Schieszl is a friendly family-run restaurant that opened in 1896. The menu is Hungarian with a German accent that reflects the family's heritage. Most dishes come in small metal pots with German-style sauerkraut and seasonal vegetables are added to many. My perfectly crisp roasted half duck served with steamed cabbage, for example, was complemented by a mixture of autumn root vegetables on one visit. Fatty pork knuckle (a Hungarian favorite) is served three ways—baked with steamed cabbage, boiled, and with sausage. The *käsespätzle*—Bavarian baked dumplings with two kinds of cheese—is a better choice for non-meat eaters than the typical vegetarian options. The family makes all of the wine they serve here (with the exception of a

ETHNIC EATING

....

E XPLORING BUDAPEST'S HUNGARIAN RESTAU-
RANTS CAN KEEP YOU BUSY FOR A WHILE. BUT
Hungary's cuisine has always been open to foreign
influences, and since the end of Communism Budapest has
become a cosmopolitan city, with a good number of foreigners choosing either to live here or to visit. No guide to
dining in Budapest would be complete without mentioning the city's international restaurants, which have
added so much to the quality and the diversity of its dining scene. These days just about any type of foreign
cuisine can be found here (the city is especially strong in
Italian and Indian food), and the choices are increasing
all the time. While I have chosen to focus on Hungarian
restaurants in this book, here is a list of ten of my favorite international restaurants.

MARQUIS DE SALADE
Azerbaijani/Causcasian

VI. HAJÓS UTCA 43 ✦ TEL: 302-4086 ✦ CASH ONLY

MAINS ◇◇-◇◇◇ ✦ WINE ★★★ ✦ OPEN DAILY 11AM *to* 1AM

M3 (*to Nyugati Pályaudvar or Arany János utca*)

HONG KONG *Chinese*

XIII. BÉKE UTCA 26 ✦ TEL: 329-7252

TAIWAN.ETTEREM@AXELERO.HU ✦ CC ✦ MAINS ◇-◇◇◇◇

(*more for the lobster!*) ✦ WINE ★★ ✦ OPEN DAILY NOON *to* 11PM

TRAM 14 (*to Frangepán utca*), TRAM 50 (*to Béke tér*)

BARAKA RESTAURANT AND LOUNGE
International/Fusion

VI. ANDRÁSSY ÚT 111 (*Andrássy Hotel*) ✦ TEL: 483-1355

WWW.BARAKARESTAURANT.HU ✦ CC ✦ MAINS ◇◇◇◇

WINE ★★★★ ✦ OPEN DAILY NOON *to* 3PM, 6 *to* 11PM

M1 (*to Bajza utca*)

IL TERZO CERCHIO *Italian*

VII. DOHÁNY UTCA 40 ✦ TEL ✦ 354-0788

WWW.ILTERZOCERCHIO.HU ✦ CC

MAINS ◇◇-◇◇◇ ✦ PASTAS ◇-◇◇ ✦ WINE ★★★★

OPEN DAILY NOON *to* 11:30PM
M2, TRAM 4, 6 (*to Blaha Lujza tér*)

PÁVA *Italian*

V. ROOSEVELT TÉR 5-6 (*Four Seasons Gresham Palace Hotel*)
TEL: 268-6000 ✦ WWW.FOURSEASONS.COM/BUDAPEST
CC ✦ MAINS ◇◇◇◇ ✦ WINE ★★★★★ ✦ OPEN MONDAY
through SATURDAY 6 *to* 10:30PM ✦ TRAM 2, 2A (*to Roosevelt tér*)

SUSHI SEI *Japanese*

III. BÉCSI ÚT 38-44 ✦ TEL: 240-4065 ✦ CC
BENTO BOXES AND SUSHI SETS ◇◇-◇◇◇✧ ✦ WINE ★★
OPEN DAILY NOON *to* 10PM ✦ BUS 6, 60, 86 (*to Kolosy tér*),
HÉV (*to Szépvölgyi út*)

SALAAM BOMBAY *Indian*

V. MÉRLEG UTCA 6 ✦ TEL: 411-1252
WWW.SALAAMBOMBAY.HU ✦ CC ✦ MAINS ◇◇-◇◇◇
WINE ★★ ✦ OPEN DAILY NOON *to* 3PM, 6 *to* 11PM
M1, M2, M3, TRAM 49 (*to Deák Ferenc tér*)

HAXEN KIRÁLY ÉTTEREM *German*

VI. KIRÁLY UTCA 100 ✦ TEL: 351-6793
WWW.HAXEN.HU ✦ CC ✦ MAINS ◇◇-◇◇◇ ✦ WINE ★★
OPEN MONDAY *through* FRIDAY NOON *to* MIDNIGHT,
SATURDAY NOON *to* 1:30AM ✦ M1 (*to Vörösmarty utca*),
TRAM 4, 6 (*to Oktogon*)

KÉT SZERECSEN *Mediterranean*

VI. NAGYMEZO UTCA 14 ✦ TEL: 343-1984
WWW.KETSZERECSEN.HU ✦ CC ✦ MAINS ◇-◇◇◇
WINE ★★★ ✦ OPEN MONDAY *through* FRIDAY 8AM *to* 1AM,
SATURDAY *through* SUNDAY 9AM *to* 1AM ✦ M1 (*to Opera*),
TRAM 4, 6 (*to Oktogon*), TROLLEY 70, 78
(*to Nagymezo utca or Andrássy út*)

MALOMTÓ ÉTTEREM *International*

II. FRANKEL LEÓ ÚT 48 ✦ TEL: 336-1830
WWW.MALOMTO.HU ✦ CC ✦ MAINS ◇◇-◇◇◇
WINE ★★★★ ✦ OPEN DAILY NOON *to* 11PM ✦ TRAM 17
(*to Szent Lukács Gyógyfürdő*), BUS 6, 60, 86
(*to Császár-Komjádi Uszoda*)

pinot noir from Pécs) in the attached winery. The Schieszls make quite a large variety of both reds and whites with grapes from various regions. They recommend several appetizers to go with their wine, like steak tartare, a cold farmer's plate (with home-made sausage, smoked knuckle with horseradish, and cheese), *zsíros kenyér*, and a plate of local goat cheese. With its vaulted stone ceiling and walls made to resemble a wine cellar, the place makes you feel like you've traveled to a countryside inn. While the wine is better than your average homemade plonk, it's not life-changing. Still, it always feels like somewhat of an honor to taste wine that someone has proudly made, which mitigates any faults it may have. It's possible to visit the winery with prior notice, but not during the winemaking period.

BUDAKALÁSZ, BUDAI ÚT 83 ✦ TEL: (26) 340-465

WWW.SCHIESZL.HU ✦ CASH ONLY ✦ MAINS ◇◇ ✦ WINE ★★

OPEN MONDAY *through* FRIDAY NOON *to* 10:30PM, SATURDAY 11AM

to 10:30PM, SUNDAY 11AM *to* 9:30PM ✦ HÉV (*to Budakalász*)

Be sure to get off at the first Budakalász stop. Cross the tracks and take Batsányi utca (next to the station house), which leads to Budai út. The restaurant is on the right.

ZÖLD KAPU VENDÉGLO

P EST TENDS TO HAVE THE MORE STYLISH EATERIES, WHILE BUDA HOLDS THE GREAT OLD-SCHOOL HUNGARIAN restaurants. Traditionally, Óbuda was a neighborhood full of small simple restaurants with leafy green gardens and predict-able menus. They were casual places with good, cheap house wine, where you could pop in for dinner a few times a week. Zöld Kapu—named for its big green gate—is this kind of place. The menu is unapologetically Hungarian (long and overwhelming),

offering all of the classic standards like pork chops with *lecsó*, lots of fried and breaded things, and all sorts of *paprikás* dishes. The dishes have cute names like "piggy in the pan" (tenderloin medallions fried in an onion and sausage ragout) or "plate of abundance" (pork stuffed with sausage and chicken liver, roasted chicken, roasted turkey, and mixed garnish). You'll find massive portions here, which make appetizers and

desserts seem like unnecessary acts of punishment on your stomach (though they're surprisingly light, if you can say that about such big portions). Eating outdoors at one of the tables under the awning in the backyard is the real reason to come here. With its brick floor, green benches, and red-and-white-checked tablecloths, the place feels like an elderly aunt's well-kept country patio. There are geraniums in the window, potted plants everywhere, and all is neat and orderly. The inside is also pleasant, with long wooden tables, antique knick-knacks scattered throughout, and a gallery that feels like a pub. Wine drinkers would be better off skipping the wines by the glass and going for one of the few decent low- to medium-priced bottles. Every neighborhood should be so lucky as to have a Zöld Kapu serving good honest food.

III. SZOLO UTCA 42 ✦ TEL: 387-7028 ✦ CASH ONLY

MAINS ◇-◇◇ ✦ WINE ★ ✦ OPEN DAILY 10AM *to* 10PM

BUS 6, 86 (*to Flórián tér*)

UPSCALE

....

GUNDEL ÉTTEREM

N O OTHER RESTAURANT IN HUNGARY SPARKS AS MUCH DISAGREEMENT AS GUNDEL, THE COUNTRY'S MOST FAMOUS. It's too expensive, it's overrated, and the food isn't as good as it used to be, say some. It's part of Hungary's history and the extravagance and opulence are worth the price, counter others. There's truth in both of those arguments. The restaurant has a long, fascinating history, which began in 1910 when it was opened by twenty-seven-year-old Károly Gundel. Like his father, restaurateur János Gundel, many of Károly's dishes have gained permanent places in the Hungarian kitchen. The younger Gundel

ran the restaurant until it was nationalized in 1949. In 1992, it was purchased, restored, and reopened by George Lang and Ronald Lauder. In 2004, the Danubius Hotel Group bought the majority stake in Gundel. Consider that Károly Gundel was a man who "has contributed more to the fame of Hungarian cooking than any other man and who is ranked by connoisseurs all over the world in a class with such restaurateurs as Escoffier and Voisin," according Joseph Wechsberg's 1948 profile of the great man in the *New Yorker*. But also consider that Gundel is now owned by a corporation, and it's no wonder that it can't live up to its former glory. But Gundel has always been the kind of place where royalty and heads of state dine when they're in town, and it still is.

The food at Gundel is exquisite, there's live classical and gypsy music, and a pleasant dining area in the garden. The main dining room is filled with original late-nineteenth-/early-twentieth-century paintings by Hungarian artists like Mihály Munkácsy and József Rippl-Rónai, crystal chandeliers, gilt, and fancy plasterwork. The menu is based on the refined French-influenced Hungarian dishes that Károly Gundel served as well as lighter versions of Hungarian classics. To start, there's caviar, a duo of house-smoked salmons, house-smoked catfish with herb sauce and tarragon potato salad, or smoked king prawn with hazelnut sauce and crispy vegetable straws. There are soups like foie gras potage with Cognac and chanterelles or pheasant broth with stuffed morels flavored with Tokaji *szamorodni*. The menu is heavy on goose liver, with seven different dishes including cold-smoked goose liver, a house specialty. There's game when it's in season, chateaubriand carved tableside, and fish dishes (like pan-roasted *fogas* fillet Gundel-style, on spinach with Egri chardonnay sauce). Or there's the duck trio (with a pink-roasted breast, crispy leg, and grilled liver with garlicky prunes and sautéed cabbage noodles) or the whole rack of lamb carved tableside. The long dessert list has classics like *Dobos torta*, Godiva bonbons served with three different dessert wines, and Gundel *palacsinta* (try it flambéed with green walnut liquor). There are also five-, six-, or seven-course tasting menus with wine pairings. The wine list is massive and offers nearly two dozen varieties of wine from Gundel's own wineries in Tokaj and Eger. There are ways to enjoy Gundel's opulence more frugally, like the three-course lunch menus and the elaborate Sunday brunch buffet. Gundel also runs the more affordably priced Bagolyvár and the 1894 Food & Wine Cellar (see pages 117 and 155). Everyone seems to have an opinion on Gundel. If you've got the money, I'd say go try it and enjoy it. Make reservations; men must wear jackets at dinner.

XIV. ÁLLATKERTI ÚT 2 ✦ TEL: 468-4040 ✦ WWW.GUNDEL.HU
CC ✦ MAINS ◇◇◇-◇◇◇◇ ✦ WINE ★★★★★
OPEN DAILY NOON *to* 4PM, 6:30PM *to* MIDNIGHT
M1, 30, TROLLEY 75, 79 (*to Hősök tere*)

KACSA VENDÉGLO

NOTHING ABOUT THIS SLIGHTLY NEGLECTED-LOOKING BUILDING REVEALS THAT ONE OF BUDAPEST'S MOST refined restaurants is hiding inside. As the name implies, *kacsa* (duck) is the house specialty (and also the name of the restaurant's cross street). The place exudes Old World style, from the violin and piano duo to the crystal lamps and the wine-colored wallpaper. An army of waiters wearing red vests hovers: one brings bread, another pushes a cocktail cart, yet another takes the orders, and a wine steward handles the wine. Silver domes are lifted simultaneously to reveal the gorgeously composed dishes on blue and gold Zsolnay china. For starters, there are dishes like smoked deer ham with house-made pickled cheese and pheasant consommé garnished with a goose-liver-stuffed potato puff. Duck, though, is the best choice. Starters include duck-filled strudel with dill and paprika sauce and duck breast tartare. There are seven main courses featuring duck. Duck Tisza style has crispy skin and is served with *lecsó* and foie gras. The Moulard duck breast with a mound of mashed apple and grilled goat cheese is a fine choice, though not as good as the crispy duck with sour cherry sauce. There's also the classic combination of duck with mashed potatoes and red cabbage. There are plenty of fish options, like grilled pike perch fillet with crayfish butter and anchovy ragout. And there are game dishes, like venison steak with wild mushroom sauce. Kacsa isn't cheap, but the food and service are top notch. The wine list, however, is a bit over-the-top with few wines poured by the glass. The roughly sixty types of Hungarian wine on the list have shockingly high markups. Reservations are highly recommended.

I. FO UTCA 75 ✦ TEL: 201-9992 ✦ WWW.KACSAVENDEGLO.HU

CC ✦ MAINS ◇◇◇-◇◇◇◇ ✦ WINE ★★★★ ✦ OPEN MONDAY *through* FRIDAY NOON *to* 3PM, 6PM *to* 1AM, SATURDAY *and* SUNDAY 6PM *to* 1AM ✦ M2, HÉV, BUS 60, 86, TRAM 19, 41 (*to Batthyány tér*)

KISBUDA GYÖNGYE ÉTTEREM

KISBUDA GYÖNGYE'S PREDECESSOR OPENED IN 1976 IN A FORMER FOURTEENTH-CENTURY INN. TODAY'S "PEARL of Little Buda" opened in 1992 in a run-down neighborhood in Óbuda when the original establishment closed for restoration. Since then it has become a favorite among Budapest's politicians and artists. It's small and homey, just as nice for romantic dinners as for discreet business lunches. The walls of the two small dining rooms are covered with mismatched pieces of antique furniture like headboards and armoire doors. There are sideboards filled with old silver and a piano in the center is draped with Oriental rugs. During dinner a pianist takes special requests. Kisbuda Gyöngye's menu changes seasonally and includes up-market dishes, creative takes on Hungarian classics,

and dishes that are not particularly Hungarian (crème brûlée or arugula salad with basil dressing and fried sheep cheese). This is a worthy place to sample Hungarian goose liver, especially the signature cold appetizer with foie gras three ways and a glass of Tokaji *aszú*. Other starters include pheasant broth, or there could be roasted goose liver with baked squash. Goose liver is also usually featured as a main course, such as the braised goose liver with apples in a rose-petal sauce. Delicate pike perch could come whole roasted, or served Hungarian style with *lecsó*. There's roasted duck with red cabbage and parsley potatoes, beef steak Hungarian style with *lecsó* and goose liver, and Hungarian Grey beef with porcini mushrooms. Dessert could be chestnut purée with whipped cream, curd cheese pie, or lemon sorbet in an almond cup. The wine list is mostly Hungarian, with only a few inexpensive

options and a nice dessert wine selection. Service is friendly and attentive, and the kitchen is always reliable. Sit outside in the shaded courtyard when the weather is warm, but be sure to check out the ceiling fresco inside. Reservations are recommended.

III. KENYERES UTCA 34 ✦ TEL: 368-6402 ✦ WWW.REMIZ.HU
CC ✦ MAINS ◇◇-◇◇◇◇ ✦ WINE ★★★ ✦ OPEN MONDAY *through*
SATURDAY NOON *to* MIDNIGHT ✦ TRAM 17 (*to Podolin utca*)
BUS 60 (*to Selmeci utca*)

MÚZEUM KÁVÉHÁZ ÉTTEREM

MÚZEUM OPENED IN 1885 ON THE SITE OF ANOTHER COFFEEHOUSE. THE PARLIAMENT WAS THEN LOCATED around the corner and this place was popular with government officials, students, and writers. Though it calls itself a kávéház étterem, Múzeum is actually an elegant restaurant. It serves good versions of Hungarian classics with slightly contemporary touches. Waiters wear pinstriped vests and bowties and say things like "for your pleasure" when they place *amuse bouches* on the table. One wall of the lofty room is mirrored, topped with a fresco by painter Károly Lotz, who painted frescoes in many of Budapest's public buildings, but Zsolnay tiles and mosaics dominate. The soft pink linens and the iron chandeliers look fit for a medieval castle, but the brightly lit "show kitchen" with hanging copper pots and displays of raw seafood doesn't fit in. Though it would be tempting to write Múzeum off as just another historic restaurant that rests on its reputation, chef Lajos Bíró (who also runs the kitchen at Bock Bisztró) hasn't let that happen. To start, there's an excellent version of tenderloin *gulyás* and a thick mushroom soup. A mound of catfish stew with paprika sauce and forest mushrooms served with delicate *túrós csusza* on a big white fish-shaped plate is fantastic, and so is the tender-roasted lamb knuckle with forest mushrooms and pea sauce. On the other hand, the veal *paprikás* could be better. There's also classic stuffed cabbage, grilled goose liver, crispy goose leg with steamed cabbage, and wild duck legs with orange sauce. Like most traditional Hungarian restaurants, the dessert selection is limited. The wine list holds more than seventy bottles of Hungarian wine, but just half a dozen by the glass. There's a pianist in the evenings. Reservations are a good idea.

VIII. MÚZEUM KÖRÚT 12 ✦ TEL: 267-0375
WWW.MUZEUMKAVEHAZ.HU ✦ CC ✦ MAINS ◇◇◇-◇◇◇◇
WINE ★★★★ ✦ OPEN MONDAY *through* SATURDAY NOON *to*
MIDNIGHT ✦ M2, TRAM 49 (*to Astoria*)

REMÍZ KÁVÉHÁZ ÉS SÖRÖZO

Remíz ("tram depot") is so named because the yellow city trams rest out front at night. Like its sister restaurant, Kisbuda Gyöngye, Remíz is a chic place that attracts politicians and celebrities. The expansive garden is the restaurant's best feature and is a popular site for weddings. Spending a summer night out here feels like being at a sophisticated garden party. Inside is also nice, with several different rooms that feel quite homey (though not in the same cozy way as Kisbuda Gyöngye). The menu changes monthly and has lots of similarities with Kisbuda Gyöngye's. To start, there are soups like consommé with matzo balls or homemade pasta, and French onion soup. There are starters like goose liver and truffle cream with toast, green peppers stuffed with eggplant mousse, and goose cracklings with red onions. Main courses include Hungarian dishes like crispy suckling pig with fresh horseradish and crispy goose leg with braised cabbage, as well as dishes that aren't so Hungarian like breaded lamb chops with tzatziki and spicy potatoes or Mexican chicken wings. The luscious goose liver risotto with basil and chanterelles is worth trying, and so is the fillet of pike perch with creamy spinach and jasmine rice. The bakery turns out a host of sweets and chocolates for dessert, and is known for its wedding cakes that are as delicious as they are beautiful. Whether it's tiramisu, strudel, crème brûlée, profiteroles, or a soufflé, it's all good. Remíz's wine list is primarily Hungarian and offers a good range of wine. Like Kisbuda Gyöngye, everything from the service to the food is smooth. There's also a winter "grill salon" that serves up spare ribs and barbecue during the cold months.

II. BUDAKESZI UTCA 5 ✦ TEL: 275-1396 ✦ WWW.REMIZ.HU
CC ✦ MAINS ◇◇-◇◇◇◇ ✦ WINE ★★★★ ✦ OPEN DAILY 9AM *to* MIDNIGHT ✦ TRAM 56 (*to Akadémia utca*), BUS 22, 158 (*to Szépilona*)

WINE RESTAURANTS

1894 BORVENDÉGLO

UPSTAIRS, GUNDEL IS ALL ABOUT EXTRAVAGANCE. DOWN-STAIRS, WHAT WAS ONCE GUNDEL'S WINE CELLAR IS now a more casual, less expensive restaurant—the 1894 "Wine Restaurant" (named for the year the building was built). Eat here to try Gundel's food at more reasonable prices. Tables are fitted with country-style white tablecloths and wine-colored runners, huge wine glasses, and Zsolnay china. Start with the *borkorcsolyák* (snacks to accompany wine), which are little bowls of spreads like creamy herbed goat cheese, ricotta, or tomato tartare. The soups—like *gulyás* and venison soup with tarragon—shouldn't be skipped. The pleasantly brief menu has just under a dozen main courses. The roe deer and red wine *pörkölt* (served around a mound of sheep cheese dumplings) is a stand-out, while the pink duck breast braised in merlot (with fruit and potato croquettes), the pan-fried *fogas* fillet (with Savoy cabbage with white wine sauce), and the paprika-seasoned grilled catfish (served over pasta) are other fine choices. Desserts are traditional, like a strudel trio, chestnut purée, and *Somlói galuska* (a sponge cake concoction with whipped cream, chocolate sauce, raisins, and nuts). The food is cooked by the same chefs who prepare the food upstairs, and while it's not as showy, it is excellent. The idea behind 1894 is that people should feel equally welcome whether they're dropping in for a glass of wine and some *borkorcsolyák*, or for a full meal. The three- and four-course tasting menus with seven or eight tasting glasses of wine (0.6 dl) are great values. Aside from the drowsy accordion player, the place is usually pretty quiet, even on weekends. There are wine "happy hours" daily from 5pm to 7pm when glasses are poured at a discount. The wine, which comes from every region of Hungary, changes monthly. The one downside to the restaurant is the often disinterested service.

XIV. ÁLLATKERTI ÚT 2 ✦ TEL: 468-4044

WWW.GUNDEL.HU/BORVENDEGLO ✦ CC ✦ MAINS ◇◇-◇◇◇

WINE ★★★★ ✦ OPEN MONDAY *through* SATURDAY 6 *to* 11PM

M1, 30, TROLLEY 75, 79 (*to Hosök tere*)

ANDANTE BORPATIKA

IN A COUNTRY THAT TAKES ITS WINE SO SERIOUSLY, IT'S SURPRISING THAT THERE AREN'T MORE WINE BARS IN the capital. Andante—owned by Villány winemaker Zsolt Tiffán and singer Ákos Kovács—is one of the few. The location on the Buda riverbank next to the Chain Bridge couldn't be better, and the views are fantastic. But its real draw is its serious selection of wine, and the simple, tasty food served with it. Almost a dozen of Tiffán's own wines are sold by the glass (and others just by the bottle or magnum). Even though Tiffán's reds are some of Hungary's best, Andante's thorough wine list offers wines from other regions and winemakers, both well established and lesser known. The wine selection here is solely Hungarian, with the exception of a few bottles from ethnic-Hungarian winemakers in Aradhegyalja in Transylvania. Good wine naturally deserves good food, which Andante has. Though there's only cold food served family style on big plates—like cheese, coldcuts, and dips—it can serve either as a light snack or be substantial enough to be a meal. There are heartier meat dishes like smoked goose breast with red onion marmalade (a specialty of the house), smoked ox tongue, goose-liver confit, roasted duck breast, Mangalica sausage, and more. There's smoked trout, smoked salmon, pâté, and seven types of goat cheese (including one aged in pumpkin-seed oil and a chocolate-covered goat cheese for dessert). It's enough to make you want to keep ordering wine just so you can sample more food. If there's anything wrong with Andante, it may be that it feels a bit formal for a wine bar.

I. BEM RAKPART 2 ✦ TEL: 457-0807

WWW.ANDANTE-BORPATIKA.HU ✦ CC ✦ MAINS ◇-◇◇◇

WINE ★★★★ ✦ OPEN SUNDAY *through* THURSDAY

4PM *to* MIDNIGHT, FRIDAY *and* SATURDAY 4PM *to* 2AM

TRAM 19, BUS 86, 16, 105 (*to Lánchíd*)

BOCK BISZTRÓ

WINEMAKERS HAVE LONG BEEN OPENING BED AND BREAKFASTS IN THE COUNTRYSIDE TO CATER TO wine tourists. József Bock, Hungary's 1997 winemaker of the year, was the first to open his own wine bistro in Budapest (inside of the gorgeously renovated Corinthia Grand Hotel

Royal). Executive chef Lajos Bíró (also of Múzeum Étterem) runs the kitchen, while Bock is busy in Villány actually making the wine. The wine list features about twenty of Bock's own wines (he's known for his big reds), more than forty wines by the glass, and wine from other winemakers and regions. The place has a Mediterranean feel with cured Spanish hams hanging from the ceiling and a partially open kitchen. At the same time it's proudly Hun-

garian, decorated with scenes of war-torn Budapest. The menu mixes Spanish and Hungarian in a delicious way. There's a great variety of *borkorcsolyák*, half a dozen types of crostini, and both Spanish and Hungarian tapas. Or choose from the cheese and cured meat in the display. More substantial starters include dishes like smoked goose-breast carpaccio with a pear salad or *lecsó* with house-made sausage. There might also be deer carpaccio, ravioli with paprika cream sauce, or a wonderful horseradish soup with ham chips. Ask your waiter to translate the daily specials scrawled on the blackboard. The menu is just the right size, with main courses that include good things like grilled goose liver paired with ginger parfait, chicken breast "barrique style" with fried potatoes, and grilled pike perch with porcini mushrooms. Dessert highlights include orange tiramisu and sweet polenta with poppy seed and plum sauce. Service is detail oriented, and the servers are eager to recommend different wines with each course. There are monthly wine-tasting dinners and during the warm months there's a *fröccs* garden outside. As the place only seats about three dozen diners, reservations are recommended.

VII. ERZSÉBET KÖRÚT 43-49 ✦ TEL: 321-0340
WWW.BOCKBISZTRO.HU ✦ CC ✦ MAINS ◇◇-◇◇◇
WINE ★★★★★ ✦ OPEN MONDAY *through* SATURDAY
NOON *to* MIDNIGHT ✦ TRAM 4, 6 (*to Király utca*)

BORBÍRÓSÁG

THERE SHOULD BE MORE RESTAURANTS LIKE BORBÍRSÁG, LOCATED BEHIND THE CENTRAL MARKET HALL. THE WINE list has 170 selections from throughout Hungary, about sixty by the glass, and ten types of spritzers. There's wine in all price categories and reasonably priced good food to boot, reaffirming that wine needn't be a luxury. Borbíróság is a casual place with exposed brick walls and tables covered in brown paper. A few tables are scattered outside when the weather warms up, and there's a musty cellar below that smells like a winery, with vaulted ceilings and wine behind iron gates. The menu mostly offers simple, classic Hungarian dishes and is laid out as "a gastronomic journey through Hungary." Dishes from each region are listed with wine recommendations. To start, there are appetizers like steak tartare, cold goose liver, Alföldi *gulyásleves*, or porcini mushroom soup. For main courses there's veal *paprikás* with *juhtúrós sztrapacska* (potato dumplings with sheep's cheese), roasted chicken with apple sauce and *röszti* potatoes, or roasted pike perch with béarnaise sauce. On one visit my oversized chunk of goose liver served with mashed potatoes and apricot sauce was absolutely luscious, especially with the server's recommended wine. On other visit a sliced goose breast with brown sauce and bread dumplings was good, and so was the duck cooked pink in green pepper sauce, although it was overwhelmed by a huge pile of fries. Vegetarian options are better than usual, with dishes like vegetable strudel with cheese sauce and a chanterelle omelet. A little glass of sweet Tokaji *aszú* for dessert is a good option, and there's also the tasty *mákos guba*. The two-course lunch menu is a steal, but not as tasty as the regular menu items. A good way to sample Hungarian wine on a budget is the half-price happy hour from 4 to 5pm.

IX. CSARNOK TÉR 5 ✦ TEL: 219-0902 ✦ WWW.BORBIROSAG.COM
CC ✦ MAINS ◇-◇◇◇ ✦ WINE ★★★★ ✦ OPEN DAILY NOON *to*
MIDNIGHT ✦ M3 (*to Kálvin tér*) TRAM 49 (*to Fovám tér*)

MALIGÁN BORÉTTEREM

THIS GEM OF A RESTAURANT IS HIDDEN BELOW GROUND ON A BUSY BUDA STREET. MALIGÁN TAKES ITS WINE seriously, with two sommeliers and a list offering hundreds of bottles and nearly two dozen monthly changing wines poured in tasting portions. Maligán bridges elegant and casual, with exposed brick walls and racks of wine lending a cozy mood. The service is friendly and professional, and servers do the almost unheard-of in Hungary: they return multiple times. Fine wine deserves fine food and the brief menu is loaded with tempting choices. House-made bread flecked with cracklings and *körözött* is served to start. Appetizers include sliced venison with giant capers and spiced goat cheese or escargot with garlic truffled butter. Soups could be roe ragout soup with juniper, chestnut and potato dumplings, or creamy mushroom with grilled pullet and potato dumplings. Main courses could be roasted Mangalica pork and Hungarian Grey beef with burgundy sauce and *lecsó*, or rare duck breast with strawberry ragout cooked in pinot noir and served with truffled gnocchi. There could be a lamb steak with chili, honey, and minty potato salad or hare cooked in a clay pot Provençal style. Maligán's kitchen takes advantage of Hungary's bounty of gorgeous products—fruits and vegetables, truffles, morels, goat cheese, honey, and heritage-breed meats. And the wine! They experiment with wine in a way rarely seen in Hungarian restaurants, creating things like Vylyan portugieser soup and wine granita. Don't come when time is limited, as many of the best dishes take up to forty minutes to prepare. Maligán's wine list is like the bible of Hungarian wine, and it's hard to imagine a better place for a wine-accented dinner. There's a good variety of *törköly pálinka*, or Hungarian grappa, made by some of Hungary's top winemakers, and about a dozen cheeses to top a meal. Maligán is proof that Hungarian food can be exciting and innovative. Reservations are recommended.

III. LAJOS UTCA 38 ✦ TEL: 240-9010 ✦ WWW.MALIGAN.HU
CC ✦ MAINS ◇◇-◇◇◇ ✦ WINE ★★★★ ✦ OPEN DAILY NOON *to* 11PM ✦ BUS 6, 60, 86 (*to Kolosy tér*), HÉV (*to Szépvölgyi út*)

ECLECTIC HUNGARIAN

ARCADE BISTRO

ARCADE BISTRO IS CAFÉ KÖR'S (*see page 165*) POSHER SISTER IN BUDA. IT'S A TINY PLACE WITH A COLUMN of flowing water in the center. The front wall is all windows and oversized contemporary paintings cover the others. You can expect the same top-notch quality as at Kör and service here is among the best in town. Order a bottle of wine and your glass is topped after practically every sip. Before you realize something is missing, a server arrives to help. As at Kör—popular for its reliably delicious menu—simplicity is Arcade's best feature. Take the deep-fried pike perch, for example. Two ample, perfectly breaded, not at all greasy fillets of delicate pike perch are served with a little bowl of caper mayonnaise and a mound of plain rice. It couldn't be simpler, yet it was memorably good. A little fancier, the house-smoked beef tenderloin with walnut sauce is served with linguine with Gorgonzola sauce and was simply perfect. The one soup on the winter menu, *húsleves*, is also one of the few traditional Hungarian dishes on the menu (veal *paprikás* is another). Other starters include beef carpaccio with arugula and Parmesan, grilled goose liver with fried brioche and sherry sauce, and goose-liver pâté with blueberries. Goose liver also features as a main course, with fried onions and mashed potatoes. There's wild duck baked with vegetables, and lamb chops with red pepper sauce. The plate of complimentary sweets will tempt you to stick around for one of their rich desserts, which include chocolate mousse, crème brûlée with chestnuts, and curd cheese soufflé with hot strawberries. While Arcade's wine list is great in terms of its selections—which include some top French and Hungarian selections—it is pricey (and geared toward the expense accounts that many of the business-suit-clad diners are probably using). On the plus side, all except the very top wines are offered by the glass. Reservations are necessary.

XII. KISS JÁNOS ALTÁBORNAGY UTCA 38 ✦ TEL: 225-1969

WWW.ARCADEBISTRO.HU ✦ CC ✦ MAINS ◇◇-◇◇◇◇

WINE ★★★★ ✦ OPEN MONDAY *through* SATURDAY 11AM *to* 4PM

and 6PM *to* MIDNIGHT ✦ TRAM 61 (*to Királyhágó utca*)

TRAM 59 (*to Kiss János Altábornagy utca*)

ARTICSÓKA

NTIL SWANKY ARTICSÓKA UNDERWENT A COMPLETE MAKEOVER, IT WAS MEDIOCRE AND UNMEMORABLE. Now it has the wide open feeling of an old converted warehouse, with enormous crystal chandeliers contrasting with the industrial flavor. Done out in black and gold, a rectangular mosaic of broken glass dominates one wall and white tablecloths brighten the place up. There's also a rooftop garden. But it's the food that commands the most attention. Don't pass on the soup. After one visit it was hard to say which was better: a pear soup with ginger, lamb-liver dumplings, and sage, or a goat cheese soup with herbs and toasted sun-dried tomato ciabatta. For starters there's also tuna carpaccio with arugula sorbet or figs with Gorgonzola and Parma ham. If it's available, try the veal ravioli with bacon (they call it "ravioli with veal salt in bocca," a successful interpretation of the classic veal *saltimbocca*). The "giant crab" was also good, with a sweet chili sauce and a little salad (but it turned out to be a few giant prawns rather than a crab). Other reliable main courses include steak served over balsamic beet carpaccio, herb crusted branzino with spinach and artichoke ragout, or lamb prepared three ways. In Hungarian the name Articsóka is a play on words: *csóka* is a member of the crow family (it's the restaurant's trademark, a whimsical version of which dominates one wall) and the "art" part refers to the back theater which hosts concerts and performances. Of course, *articsóka* also has a culinary meaning, artichoke. The wine list is fairly expensive, and overwhelmingly French, but there are several options on the cheaper side. There are a few Hungarian wines available, but it would be nice to see more. All wines are also poured by the glass or in tasting portions. Reservations are recommended.

VI. ZICHY JENO UTCA 17 ✦ TEL: 302-7757 ✦ WWW.ARTICSOKA.HU
CC ✦ MAINS ◇◇-◇◇◇ ✦ WINE ★★★★ ✦ OPEN DAILY NOON *to*
MIDNIGHT ✦ M3 (*to Arany János utca*), M2 (*to Opera*)
TROLLEY 70, 78 (*to Zichy Jeno utca*)

CAFÉ BOUCHON

AFÉ BOUCHON IS A FRIENDLY FRENCH-STYLE BISTRO ON A QUIET STREET. IT SEEMS TO EFFORTLESSLY manage being stylish and classy, without being the least bit snobbish. There are Hungarian dishes, like the Bouchon plate with Hungarian sausage, goose cracklings, and goose liver and the *Somlói galuska* for dessert. But most are a happy marriage of Hungarian ingredients and French style. The menu is compact with a list of daily specials to round it out. You'll start with a pot of Bouchon's complimentary house tomato marmalade and warm bread. Then try the Tokaj grape salad (apples, Camembert, walnuts, and greens tossed with Tokaji *aszú* vinaigrette) or the goose-liver pâté. Main courses include tender slices of beef tenderloin stuffed with Gorgonzola (with buttery green beans and carrots), a thick grilled duck steak (with honey cherry sauce and almond potato croquettes), or grilled smoked goat cheese and mozzarella. In another nod to traditional Hungarian cuisine, there's beef *pörkölt* cooked in red wine. Or order a combination plate with three different dishes. There are also reasonably priced four-course Hungarian tasting menus to consider and daily two- and three-course "business lunches." One of Bouchon's best features is its service. On one visit my server suggested that we order main courses in half portions so we'd have room for dessert. We thanked him after tasting the big chunk of flourless chocolate cake he recommended. The crêpes Suzette flambéed with Grand Marnier are also worth sampling. Despite the French influence at Bouchon, the wine list is wholly Hungarian, with the exception of a few bottles of Veuve Clicquot. The well-balanced (and reasonably priced) wine list has just thirty or so wines. Opened in 2003 by a former waiter at Café Kör, Bouchon is one of the better values of Budapest's white-tablecloth restaurants. Reservations are recommended.

VI. ZICHY JENO UTCA 33 ✦ TEL: 353-4094

WWW.CAFEBOUCHON.HU ✦ CASH ONLY ✦ MAINS ◇◇-◇◇◇

WINE ★★★ ✦ OPEN MONDAY *through* SATURDAY 9AM *to* 11PM

M2 (*to Opera*), TROLLEY 70, 78 (*to Zichy Jeno utca*).

CAFÉ GUSTO

OZY LITTLE CAFÉ GUSTO IS THE POLAR OPPOSITE OF SO MANY BUDAPEST RESTAURANTS WITH ENCYCLOPEDIC menus and empty dining rooms. Gusto has a tiny menu of cold salads, sandwiches, and appetizers, but it is almost always full. I hardly mind the lack of hot food because everything else on the menu is so good. Order the *vegyes ízelíto*, the "sampler plate," and you'll get a massive portion of a little of everything:

smoked salmon with horseradish cream, slices of buttery goose liver, melon and cured ham, carpaccio, and several different salads. It's ideal for nibbling while slowly polishing off a bottle of wine. There are also things like pasta salad, cheese plates, and seafood salads. Even the ubiquitous (and usually sketchy) *meleg szendvics* (warm sandwich) is good here, with tomatoes and ham under melted Parmesan cheese. Like its menu, the café is also tiny. Inside are just seven tables, and comfy big sofas at either end of the room. An oil painting of a stern-looking, old politician hangs prominently on the wall, as if he's keeping watch. An outdoor patio is enclosed by a plastic tent so it can be used year-round, which nearly doubles the size of the place. For dessert, there's tiramisu, which adds another reason to come here: it goes down perfectly with an afternoon coffee.

II. FRANKEL LEÓ ÚT 12 ✦ TEL: 316-3970 ✦ CASH ONLY

MAINS ◇-◇◇ ✦ WINE ★★ ✦ OPEN MONDAY *through* SATURDAY

10AM *to* 10PM (*hours are sometimes erratic*)

TRAM 4, 6 (*to Margit híd, Budai hídfo*)

CAFÉ KÖR

"CAFÉ CIRCLE," JUST A FEW STEPS FROM THE BASILICA, IS A FAVORITE AMONG BUDAPEST FOODIES, WHO KNOW there will always be a long list of tempting dishes scrawled on the wall. The atmosphere is everything you'd expect in a good bistro—fresh flowers, soft orange walls, crisp white tablecloths, vintage green lamps, and professional servers. The place is small, however, and tables can feel cramped at times. The menu is not known for its creativity, but for its consistency. Whatever you order will be about as good as it can possibly get in the hands of chef Ádám Répás, who mixes Hungarian, French, and Continental styles. He doesn't overly dress anything, instead letting the ingredients shine. While the regular menu offers Kör's standards, it's the daily specials that keep many regulars coming back. There are more than half a dozen crispy green salads to choose from—like arugula salad with avocado, salmon salad with balsamic vinegar, or roasted goat cheese over mixed greens. The steak tartare is among the best in town and the goose-liver pâté with Cognac is equally good. Specials almost always include some sort of classic Hungarian dish, like *pörkölt* (which benefits from top ingredients and a lighter touch in Kör's kitchen). Recommended main courses include Wiener schnitzel (made from veal, as it should be), a tasty duck breast served with tangerine sauce, and beef tenderloin slices with potatoes and roquefort. Anything that includes roasted goose liver is always a good bet, like the roast goose liver with apples, cranberries, and potatoes. The dessert menu features classics like *Somlói galuska*, *mákos guba*, *Gundel palacsinta*, and chestnut purée with sour cherries. But don't hesitate if there's a simple warm apple pie with ice cream or doughnuts. The short wine list is well done, with about three dozen well priced Hungarian wines sold both by the glass and the bottle. There's breakfast until noon. Reservations are essential. Once you try Café Kör, you may not go anywhere else.

V. SAS UTCA 17 ✦ TEL: 311-0053 ✦ WWW.CAFEKOR.COM
CASH ONLY ✦ MAINS ◇◇-◇◇◇ ✦ WINE ★★★ ✦ OPEN MONDAY
through SATURDAY 10AM *to* 10PM ✦ M3, BUS 15 (*to Arany János utca*)

CAFÉ PIERROT RESTAURANT

THE CASTLE DISTRICT IS GENERALLY BEST AVOIDED WHEN IT COMES TO DINING. MOST RESTAURANTS THERE SERVE over-priced, mediocre food, with waiters who know they'll never see you again (and act accordingly). Luckily, there's at least one exception. Café Pierrot hasn't made itself into an overdone folkloric place, as many of the castle's restaurants unabashedly do. Though it's not cheap, Pierrot has more than its location going for it. The eponymous French pantomime character of the restaurant's name is depicted in a floor-to-ceiling painting in the center of the restaurant. The theater theme continues throughout the elegant restaurant with masks, puppets, and old black-and-white drawings. Located in a thirteenth-century building a stereo plays jazz when there's no live piano music. To start things off, the servers bring baskets stuffed with several types of good, fresh bread and rolls and herbed butter. The menu is long enough to make decision-making difficult, but not too long as to overwhelm. There are quite a few Hungarian dishes mixed in with Italian, French, and others that are clearly not Hungarian. There are Hungarian starters like a goose-liver trilogy, *gulyás* soup, and Hortobágyi pancakes. Hungarian main course options include wild boar goulash (which is actually *pörkölt*), beef tenderloin Budapest-style (with goose liver and a pepper and tomato sauce), and grilled goose liver with caramelized apples and potatoes. Or go the non-Hungarian route with a big salad (like the crispy mixed green salad with sautéed porcini mushrooms, shaved Parmesan, and pine nuts). There are half a dozen pasta and risotto dishes, including champagne risotto with garlicky frog legs. There's pepper-crusted yellow fin tuna cooked rare and served with creamy spinach and roasted vegetables or roasted breast of guinea fowl served with grape fennel sauce and potato purée. You can't get any more decadent than the Mangalica tenderloin with morel and truffle ragout and goose-liver sauce. End with the dessert assortment that includes small portions of three different desserts. The compact, but expensive, wine list has a nice range of almost entirely Hungarian wine, which includes mid-priced wines.

I. FORTUNA UTCA 14 ✦ TEL: 375-6971 ✦ WWW.PIERROT.HU
CC ✦ MAINS ◊◊◊-◊◊◊◊ ✦ WINE ★★★ ✦ OPEN DAILY 11AM *to*
MIDNIGHT ✦ VÁRBUSZ (*to Szentháromság tér*)

CARNE DI HALL

CARNE DI HALL IS IN A VAULTED CELLAR ACROSS FROM THE DANUBE. THE STYLISH PLACE IS INVITING WITH irresistible smells and sounds bursting from the swinging kitchen doors. Touches like fresh flowers, thick linen napkins, and heavy cutlery on the blonde wood tables make you want to settle in for a long leisurely dinner. Much of the menu is Hungarian, or at least uses Hungarian ingredients. (However, as its name implies, meat plays a big role here, and much of the beef comes imported from Uruguay.) From starters like beef carpaccio and beef tartare to main courses like thyme-accented rack of deer or veal steak with porcini risotto, this is a place for carnivores. The list continues: Angus rump steak, Angus tenderloin, a crispy half duck. But despite the kitchen's familiarity with meat, not everything always works. On one visit, the oven-baked knuckle of pork with rosemary potatoes and fried garlic mousse was a letdown. The grilled duck liver with chamomile sauce, however, was perfectly browned and tender on the inside. There's even a mixed green salad with stir-fried filet mignon strips. You're famished? Try the one-kilogram tenderloin steak (more than thirty-five ounces) with fries, called the "oh la la Carne Di Hall." I can't vouch for it, but the waiter confirmed that it takes at least two big eaters, sometimes three, to finish it. Not everything is carnivorous. There are a few pastas, like ravioli stuffed with porcini with cream sauce, and the soups are lovely, especially a creamy pecorino soup with basil that I once sampled. For dessert try the signature decadent rich chocolate cake with vanilla ice cream and candied orange rind. Or the dessert menu could include a walnut soufflé or house-made poppy-seed-stuffed crescent rolls. The thoughtful wine list is mostly Hungarian, with a few Italian, Chilean, Australian, and French additions.

I. BEM RAKPART 20 ✦ TEL: 201-8137
WWW.CARNEDIHALL.COM ✦ CC ✦ MAINS ◇-◇◇◇
(*more for the 1 kg steak!*) ✦ WINE ★★★★ ✦ OPEN DAILY NOON *to*
MIDNIGHT ✦ M2 (*to Batthyány tér*), TRAM 19, 41 (*to Halász utca*)

CSALOGÁNY 26

CSALOGÁNY 26 IS RATHER UNCREATIVELY NAMED FOR ITS ADDRESS, BUT THE FOOD IS ANYTHING BUT BORING. While one of the dining room's main features—a TV screen focused on what's cooking in the kitchen—may seem a bit over-done, it actually works well. Otherwise, besides the green-checked tablecloths and a few oil paintings, there's little else in the spare but tasteful dining room to take the focus off the food, which leans toward simplicity, featuring lots of herbs and green salads with some of the main courses. It's not exactly Hungarian (although there's the occasional Hungarian dish), but it does often feature special Hungarian ingredients like Mangalica pork. The menu changes frequently and might offer soups like sweet potato with salmon, wild mushroom, lentil with blood sausage, or cold plum. Next courses could be beet gnocchi with smoked cod, truffle risotto with bone marrow, or a duck liver terrine. Main courses might include roasted farm-fresh pullet served with new peas and mashed potatoes, beef tenderloin medallions with Port and mushroom sauce, or roasted lamb with spinach. There's usu-ally some sort of cheese course, and dessert tends to feature lots of fruity items (although it could also be something more sig-nificant like tiramisu or chocolate cake with pineapple sauce). Csalogány 26's menu writer tends towards understatement, with the sparse menu descriptions hardly doing justice to the perfectly cooked dishes that come from behind the kitchen's sliding doors. One of the best things about Csalogány 26 is its daily lunch menu which offers a well-priced two- or three-course selection. And unlike many restaurants with cheap lunch menus, it doesn't skimp on the quality. Like the menu itself, the wine list is also short but well priced, with selections from ten winemakers including top wine-maker, Imre Györgykovács, from the tiny Somló region and lesser-known ones like Sándor Tóth from the Balaton-felvidék region. The place is small and fills up with neighborhood office workers for lunch. Reservations are recommended.

I. CSALOGÁNY UTCA 26 ✦ TEL: 201-7892

WWW.CSALOGANY26.HU ✦ CC ✦ MAINS ◇◇-◇◇◇

WINE ★★★ ✦ OPEN MONDAY *through* FRIDAY NOON *to* 11PM

SATURDAY 6PM *to* 11PM ✦ M2, HÉV, BUS 60, 86

TRAM 19, 41 (*to Batthyány tér*)

GERLÓCZY KÁVÉHÁZ

WNED BY CHEESE GURU TAMÁS NAGY (WHO HAS A CHEESE SHOP DOWN THE STREET AND A SALAMI SHOP next door, see pages 298 and 302), the Gerlóczy is probably as close as you'll get to a Parisian atmosphere in Budapest. There's non-smoking seating in an upstairs gallery. But downstairs at the small marble-topped tables next to the semi-open kitchen is the best place to be. This bustling restaurant, which is centrally located between Deák tér and Astoria, has lots going for it. When the weather is warm, the sidewalk on the pretty square out front turns into one of the nicest open-air dining areas in central Pest. Fresh oysters arrive every Thursday, straight from Brittany. A variety of breads and pastries are house-baked daily. There's live music nightly. It's a great place for breakfast (which is served

until noon), whether it's just a buttery croissant and coffee or ham and eggs. Though the atmosphere is Parisian, the food is a jumble of Hungarian and French, with a little Italian thrown in. The seasonally changing menu features decadent dishes like creamy black-mussel soup, duck-liver ravioli with blackberries and porcini mushrooms, and chili-dusted lamb shank with polenta. There are always a few pastas, like lasagna with spinach and salmon cream sauce and tagliatelle with shrimp and mussels. There's also *pörkölt*, *gulyás*, and potatoes *paprikás*. The duck liver specialties steal the spotlight, however, with choices like duck-liver pâté with walnuts, blackcurrant sauce, and walnut bread or roasted duck liver with caramelized apricot flavored with rosemary and mashed potatoes. Of course, there's also the cheese. If there were ever a place where forgoing dessert in favor of a cheese plate would be a good idea, it's here. Even better, do both. For dessert there's a fancy chocolate soufflé as well as a home-style milk pie, which has been dressed up just a little bit. There are decently priced, mostly mid-range wines by the glass to choose from on the wine list, and a few dearer ones. The list is overwhelmingly Hungarian, with the main exception being a few French Champagnes. Despite all of the good choices on the menu, the kitchen can have bad days (and so can the servers). Have brunch, read a newspaper, have a glass of wine, this is the kind of place to go at any time of the day.

V. GERLÓCZY UTCA 1 ✦ TEL: 235-0953 ✦ WWW.GERLOCZY.HU

CC ✦ MAINS ◇◇-◇◇◇◇ ✦ WINE ★★★ ✦ OPEN MONDAY *through* FRIDAY 7AM *to* 11PM, SATURDAY *and* SUNDAY 8AM *to* 11PM M1, M2, OR M3 (*to Deák tér*)

GRESHAM KÁVÉHÁZ

THE LIGHT-FLOODED LOBBY OF THE FOUR SEASONS GRESHAM PALACE HAS A CHANDELIER MADE FROM hundreds of glass leaves, a sparkly Italian-style mosaic floor, and is topped with a glass cupola. Look carefully at the Zsolnay tiles covering the lobby, and you'll see which are the originals and which are the replicas added during the building's five-year $110-million renovation. The Gresham Kávéház sits on the site of a 1930s café of the same name. It's really more of a restaurant than the café it claims to be, with a full menu, a lengthy wine list, and an absolutely gorgeous dessert case that looks more like a modern art gallery. It's more casual (and slightly less expensive) than Páva, the hotel's acclaimed Italian restaurant next door. A team of waiters quietly scurries around making sure that the orchids are perfectly arranged on each table, the lighting is just so, and that every piece of heavy silverware is precisely. Breadbaskets are filled with at least four types of soft, warm, house-baked bread. Start with an asparagus soup with white truffle oil or a trio of goose liver. For main courses try the stuffed goose leg and the pink-roasted goose breast served with braised beans and sausage, or the sirloin steak with fries, wilted spinach, and béarnaise sauce. Just about the only Hungarian option on one visit was the chicken *paprikás* with dumplings and a cucumber salad. The Gresham also has sandwiches and burgers (probably the most expensive in town). Do order dessert, they taste even

better than they look. The wine list holds a great selection of Tokaj wines, lots of Italian, and a few French offerings. From Thursday through Saturday nights a fantastic jazz band led by Károly Nyári plays from 7pm.

V. ROOSEVELT TÉR 5-6 (*Four Seasons Gresham Palace Hotel*)
TEL: 268-5110 ✦ WWW.FOURSEASONS.COM/BUDAPEST
CC ✦ MAINS ◇◇◇-◇◇◇◇ ✦ WINE ★★★★★ ✦ OPEN MONDAY
through SATURDAY 6:30AM *to* 10PM, SUNDAY 7AM *to* 10PM
TRAM 2, 2A (*to Roosevelt tér*)

KLASSZ

Klassz replaced the popular vörös és fehér (red and white) wine bar/restaurant in early 2007. The walls are covered in different floral patterns and light floods through the big windows opening from Andrássy út. A high window exposes the kitchen above (although all you see is stainless steel and the chef's toques). Service is quick and casual, while the whole place gives off a cheery vibe. But the food is the real standout (starting with the house-baked bread, which might be Budapest's best), and it's surprisingly reasonably priced considering the stellar location. The one-page menu changes frequently and might offer soups like cream of eggplant and arugula, haricot bean, or cream of strawberry. Salads are excellent—the marinated salmon with horseradish-flavored whipped cream served with a crispy green salad with cherry tomatoes. The food is not traditional Hungarian, although there are Hungarian influences like the beef stew, the steak with *lecsó*, and the strudel for dessert. The duck breast (served perfectly pink in the center) could be served with tomato honey sauce and sautéed Nappa cabbage or with cherry sauce and risotto. Pullet makes frequent appearances, and I've had it served with mashed potatoes and mâche salad. There may be roasted leg of lamb with tarragon cabbage and onion potatoes, or vegetarian pasta dishes like Gorgonzola risotto and penne with tomatoes. A simple cheese tart topped with strawberries and strawberry sauce is a perfect end. Klassz is connected with the Bortársaság wine shop (see page 307), and the wine list reflects this. Just one page, it has a nice variety of prices. It's a great place to sample wine from some of the smallest wineries in a country full of small wineries. Klassz is a slang word that means something along the lines of "super" or "great," which is exactly what the place is.

VI. ANDRÁSSY ÚT 41 ✦ CC ✦ MAINS ◇-◇◇◇ ✦ WINE ★★★★
OPEN MONDAY *through* SATURDAY 11:30AM *to* 11PM, SUNDAY
11:30AM *to* 6PM ✦ M1 (*to Opera*)

M.

M. HAS THE WARMTH AND PERSONALITY OF A GOOD NEIGHBORHOOD RESTAURANT. BUDAPEST IS IN SHORT supply of eateries serving creative food at reasonable prices—M. is one of the few. The mismatched tables are covered with burlap and brown paper and the walls are plastered with brown paper covered in black marker drawings. Everything from a ceiling fan and a telephone to stacks of books and an Oriental rug is drawn on the wall. Even the curtains are brown paper cut-outs. The place is small—with just four tables downstairs and about double that upstairs—and service is low-key. Despite the low-budget atmosphere, they don't skimp on the food and the menu changes weekly. If there happens to be duck breast served with polenta and grape sauce on your visit, order it. Perfectly cooked, it's tender with hints of star anise and red peppercorns. On another visit I sampled an excellent tender pork chop from a suckling pig covered with panko crumbs and served in a cast-iron skillet with mashed potatoes and red-pepper compote. You can count on other imaginative menu items like zucchini and mint soup with mini balls of mozzarella or goose liver and apple ragout served with asparagus-flecked jasmine rice. There are few Hungarian items on the menu, but occasionally you'll find a catfish stew with *túrós csusza* served with chunks of Mangalica ham. There's a surprising attention to detail concerning the food that is a bit unexpected after seeing the DIY dining room. While the menu is refreshingly brief, an expanded wine list would be nice. Food like this deserves a list of more than a few wines, which specify neither the winery nor the vintage.

VII. KERTÉSZ UTCA 48 ✦ TEL: 342-8991
WWW.RAJZOLTETTEREM.HU ✦ CASH ONLY ✦ MAINS ✧-✧✧
WINE ★ ✦ OPEN MONDAY *through* SATURDAY NOON *until* THE
LAST GUEST LEAVES, SUNDAY 6PM *until* THE LAST GUEST
LEAVES ✦ TRAM 4, 6 (*to Király utca*), TROLLEY 70, 78 (*to Teréz körút*)

CHEAP LUNCH SPOTS

EBÉDLO-KÁVÉZŐ

EATING AT THIS NO-NAME *ÉTKEZDE* FEELS LIKE LUNCHING IN A GRANDMOTHER'S SPOTLESS, HOMESPUN KITCHEN. The standard Hungarian food like *palócleves*, *húsleves*, *paprikás*, and *pörkölt* won't win any culinary competitions, but it's tasty and respectable, particularly the dishes that come with the homemade *galuska*. The blue and white flowery tablecloths, dried flower arrangements, houseplants, needlepoint, and hanging plates on the walls add to that grandmotherly feeling, as do the chipped plates and the help-yourself attitude concerning the pickled salads and desserts sitting on the counter. The daily menu is written on a board by the kitchen, which is where you order and pick up your food. Although it's written only in very hard-to-read Hungarian, the kitchen is half open so non-Hungarian speakers can just point if they see something appealing. The place is popular with students and staff from the nearby Central European University business school. Lunch here is also a good way to top off a visit to the Lukács baths, which are just across the street and always seem to induce hunger. Unlike the average *étkezde*, coffee is served here.

II. FRANKEL LEÓ ÚT 36 ✦ CASH ONLY ✦ MAINS ◇
OPEN MONDAY *through* FRIDAY 11AM *to* 5PM ✦ TRAM 4, 6
(*to Margit híd, Budai hídfo*)

KÁDÁR ÉTKEZDE

BUDAPEST'S VERSION OF A HECTIC LOWER EAST SIDE CAFETERIA, KÁDÁR ÉTKEZDE IS IN THE CENTER OF the old Jewish quarter. Kádár is always packed with regulars, and tourists who find their way to this seventh-district institution known for its Jewish specialties. The place is particularly busy on Saturdays when a line of hungry customers wait for tables. Cholent (*sólet*)—a Jewish bean stew which can be had with additions like goose leg, smoked ham, pork knuckle, or hard-boiled egg—is served only on Saturdays. The food here is home-style Hungarian and it's always wonderful (although a little more seasoning sometimes wouldn't hurt). The duck with red cabbage is excellent, and so is the goose liver

when they have it. The many types of boiled beef aren't as boring-tasting as they sound. Kádár's stuffed cabbage is about as good as it gets. I always love the dessert of the day, especially when it's *vargabéles* (a cake made from pasta and strudel dough). The daily specials tend to run out long before the lunch rush is over.

The kind long-time waitresses (who wear old-school toeless white boots) are just as impressive as the food. They must be the hardest-working waitresses in Budapest, pushing through the tightly packed tables to the kitchen, arms stacked with plates. Charming photographs of Hungarian celebrities and sportsmen cover the walls, and the proprietor stands at the door in a white coat, welcoming customers and collecting their money when they leave. Soda water is the drink of choice here, and each table is fitted with a bottle of it. Remember how many glasses you've had and count your slices of bread. Don't forget to go back and tip the waitresses after you've paid your bill at the door, and be prepared to share a table with strangers.

VII. KLAUZÁL TÉR 9 ✦ TEL: 321-3622 ✦ CASH ONLY

MAINS ◇ ✦ OPEN TUESDAY *through* SATURDAY 11:30AM *to* 3:30PM

M1, M2, M3 (*to Deák tér, Astoria, or Blaha Lujza tér*), TROLLEY 74 (*to Nyár utca or Nagy Diófa utca*), TROLLEY 70, 78 (*to Nagymezo utca*)

KÍVÁNSÁG ÉTKEZDE

HUNGARIAN HOSPITALITY IS LEGENDARY, AND MEALS IN HUNGARIAN HOMES USUALLY INVOLVE HUGE PORTIONS of what most people would call comfort food. Unfortunately, most of us aren't treated to home-cooked meals every day, but the next best thing would be having lunch at the Kívánság Étkezde. This simple, no-frills place must be no bigger than 200 square feet, with a gallery that holds a few additional tables. The place really does feel like someone's house, with mismatched tablecloths and dusty artificial flowers. Before the kitchen officially opens, the ground-floor tables fill up with neighborhood pensioners who chat as if they have been meeting there daily for years. Peek into the kitchen on your way in and you'll see Laci *bácsi* ("Uncle" Laci) preparing heavy, hearty dishes like bean soup with smoked meat, *húsleves*, *fozelék*, *Brassói aprópecsenye*, grilled pork, fried cheese, and fried mushrooms. My personal favorite is the *Mátrai borzaska*, a big breaded pork cutlet topped with sour cream, cheese, and garlic, served with both rice and fries. Order a pickled salad to accompany it, and save room for dessert if it happens to be offered that day (sometimes a pasta dish is offered instead). Be prepared to either practice your Hungarian or do a lot of pointing, as the menu is only in Hungarian and no English is spoken. This isn't the place to go for a business lunch or to impress a date, but it is the kind of place that you'll remember when you get hungry for some straightforward home-style Hungarian food that you don't want to pay a lot of money for.

VII. ALSÓERDOSOR UTCA 36 ✦ TEL: 352-1450 ✦ CASH ONLY
MAINS ◇ ✦ OPEN MONDAY *through* FRIDAY 11:30AM *to* 4PM
TRAM 4, 6 (*to Wesselényi utca*), TROLLEY 74 (*to Almássy tér or Szövetség utca*), BUS 7, 78 (*to Huszár utca*), M2 (*to Keleti pályaudvar*)

RÓMA ÉTELBÁR

LOCATED INSIDE OF AN UNATTRACTIVE BLOCKY BUILD-ING COVERED WITH GRAFFITI, THE RÓMA IS A SIMPLE place that serves better than average *étkezde* food. Workers from the neighborhood office buildings come here for hearty classics like *húsleves* (usually offered with matzo balls, liver dumplings, or semolina dumplings), fried cheese or mushrooms, Wiener schnitzel, *fozelék*, fried liver, *cigánypecsenye*, *hagymás rostélyos*, and turkey Kiev. There's usually one pasta or *palacsinta* dish and one dessert offered daily. To see what the menu has on offer on a particular day, check out the web site which posts the daily menu (in Hungarian only). When weather permits, tables and fold-up chairs are set out on the sidewalk, more than doubling the size of the place. Csalogány utca, which is one of the ugliest streets in Buda, isn't an ideal location for outdoor dining, but it's more pleasant than the tiny interior. Coffee is also served here.

I. CSALOGÁNY UTCA 20 ✦ TEL: 201-4545
WWW.CONTROLL.HU/ROMA ✦ CASH ONLY ✦ MAINS ✦
OPEN MONDAY *through* SATURDAY 11AM *to* 4PM ✦ M2 *or* HÉV,
BUS 60, 86, TRAM 19, 41 (*to Batthyány tér*)

OPEN-AIR DINING

....

MOST OF BUDAPEST'S RESTAURANTS, CAFÉS, AND BARS SET UP SOME FORM OF OUTDOOR DINING when the weather warms up, even if it is just one or two rickety plastic garden tables on a busy sidewalk. But a few of them do it in true style with courtyard patios, Parisian-like sidewalk seating, or gardens transformed into outdoor dining rooms far from the honking horns and screeching wheels. To escape even further into the *al fresco* mode, head up into the Buda hills to a garden restaurant surrounded by tall trees and fresh air. When it chills off in the evening, servers at most restaurants kindly hand out plaid blankets to throw over your shoulders. Liszt Ferenc tér and Ráday utca are lined with cafés and bars which all set up substantial sidewalk dining areas when weather permits. For a bigger variety of outdoor eating and drinking options, check out these addresses:

Angelika (page 232) for coffee and cakes on a multi-level terrace next to the Danube and opposite the Parliament.

Bagolyvár (page 117) for traditional Hungarian food in a garden in City Park.

Bambi Presszó (page 228) for beer and wine spritzers on the smoky patio of a Socialist-style café.

Budai Cukrászda (page 214) for luscious Szamos Marcipán cakes and chocolates on a patio in Buda.

Café Eckermann (page 236) for sipping coffee in a tiny hidden garden-like courtyard off Ráday utca.

Café Pierrot Restaurant (page 167) for outdoor dining in the castle.

Café Vian (page 239) for drinks, light food, and people watching on Liszt Ferenc tér.

Ezüst Ponty (page 120) for typical Hungarian food on a shaded patio in the Buda hills.

Fészek (page 121) for an inner-city courtyard transformed into a dining room.

Gerlóczy Kávéház (page 171) for Parisian-style sidewalk dining on a pretty downtown square.

Gundel (page 144) for elegant dining with live music next to the zoo in the City Park.

Kéhli Vendéglo (page 126) for classic Hungarian food in a cobblestoned Óbuda garden shaded by chestnut trees.

Kisbuda Gyöngye (page 148) for refined courtyard dining under the shade of an old chestnut tree.

Le Café Alexandre Dumas (page 241) for Danube-side snacks and drinks on the terrace of the French Institute.

Menza Étterem és Kávézó (page 131) for dining and drinking on sidewalk tables on Liszt Ferenc tér.

Náncsi Néni (page 135) for a countryside atmosphere in the Buda hills, complete with live music at night and a playground for the kids.

Régi Sipos Halászkert (page 138) for eating fish in a pretty, old-fashioned courtyard turned "fishgarden."

Remíz (page 154) for dining among local celebs and politicians in a garden-party-like atmosphere, complete with an outdoor grill.

Szépkilátás Cukrászda (page 226) for a pre- or post-hike calorie splurge on Sváb hill.

Zöld Kapu Vendéglo (page 142) for generous portions of Hungarian food on red-checked tablecloths in a perfectly kept patio.

STRAIGHT FROM THE BUTCHER

WHEN MEAT-LOVING LOCALS WANT A CHEAP LUNCH ON THE GO, THEY'LL GO TO A *HÚS-HENTESÁRU bolt* (butcher shop), which serves freshly cooked sausages on paper plates with thick slices of bread and a pile of mustard. There's usually a variety of sausages (pork, liver, and blood), and sometimes breaded meat, roasted chicken, or other roasted meats. There's often a small selection of pickles or hot pickled peppers to go with your choice. Not all butchers do this; the ones that do will have counters where customers stand and quickly devour their sausages, and there may be a sign that says "*Grill*." Remember, these shops are foremost butcher shops and the prepared snacks are just a side business. Since you're being served by a butcher rather than a waiter, service may be gruff, it's almost always standing only, English is rarely spoken, and you'll be eating among display cases of raw meat while white-coated butchers do their work behind. These are just a few of the best butchers who serve prepared food.

GASZTRÓ HÚS-HENTESÁRU

THIS IS ONE OF THE BEST SMALL BUTCHERS IN THE CITY. CHECK OUT THE LONG LIST OUTSIDE OF THE day's offerings, and let the smell of sizzling sausages tempt you inside.

II. MARGIT KÖRÚT 2 ✦ TEL: 212-4159 ✦ CASH ONLY
OPEN MONDAY 7AM-6PM, TUESDAY *through* FRIDAY 6AM *to* 6PM
SATURDAY 6AM *to* 1PM ✦ TRAM 4, 6 (*to Margit híd, Budai hídfo*)

PETRÓ HÚS-HENTESÁRU

JUDGING BY FOOT TRAFFIC, THIS BUTCHER SHOP MUST BE ONE OF THE CITY'S MOST POPULAR. LOCATED ON busy Moszkva tér, this place is always crowded. Regulars come to the stand-up tables to eat sausages or chunks of fried pork, accompanied by a generous scoop of horseradish from a big bowl next to the register. There's a huge tub of crispy cracklings sitting on the end of the counter, and at least half a dozen black-boards propped up outside advertising their goods.

II. MARGIT KÖRÚT 105 ✦ TEL: 316-5697 ✦ CASH ONLY
OPEN MONDAY *through* FRIDAY 6AM *to* 7PM, SATURDAY 6AM *to* 1PM
M2, BUS 5, 21, 22, 28, 39, 49, 56, 90, 128, 156, TRAM 4, 6 18, 56, 59,
61, 118 (*to Moszkva tér*)

ÁRPÁD HENTESBOLT

THE KÖRÚT, WITH ITS PLETHORA OF GYROS AND FAST-FOOD CHINESE JOINTS, ISN'T THE PLACE FOR FINE dining. Instead, come here for sausages and roasted pork.

VII. ERZSÉBET KÖRÚT 24 (*in the entrance of the Plusz Diszkont store*)
TEL: (26) 370-400 ✦ CASH ONLY ✦ OPEN MONDAY *through*
FRIDAY 7AM *to* 8PM, SATURDAY 7AM *to* 3PM
TRAM 4, 6 (*to Wesselény utca*)

HEGYVIDÉK HÚSÁRUHÁZ

THIS EXCELLENT BUTCHER SHOP, WHICH HAS BEEN IN OPERATION SINCE 1936, SERVES THE TYPICAL HOT choices, including excellent roasted chicken. Another reason to come is for their stock of wild boar and venison meat in the freezer case.

XII. BÖSZÖRMÉNYI ÚT 36/A ✦ TEL: 356-6902 ✦ CASH ONLY
OPEN MONDAY *through* FRIDAY 6:30AM *to* 7PM, SATURDAY 6:30AM
to 1PM ✦ TRAM 59, BUS 102, 105, 112 (*to Apor Vilmos tér*)

HÚS-HENTESÁRU

NOT FAR FROM THE LEHEL TÉR MARKET, THIS BUTCHER IS A POPULAR NEIGHBORHOOD BUDGET-LUNCH SPOT.

XIII. CSANÁDY UTCA 8 ✦ TEL: 350-2927 ✦ OPEN MONDAY
through FRIDAY 7AM *to* 5:30PM, SATURDAY 7AM *to* NOON
M3 (*to Lehel tér*), TROLLEY 76 (*to Hegedus Gyula utca*), BUS 15
(*to Radnóti Miklós utca*)

CHILD-FRIENDLY EATING

THE GOOD NEWS IS THAT HUNGARIANS TEND TO ADORE CHILDREN. EVERYONE, IT SEEMS, FROM THE little old lady in the grocery line to the tough-looking security guard makes a big fuss over kids. Waiters are generally patient and understanding when it comes to dining with children, even when their crying doesn't make them look so cute anymore. The bad news is that restaurants rarely have children's menus. Of course, that's only bad news for children who have their hearts set on eating chicken fingers and fish sticks. In Hungary children tend to grow up eating pretty much the same food as the rest of the family. Instead of animal-shaped pasta, they'll break their teeth in on *lecsó*, *pörkölt*, and *gulyás*, which is probably why so few restaurants offer special menus for the young ones. Many restaurants will, however, let you order half portions. Most (but not all) have highchairs for babies, and some may have booster seats for older kids. The hardest part, really, about dining with children in Hungary is that many restaurants don't have separate non-smoking sections, and if they do, it's often just a few tables in the corner with nothing to separate them from the second-hand smoke. There are a few exceptions: Centrál Kávéház offers a children's menu and a Sunday brunch with clowns and other entertainment. In the Buda hills, Náncsi Néni, Ezüst Ponty, and Remíz (see pages 135, 120, and 154) have little playgrounds in their garden dining areas to help keep children entertained.

CHAPTER 6:

....

COFFEE, SWEETS, AND DRINKS

A jó kávé legyen fekete mint az ördög, forró mint a pokol és édes mint a csók.

Good coffee should be black like the devil, hot like hell, and sweet like a kiss.

Hátra van még a feketeleves.

The black soup is still to come.

(The worst is yet to come. During the Turkish occupation unpleasant business wasn't discussed until coffee, the "black soup," was served.)

—HUNGARIAN PROVERBS

THE TABLE THAT WAS THE LAST ONE ON THE RIGHT IN THE ROOM AND WAS TWICE AS LONG AS THE others was the table where Hungarian literature at that time was directed from.

—*The Happy Younger Days of Mór Jókai*,
GYULA KRÚDY

SWEETS, CAKES, & DESSERTS

(Édesség, Sütemény, and Desszert)

·······························

I F HUNGARIANS SEEM TO BE ADDICTED TO DESSERTS, IT'S FOR GOOD REASON: THEY'RE EVERYWHERE. DESSERTS are a way of life, so important that old customs are rarely tinkered with. Modernized versions of classical desserts are rare, and exquisite Austro-Hungarian-monarchy-style cakes are still the fashion. Hungary has one of the great baking traditions of Europe and is deservedly renowned for its fancy layered cakes (*torta*) and flavorful home-baked ones. The Hungarian pastry kitchen is varied, and stretches from the refined seven-layer *Dobos torta* to the countless everyday cakes that Hungarian cooks seem to be able to throw together at a moment's notice. Hungarians take their desserts seriously, and no family meal is complete without something sweet. Hungarian desserts are rich and flavorful, bringing out the most from simple ingredients like poppy seeds, apricots, plums, butter, or nuts. Like everything else in the Hungarian kitchen, desserts have been heavily influenced by other cultures over the centuries, especially Turkish (who introduced filo dough), Italian (who introduced many new ingredients), Austrian (who popularized fancy tortes), and nineteenth-century French chefs who made fancy cakes and tarts popular. Still, many small shops stock mass-produced cakes and it can be easier to find a bad *cukrászda* (pastry shop) than a good one if you don't know where to go.

There's quite a difference between the desserts that you will find in the restaurants, at the coffeehouses, and in homes. Coffeehouses are the places to go for fancy layer cakes and elegant pastries, while restaurants traditionally serve things like *palacsinta* (pancakes), and *rétes* (strudel). There's a huge variety of home-style cakes, and the commonly made yeast-raised cakes are hardly ever found at restaurants. *Aranygaluska*, or "golden dumplings," is one of the best home-baked creations: yeast-raised round dumplings squished in a baking pan, brushed with melted butter, flavored with apricot jam and ground walnuts, and eaten hot. Another is *fánk* (doughnuts), which are sometimes called *farsangi fánk* (Carnival doughnuts) since they were traditionally prepared during the Carnival season. *Marcipán* (marzipan) is an important ingredient in Hungarian desserts and is what one of the country's most famous pastry dynasties, Szamos Marcipán, has based itself on.

Some of the desserts you can expect to find in Hungary are: *Rétes*, or strudel, introduced by the Turks in the sixteenth century, but now just as Hungarian as paprika. It's most commonly filled with curd cheese, cherries, apples, or poppy seeds (or a combination). It can even be savory and stuffed with cabbage or curd cheese and dill. *Vargabéles* is a cake made from noodles and curd cheese cooked between layers of strudel dough. *Somlói galuska* was created at Gundel, and is now ubiquitous. It includes chunks of chocolate and vanilla sponge cake flavored with rum, vanilla custard, raisins, and walnuts, drenched in chocolate syrup and whipped cream. *Palacsinta*—Hungary's version of crêpes—can be filled with virtually anything, but the traditional fillings, like curd cheese, jam, walnuts, and chocolate, are the best. *Gundel palacsinta*, created by Károly Gundel, are pancakes stuffed with walnut filling and topped with chocolate sauce (traditionally it wasn't served flaming). *Csúsztatott palacsinta*, "slipped pancakes," generally is a homemade dessert consisting of layers of pancakes spread with apricot jam or chocolate, stacked high to look like a cake, and topped with meringue. *Túrós gombóc* are curd cheese dumplings slathered with buttery bread crumbs and served with sweetened sour cream sauce. *Szilvásgombóc* are plum dumplings made with potato dough, which can be eaten as a dessert or a meal. *Mákos guba* is bread pudding slathered in poppy seed sauce. *Gesztenyepüré* is chestnut purée flavored with rum, and topped with whipped cream. The *Ischler* is a chocolate-glazed cookie filled with fruit preserves. The *kürtoskalács* originated in Transylvania, and is now most commonly found at festivals and fairs. It's a long thin strip of dough wrapped around a metal spit, brushed with sugar, and rotated in an oven or over a fire until it's cooked and the sugar has caramelized. *Almás pite* is apple pie (served in squares rather than wedges). *Diótorta* is walnut cake and *mogyorótorta* is hazelnut cake. *Flódni* is a traditional Jewish dessert of ground walnut paste, poppy seeds, and apples between thin layers of pastry. *Meggyes piskóta* is cherry sponge cake. *Püspökkenyér*, or "bishop's cake," is the Hungarian version of fruit cake. *Túrós lepény*, or "cheese pie," is curd cheese filling between two layers of short crust. *Túrótorta* is cheesecake made with curd cheese.

In coffeehouses you're likely to find more elaborate cakes such as: the *Dobos torta*, which was invented in the late 1800s by József Dobos, one of Hungary's most famous pastry chefs. It is five layers of vanilla sponge cake, each smothered with chocolate buttercream icing, and topped with thin wedges of caramel-glazed sponge cake. *Stefánia torta* is similar but the top is dusted with cocoa powder instead of topped with caramel. The *Esterházy torta* is layers of rich walnut cake, spread with cream, and topped with a thin layer of fondant. *Fekete-erdo torta* is Black Forest cake (chocolate layers with sour cherries, lots of whipped cream, and chocolate shavings). *Francia krémes* is two crisp pieces of puff pastry stuffed with cream filling and a layer of whipped cream and topped with coffee-flavored icing. *Gerbeaud szelet* (or *Zserbó szelet*) was created by Swiss pastry chef Emile Gerbeaud. It is thin layers of sweet yeast cake, apricot jam, and ground walnuts, topped with a chocolate glaze. The *Indiáner* is a pastry stuffed with whipped cream and glazed with chocolate. *Kardinális szelet* is sponge cake with a thick layer of meringue, with jam or fruit sometimes sandwiched between. *Linzertorta*, which originated in Austria, has a crust made from ground almonds or walnuts, which is spread with jam and topped with a pastry lattice top. *Lúdláb torta* is a thin chocolate sponge cake topped with chocolate mousse and a layer of brandy-soaked cherries, and smothered with shiny chocolate glaze. *Orosz krém torta*, "Russian cream cake," is a light sponge cake topped with a thick layer of creamy filling flavored with rum and candied fruits and raisins, and topped with whipped cream. *Rákóczi túrós* has a short crust, a baked curd cheese filling, and a meringue and apricot jam topping. The *Rigó Jancsi* is squares of chocolate mousse sandwiched between two layers of chocolate cake topped with a chocolate glaze. It was named for a late-nineteenth-century event that scandalized Europe: a Belgian baroness fell in love with a Hungarian gypsy violinist (named Rigó Jancsi), slipped her diamond ring onto his finger, and ran away with him. Although it was created in Vienna, the *Sacher torta* is ubiquitous in Budapest. It's two layers of firm chocolate cake with apricot glaze in the center, chocolate glaze on top, and a dollop of fresh whipped cream.

COFFEEHOUSE CULTURE

T HE TABLES OF BUDAPEST'S GRAND OLD COFFEE-HOUSES ONCE SERVED AS OFFICES AND SECOND homes to some of Hungary's greatest writers, artists, and intellectuals. Books were written, plays were penned, and literary journals were edited at the small marble tables in the elegantly furnished coffeehouses whose lists of regulars read like

the who's who of the Hungarian art and literary scene. One of the few happier legacies of the 150-year Turkish occupation was the arrival of coffee in Hungary, which gave Budapest a head start in the Central European coffeehouse scene that defined social life from the end of the nineteenth-century until 1940. From Belgrade to Prague, small cramped apartments were what fuelled the legendary coffeehouse culture. People went to cafés not just to relax, but to work, and regulars even received messages at their tables. Coffeehouses were welcoming places that functioned as extensions of the home, where people could socialize, talk business, or sit for hours nursing a cup of coffee while reading the newspapers.

They were also affordable, and many cafés offered subsidies to writers, like cheap "writer's plates" of sausage, bread, and cheese or free pens and paper. Everybody in the different intellectual circles knew each other, and knew at which coffeehouses their friends and colleagues could be found. Different coffeehouses had different customer bases: some attracted mostly painters or sculptors. Others attracted writers, artists, or intellectuals. Regulars had their favorite tables kept on constant reserve, and waiters were known to be discreet, even offering credit to their favorite customers. Not just for the intellectual classes, coffeehouses also attracted families or people who simply wanted to eat. Menus were typically long, some were open twenty-four hours daily, and many had live music.

Around 1900 coffeehouses became more luxurious, decorated with gold gilt, mirrors, and crystal chandeliers. They tried to outdo each other in terms of glitter and elegance, and the New York Café (see page 207) surpassed them all. The two wars weakened coffeehouse culture, and Communism and nationalization

eventually destroyed it, in addition to the class of intellectuals who frequented coffee houses.

From the *kávéház* grew the grungy *eszpresszó* where the actual coffee, rather than the atmosphere and conversation, was the main function. The *eszpresszó* was simple and more working class, which corresponded with the mood of the times. They were smoky, unattractive places with surly waitresses. And the ones that are left still are. Don't go to the *eszpresszó* for its culinary value, but for its stuck-in-time 1960s Communist-era atmosphere. While the *eszpresszó* once offered food—and sometimes live music and dancing—it's now mainly a place to drink cheap beer or coffee, with a large portion of nostalgia on the side. Expect linoleum-covered floors, bad lighting, coffee served in little glass cups, plastic ashtrays full of stubbed-out cigarettes, and red vinyl seating. These places are dives, for sure, but they offer one of the last glimpses into the Budapest of the decades before the city began to crawl out from behind its dusty mask and reassert itself as a cosmopolitan European capital.

Budapest still has a few grand old coffeehouses left, but most are long gone. The New York Café and the Centrál Kávéház were both restored and reopened. While there are no signs left of the New York's literary past since its posh renovation, the Centrál feels more like I would have imagined it did back in the coffeehouse era. Others like the Gerbeaud, Ruszwurm, and Hauer have been around since that era (or even earlier), and are also excellent pastry shops. Coffeehouses no longer play the important intellectual role in Hungarian society that they once did. But Budapest still has plenty of cafés, which are as popular as ever. Times have definitely changed, but cafés are still vital to the social life of the city, although in a different way. Visit any café on a few occasions, and you're bound to see regulars. They'll still be sipping their coffee, but chances are they'll be using the free wireless Internet rather than penning the next great novel.

COFFEE TRANSLATOR

STRONG KÁVÉ IS A BASIC NECESSITY FOR MOST HUNGARIANS. HUNGARIANS DRINK THEIR COFFEE IN A similar fashion to the Italians, but an espresso here is larger and less concentrated. Hungarians also prefer to drink their coffee sitting down, though it is now possible to get coffee-to-go in paper cups. The preferred method for making coffee at home is the old-fashioned stovetop espresso percolator. Coffee is often served in little demitasse glasses, although in nice cafés you'll get the classic treatment: coffee delivered on a silver tray in a nice porcelain cup and saucer, with a little demitasse of mineral water on the side, and a cookie or chocolate on the plate. When you need your caffeine fix, there's some essential vocabulary to know in order to avoid disappointment or confusion. Most cafés also have lengthy lists of their own coffee concoctions.

amerikai kávé: American coffee; which is a weak filter coffee. Hotels generally serve it, but most cafés and restaurants don't.

árkádia kávé: Espresso with cinnamon and honey, topped with whipped cream.

cappuccino: Cappuccino; instead of milk, it could be served with gobs of whipped cream.

dupla kávé: Double espresso.

forró csokoládé: Hot chocolate.

hosszú kávé: "Long coffee," an espresso with hot water added.

ir kávé: Irish coffee.

jeges kávé: Iced coffee.

kávé: Espresso; also called *eszpresszó, presszókávé,* or *fekete.* If you simply ask for a

coffee, this is what you'll get.

koffeinmentes kávé: Decaffeinated coffee; not available everywhere.

Mária Terézia kávé: Espresso with orange liqueur and whipped cream.

mélange: This typically Viennese coffee is made with half Viennese light-roasted coffee and half steamed milk, and sometimes topped with foamed milk.

rumos kávé: Espresso with rum.

Sissi kávé: Espresso with Sissi-brand apricot cream liquor.

tea: Tea.

tejeskávé: "Milky coffee," half milk and half espresso.

CLASSIC COFFEEHOUSES

CAFÉ GERBEAUD

W ITH ITS CENTRAL LOCATION ON VÖRÖSMARTY TÉR AND THE BEGINNING OF VÁCI UTCA, AND ITS LUSCIOUS pastries, it's really not a surprise that Gerbeaud is so firmly on the beaten tourist track. Swiss pastry chef Henrik Kugler—who came from a family of bakers and had worked throughout Europe by the time he arrived in Budapest—opened the café in 1858. It was called Kugler back then and was located a few blocks away. By the time it moved to its present location in

1870, it was known as one of the finest in town, and still is today. In the 1880s Kugler joined forces with Emile Gerbeaud, another Swiss pastry chef, who took over and continued to improve on Kugler's legacy. While the coffeehouses of that period all had reputations for being lush and ornately furnished, George Lang called the Gerbeaud "the Taj Mahal of them all, its high-ceilinged, gold, marble, and stucco complex of giant rooms suggesting the cozy splendor of a museum or a church." The place is still as exquisite as ever (it was renovated in 1997), with crystal chandeliers and a long and very tempting pastry counter filled with thick cakes, shiny marzipan concoctions, and chocolate truffles. Each room is different, and a large terrace opens on the square when the weather is warm. Gerbeaud's reputation for fine pastries and chocolates is justly deserved—here you'll find some of the finest in Hungary, and maybe even Europe. But the prices are also higher than the average, and the constantly flashing cameras can get a bit annoying. There are few wines available here, but the sweet Gerbeaud cuveé is worth trying—it's made in Tokaj exclusively for Gerbeaud by János Árvay. The Gerbeaud empire takes its marketing seriously—there's even a gift shop complete with products with Gerbeaud's own label. Gerbeaud also operates a delivery service called Gerboy (Tel: 429-9026). The Gerbeaud Sörház (Tel: 429-9022; Open daily noon-midnight) in the basement is a pub that offers full meals and house-brewed beer.

V. VÖRÖSMARTY TÉR 7 ✦ TEL: 429-9020 ✦ WWW.GERBEAUD.HU

CC ✦ OPEN DAILY 9AM *to* 9PM ✦ M1 (*to Vörösmarty tér*)

CENTRÁL KÁVÉHÁZ

O F THE BATCH OF CLASSIC COFFEEHOUSES THAT ONCE DEFINED BUDAPEST'S COFFEEHOUSE CULTURE, THE Centrál is one of the few that has managed to retain what I imagine was the old *kávéház* atmosphere that made the places such city institutions. While some coffeehouses now feel more like tourist traps than old literary haunts, the Centrál is still the

kind of place where you can stay and sip coffee all day long if you want to, and even add a meal and a few glasses of wine without breaking your bank account. It first opened in 1887 and was open non-stop to accommodate the artists, writers, and intellectuals who made the place their second home. Some of Hungary's best twentieth-century writers (whose names you'll recognize from street signs) were regulars here: Endre Ady, Frigyes Karinthy, Zsigmond Móricz, Mihály Babits, Dezso Kosztolányi, and Gyula Krúdy. The various sections of the café are named for publications that were once edited at its tables and there are silhouettes depicting famous writer customers on the walls. The café closed in 1949 when the building was nationalized, and the elegantly decorated place functioned as a cafeteria, an arcade, and a university club before being resurrected in 2000 complete with its old welcoming atmosphere and classy prewar look with shades of soft green and orange, gold and brass, and pretty pink flowers on the ceiling. The gallery upstairs is a full restaurant (see page 119), while downstairs is the café where meals can be eaten as well. While the food here is consistently good, the service is downright slow and disinterested more often than not. There's live piano music Wednesday through Friday from 6pm to 10pm, and on Sunday from 11am to 4pm.

V. KÁROLYI MIHÁLY UTCA 9 ✦ TEL: 266-2110

WWW.CENTRALKAVEHAZ.HU ✦ CC ✦ OPEN DAILY 7AM *to*

MIDNIGHT ✦ M3, BUS 5, 7, 7A, 8, 15, 78, 112, 173 (*to Ferenciek tere*)

HAUER CUKRÁSZDA

THE HAUER CUKRÁSZDA IS ONE OF THE SEVERAL OLD-STYLE COFFEEHOUSES THAT HAVE BEEN RESTORED and reopened in Budapest. While it's nowhere near as elegant as the New York, and it lacks the fine details that make the Centrál Kávéház so gorgeous, it's always nice to drink coffee and eat cake in a café that helped make Budapest one of the café capitals of early twentieth-century Europe. Marble-topped tables sit on the rose-and-black-patterned terrazzo floor, the lamps are art nouveau style, and mirrors on the white molded paneling in the front room make the place seem more spacious. It lacks the sophistication that other traditional coffeehouses have, and the conference facilities in the back are a bit dreary. But, like a true coffeehouse should, it attracts a wide range of customers, from elegantly dressed old ladies with all afternoon to spare, to office workers rushing to gulp down their coffee. It also fulfills another coffeehouse requisite: it serves excellent pastries. Head towards the back and check out the display cases full of historical mementos like old china and silver, menus from the 1930s, and awards that date up to the present.

VIII. RÁKÓCZI ÚT 47-49 ✦ TEL: 323-1476
WWW.HAUERCUKRASZDA.HU ✦ CASH ONLY ✦ OPEN DAILY
10AM *to* 9PM ✦ M2, BUS 7, 78, TRAM 4, 6 (*to Blaha Lujza tér*)

LUKÁCS CUKRÁSZDA

THE LUKÁCS IS ANOTHER OF BUDAPEST'S COFFEE-HOUSES THAT HAS RECENTLY BEEN REBORN. THE PLACE was founded by the Lukács family in 1912, was nationalized in 1949, and then transformed into the cafeteria for the secret police who worked down the street at Andrássy út 60 (now the House of Terror Museum). It was reopened and restored in the 1990s, but sharing an entrance with a bank isn't very classy, and the place has always felt a bit forgotten to me. It was recently renovated and the gold gilt, crystal, mirrors, and fancy stucco work look better than ever (although the bank entrance still doesn't look any better). The menu has also been upgraded, and although the extensive selection of pastries is tasty, it's among Budapest's priciest. The Lukács also offers house-made macaroons (a rarity in Budapest), as well as a small selection of heavier fare for breakfast and lunch.

VI. ANDRÁSSY ÚT 70 ✦ TEL: 302-8747

WWW.LUKACSCUKRASZDA.COM ✦ M1 (*to Vörösmarty utca*)

MUVÉSZ KÁVÉHÁZ

I CAN'T HELP BUT LOVE THE MUVÉSZ COFFEEHOUSE. THE "ARTIST COFFEEHOUSE" IS GRAND AND MAJESTIC. OR at least it used to be. Like a glamorous woman who has grown old and never changed her ways or her style, despite the wrinkles and sags, the Muvész feels a bit past its prime these days. But its faded elegance is just what makes it so lovable. Located a few steps from the Opera House, the place is one of the few classic old

coffee houses that hasn't been renovated. Smokers congregate in the front room, where the stuffed pastry case is also located. Back in the main room lined with dignified green-and-white-striped wallpaper (which also needs updating), there are big mirrors, candelabras, gold molding, and fancy crystal chandeliers. The walls are dotted with dark oil paintings, and the little marble-topped tables are often occupied with regular customers. During

the warm months tables are set up on the sidewalk to tempt those passing by to pop in for a coffee or a glass of wine. Founded in 1898, Muvész is a Budapest institution.

VI. ANDRÁSSY ÚT 29 ✦ TEL: 352-1337 ✦ CASH ONLY
OPEN DAILY 9AM *to* 11PM ✦ M1 (*to Opera*)

NEW YORK CAFÉ

O F ALL BUDAPEST'S LITERARY-MINDED CAFÉS, THE LEG-
ENDARY NEW YORK CAFÉ (KÁVÉHÁZ) WAS ARGUABLY
the most beloved. The eclectic Italian Renaissance-style building was built in 1894 to house the New York Insurance Company, but it was best known for its café, which was a hangout for Budapest's prewar literary circles. It offered cheap "writer's plates" for the penniless writers who were there day and night.

The story goes that one of its regulars, writer Ferenc Molnár, marched the café's keys down to the Danube and threw them in, so the place would never close its doors. It suffered the same fate as many cafés during the Communist era, functioning as a sporting goods store and travel agency for a while before reopening as a not-so-luxurious café. When the Italian Boscolo hotel group bought the building it was in such bad condition that netting was protecting pedestrians from falling pieces of stucco. In the spring of 2006, after a lengthy renovation, the café reopened along with a posh hotel. It was renovated down to the last detail, with Hungarian and Italian artists working for three years on the ceiling frescoes alone. The plethora of gilt, marble, and crystal is now probably shinier than it has ever been, and the place feels more like a palace than a café. Acclaimed restaurant designer Adam Tihany (who was born in Transylvania) worked on the café, which means that modern elements are mixed in with the original features. At the upstairs cigar bar, which is fitted with plush red carpets and red lamps, cigars are kept in old bank safes. The Mély Víz ("Deep Water") restaurant sits below the café and serves Italian and Hungarian food. At the café, a small menu offers a disappointingly small (and expensive)

dessert selection. Although it is undoubtedly a gorgeous and much-needed renovation job, the atmosphere of the New York has changed along with the ownership. Before its renovation, it was a comfortable, reasonably priced place where, if you thought hard enough, you could imagine magazines being edited and novels written. These days, no writer I know would have the bank account to be spending his days here. It was once considered Budapest's finest café and restaurant, but now it exists mainly for tourists. Still, though the café is now part of the Boscolo Hotel, it belongs as much to the city as to the hotel and is worth visiting. The New York has always been the grandest café in Budapest, and it still is.

VII. ERZSÉBET KÖRÚT 9-11 (*New York Palace Boscolo Hotel*)

TEL: 886-6111 ✦ WWW.NEWYORKPALACE.HU ✦ CC ✦ OPEN DAILY 9AM *to* MIDNIGHT ✦ M2, TRAM 4, 6 (*to Blaha Lujza tér*)

RUSZWURM CUKRÁSZDA

O F ALL BUDAPEST'S HISTORIC PASTRY SHOPS, RUSZ-WURM WINS IN THE CATEGORY OF QUALITY. FOUNDED in 1827 in the Buda Castle, it's not an exaggeration to call this Biedermeier-style *cukrászda* cozy. It's small, and very much on the tourist track, which means that it's often difficult to get a

table. Long before the place was Ruszwurm, it housed a Turkish biscuit baker. Despite its stormy history—which includes having survived the sieges of 1849 and 1944–45, being nationalized in 1951, and closing for a few years—today's Ruszwurm still has some of Budapest's best cakes and pastries. The place isn't named for its founder, but for an apprentice who came to own the shop a few generations later. During its heyday in the nineteenth century it was favored by aristocrats

and government officials, and Queen Elisabeth ("Sissi" to the Hungarians) even shopped here. Ruszwurm suffered under Communism and was eventually bought in 1994 by the Szamos Marcipán family and resurrected to its old glory. Though everything else has, it seems as if nothing about the décor has changed over the years. The pastry case in front of the cherry and mahogany counter is jammed full of tantalizing options, which in this instance really do taste as good as they look. Especially worth trying are the Ruszwurm *krémes* and the chocolaty Ruszwurm *torta*.

I. SZENTHÁROMSÁG UTCA 7 ✦ TEL: 375-5284

WWW.RUSZWURM.HU ✦ CASH ONLY ✦ OPEN DAILY

10AM *to* 7PM ✦ VÁRBUSZ (*to Szentháromság tér*)

PASTRY SHOPS

AUGUSZT CUKRÁSZDA

THE OLD AUGUSZT CUKRÁSZDA WAS KNOWN AS THE GERBEAUD OF BUDA. JUDGING BY FADED OLD BLACK and white photos of the place, it was every bit as grand as the Gerbeaud is today. The company was established in 1870 when pastry chef Elek Auguszt opened his first shop in the Tabán (the area behind the Buda Castle) and later generations of the family joined the trade and continued to add shops and cafés. Wars, revolutions, and nationalization disrupted the business, but today the fifth generation of Auguszts have three shops in Budapest. The original shop on Krisztina tér was bombed and destroyed during the 1944–45 siege of Budapest, and was only reopened two years later. The company was nationalized in 1951 and the family was then deported. When they returned in 1957 they opened the shop on Fény utca, which was turned into a café in 2003; two more have opened since. The Kossuth Lajos utca shop is in the courtyard of a protected building on a major downtown street; the Sasadi út shop is in an old villa next to the Farkasréti Cemetery, which adds garden tables during the summer; and the Fény utca shop is behind the Mammut shopping center, with seating on the second level. In addition to a wide variety of rich and creamy cakes and pastries, they serve excellent ice cream in the summer.

II. FÉNY UTCA 8 ✦ TEL: 316-3817

WWW.AUGUSZTCUKRASZDA.HU ✦ CASH ONLY

OPEN TUESDAY *through* FRIDAY 10AM *to* 6PM, SATURDAY 9AM *to* 6PM ✦ TRAM 4, 6 (*to Széna tér*), M2, BUS 5, 21, 22, 28, 39, 49, 56, 90, 128, 156, TRAM 18, 56, 59, 61, 118 (*to Moszkva tér*)

V. KOSSUTH LAJOS UTCA 14-16 ✦ TEL: 337-6379 ✦ CASH ONLY

OPEN MONDAY *through* FRIDAY 10AM *to* 6PM ✦ M3, BUS 5, 7, 15, 78 (*to Ferenciek tere*), M2, TRAM 49 (*to Astoria*)

XI. SASADI ÚT 190 ✦ TEL: 249-0134 ✦ CASH ONLY

OPEN WEDNESDAY *through* SUNDAY 10AM *to* 6PM

TRAM 59, BUS 8, 53 (*to Farkasréti tér*)

BUDAI CUKRÁSZDA

SINCE THIS PLACE IS PART OF THE SZAMOS MAR-
CIPÁN DYNASTY, YOU CAN BE SURE THAT THE CAKES,
pastries, and chocolates will be top-notch. It's a neighborhood favorite and when the large shaded terrace is open, the
tables are packed with people from the neighborhood, their children, and their dogs. Those who don't want to stay get ice cream
cones instead. The cases of desserts inside are lined with colorful
mignons, layered cakes, and dozens of types of bonbons and
truffles. They make a particularly good *francia krémes* and the
fekete-erdo torta (Black Forest cake) is also a favorite. The cozy
inside—decorated in Old World antique style—is fairly small
and is perfect for warming up on chilly days.

XII. BÖSZÖRMÉNYI ÚT 44-46 ✦ TEL: 355-1728
WWW.SZAMOS.HU ✦ CC ✦ OPEN DAILY 10AM *to* 7PM, SUMMER
10AM *to* 8PM ✦ TRAM 59, BUS 102, 105, 112 (*to Apor Vilmos tér*)

DAUBNER CUKRÁSZDA

THE LINES STRETCHING OUT THE DOORS OF THIS
LONG, LOW BUILDING AT PRACTICALLY ALL HOURS SAY
everything you need to know about Daubner's popularity.
Despite its non-central location, Daubner must be Budapest's
busiest pastry shop, and one of its largest. You'll find the full

spectrum of Hungary's desserts here: rows of *torta* with thick layers of cream and chocolate, thick slices of strudel, delicate cookies, colorful parfaits, tubs of *pogácsa*, and even ice-cream cakes. The *bejglis* disappear as fast as they come out of the oven around Christmas. The house-made ice cream sold in the summer (which makes the lines even longer) is some of Budapest's best. At the busiest times, especially on the weekends, space is tight, lines move slow, and people sit on the wall out front eating their cakes. There are no tables, just a standing bar. The place was opened by Béla Daubner in 1901, and is run today by his grandson, using the same recipes that his grandfather and father before him used. Daubner recently expanded to the building next door, where there's a smaller selection of pastries for sale, but there are tables for sitting down to eat properly, which doesn't seem to have made the lines any shorter.

II. SZÉPVÖLGYI ÚT 50 ✦ TEL: 335-2253
WWW.DAUBNERCUKRASZDA.HU ✦ CASH ONLY ✦ OPEN
DAILY 9AM *to* 7PM ✦ TRAM 17, BUS 6, 60, 86 (*to Kolosy tér*)

EURÓPA CUKRÁSZDA & KÁVÉHÁZ

THOUGH THIS PLACE DOESN'T HAVE THE CHARM THAT THE OLD COFFEEHOUSES DO, IT'S FINE FOR COFFEE and cake on the *körút*. The clientele is a mix of old ladies in fur coats, men in business suits, and people just popping in for a quick snack or caffeinated pick-me-up. It tends to get smoky, even in the non-smoking section. The gallery upstairs, with green carpeting and random paintings on the wall, is quieter. Watching the busy street below from the comfortable couch-like seats is an advantage to sitting up here. The choice of desserts is extensive, and all of the usual suspects are featured in the pastry case. The house specialty, the *Európa torta*, is a rather dry chocolate sponge cake layered with rum-flavored whipped cream and chestnut cream and topped with chocolate icing. There are also a few heartier dishes, mostly cold salads and sandwiches, on the menu. There are omelets and eggs for breakfast, but cake is really the thing to order here. If you're in a rush, go next door to the *cukrászda* for the same pastries, only quicker and cheaper, which can be eaten standing up.

V. SZENT ISTVÁN KÖRÚT 7-9 ✦ TEL: 312-2362

WWW.EUROPAKAVEHAZ.HU ✦ CASH ONLY ✦ OPEN DAILY

9AM *to* 11PM MAY *through* OCTOBER, 9AM *to* 10PM NOVEMBER

through APRIL ✦ TRAM 4, 6 (*to Jászai Mari tér*)

FROHLICH CUKRÁSZDA

THIS FAMILY-RUN BAKERY HAS BEEN AN INSTITUTION IN THE SEVENTH DISTRICT'S OLD JEWISH NEIGHBORHOOD, as well as in the Jewish community, since it was founded in 1953 by György Frohlich. The kosher bakery is also a fixture in the Jewish community, and is the best place in town to sample Jewish specialties like the *flódni*, Hannukah donuts, challah bread, and other special holiday treats for Purim and Rosh Hashanah. It was recently brightened up a bit with some orange paint, but besides that you get the idea that not much has changed over the years at the Frohlich. Spend any time sitting with your coffee and cakes, and you're likely to run into tourists from around the world, including many Israelis who have come to Hungary to see the land of their ancestors. If you have to choose just one thing from the pastry case, make it the *flódni*, which is the specialty of the house. Regardless, this no-frills bakery is a must-visit.

VII. DOB UTCA 22 ✦ TEL: 267-2851 ✦ WWW.FROHLICH.HU
CASH ONLY ✦ OPEN MONDAY *through* THURSDAY 9AM *to* 8PM
FRIDAY 7:30AM *to* 6PM, SUNDAY 10AM *to* 4PM
M2, TRAM 49 (*to Astoria*)

IGRINYI CUKRÁSZDA

T HE IGRINYI CUKRÁSZDA HAS BEEN AROUND SINCE 1938. LOCATED IN THE OLD SEVENTH-DISTRICT JEWISH neighborhood, all of the pastries made here are good. The only problem is that there's not enough of them! The pastry case is, sadly, usually half empty. But that just gives you more time to concentrate on what is there. One of the usual fixtures is the *Krakkói mákos*, which is a bottom layer of crumbly pastry, topped with poppy seed filling, and a thick layer of meringue. There are excellent home-style fruit cakes, most notably the thin, very tasty, plum cake. During the warm months there's good ice cream. There are no tables at the Igrinyi, just a standing counter.

VII. WESSELÉNYI UTCA 32 ✦ TEL: 341-4922 ✦ CASH ONLY
OPEN TUESDAY *through* SATURDAY 10AM *to* 7PM ✦ M2, TRAM 4, 6
(*to Wesselényi utca*), TROLLEY 74 (*to Nyár utca or Nagy Diófa utca*)

JÉGBÜFÉ

O NE OF THE BEST PEOPLE-WATCHING SPOTS IN BUDA-PEST IS THE STAINLESS-STEEL COUNTER IN FRONT OF the long windows at Jégbüfé. It faces busy Ferenciek tere, with rocky Gellért Hill visible across the bridge. Jégbüfé, which opened in 1952, is one of Budapest's busiest pastry shops and many of Budapest's pastry chefs get their start in its bustling kitchen. Here's the drill: walk from one end of the long pastry shop to the other, examining the tempting confections behind the glass. When you've spotted yours, pay at the cashier, and bring your receipt back over to the pastry case to pick up your prize. There are no seats or tables, just the stand-up counter where you can eat and drink in peace while commuters and pedestrians scurry around outside. Ice cream is a big business here during the summer, but be sure you get the house-made variety rather than the commercially-made kind they also sell. While many people

swear by the pastries and cakes at Jégbüfé, they aren't Budapest's best (they can be too gelatinous and sugary). The one thing that I can never resist, however, is the buttery *pálmalevél* (palmier), which is a perfect match for the strong coffee.

V. FERENCIEK TERE 10 ✦ TEL: 318-6205 ✦ WWW.JEGBUFE.HU
CASH ONLY ✦ OPEN MONDAY, TUESDAY, THURSDAY *through*
SATURDAY 7AM *to* 9:30PM, WEDNESDAY 7AM *to* 8:30PM
SUNDAY 8AM *to* 9:30PM ✦ M3 (*to Ferenciek tere*)

KOVÁCS CUKRÁSZDA

THIS PASTRY SHOP HAS A BIGGER SELECTION OF CAKES AND SWEETS STUFFED INTO ITS FORMICA pastry cases than many shops three times its size. The place is totally old school, with faux-wood cabinets, a stern-looking *néni* taking orders, and a worn grey-tiled floor. There's the usual selection of fancy cream-filled layer cakes, as well as *pogácsa*, simple home-style cakes (such as an excellent plum cake), and chocolate-and-marzipan-covered petits fours. They also do a big business in special order cakes and *bejglis* for Christmas. The man behind the shop, pastry chef Sándor Kovács, works in the kitchen behind an old brown-and-white-checked curtain. There

are two tiny tables with small wobbly stools where most customers quickly and quietly slurp down their coffee and cake, and then
come back the next day for more.

VIII. BRÓDY SÁNDOR UTCA 23/A ✦ TEL: 338-1398

CASH ONLY ✦ OPEN TUESDAY through FRIDAY 10AM to 6PM

SATURDAY 9AM to 2PM ✦ TRAM 4, 6 (to Rákóczi tér)

LÁSZLÓ CUKRÁSZDA

THIS PLEASANT LITTLE PASTRY SHOP HAS BEEN RUN
BY PASTRY CHEF JÓZSEF LÁSZLÓ SINCE 1970. IT'S
popular with students from the nearby technical university,
as well as pensioners having afternoon coffee and cake at the five
tiny tables in the sparklingly clean one-room place. A refrigerator
case is filled with tempting cream-filled layer cakes like *Stefánia
torta*, *lúdlábtorta*, *mogyorótorta*, and *francia krémes*. But the
place is best known for its *kuglóf*—which is a sort of moist coffee
cake, with various types of filling, baked in a Bundt pan. It's
baked every Friday, and is available after 2pm. They also do an
excellent job with the more simple things like tiny *pogácsa*,
cookies, and small crispy *pálmalevelek* (palmiers), and they serve
ice cream when the weather calls for it.

XI. BUDAFOKI ÚT 53 ✦ TEL: 365-8496

WWW.SZAKINFO.HU/LASZLO_CUKRASZDA/INDEX.HTML

CASH ONLY ✦ OPEN TUESDAY through SUNDAY 9AM to 6PM

BUS 86 (to Karinthy Frigyes út), TRAM 6 (to Budafoki út)

NÁNDORI CUKRÁSZDA

DURING THE WEEKS BEFORE CHRISTMAS THE STAFF
HERE ARE BUSY WRAPPING POPPY SEED AND WALNUT
stuffed *bejglis* as fast as they come out of the oven. This
bakery has been serving some of the city's best cakes and desserts
since 1957, which was long
before all of the other eating and drinking spots
arrived on Ráday utca. In
1988 the name was
changed from the Varga to
the Nándori when baker
László Nándori took over.

The walls are plastered with awards and recognitions that Nándori has won, and the regular customers pouring in throughout the day buying bags of pastries to go are testimony to the quality. The place makes gorgeous classic cakes, like the *Dobos torta*, *Orosz krém torta* (Russian cream cake), and all the other Hungarian favorites. But the simpler ones like the *Rákóczi túrós*, the *mézeskrémes* (layers of honey cake stuffed with apricot jam and cream), and the *szilvás pite* (plum cake) might be even better. Baking *pogácsa* should be pretty straightforward, but it can be hard to find good pogácsa in this age of commercial baking and this is one of the things Nándori does best, usually in varieties like sheep cheese, Roquefort, potato, butter, and olive. It's hard to resist buying a little bag to nibble on while you're wandering down Ráday utca. Coffee is served, but competition can be fierce for the two small tables by the door.

IX. RÁDAY UTCA 53 ✦ TEL: 215-8776 ✦ WWW.NANDORI.HU
CC ✦ OPEN MONDAY *through* SATURDAY 7:30AM *to* 6PM
TRAM 2, 2A, 4, 6, BUS 15 (*to Boráros tér*)

PILLÓK CUKRÁSZDA

THIS FRIENDLY SWEET SHOP OPENED IN 2006 IN THE FORMER SPACE OF A GREENGROCER, AND HAS significantly brightened up this end of Batthyány utca. Kids tumble in from the school across the street for ice cream when the weather is warm, or cakes when it's cold. They take special orders for decorative, sugary cakes. But the simplest things here are the best, like the not-too-sweet cookies. The *pogácsa* is also excellent (especially the version with cracklings). The fact that it's open late (for Hungary) on Saturday and Sunday is an added bonus.

I. BATTHYÁNY UTCA 15 ✦ TEL: 201-1652 ✦ WWW.PILLOK.HU
CASH ONLY ✦ OPEN MONDAY *through* FRIDAY 7AM *to* 6PM
SATURDAY *and* SUNDAY 10AM *to* 6PM ✦ M2, BUS 60, 86
TRAM 19 (*to Batthyány tér*)

ROYAL KÁVÉHÁZ & SZAMOS MARCIPÁN CUKRÁSZDA

FIRST OPENED AS A HOTEL IN 1896, THE CORINTHIA GRAND HOTEL ROYAL SUFFERED TERRIBLY FROM DECADES of neglect and misuse until it underwent an extensive, expensive renovation and reopened at the end of 2002. Although it's located on one of Budapest's most heavily trafficked roads, once you ascend the grand staircase to the lobby, it's easy to forget about the outside world. With inner courtyards and glass and wrought-iron ceilings, there is natural light everywhere in this hotel that feels like it goes on forever, and it's worth poking around the lobby even if you're not staying here. Luckily, non-guests can also appreciate the luxury by nibbling on cake and sipping cappuccino at Szamos Marcipán's toniest coffeehouse. Enter from the street (or from the hotel), and check out the pastry case before taking a seat at one of the white marble tables. There's a separate room with big comfy couches reserved for smokers, and there's occasional live gypsy music. As usual, the Szamos cakes and chocolates available here are first rate.

VII. ERZSÉBET KÖRÚT 43-49 (*Corinthia Grand Royal Hotel*)
TEL: 479-4000 ✦ WWW.SZAMOS.HU,
WWW.CORINTHIAHOTELS.COM ✦ CC
OPEN DAILY 9AM *to* 8PM ✦ TRAM 4, 6 (*to Király utca*)

SZALAI CUKRÁSZDA

TIME HAS PRACTICALLY STOOD STILL AT THIS LITTLE FAMILY-RUN BAKE SHOP A FEW BLOCKS FROM THE Parliament, at least that's the feeling you get from the décor and the old-fashioned red scale sitting on the counter. The walls could have used a new coat of paint long ago, the grey tile floor looks a bit dull, and the Formica tables and red chairs look dated. Meanwhile the gilt mirror looks a little out of place next to the cheap wood paneling. But this is what makes this *cukrászda* so charming. The walls are dotted with awards and certificates from generations of the Szalai family, who run the place (and who used to own the Európa Kávéház), which is one of Budapest's favorite little *cukrászdas*, turning out classics like *francia krémes* and *rétes*.

V. BALASSI BÁLINT UTCA 7 ✦ TEL: 269-3210 ✦ CASH ONLY
OPEN WEDNESDAY *through* SUNDAY 9AM *to* 7PM (*winter*), TUESDAY
through SUNDAY 9AM *to* 7PM (*summer*) ✦ M2 (*to Kossuth Lajos tér*)
TRAM 2 (*to Szalay utca*)

SZAMOS MARCIPÁN

HUNGARY'S MOST RENOWNED CONFECTIONER AND CHOCOLATIER HAS RETAIL OUTLETS AND CAFÉS throughout the city, but is essentially still a family business. Mátyás Szamos, the company's founder, grew up in Szentendre and learned how to make marzipan roses when he was an apprentice confectioner in the 1930s. He built up his chocolate and marzipan empire from there with the help of his family. Mátyás died in 2002, but his children and grandchildren still run the company, which is based in Pilisvörösvár (ten miles from Budapest). One of the secrets to the company's success, it claims, is that their chocolate products are exclusively made from cocoa butter. The Párizsi utca shop is the flagship, and other Szamos shops (with smaller selections) are scattered in malls around the city. All carry chocolate-covered marzipan, truffles, and bonbons (be sure to sample the white chocolate shells filled with dark caramel or the rum-flavored truffles). Tasty cakes and coffee can also be had and whole cakes can be specially ordered and custom-decorated. You'll also find flowers, animals, fruit, and cartoon characters fashioned out of marzipan. Entire cakes can be ordered draped in marzipan designs of your choice. Budai Cukrászda, Szépkilátás Cukrászda, Ruszwurm, and the Royal Kávéház & Szamos Marcipán Cukrászda are affiliated with Szamos.

V. PÁRIZSI UTCA 3 ✦ TEL: 317-3643

WWW.SZAMOS.HU ✦ CC ✦ OPEN DAILY 10AM *to* 7PM ✦ M1 (*to Vörösmarty tér*), M3, BUS 5, 7, 15, 7 (*to Ferenciek tere*)

SZÉPKILÁTÁS CUKRÁSZDA

ALTHOUGH IT'S A BIT OF A TREK FROM THE CITY CENTER, THIS HAS BECOME ONE OF MY FAVORITE PLACES TO GO on a weekend afternoon after a hike in the Buda hills. And I'm not the only one—it attracts an unusually high number of expats, and is especially popular with families. The pastries, cakes, and chocolates at the Szépkilátás (which translates as "beautiful view") are well worth the ride up the hill on the cogwheel train, and are among the best in town (and the view from the train windows is beautiful). The *cukrászda* (affiliated with Szamos Marcipán) is in an old house that has retained its homey atmosphere, with colorful walls and a few small dining rooms. I'm preferential to the chocolate cakes, like the truffle *torta* and the *Rigó Jancsi*, but the *francia krémes* is also fantastic, as is everything else here.

XII. SZÉPKILÁTÁS UTCA 1 ✦ TEL: 391-7740 ✦ WWW.SZAMOS.HU

CC ✦ OPEN DAILY 9AM *to* 7PM

COGWHEEL TRAIN, BUS 21, 90 (*to Svábhegy*)

TÖRÖK SÜTEMÉNYEK

THIS LITTLE TURKISH PASTRY AND SANDWICH SHOP IS DELIGHTFUL, WHETHER YOU HAVE A SWEET TOOTH OR crave something more substantial. Many of the cookies, candies, and sweets come straight from Turkey, and the small moist cookies filled with date purée are especially tasty. The several varieties of baklava (including a Hungarian-accented *túró* baklava) are house-made. While burek is found in many countries that were formerly part of the Ottoman Empire, this shop is one of the few places in Budapest where you'll find flakey burek, which is also house-made. Sandwiches, like falafel, eggplant, and olive salad are made with pita bread. You'll also find Turkish yogurt and other treats like sesame-seed-coated pretzels, Turkish delight, and halva (a Middle Eastern confection made from ground sesame seeds and honey).

VIII. BRÓDY SÁNDOR UTCA 27 ✦ TEL: 266-6697 ✦ CASH ONLY
OPEN MONDAY *through* FRIDAY 6:30AM *to* 7PM, SATURDAY
9AM *to* 5PM ✦ TRAM 4, 6 (*to Rákóczi tér*)

ICE CREAM

GOOD ICE CREAM CAN ALSO BE FOUND AT DAUBNER CUKRÁSZDA, AUGUSZT CUKRÁSZDA, AND AT THE STALL SET UP IN FRONT OF GERBEAUD WHEN THE WEATHER IS WARM (see pages 213, 214, and 199).

BUTTERFLY FAGYLALTOZÓ

THERE'S CERTAINLY NO SHORTAGE OF GOOD SWEETS IN HUNGARY, BUT IT'S HARD TO FIND GOOD ICE CREAM. Even many dedicated ice cream shops sell mass-produced ice cream rather than making their own. No bigger than a closet, this one of Budapest's best and most popular ice cream shops.

VI. TERÉZ KÖRÚT 22 ✦ CASH ONLY ✦ OPEN MONDAY *through*
FRIDAY 10AM *to* 7PM, SATURDAY 10AM *to* 2PM
(*Closed mid-December-February*) ✦ M1, TRAM 4, 6 (*to Oktogon*)

GELATO-OLASZ FAGYIZÓ

JUST DOWN THE STREET FROM CENTRÁL KÁVÉHÁZ, THIS PLACE IS NO MORE THAN A COUNTER STOCKED with tubs of the city's best creamy ice cream. Pay first, and then choose your flavors at this long-time favorite gelato stand. If you can resist all the others, try one of the distinctively Hungarian flavors like poppy seed (*mák*), cinnamon (*fahéj*), curd cheese (*túró*), or rice (*rízs*).

V. IRÁNYI UTCA 21/23 ✦ CASH ONLY ✦ OPEN DAILY 11AM-11PM
(*closed November-April*) ✦ M3 (*to Ferenciek tere*)

V. VÁCI UTCA 69 ✦ CASH ONLY ✦ OPEN DAILY NON-STOP
(*closed November-April*) ✦ TRAM 2, 2A, 49 (*to Fovám tér*)

GELATTI

THE COLORFUL TUBS OF CREAMY ICE CREAM TEMPT PASSERS-BY TO COME IN FOR A FEW SCOOPS. JUST off of Váci utca, this shop sells very good house-made ice cream in dozens of flavors.

V. KÍGYÓ UTCA 8 ✦ TEL: 06-70/387-5829 ✦ CASH ONLY
OPEN DAILY 11AM *to* 10PM ✦ M3, BUS 7, 173 (*to Ferenciek tere*)

ESZPRESSZÓS

BAMBI ESZPRESSZÓ

ALTHOUGH I CAN'T SAY FOR SURE BECAUSE I WASN'T THERE, THE BAMBI LOOKS AS IF IT HASN'T CHANGED a bit since the 1960s. The large patio on pleasant Frankel Leó út is enough reason alone to come here, but you're missing out on the whole *eszpresszó* experience by not peeking inside. The tiny tables are covered with frilly lace-like tablecloths, faux red-leather benches line the walls, and the miniature stools are matching red. Don't come here if you have a problem with secondhand smoke—the ashtrays on every table prove that smoking is very welcome here. The place attracts a mixed bag of people:

pensioners eating plates of *virsli* and mustard for dinner, yuppies in pinstriped suits drinking beer or spritzers, and students who like the cheap alcohol. At closing time the manager walks around sweetly ringing a little bell and asking everybody to finish up their drinks. If you visit any *eszpresszó*, make it the retro Bambi, which is one of the most popular.

II. FRANKEL LEÓ ÚT 2-4 ✦ TEL: 212-3171 ✦ CASH ONLY
OPEN MONDAY *through* FRIDAY 7AM *to* 10PM, SATURDAY *and*
SUNDAY 9AM *to* 9PM ✦ TRAM 4, 6 (*to Margit híd, Budai hídfö*)

TERV ESZPRESSZÓ

TERV ESZPRESSZÓ IS NAMED FOR THE FIVE-YEAR PLANS THAT USED TO BE DECLARED DURING THE COMMUNIST era. The era of the *terv* is also the major decorating theme here: the walls are plastered with old ads, black-and-white photos, and newspaper clippings. Old bottles, tins, pots, and pans from the Communist period hang from the walls. The crowd here is half cosmopolitan hipster and half hard-core old-timers staring into their beer mugs until closing time. Smoking seems to be encouraged, and the beer selection includes almost two dozen bottled beers.

V. NÁDOR UTCA 19 ✦ TEL: 269-3132 ✦ CASH ONLY ✦ OPEN
MONDAY *through* SATURDAY 9AM *to* MIDNIGHT, SUNDAY
10AM *to* 11PM ✦ M3 (*to Arany János utca*)

CAFÉS WITH FOOD

ANGELIKA KÁVÉHÁZ

VISIT THE GORGEOUS PALE YELLOW SZENT ANNA TEMPLOM (CHURCH OF ST. ANNE)—WHICH IS ONE OF Budapest's prettiest churches—and then stop at the Angelika for coffee. The Angelika actually shares a building with the church. It occupies a ground-floor wing, and has a spacious multi-level patio, with direct views of the Parliament and the Danube, as well as pleasant Batthyány tér. Inside it's dark, and the air is slightly stale from the leftover cigarette smoke, making it not feel very conducive to eating. There are comfy, rather surreal-looking couches, and several different rooms. While the patio is generally bustling, it's not unusual to find yourself with a room to yourself inside. The place could use a new coat of paint (and could stand to lose the heavy fabric draped over the light fixtures), but it's a fine place to unwind with a drink, especially since the neighborhood doesn't have many cafés.

I. BATTHYÁNY TÉR 7 ✦ TEL: 201-0668

WWW.ANGELIKAKAVEHAZ.HU ✦ CASH ONLY ✦ MAINS ◇◇-◇◇◇

OPEN DAILY 9AM *to* MIDNIGHT ✦ M2, TRAM 19, HÉV, BUS 11,

39, 60, 86 (*to Batthyány tér*)

ASTORIA CAFÉ MIRROR

THE ASTORIA HOTEL AND ITS COFFEEHOUSE IS A SAD EXAMPLE OF WHAT HAPPENS WHEN A GRAND AND once luxurious hotel grows old and doesn't age well. The Astoria was once one of the city's finest classic hotels, but is now a tired, dusty remnant of its former self. Built in 1914 in French Empire style, the interior is full of turn-of-the-century atmosphere. Even though much of the place has undergone some serious refurbishments between 2004 and 2006, the coffeehouse still lacks spirit, despite its high prices. The café does have a few important things going for it: a great location, lots of history, and despite its lack of style (a dessert case in the middle of the room, disinterested servers, and a gallery that seems to be used for storage), it has what could be a great space with big crystal chandeliers, marble columns, and gold molding. While you could say that the hotel evokes Old Budapest, I'd like to think that Old

Budapest had more life to it. That said, it still has more character than most hotel cafés in this price range.

V. KOSSUTH LAJOS UTCA 19-21 (*Hotel Astoria*) ✦ TEL: 889-6000
WWW.DANUBIUSHOTELS.COM/ASTORIA ✦ CC ✦ MAINS ◇-◇◇
OPEN DAILY 7AM *to* 11PM ✦ M2 (*to Astoria*)

BALETTCIPO

THIS IS THE KIND OF PLACE I COULD EASILY IMAGINE MAKING MY DAILY LUNCH HANGOUT IF I WORKED IN THE area, or my weekly Sunday afternoon cappuccino destination if I lived nearby. In fact, Balettcipo is nice just about any time of the day, especially when the sun is shining and the tables are set up outside on the semi-pedestrianized street. There are light dishes like dips, salads, sandwiches, and pâté, for when this is just a stop before dinner somewhere else. Or there are heavier options like burgers, steak sandwiches, or filet mignon topped with caramelized onions and red wine chili sauce. There's little that's Hungarian about the menu, but it somehow doesn't give off that fusion-snobby international vibe that infects so many Budapest cafés. Inside is just as welcoming as out, with loft seating behind wrought-iron bars, and polished but comfy dark-wood fittings and tables. Balettcipo—which means "ballet shoe" in Hungarian (there's a pair hanging in the door as a reminder)—is named for the café's predecessor, which was opened in the same spot by a former ballerina in 1948. Located behind the Opera, Balettcipo is a great reason to stray from pricey Andrássy út. My only complaint is that the wine list is a bit weak.

VI. HAJÓS UTCA 14 ✦ TEL: 269-3114 ✦ WWW.BALETTCIPO.HU
✦ CASH ONLY ✦ MAINS ◇-◇◇◇◇◇ ✦ OPEN MONDAY *through*
FRIDAY 10AM *to* MIDNIGHT, SATURDAY *and* SUNDAY NOON *to*
MIDNIGHT ✦ M1 (*to Opera*)

CAFÉ ALIBI

POPULAR WITH STUDENTS FROM THE NEARBY UNIVERSITIES AND OTHER INTELLECTUAL-LOOKING TYPES, Café Alibi is the kind of place that makes you want to pull out a pad of paper and start writing, or get a caffeine buzz while reading that book you've been meaning to start. I like Café Alibi any time of the day: for a filling breakfast, an afternoon coffee, a

mid-afternoon glass of wine, or a light dinner. And I'm not alone. The names of regular customers are engraved into brass plaques attached to the backs of bar stools. The place is cozy with splotchy mustard walls, dark café tables, and a big antique cash register on the bar. Service is casual and friendly, and the food is decent, but not outstanding. They do a better job with the big salads, especially the salad Niçoise, than with the more substantial entrées. There are weekly specials and, like any good café should, it offers light snacks. Desserts are more home-style than the fancy layered cakes served in the traditional coffee houses. The compact wine list, like the café itself, is straightforward: three whites, one rosé,

three reds, and one dessert wine. Café Alibi is also the site of
occasional Monarchia wine dinners, which usually feature five
courses matched with different wines.

V. EGYETEM TÉR 4 ✦ TEL: 317-4209 ✦ WWW.CAFEALIBI.HU
CC ✦ MAINS ◇-◇◇ ✦ OPEN MONDAY *through* SATURDAY 8AM *to*
11PM, SUNDAY 9AM *to* 5PM ✦ M3, TRAM 49 (*to Kálvin tér*)

CAFÉ ECKERMANN

THE GOETHE-INSTITUT, ALONG WITH ITS CAFÉ, MOVED TO RÁDAY UTCA IN EARLY 2006. WHILE I'M NOT A FAN of the new building, the café is still charming. It's a magnet for German speakers and German expats, who leaf through the German newspapers while sipping their coffee and chewing their croissants. The small menu changes daily and offers things like sandwiches, hummus, pastas, and cakes. There's an enclosed patio in the back courtyard which is a pleasant escape from busy Ráday utca when the weather is warm. The Institute itself offers a full program of films, concerts, theater, and lectures for the German-minded. While the café still needs a little breaking in to feel as cozy as the old one, it'll get there.

IX. RÁDAY UTCA 58 ✦ TEL: 786-0795
WWW.GOETHE.DE/BUDAPEST ✦ CASH ONLY ✦ MAINS ◇
OPEN MONDAY *through* FRIDAY 8AM *to* 11PM
SATURDAY 10AM *to* 11PM, SUNDAY 10AM *to* 10PM
TRAM 2, 2A, 4, 6, BUS 15 (*to Boráros tér*)

CAFÉ FACTORY

BORED WITH CAPPUCCINO? ORDER A VIENNESE CAFÉ CRÈME, AN ITALIAN MACCHIATO, OR JUST STICK TO A Hungarian *dupla*. Café Factory takes its coffee so seriously that it offers at least six different brands of coffee beans—Segafredo, Danesi, Dall-mayr, Vergnano, Meinl, and Manuel—and the barista prepares more than two dozen coffee specialties. Several coffee grinders sit behind the long cherry-wood bar, and stacks of creamers, saucers, and cups sit on the bar next to the two huge espresso machines. There's a small menu with a few salads, and more substantial dishes like a beef sirloin with bacon and duck

liver. But coffee is really the thing here, and the low-key atmosphere is conducive to lingering. Floor-to-ceiling windows flood the smoky room with light, small round wooden tables cover the hardwood floor, and an odd-shaped gallery provides upstairs seating. Music blares from the stereo, and the espresso machine never stops hissing.

VI. JÓKAI UTCA 28 ✦ TEL: 269-4923 ✦ WWW.CAFEFACTORY.HU
CASH ONLY ✦ MAINS ✧-✧✧ ✦ OPEN DAILY 10AM *to* 11PM
M3, TRAM 4, 6 (*to Nyugati pályaudvar*)

CAFÉ FARGER

JUST ACROSS FROM ROOSEVELT TÉR, THIS MODERN CAFÉ SERVES EXPERTLY PREPARED COFFEE, AS WELL as salads and sandwiches. With its floor-to-ceiling windows, hardwood floors, and palm trees, the place is airy. The wireless Internet access and plush couches and armchairs make it particularly inviting. The contemporary paintings on the walls are for sale, and a stack of magazines by the door provides ample reading material.

V. ZOLTÁN UTCA 18 ✦ TEL: 373-0078 ✦ WWW.FARGERKAVE.COM
CC ✦ MAINS ✧ ✦ OPEN MONDAY *through* FRIDAY 7AM *to* 8PM,
SATURDAY *and* SUNDAY 9AM *to* 4PM ✦ M2 (*to Kossuth Lajos tér*)

CAFÉ FIVE

DESPITE BEING ON A LOUD AND BUSY STREET IN AN OFFICE-LIKE SPACE WITH LOW CEILINGS, IF YOU HAPPEN to be in Újpest, Cafe Five is a pleasant place for a coffee or a sandwich. It's a stylish little café (if you ignore the paintings), with leather chairs and dark wood tables. For breakfast there are eggs, and the decent sandwiches come on ciabatta or baguettes. The place is popular with neighborhood office workers, who come for the huge tea selection and more than a dozen types of hot chocolate. They also have coffee to go.

IV. ÁRPÁD ÚT 53 ✦ TEL: 272-0360 ✦ WWW.CAFEFIVE.HU
CASH ONLY ✦ MAINS ✧ ✦ OPEN MONDAY *through* THURSDAY
8AM *to* 10PM, FRIDAY 8AM *to* MIDNIGHT, SATURDAY 11AM *to*
MIDNIGHT, SUNDAY 11AM *to* 10PM ✦ M3 (*to Újpest-Központ*)

CAFÉ VIAN

I T'S HARD TO BELIEVE THIS PLACE WAS ONCE A LAUN-
DERETTE. CAFÉ VIAN IS A BRIGHT, SPACIOUS CAFÉ, WITH
splashy modern art on the walls, and a constant trickle of
people coming and going. It's stylish, but not overbearingly so,
like other Liszt Ferenc tér eating and drinking spots. Unlike many
of the square's addresses, which seem to be occupied by some new
high-concept place every season, Vian is dependable, especially
when the weather is warm and the sidewalk tables are out. Most
come for coffee or drinks, but Vian has a full menu that's reasonably priced considering its prime location. But don't expect any
life-changing culinary moments to occur here. Like any good
café, there's something for any time of the day: omelets for
breakfast, salads and sandwiches for lunch, a cheese plate for a
late afternoon snack, and goose liver cooked in Tokaji *aszú* for a
deliciously rich dinner. The tall windows, comfy armchairs and
couches, low lighting, and not-too-loud music makes the place a
good spot for a chat or a light bite, even better if you can sit outside. The wine list offers just a few choices, cocktails seem to be
the drink of choice. The manager wanders around making sure
everyone is taken care of, and all of the waitresses, it seems,
are pretty blondes.

VI. LISZT FERENC TÉR 9 ✦ TEL: 268-1154 ✦ WWW.CAFEVIAN.COM
CC ✦ MAINS ◇-◇◇ ✦ OPEN DAILY 9AM *to* 1AM
M1, TRAM 4, 6 (*Oktogon*)

CALLAS CAFÉ

L OCATED NEXT TO THE OPERA, CALLAS HAS A PRIME
ADDRESS ON ANDRÁSSY ÚT THAT MAKES IT AN IDEAL
PLACE to pop in for a drink or a snack if you happen to be in
the neighborhood. The art deco interior has cavernous vaulted
ceilings, lots of tall windows, and fancy ceiling and wall adorn-
ments. It's not one of Budapest's old-time coffeehouses, although
from its interior you might think it is. The place serves yogurt,
eggs, ham, and pastries for breakfast. There's a dessert selection
available throughout the day. And there is a sushi bar and an
extensive menu that offers everything from Caesar salad and

lasagna to chicken *paprikás* and Australian kingfish. I'll keep coming to Callas for coffee, pastry, or a glass of wine from the decent wine list. But rather than tempt, the all-over-the-place menu scares me off. When the weather is warm, tables are set up facing Andrássy út and the Opera.

VI. ANDRÁSSY ÚT 20 ✦ TEL: 354-0954 ✦ WWW.CALLASCAFE.HU
CC ✦ MAINS ◇◇◇-◇◇◇◇ ✦ OPEN MONDAY *through* FRIDAY 8AM *to* 2AM, SATURDAY *and* SUNDAY NOON *to* 2AM ✦ M1 (*to Opera*)

GODOT KÁVÉHÁZ

THE GODOT WAS HUNGARY'S FIRST STAND-UP COMEDY CLUB, BUT NON-HUNGARIAN SPEAKERS, UNFORTUNATELY, won't be able to experience that aspect of the place. But they can stop in for a coffee, or something stronger from the fully stocked bar. There's an art gallery attached (*open Monday through Friday, 10am to 6pm*) which showcases Hungarian contemporary art. And with its stripy painted bar, dim lights, and artistic bent, it's not surprising that the clientele here is more artsy than the average crowd of café-goers. The small menu offers salads, sandwiches, standard appetizers like hummus and tzatziki, and main courses like lasagna and steaks. Stand-up comedy events are held Thursday through Saturday, so the café doors close at 5pm (unless you happen to be staying for the show).

VII. MADÁCH IMRE TÉR 8 ✦ TEL: 322-5274 ✦ WWW.GODOT.HU
CC ✦ MAINS ◇-◇◇◇◇◇ ✦ OPEN MONDAY *through* FRIDAY 9AM *to* MIDNIGHT, SATURDAY 5PM *to* MIDNIGHT
M1, M2, M3, TRAM 49 (*to Deák tér*)

KÜLVÁROSI KÁVÉHÁZ

STEPPING INTO THIS CAFÉ IN THE OLD SECTION OF ÚJPEST FEELS LIKE STEPPING BACK IN TIME. THERE are dainty velvety chairs and couches and antique light fittings. The working fireplace with a marble hearth makes it perfect for a cold winter day. An intricate wood and stained-glass wall separates the café in the front room from the fancier restaurant in the back room, and there are a few tables in the garden in the warm months. The walls are lined with pen-and-ink drawings of famous Hungarian movie stars, and the piano is the centerpiece of the room. The name means "suburban café," but it feels more like a place that has been forgotten by time. In fact, it isn't even particularly old. Külvárosi only opened in 1993, but manages to conjure up images of Gyula Krúdy sitting in turn-of-the-twentieth-century cafés. The restaurant offers a perfectly tempting Hungarian menu, which is heavy on the duck and goose. With starters like goose broth with matzo dumplings or goose cracklings with onions, and main courses like a mixed goose platter or roast wild boar, it's easy to imagine spending extended amounts of time here.

IV. ISTVÁN UTCA 26 ✦ TEL: 379-1568 ✦ CC ✦ MAINS ◇◇-◇◇◇
OPEN DAILY 9AM *to* 11PM ✦ M3 (*to Újpest-Központ*)

LE CAFÉ ALEXANDRE DUMAS

S IT OUT ON THE PATIO WITH AN ESPRESSO OR A CROQUE MONSIEUR, AND YOU COULD ALMOST IMAGINE THAT you were in Paris. That is, until you take in the fantastic Danube and Chain Bridge view, which is one of the best from any of the city's cafés (once you look past the busy quay, directly in front). Inside, two computers with Internet access are free for customers to use. Floor-to-ceiling windows flood the place with light, and a steel staircase in the center of the café leads to the upstairs exhibition space. The small menu offers French dishes like salads, a quiche and tart of the day, cheese and charcuterie plates, and crème caramel. Even the clientele here—which always includes a few French speakers and singles nursing coffee and reading books—has that Parisian feel.

I. FO UTCA 17 (*French Institute*) ✦ TEL: 225-8417
WWW.INST-FRANCE.HU ✦ CASH ONLY ✦ MAINS ◇-◇◇
OPEN MONDAY *through* FRIDAY 8:30AM *to* 9PM, SATURDAY 10AM *to* 2PM ✦ M2 (*to Batthyány tér*), TRAM 19 (*to Halász utca*)

MANDRAGÓRA KÁVÉHÁZ

W HILE MANDRAGÓRA DOES HAVE A FULL MENU, IT'S BETTER TO SKIP THE FOOD. COME HERE FOR the great selection of reasonably priced Hungarian wines, preferably after soaking in the nearby Király bathhouse. The place, which is in a cellar in a neighborhood with few other cafés, looks almost thrown together, with brightly painted walls to lighten things up. Looking at it from the outside, where there are tables on a patio when the weather is warm, it's hard to make out what this place is about. It certainly doesn't look as if it would serve more than forty wines, and pour about half of them by the glass. The best seats in the house are the big leather chairs and sofas in the smoking room.

II. KACSA UTCA 22 ✦ TEL: 202-2165

WWW.MANDRAGORAKAVEHAZ.HU ✦ CC ✦ MAINS ◇◇-◇◇◇

OPEN MONDAY *through* SATURDAY 10AM *to* MIDNIGHT

M2 (*to Batthyány tér*), TRAM 4, 6 (*to Mechwart liget*)

BUS 60, 86 (*to Bem József tér*)

NELSON CAFÉ

THERE'S A CLUSTER OF SMALL CAFÉS ACROSS THE STREET FROM THE DOHÁNY UTCA SYNAGOGUE. BUT I prefer the Nelson Café a little further down the street, where a cafe latte comes in a mug the size of a soup bowl and the servers are friendly. There are a few comfy couches in the front, big windows that roll away when it heats up, and lively music blasting from the stereo. The food is decent, if simple, and it attracts neighborhood office workers (who also keep the delivery guy busy). The two-course lunch menu is a bargain, and simple breakfast dishes are also served.

VII. DOHÁNY UTCA 12 ✦ TEL: 411-1804

WWW.NELSONCAFE.HU ✦ CC ✦ MAINS ◇ ✦ OPEN MONDAY

through FRIDAY 7AM-MIDNIGHT, SATURDAY *and* SUNDAY 8AM *to*

MIDNIGHT ✦ M2, TRAM 49 (*to Astoria*)

PETIT CAFÉ VIAN

PLEASANT "SMALL" CAFÉ VIAN IS LOCATED JUST EAST OF SZABADSÁG TÉR. IT DOESN'T PAY AS MUCH ATTENTION to style as its bigger sister on Liszt Ferenc tér does. It's a friendly place, with a cluttered bar and Mediterranean-orange walls plastered with postcards. Two comfy couches are fine places to flip through the magazines and newspapers on hand. The menu here, too, is lighter than Café Vian's, with simple sandwiches (on croissants, baguettes, or panini), salads, and desserts (including a few gluten-free and sugar-free cakes). Be aware that when one person lights up, the whole place fills with smoke.

V. HERCEGPRÍMÁS UTCA 21 ✦ TEL: 269-2451
WWW.CAFEVIAN.COM ✦ CASH ONLY ✦ MAINS ◇
OPEN MONDAY *through* FRIDAY 7:30AM *to* 7PM
M3 (*to Arany János utca*)

SPINOZA HÁZ

NAMED FOR THE SEVENTEENTH-CENTURY DUTCH PHI-LOSOPHER BARUCH SPINOZA, THE SPINOZA HOUSE opened in 2003 with the aim of bringing Dutch culture to Budapest and promoting Hungarian culture in the Netherlands. The classy, artsy place is in the heart of the reawakening old Jewish quarter and houses a café/restaurant with a performance space in the rear. Temporary art or photo exhibitions grace the bright red walls, and there's a full program of entertainment—concerts, lectures, comedy, and cabaret—which aren't only Dutch related. It's worth checking the monthly program, and having a coffee in the art-nouveau-style café while you're at it. Sit at the round table in the corner nook which has curtains for privacy, or in the gallery with wrought-iron railings. The kitchen is a bit uneven. I've had some great dishes here, most memorably the cheese soup (made with trappista, edam, and smoked cheese). But there have also been disappointments, like overcooked liver wrapped in bacon. The Dutch influence carries over to the kitchen, with cheese showing up as a frequent ingredient. If you need inspiration (or your tired feet need a break from the city streets), there are free concerts on Wednesdays at 1pm.

VII. DOB UTCA 15 ✦ TEL: 413-7489 ✦ WWW.SPINOZAHAZ.HU
CC ✦ MAINS ◇◇-◇◇◇ ✦ OPEN DAILY 11AM *to* 10:30PM ✦ M1, M2,
M3 (*to Deák tér*), M2, TRAM 49, BUS 7 (*to Astoria*)

SMALL AND COZY

BALZAC CAFÉ

GOOD COFFEE AND GOOD HOT CHOCOLATE, BUT HARDLY ANY ROOM TO SIT AND ENJOY IT AT THIS TINY NEIGHBOR-hood coffee shop. There are just two small tables, but you could always get it to go (along with a croissant or a bar of Belgian chocolate).

XIII. BALZAC UTCA 44/B ✦ TEL: 350-2621
WWW.BALZACAFE.HU ✦ CASH ONLY ✦ OPEN MONDAY *through*
FRIDAY 8AM *to* 6PM, SATURDAY 9AM *to* 2PM ✦ BUS 15 (*to Radnóti Miklós utca*), BUS 133 (*to Csanády utca*), TROLLEY 76 (*to Hegedus Gyula or Csanády utca*), TROLLEY 79 (*to Radnóti Miklós utca*)

CAFÉ 22

WITH SO MANY CAFÉS TO CHOOSE FROM, THERE'S REALLY NO NEED TO DRINK COFFEE FROM A STYROFOAM cup. But I make an exception for Café 22's fair-trade coffee (from Robert's Coffee, a Finnish company). With just three small tables and a few bar stools that are usually occupied by neighborhood office workers, coffee to go is sometimes a must here, and it's worth it for one of Café 22's smooth, creamy lattes. This tiny cheerful café serves a few snacks like cake and thick, American-style cookies.

VII. SÍP UTCA 22 ✦ TEL: 06-30/942-2605 ✦ CASH ONLY
OPEN MONDAY *through* FRIDAY 8:30AM *to* 6PM
M2, TRAM 4, 6 (*to Astoria*)

CAFÉ ALKOHOLOS FILC

THIS TINY CAFÉ, ACTUALLY MORE OF A BAR, IS LIKE AN EXTENSION OF KÁROLY SZALÓKY'S EMPIRE OF CONTEM-porary art galleries on Várfok utca. When he began opening art galleries here in 1990, Szalóky turned this street under the castle into the place to go to check out Hungarian contemporary

art. The Alkoholos Filc (which translates as "felt-tip pen") is like an art gallery itself with walls covered with colorful canvases by artists such as Imre Bukta, János Szirtes, Péter Ujházi, and István Nádler. The place is so small that there's only room for a few tables inside, but a makeshift terrace opens when the weather is warm. The cocktails are interesting, and there's a good selection of wine by the glass, but the food selection is slim. Visit the Várfok Gallery (Várfok utca 14) and the Portál Gallery (Várfok utca 8) while you're in the area, or for more inspiration check out the list of neighborhood art galleries posted on the door.

I. VÁRFOK UTCA 15/B ✦ WWW.VARFOK-GALERIA.HU
CASH ONLY ✦ OPEN MONDAY *through* SATURDAY 9AM *to* 10PM
M2, TRAM 4, 6, 18, 56, 59, 61, 118, BUS 5, 21, 22, 28, 39, 49, 56, 90, 128, 156 (*to Moszkva tér*)

CAFÉ CRÉME CORNER

CAFÉ CRÉME CORNER GETS ITS NAME FROM ITS CORNER LOCATION, WHERE BATTHYÁNY UTCA AND HATTYÚ UTCA meet in a V-shaped intersection. The place is a semi-circle, with rounded walls and big curvy windows. Tastefully decorated (apart from the Pepsi placemats), with glass-topped tables, gilt mirrors, and cheery yellow walls, this cute storefront café is a welcome addition to a neighborhood with few cafés. With just six small tables, there's barely room for the waitress to squeeze by with the cappuccino. But tables are added to the patio outside when weather permits. A limited menu—just a few salads and sandwiches—make coffee the choice menu item, although a bar stocks hard liquor.

I. HATTYÚ UTCA 2 ✦ CASH ONLY ✦ OPEN MONDAY *through* FRIDAY 8AM-11PM, SATURDAY *and* SUNDAY 10AM *to* 11PM M2, BUS 60, 86, TRAM 19, 41 (*to Batthyány tér*), M2, BUS 5, 21, 22, 28, 39, 49, 56, 90, 128, 156, TRAM 4, 6 18, 56, 59, 61, 118 (*to Moszkva tér*)

FÉL NYOLC

THIS CUTE LITTLE CAFÉ IS A PERFECT ESCAPE FROM THE MORE TRENDY PLACES IN THE NEIGHBORHOOD. The walls are lined with black-and-white photos of celebrities such as Dustin Hoffman and Alfred Hitchcock. It's a warm place with red walls, red wood, and tables stuffed into every small nook and cranny downstairs and in the gallery. The coffee is good, and the croissants are decent.

V. MADÁCH IMRE TÉR 5 ✦ CASH ONLY ✦ OPEN MONDAY *through* FRIDAY 7:30AM *to* 7:30PM, SATURDAY 8AM *to* 2PM ✦ M1, M2, M3, TRAM 49 (*to Deák tér*)

GRISSINI KÁVÉZÓ

THERE'S A LOT CRAMMED INTO THIS ODD COMBINA-TION OF A CAFÉ AND AN ITALIAN FOOD SHOP. THE tiny room is lined with shelves stocked with pastas, bread-sticks, sauces, biscotti, olive oil, and other Italian products. The coffee here is excellent but there are just a few tiny tables. A small menu offers snacks like salads, bruschetta, and crostini, and a refrigerator holds a few unappetizing looking pre-made sandwiches. In true Italian fashion, neighbors stop by to gulp down their coffee standing at the tiny bar.

XIII. HEGEDUS GYULA UTCA 23 ✦ TEL: 320-4720
WWW.GRISSINI.HU ✦ CASH ONLY ✦ OPEN MONDAY *through*
FRIDAY 8AM *to* 10PM, SATURDAY 10AM *to* 10PM ✦ M3, TRAM 4, 6
(*to Nyugati pályaudvar*), TROLLEY 76, 79 (*to Radnóti Miklós utca*)

JAVA CAFFÉ

THOUGH ONE OF THE HIGHLIGHTS HERE IS THAT THERE'S GOOD COFFEE TO GO, IT'S A NICE ENOUGH PLACE TO take your coffee sitting down. Just down the street from Szabadság tér, the few tables downstairs are often full. In the smoky upper level there are couches and a counter overlooking the monument to Lajos Batthyány. Despite the good coffee and the cheerfulness, you're not missing much by passing on the sweets. If the pre-made sandwiches aren't appealing, there are also warm panini-like sandwiches.

V. AULICH UTCA 7 ✦ TEL: 311-2251 ✦ CASH ONLY
OPEN MONDAY *through* FRIDAY 7AM *to* 7PM, SATURDAY
9AM *to* 2PM ✦ M2 (*to Kossuth tér*)

KÁVÉSZÜNET

TUCKED AWAY ON A QUIET STREET JUST A FEW BLOCKS AWAY FROM THE PARLIAMENT, "COFFEE BREAK" IS dark and smoky, even during daylight hours. If it were better lit, the DIY décor (like the upholstery nailed to the walls) would be more noticeable. This way, it feels like a quiet secret—a place to escape between meetings for a solo cup of coffee with a book or for a private beer with a friend. It's central, but manages to be hidden at the same time.

V. GARIBALDI UTCA 5 ✦ TEL: 06-70/635-5544
WWW.KAVESZUNET.UW.HU ✦ CASH ONLY ✦ OPEN MONDAY
through THURSDAY 9:30AM *to* 6PM, FRIDAY 9:30AM *to* MIDNIGHT
M2 (*to Kossuth Lajos tér*)

PALMETTO CAFÉ

THIS FRIENDLY CAFÉ PREPARES EXCELLENT COFFEE, BUT THE SMALL, WINDOWLESS BACK ROOM CAN BE A bit claustrophobic. The owners have turned this space—which formerly was a clothing store—into a comfortable neighborhood haven for coffee drinkers. The pastries like *flódni* and carrot cake are pretty good, there are sugar-free desserts, and coffee to go. The walls behind the counter are covered with blackboards listing the coffee products, and coffee beans from around the world are for sale, roasted either Viennese (light), French (medium), or Italian (very dark) style.

XIII. CSANÁDY UTCA 4/B ✦ TEL: 350-3227
WWW.PALMETTOCAFE.HU ✦ CASH ONLY ✦ OPEN MONDAY
through THURSDAY 10AM-7PM, FRIDAY 10AM *to* 6PM, SATURDAY
10AM *to* 1PM ✦ M3 (*to Lehel tér*), TROLLEY 76, BUS 133 (*to Váci út*)

SIR MORIK KÁVÉZÓ

SIR MORIK IS AN OLD NAME IN THE HISTORY OF HUNGARIAN COFFEE AND THERE ARE SHOPS BEARING HIS name around the country. The Nádor utca location is a fine place to sit down with a cup of coffee. The smaller Ráday utca location isn't as appealing because of all the other choices within steps of it. They both sell coffee beans and have small selections of croissants and cakes.

V. NÁDOR UTCA 5 ✦ CASH ONLY ✦ OPEN MONDAY *through* FRIDAY
7:30AM-7PM, SATURDAY 9AM *to* 5PM
M1, M2, M3, TRAM 49 (*to Deák tér*)

IX. RÁDAY UTCA 15 ✦ TEL: 215-2444 ✦ CASH ONLY
OPEN MONDAY *through* FRIDAY 8AM *to* 7PM, SATURDAY *and*
SUNDAY 9AM *to* 5PM ✦ M3, TRAM 49 (*to Kálvin tér*)

WALZER CAFÉ

THE MOST CASUAL PLACE TO HAVE COFFEE IN THE CASTLE DISTRICT IS AT THIS MINISCULE CAFÉ WHICH HOLDS JUST four stools, and not much else besides the friendly owner. Outside it's more spacious, with tables set up in the old courtyard (and portable heaters and blankets when it's cold). There are a few types of cakes available, and the coffee is great. The Armenian-style caramel cake is excellent.

I. TÁNCSICS UTCA 12 ✦ TEL: 06-30/250-5971 ✦ CASH ONLY
OPEN TUESDAY *through* SUNDAY 10AM *to* 6PM ✦ VÁRBUSZ
(*to Szentháromság tér*)

EVERYDAY CAFÉS

CAFÉ PONYVAREGÉNY

AT CAFÉ "PULP FICTION" PEOPLE SHARE CIGARETTES, NURSE THEIR BEERS AND ESPRESSO, TYPE ON THEIR laptops, and scribble in their notebooks. There are shelves lined with books and stacked with board games like Scrabble and Battleship, and every table is equipped with a pencil and a thick notebook, full of doodles and notes from the people who sat there before. In the front corner there's an old couch, a few armchairs, and a coffee table, and the tables are covered with white folksy tablecloths and long candlesticks, fattened with wax drippings. It feels quite homey, especially with the worn Oriental rug and the floor lamps with frilly shades. There's a long list of coffee and drinks served here, but just a few small dishes. Café Ponyvaregény is a comfortable place where you could easily stay longer than intended, unless the heavy cigarette smoke bothers you.

XI. BERCSÉNYI UTCA 5 ✦ TEL: 209-5255 ✦ PONYVA@TELNET.HU
✦ OPEN MONDAY *through* SATURDAY 10AM *to* MIDNIGHT
SUNDAY 2 *to* 10PM ✦ TRAM 6, 18, 19, 49, 61, 118, BUS 3, 7, 73
(*to Móricz Zsigmond körtér*)

COFFEE-INN

LOCATED ALONG A NARROW STAIRWAY LEADING FROM FO UTCA UP TO THE CASTLE, THIS PLACE FEELS HIDDEN away although it's just a short walk from the Chain Bridge. The place is small—just a bar and a few stools on the lower level, plus a gallery with extra seating, and two rickety tables outside when the weather warms up. I've heard that the coffee is good here, as the name implies, but I always arrive too late for coffee, and take advantage of the short, but excellent wine list. All seventeen wines on the list are sold by the glass and are priced to make you want to keep drinking. Czech Krušovice beer is on tap, and the cheery place has a shelf full of games, puzzles, and cards to keep you entertained. There's nothing like a good game of pick-up sticks with a glass of wine.

I. APOR PÉTER UTCA 2 ✦ TEL: 201-2935 ✦ WWW.COFFEEINN.HU

CASH ONLY ✦ OPEN DAILY 11AM-11PM

BUS 115, 16 (*to Clark Ádám tér*), TRAM 19, 41 (*to Lánchíd*)

FOVÁROSI SZABÓ ERVIN KÖNYVTÁR

HAVE COFFEE IN A LITERARY ENVIRONMENT AT THE CAFÉ AT THE CITY'S CENTRAL LIBRARY. THE NEO-BAROQUE library is one of the city's most beautifully renovated buildings (and there's also a decent selection of English books). The nineteenth-century building is the former Wenckheim Palace, which was home to a count who was a member of Parliament. After the count died, the city bought the building and it became a library in 1931. It was renovated in 2001, and is as good a place as any to sip coffee while taking in the fine architecture. You have to have a library card (which must be paid for) to get in beyond the café, unless you smile nicely at the students checking cards. But it's worth going inside to check out the former ballroom (now a reading room) and the dining room (now the periodical reading room). Otherwise, the café on the ground floor is under a covered courtyard and is popular with students on study breaks.

VIII. REVICZKY UTCA 1 ✦ TEL: 411-5000 ✦ WWW.FSZEK.HU

CASH ONLY ✦ OPEN MONDAY *through* FRIDAY 10AM *to* 8PM

SATURDAY 10AM *to* 4PM ✦ M3, TRAM 49 (*to Kálvin tér*)

ISTITUTO ITALIANO DI CULTURA

THE ITALIAN CULTURAL INSTITUTE IS ALSO WORTH SEEING, AND YOU CAN DO SO WHILE HAVING COFFEE IN its lobby café, which is between the grand stone staircase and the imposing four-meter-high front doors. The neo-Renaissance building was designed by nineteenth-century architect Miklós Ybl, who also created the Opera House, the University of Economics, and St. Stephen's Basilica. Before Parliament was built, the Hungarian Parliament was housed here from 1866 to

1901. Since 1942 it has been the Italian Cultural Institute, which offers a full schedule of events throughout the year, like exhibitions, concerts, lectures, and films. There's little else but coffee here, just a few non-alcoholic drinks. The espresso is served Italian style, short and strong.

VIII. BRÓDY SÁNDOR UTCA 8 ✦ TEL: 483-2040

WWW.IICBUDAPEST.ESTERI.IT ✦ CASH ONLY

OPEN MONDAY *through* FRIDAY 9AM *to* 8PM

M2, TRAM 49 (*to Astoria*)

MAI MANÓ KÁVÉZÓ

L OCATED ON THE GROUND FLOOR OF THE HUNGARIAN HOUSE OF PHOTOGRAPHY, THIS PLACE IS NAMED FOR Manó Mai, the late-nineteenth-/early-twentieth-century photographer who lived and worked here. The eight-story building is one of Budapest's most interesting (worth a visit in

itself), with lots of skylights and sunlight, frescoes, wrought-iron balconies, and fancy plasterwork. The café is a thoroughly inviting place for coffee or a drink, and the other customers with their laptops and books also seem to think so, at least judging by how long they stay parked at their tables. The walls are covered with temporary photo exhibitions, and there's an old camera stuck in a nook in the wall. The closely spaced tables in the small place have seating on a couch lined with comfy pillows, and colorful rugs hang on the walls. The friendly waiter may not give you a saucer with your coffee, but you will get the oh-so-Central European demitasse of water with it. There are outdoor tables in the summer.

VI. NAGYMEZO UTCA 20 ✦ TEL: 269-5642

WWW.MAIMANOKAVEZO.HU ✦ CASH ONLY ✦ OPEN DAILY

10AM *to* 1AM ✦ M1, TRAM 4, 6 (*to Oktogon*), TROLLEY 70, 78

(*to Andrássy út*)

PRÁGA KÁVÉHÁZ ÉS TEÁZÓ

JUST A FEW STEPS FROM THE CITY'S MAIN LIBRARY AND SEVERAL UNIVERSITIES, THE BELOW-GROUND PRAGUE café and tea house is forever smoky and full of students nursing cups of tea or collecting empty beer glasses on their tables. There's a mural depicting Prague on the back wall, a few framed photos of coffee, and little else besides the worn floor, wooden café tables, and constantly hissing espresso machine. Don't come here for the food (there are just a few kinds of cookies and cakes), but come for the three dozen types of tea and the specialty coffees (including coffee cocktails).

VIII. BAROSS UTCA 8 ✦ TEL: 486-1937

CASH ONLY ✦ OPEN MONDAY *through* FRIDAY

7AM *to* 10PM, SATURDAY 9AM *to* 10PM

M3, TRAM 49 (*to Kálvin tér*)

TEAHOUSES

AROMA TEAHÁZ

THIS TINY TEAHOUSE'S COLORFUL WINDOW DISPLAY IS INVITING, AND SO IS THE SWEET FRAGRANCE OF tea when you walk inside. Since there are just a few places to sit, it isn't the most conducive to lingering over your cuppa. There's a decent selection, and loose tea can also be bought.

XIII. POZSONYI ÚT 5 ✦ TEL: 339-8428 ✦ CASH ONLY

OPEN DAILY 10:30AM *to* 7:30PM ✦ TRAM 4, 6 (*to Jászai Mari tér*)

BIG BEN TEAHÁZ

NEAR VÁCI UTCA, THIS TEAHOUSE HAS A SELECTION OF ABOUT A HUNDRED TYPES OF PREMIUM TEA FROM around the world. Sit and have a pot at the café, which is popular with students, or buy a bag to go.

V. VERES PÁLNÉ UTCA 10 ✦ TEL: 317-8982

WWW.BIGBENTEAHAZ.HU ✦ CASH ONLY ✦ OPEN MONDAY

through SATURDAY 10AM *to* 10PM, SUNDAY 2 *to* 10PM

M3, BUS 5, 7, 15, 78 (*to Ferenciek tere*)

DEMMERS TEAHÁZ

THE PROPRIETOR AT THE FÉNY UTCA LOCATION OF THIS FRIENDLY TEA-HOUSE FRANCHISE (THERE ARE ALSO locations in Austria and Poland) knows his tea, and can recommend one like a sommelier recommends a glass of wine. On one occasion when a friend and I wanted to order the same type of green tea, we were sharply told that we should order two different ones so we could each try both. We took his advice, and were glad we did after tasting the fragrant green tea flavored with lemongrass that he suggested. Tea is served in heavy Zsolnay china and the walls are lined with tea sets, tinned and boxed tea, and tea accessories (all are for sale). The proprietor lamented that the average Hungarian drinks little tea. "It's not the kind of thing they feel like they have to replace when they run out," he said, which may explain why the place has just a few seats. It does, however, stock nearly 150 varieties of tea, but alas, no pastries to nibble on with it.

II. FÉNY UTCA 1 ✦ TEL: 345-4150 ✦ WWW.TEAZO.HU
CASH ONLY ✦ OPEN MONDAY *through* SATURDAY 10:30AM *to*
7:30PM ✦ TRAM 4, 6 (*to Széna tér*), M2, BUS 5, 21, 22, 28, 39, 49, 56,
90, 128, 156, TRAM 18, 56, 59, 61, 118 (*to Moszkva tér*)

VI. PODMANICZKY UTCA 14 ✦ TEL: 302-5674 ✦ CASH ONLY
OPEN MONDAY *through* SATURDAY 11AM *to* 9PM, SUNDAY 1 *to* 9PM
M3, TRAM 4, 6 (*to Nyugati pályaudvar*)

TEAHÁZ A VÖRÖS OROSZLÁNHOZ

AT THE "RED LION TEA HOUSE," WITH ITS TWO CENTRAL LOCATIONS, BE PREPARED TO BROWSE A LIST OF AT least a hundred types of tea. There's also a small selection of teacakes, cookies, muffins, and fruit bread. The teahouses are quiet and pleasant enough, though the décor is rather typical with paper lamps, red walls, and eastern textiles. Don't come here if you're in a rush, the tea (which comes in individual teapots) takes time to prepare.

VI. JÓKAI TÉR 8 ✦ TEL: 269-0579
WWW.VOROSOROSZLANTEAHAZ.HU ✦ CC
OPEN MONDAY *through* SATURDAY 11AM *to* 11PM
SUNDAY 3 *to* 11PM ✦ M1, TRAM 4, 6 (*to Oktogon*)

IX. RÁDAY UTCA 9 ✦ TEL: 215-2101 ✦ CC
OPEN MONDAY *through* SATURDAY 11AM *to* 11PM
SUNDAY 3 *to* 11PM ✦ M3, TRAM 49 (*to Kálvin tér*)

BAR HOPPING

···································

BUDAPEST IS A GREAT BAR CITY, THOUGH COCKTAIL CULTURE IS FAIRLY NEW HERE. WHAT SETS THE BAR scene in Budapest apart, however, is its Bohemian-like bars called *Kerts* that open in the courtyards of abandoned buildings or in parks. These places come and go and locations change frequently, so check with the local press for the most up-to-date information (the best source is www.pestiside.hu). The following is by no means a complete guide to all of Budapest's bars, but these are a variety of the city's favorite spots, which should suit most drinkers' tastes.

LUXURY

···································

ADRIA PALACE BAR

────────

A PLEASANT AND MODERN HOTEL BAR LOCATED AT THE CROSSROADS OF BUDAPEST'S MAJOR TRANSPORT lines. Often features live jazz music.

V. ERZSÉBET TÉR 9-10 (*Le Meridien Hotel*) ✦ TEL: 429-5775 ✦ CC
OPEN DAILY 5PM *to* 3AM ✦ M1, M2, M3, TRAM 49 (*to Deák Ferenc tér*)

FOUR SEASONS BAR

────────

IF YOU DON'T GET A CHANCE TO STAY OR EAT IN THE SPECTACULAR FOUR SEASONS, WHICH SITS AT THE PEST terminus of the Chain Bridge, make sure to stop in for a pre-dinner drink at the hotel's bar. It's known for having the best bar snacks in Budapest.

V. ROOSEVELT TÉR 5-6 (*Four Seasons Gresham Palace Hotel*)
TEL: 268-6000 ✦ CC ✦ OPEN DAILY 11AM *to* 1AM
TRAM 2, 2A (*to Roosevelt tér*)

NEGRO CAFÉ

A SLEEK INDOOR-OUTDOOR BAR/CAFÉ SHARING A NICE COBBLED SQUARE WITH THE BASILICA, NEGRO (IT'S named after Hungary's favorite cough drop) is a key stop for Budapest's see-and-be-seen set.

V. SZENT ISTVÁN TÉR 11 ✦ TEL: 302-0136 ✦ CC
OPEN DAILY 11AM *to* 24AM ✦ M1 (*to Bajcsy-Zsilinszky út*)

SPOON CAFÉ & LOUNGE

E SPECIALLY DURING THE SUMMER MONTHS, A DRINK ON THE DECK OF THIS HIGH-END FLOATING RESTAURANT/ bar is well worth the indifferent service you may receive.

V. VIGADÓ TÉR 3 (*opposite the Intercontinental Hotel*) ✦ TEL: 411-0933
WWW.SPOONCAFE.HU ✦ CC ✦ OPEN DAILY NOON *to*
MIDNIGHT ✦ TRAM 2, 2A (*to Eötvös tér*)

MID-RANGE

A38 HAJÓ

F OR MUSIC WITH YOUR DRINKS, TRY THE A38 SHIP, A UKRAINIAN STONE-CARRIER TURNED CLUB/BAR/ restaurant/cultural center, moored on the Danube on the Buda side of Petofi bridge. With a lineup heavy on international acts and world music, there are shows nearly every night.

XI. PÁZMÁNY PÉTER SÉTÁNY ✦ TEL: 464-3940 ✦ WWW.A38.HU
OPEN DAILY 11AM *to* 4AM ✦ TRAM 4, 6, BUS 12
(*to Petofi híd, Budai hídfo*)

BUENA VISTA CAFÉ

T HE BUENA VISTA IS ONE OF THE MAIN CAFÉ-RESTAURANT-BARS ON PEST'S BUSIEST CAFÉ SQUARE, AND OFFERS several indoor and outdoor seating areas, as well as cocktails and individual "beer-taps."

V. LISZT FERENC TÉR 4-5 ✦ TEL: 344-6303
WWW.BUENA-VISTA.HU ✦ CC ✦ OPEN MONDAY *through*
FRIDAY 8AM *to* 1AM, SATURDAY *and* SUNDAY 11AM *to* 1AM
M1, TRAM 4, 6 (*to Oktogon*)

FAT MO'S SPEAKEASY

P ERENNIALLY POPULAR UNDERGROUND WATERING HOLE
NEAR PEST'S MAIN TOURIST THOROUGHFARE WITH LIVE
music on most nights.

V. NYÁRY PÁL UTCA 11 ✦ TEL: 267-3199 ✦ WWW.FATMO.HU
OPEN MONDAY *through* WEDNESDAY NOON *to* 2AM, THURSDAY
through FRIDAY NOON *to* 4AM, SATURDAY 6PM *to* 4AM, SUNDAY
6PM *to* 2AM ✦ M3 (*to Ferenciek tere*)

OSCAR AMERICAN BAR

T HIS HOLLYWOOD-THEMED COCKTAIL BAR (A.K.A. OSCAR'S)
NEAR THE BUDA CASTLE CELEBRATED ITS TENTH ANNIVER-
sary in early 2007, and is one of the best places to mingle in
(very) close quarters with the capital's party crowd.

I. OSTROM UTCA 14 ✦ TEL: 212-8017 ✦ WWW.OSCARBAR.HU
OPEN SUNDAY *through* THURSDAY 5PM *to* 2AM, FRIDAY *and*
SATURDAY 5PM *to* 4AM ✦ M2, BUS 5, 21, 22, 28, 39, 49, 56, 90,
128, 156, TRAM 18, 56, 59, 61, 118 (*to Moszkva tér*)

PICASSO POINT

W HILE BACK IN THE EARLY 1990S PICASSO POINT WAS
THE UNDISPUTED CENTER OF EXPATRIATE NIGHTLIFE
in Budapest, it is now an excellent place to avoid the hype
and flash of the city's newer bar scene.

VI. HAJÓS UTCA 31 ✦ TEL: 312-1727 ✦ WWW.PICASSOPOINT.HU
OPEN MONDAY *through* WEDNESDAY 11AM *to* MIDNIGHT,
THURSDAY 11AM *to* 2AM, FRIDAY 11AM *to* 4AM, SATURDAY
4PM *to* 4AM, SUNDAY 4PM *to* MIDNIGHT ✦ M3 (*to Arany János utca*)

SANDOKAN LISBOA SOLINGBAR

A PETITE BUT FUN TWO-LEVEL BAR/CAFÉ ON THE SLOWLY DEVELOPING PEDESTRIAN STREET BEHIND THE STATE Opera House, famous for being co-owned by the former Hungarian "adult" actress Michelle Wild.

VI. HAJÓS UTCA 23 ✦ TEL: 06-20/335-1041 ✦ OPEN MONDAY *through* FRIDAY NOON *to* 2AM, SATURDAY *and* SUNDAY 4PM *to* 2AM
M1 (*to Opera*)

TIME CAFÉ & LOUNGE

O NE OF THE MORE ESTABLISHED AND PLEASANT STOPS ALONG THE NINTH DISTRICT'S PEDESTRIANIZED CAFÉ-bar row, the Time features a large clock built into the floor in front of the bar, and a comprehensive cocktail menu.

IX. RÁDAY UTCA 23 ✦ TEL: 476-0433 ✦ WWW.TIMECAFE.HU
OPEN MONDAY *through* WEDNESDAY 11AM *to* 1AM, THURSDAY *and* FRIDAY 11AM *to* 2AM, SATURDAY 2PM *to* 2AM, SUNDAY 4PM *to* 1AM
M3, TRAM 49 (*to Kálvin tér*)

HIP

CALGARY ANTIK DRINK BÁR

A N EXTREMELY ATMOSPHERIC (I.E. STRANGE AND SOMETIME MENACING) LITTLE BAR NEAR THE RIVER IN Buda, complete with parrot and live piano music on Friday nights.

II. FRANKEL LEÓ ÚT 24 ✦ TEL: 316-9089 ✦ CC
OPEN DAILY 6PM *to* 3AM ✦ TRAM 4, 6 (*to Margit híd, Budai hídfo*)

CASTRO BISZTRÓ

DESPITE ITS NAME, CASTRO HAS NOTHING TO DO WITH CUBA OR ITS LEADER. IN 2006 CASTRO MOVED FROM Ráday utca, but didn't lose its beloved smoky-Bohemian atmosphere. The hearty Serbian food here makes this place a favorite even at lunch.

VII. MADÁCH IMRE TÉR ✦ TEL: 215-0184 ✦ WWW.CASTRO.HU
OPEN MONDAY *through* THURSDAY 9AM *to* MIDNIGHT, FRIDAY
9AM *to* 1AM, SATURDAY NOON *to* 1AM, SUNDAY 2PM *to* MIDNIGHT
M1, M2, M3, TRAM 49 (*to Deák Ferenc tér*)

KUPLUNG

KUPLUNG MEANS "CLUTCH," WHICH IS FITTING, AS THE PREMISES OF THIS POPULAR DOWNTOWN BAR WAS formerly a motorcycle repair shop. Behind unmarked doors, this smoke-filled hall has an exhibition area, a performance space, and attracts a young Bohemian crowd before the open-air courtyard bars open.

VI. KIRÁLY UTCA 46 ✦ TEL: 06-30/986-8856 ✦ OPEN DAILY 2PM
to 4AM ✦ M1 (*to Opera*)

PIAF

A LEGENDARILY BIZARRE AFTER-HOURS "KNOCK FIRST" CLUB ON PEST'S VERSION OF "BROADWAY," PIAF OFFERS TORCH tunes upstairs, and a cramped and hopping mini-disco in the basement.

VI. NAGYMEZO UTCA 25 ✦ TEL: 312-3823 ✦ OPEN SUNDAY
through THURSDAY 10PM *to* 6AM, FRIDAY *and* SAURDAY
10PM *to* 7AM ✦ M1 (*to Opera*)

SZÓDA CAFÉ

A VERY APPEALING CAFÉ-BAR IN PEST'S JEWISH QUARTER, WITH A RELAXED UPSTAIRS AND A BASEMENT AREA THAT features live music most weekends. Also offers free wi-fi.

VII. WESSELÉNYI UTCA 18 ✦ TEL: 461-0007

WWW.SZODA.COM ✦ OPEN DAILY 8AM *to* 5PM

M1, M2, M3, TRAM 49 (*to Deák Ferenc tér*)

SZIMPLA KERT

P EST'S BEST-KNOWN *ROMKERT* (OPEN-AIR BAR), SZIMPLA
KERT—NOT TO BE CONFUSED WITH PLAIN "SZIMPLA," A
few blocks away—offers both a summer beer garden, an
outdoor movie theater, and several wonderfully run-down all-
weather bar areas.

VI. KAZINCZY UTCA 14 ✦ TEL: 321-5880 ✦ WWW.SZIMPLA.HU
OPEN DAILY 5PM *to* 2AM ✦ M2, TRAM 49 (*to Astoria*)

VITTULA

A VERY SMALL AND DINGY BUT CHARMING BASEMENT HANGOUT POPULAR WITH YOUNGER MEMBERS OF Budapest's international set.

VI. KERTÉSZ UTCA 4 ✦ TEL: 06-20/527-7069 ✦ OPEN DAILY 6PM
until LATE ✦ M2, TRAM 4, 6 (*to Blaha Lujza tér*)

CHAPTER 7:

....

BUDAPEST'S MARKETS

Olcsó húsnak híg a leve.
Cheap meat produces thin broth.

Üres kamrának bolond a gazdasszonya.
An empty pantry has a foolish housewife.

—HUNGARIAN PROVERBS

EVEN AS A FULL GENERAL ON ACTIVE SERVICE, HE HAD BEEN KNOWN FOR SPARING NO EFFORTS TO SCOUR the entire city for a peach. And since his retirement he had nothing else to do but to keep a lookout for the *primeurs* of the markets and the window displays of the delicatessens. And because his disposition was such that he preferred the wildlings of nature to fruit and greens grown under glass, the first field mushroom could not thrust up its tiny pink head in the trackless forests of the Mátra mountains without the lieutenant general learning of it in Mester Street. He could sense it from the air, from the wind...

—*Spring,* GYULA KRÚDY

MARKETING

....

A LINGUISTIC NOTE TO START: *PIAC, CSARNOK,* AND *VÁSÁRCSARNOK* ALL MEAN "MARKET" IN HUNGARIAN, but they traditionally refer to different types of markets. A *vásárcsarnok* is a covered market hall (like Budapest's six traditional market halls). *Piac* means "market place" and can also refer to other types of non-food markets. *Csarnok* means "hall."

There's a grocery store two blocks from my apartment, but I'm in the habit of walking an extra fifteen minutes to the market to do my shopping. Compared to the sorry selection of wilted vegetables and mass-produced cheese at the grocery store, the market is a bounty of variety and freshness. You might not know it from the lines in the grocery store, but markets are still essential to many Budapesters. Sure, marketing takes longer than one-stop shopping, but that's part of the fun of it. The things I especially love to buy at the market—fresh goat cheese, homemade sour cream that tastes like crème fraîche, home-churned sweet butter, sausages and salami made from Mangalica pork—aren't even sold in grocery stores. The markets are fantastic places to buy dairy products. You'll find buttermilk, whey, raw milk, fresh yogurt, and more. You can get eggs so new they are still unwashed, and occasionally have a few stray feathers stuck to the shells. More than any museum, a trip to a neighborhood market will show you firsthand how intensely important food and cooking are in Hungary.

You can watch the seasons change at the markets. In the summer there are heaps of fresh produce, like juicy tomatoes, warty cucumbers for pickling, white and green asparagus for soups, cherries for eating straight from the bag, peaches, and apricots for turning into jam that will last the whole year. Year round, pale green bell peppers (which are often called Hungarian wax peppers abroad) are a mainstay. By the end of the summer they are cheap and plentiful, and home cooks buy them in multiple kilos for making *lecsó* to last through the winter. The fall brings foragers selling precious piles of wild mushrooms. Testament to the fondness for mushrooms in Hungary, most markets have specialists on duty to examine mushrooms (*gombavizsgálat*) that foragers bring to determine whether they're edible or poisonous. Winter menus rely on roots and tubers and markets are full of things like parsnips, celery root, and kohlrabi, which are necessary ingredients for a good *húsleves*. Come spring, there's a welcome abundance of non-roots like new garlic that's sliced and eaten raw, bright red radishes, tiny new red potatoes, and sweet strawberries.

A trip to the Nagyvásárcsarnok, the Central Market Hall—which is both a stunning building and a wonderful food market—should be right up there with the castle on a Budapest must-see list, even if you don't plan to buy anything. There are four other similar, but smaller, old-style market halls, which all opened in 1887. While they are examples of fine architecture—big brick buildings with lots of iron, glass, and open space—they are hardly the bustling markets that they once were, and are far less interesting than some of the city's other markets. The old market hall on Batthyány tér in Buda's first district (which opened in 1905) and the market hall at Klauzál tér in the seventh district's old Jewish quarter aren't even markets anymore, but grocery stores. The other old market halls, while still operational, pale in comparison to some of the city's other markets.

After checking out the Central Market Hall, it's worthwhile to visit a few of the other markets where you may even be the only tourist in sight. Like Budapest's distinctive neighborhoods, different markets reflect different economic circumstances and lifestyles. A visit to the weekly MOM Park Ökopiac (organic market) offers a peek into an entirely different social sphere than that at, say, the Bosnyák tér Market. The organic market is a Saturday morning ritual for the growing number of Hungarians who are passionate about organic eating and supporting organic farmers (and have the means to pay considerably more for it). On the other end of the spectrum, at the Bosnyák tér market in a working-class neighborhood of Pest, pork is the king in all shapes and forms, and most shoppers couldn't care less about organic food. Just like in other cities, many of the vendors at Budapest's markets don't actually grow their own produce, but buy it every morning at the Nagybani Piac (wholesale market). But there are still a *néni* and a *bácsi* or two ("aunt" or "uncle") who come from outside of Budapest to hawk their own products. Additionally, there's a nice cluster of food shops in the basement of the Budagyöngye Shopping Center in Buda's second district (some of which are listed in Chapter 8).

Market etiquette isn't particularly complicated. Things are priced either by weight, by the piece (*darab*, abbreviated as db.), or by the bunch (*csomó*, abbreviated as cs.). When goods are priced by weight, it's usually by the kilogram unless it's otherwise labeled. Some vendors have little plastic baskets for gathering up your pickings, while others snap at customers who attempt to pick out their own fruits and vegetables. Vendors at the Central Market are used to non-Hungarian speakers and many can speak just enough English to make for a smooth transaction. At the other markets English is rare. Don't expect a bag (they might cost extra). Serious shoppers wander around and compare prices before buying anything, as prices and quality can vary greatly from stall to stall. Snacking on greasy *lángos* is a market ritual for some. The cheap plonk served at the market bars from early in the morning attracts an entirely different crowd who have no interest in the butchers and the greengrocers.

Markets generally close for the weekend around 1pm on Saturday (except for the Lehel tér Csarnok, which is also open on Sundays). Saturday morning is the busiest market day, when shoppers stock up for a weekend's worth of meals. It's wise to avoid Mondays at the markets, when many vendors stay home. Most of Budapest's markets are run by the Municipality of Budapest's Hall and Market Management company (CSAPI). For more information visit www.csapi.hu, where the weekly average prices for fruits and vegetables at five different markets are also listed.

MARKETS IN PEST

NAGYVÁSÁRCSARNOK
(Central Market Hall)

ON THE PEST SIDE OF SZABADSÁG BRIDGE (AT THE END OF VÁCI UTCA), THE NAGYVÁSÁRCSARNOK IS Budapest's largest and grandest market of them all. It's also one of the city's top tourist attractions. Despite what it may feel like, it's not just for tourists. The market—a protected city monument—is one of Europe's finest. The airy orange and yellow brick building is full of steel beams and light flooding in through enormous windows. With its cavernous interior, the vast three-level market hall is a cathedral to food where you can spend hours browsing, shopping, and snacking.

One of the original reasons behind the construction of this market (and the smaller versions) was to improve food quality in rapidly growing late-nineteenth-century Budapest. Architects competed to design the new market hall and Samu Pecz was finally commissioned, taking home a 2,000 HUF prize. In the

THE SAFFRON STORY

....

THE LITTLE PACKETS OF "SAFFRON" THAT ARE CHEAP AND PLENTIFUL AROUND THE CENTRAL MARKET Hall and Váci utca may be tempting, but there's a reason it's so cheap. It's not actually saffron, it's safflower petals, or *sáfrányos szeklice* in Hungarian. Saffron is the world's most expensive spice because it takes about 70,000 female saffron crocus flowers to produce half a kilogram, and every step in the cultivation process is done by hand. Safflower is sometimes used as a cheap substitute. It adds color, but lacks the distinctive fragrance and flavor that saffron has. Safflower also goes by other names: false saffron, American Saffron, Mexican saffron (which grows wild in America and Mexico), dyer's saffron, bastard saffron, and zaffer. Despite the similar names, safflower isn't in any way related to true saffron.

summer of 1897, after two years of construction and with the building less than two weeks from being finished, a fire tore through it and set completion back until the following year. When it finally opened, the market became an import-export center and an important source of food supplies for both Budapest and the rest of Hungary. Strict rules were set up to maintain high quality. In the early days an aisle for wagons ran through the center, with retailers on the east side and wholesalers on the west. The market was severely damaged during World War II and was hastily repaired after the war. By 1991 it had fallen into such disrepair that it was deemed too dangerous to use and was closed until 1994 for a thorough restoration, in which even the old roof tiles were replaced by exact Zsolnay replicas.

Most of the action is on the ground level. The left aisle mostly stocks straightforward fruits and vegetables, while the sellers along the right aisle mix in more exotic produce. About halfway down the right aisle (on the left-hand side), you'll find the vendor who sells the best selection of fresh herbs in town, along with intriguing imported goodies like papayas, pitahayas, and kumquats. There are dozens of butchers here, who call out to potential customers as they walk by. This is the place to come for one-kilogram chunks of creamy duck or goose liver. There are also the stalls selling overpriced tourist-ready paprika in little sacks along with painted wooden spoons, which should be avoided. The mushroom display in the back of the market features eight cases of mushrooms, marked as edible or poisonous. In the rear wing, small farmers and producers set up wooden tables to display their hand-produced jars of jam and honey, egg noodles of all shapes and sizes, raw milk, and homemade cheeses, sour cream, and butter.

By this time you may need a coffee to keep you going. If you're standing at the beginning of the center aisle, walk straight and take your first left. You'll most likely see a line outside of a tiny window, where little glasses of dark, strong coffee are served. Nearby, in the central aisle, there's a stall selling freshly made *rétes*, still warm from the oven. Big wooden staircases in the center lead to the upper level, where there are stalls selling sausages and *lángos*. At the cheap bars, men down shots of Unicum accompanied by cheap wine. Most of the upper level is devoted to selling the mostly mediocre (and probably made in China) folk art and knick-knacks.

You'll catch whiffs of sauerkraut and vinegar as you descend into the basement. That's where the fishmongers and a clutch of vendors selling pickled vegetables are located. There's also quite a good selection of game down here, as well as a vendor selling cheap kitchen utensils. Ázsia—one of the best (and among the first) specialty international food shops to open in Budapest—is also on this level (see Chapter 8). The Central Market also has a so-called Bio Market on Wednesdays, which is little more than one family from Tököl (about ten kilometers from Budapest) selling organic products on a few folding tables in the rear of the market hall.

IX. VÁMHÁZ KÖRÚT 1-3 (*Fovám tér*) ✦ TEL: 366-3300
WWW.CSAPI.HU ✦ OPEN MONDAY 6AM-5PM, TUESDAY *through*
FRIDAY 6AM *to* 6PM, SATURDAY 6AM *to* 2PM
BIO MARKET WEDNESDAY 7AM *to* 1PM *and* FRIDAY 7AM *to* 4PM
(TEL: (24) 489-138) ✦ M3 (*to Kálvin tér*), TRAM 2, 2A, 49 (*to Fovám tér*)

BOSNYÁK TÉR PIAC

I F YOU'RE AFTER DAZZLING ARCHITECTURE, PRETTY STRINGS OF PAPRIKA, AND LEISURELY BROWSING, THIS MARKET isn't for you. Here you'll find masses of people jammed into a maze-like building, half covered and half open-air. It's chaotic, cluttered, raucous, and colorful—which is exactly how a neighborhood market should be. Even if you wanted to linger and admire the stacks of smoked bacon or the fresh peppers, chances are that you'd be pushed and shoved, forced to move on. Mothers push strollers, old ladies push metal carts, and shoppers elbow through the narrow aisles with their wicker baskets and plastic shopping bags. A booming voice shouts, "*Tessék, itt a szép paradicsom!*" (Here are the beautiful tomatoes) or, "*Tessék, itt a finom hagyma!*" (Here are the delicious onions), if a shopper happens to glance in his direction. He doesn't expect an answer, and neither do the women wearing aprons and head scarves, sweetly beckoning you to come buy their bags of spinach, jars of honey, or slabs of home-smoked lard. Ruddy men cluster around the cheap drink stands with empty mini bottles of booze and half-finished beer cans lined up on their tables. They didn't come for the fresh fruits and vegetables, but they're here every day.

This market is not for the squeamish. Much of the chicken here comes with heads, feet, and innards still attached. While chefs in America sometimes lament the difficulties of finding the more lowly cuts of meat—like tripe, goose necks, and kidneys—these are common items here. Smoked pork knuckles and dried sau-

sages dangle over the butcher counters and thick blood and liver sausages tempt shoppers from the meat cases. One butcher sells curly little smoked pig tails and buckets full of pig ears.

The low plain brick building has 1960s-style lettering carved into stone above the entrance. Florists and plant sellers congregate in the rear, while off to the side a junk market stocks cheap shoes, bags, toys, and clothes. A market highlight is the two stalls selling home-style cookies and cakes (look for the small sign, "*Nápolyi Édesség*," near the entrance in the middle aisle). Cardboard boxes with handwritten labels are stuffed with a variety of not-too-sweet buttery Linzer cookies, Ischler cookies, and nut cookies as well as layered desserts like Gerbeaud slices, *mézeskrémes*, and *Rákóczi túrós*. For an everyday, gritty, bustling market experience, skip the Central Market Hall and take the fifteen-minute bus ride from the Keleti railway station to Bosnyák tér.

XIV. CSÖMÖRI ÚT 9-11 ✦ TEL: 273-3144 ✦ OPEN MONDAY 6AM *to* 5PM, TUESDAY *through* FRIDAY 6AM *to* 6PM, SATURDAY 6AM *to* 2PM
BUS 7, 24, 32, 70, 73, 77, 132, 173, TRAM 3, 62 (*to Bosnyák tér*)

LEHEL TÉR CSARNOK

YOU'LL KNOW YOU'VE ARRIVED AT THE LEHEL TÉR MARKET WHEN YOU SEE THE BIZARRE-LOOKING BRIGHT RED, yellow, and blue building that looks like a ship, complete with a Hungarian flag waving from the mast. It was built in 2003, to mixed reviews from Buda- pesters, to replace the old market on the same site. This building— full of glass and blue steel raf- ters—was designed by László Rajk, son of the Hungarian Communist Interior Minister of the same name who was the victim of a notorious Stalinist show-trial and executed for conspiracy in 1949. He officially became a non-person and was only given a public burial weeks before the failed 1956 Hun- garian Revolution. As well as being an architect, Rajk Jr. was also involved in politics.

However you feel about the theme-park-like building, the food market inside is one of the city's best. Meat is king here, and if you ever forget that every animal once came with a head, feet, and ears, here you'll be reminded. Stacks of *szalonna* and tubs of *teperto* sit on the counters. Smoked ribs and knuckles, salamis of all sizes, links of sausages, and pieces of smoked goose and duck hang from above. You'll never look at the sorry supermarket cases full of ground beef and flimsy steaks the same way again after seeing the dozens of butchers here, which prove there's more out there than just the common cuts of meat that most supermarkets stock these days. Hungarians are fond of cooking these cheaper, flavorful, fatty, and tough cuts of meat, and they do it well.

Plenty of fruit and vegetable vendors sell whatever is in season. While the selection is big, there are few exotic choices. Other highlights include a specialized mushroom store ("*Gomba Szakbolt*"), a honey store near the entrance, and a fantastic dairy shop with locations on the ground floor and the first floor ("*Tejbolt*").

The dairy stocks homemade (házi) everything—butter,cheese, yogurt, kefir, cream, and sour cream—as well as a few imported cheeses. On the upper level the Táplálék Allergia Centrum (Tel: 288-6833; Open Monday through Friday 7:30am to 6pm, Saturday 7:30am to 1pm) specializes in glu- ten-free products. Every market

has a near-Eastern specialty store, and this one is in the basement (the Kis Piac), where bags of pistachios, rice, lentils, and garbanzo beans crowd the floor. Noodles, sauces, tubs of olives, fresh pita bread, loose spices, and baklava are also sold at this Keleti Foszerek-Cse- mege ("eastern spice and delicacy").

XIII. LEHEL TÉR ✦ TEL: 340-2942 ✦ OPEN MONDAY *through* FRIDAY 6AM *to* 8PM, SATURDAY 6AM *to* 2PM, SUNDAY 6AM *to* 1PM M3, TRAM 1, 14, BUS 4, 15, 133, TROLLEY 76, 79 (*to Lehel tér*)

RÁKÓCZI TÉR VÁSÁRCSARNOK

ANOTHER OF THE ORIGINAL GRAND MARKET HALLS—IN A GORGEOUS BRICK, GLASS, AND STEEL BUILDING— the Rákóczi tér Market Hall was badly damaged by a fire and nicely reconstructed and reopened in 1991. The spacious place has the same enormous ceilings and windows as the Central Market Hall, but this one has only a ground level. Although there are lots of junk stores mixed in with the food stalls, it remains a decent centrally located market—almost a small-scale version of the Central Market Hall. Butchers with the typical hanging sau- sages and salamis, tubs full of cracklings, and stacks of lard are numerous here. There's a fishmonger, and a vendor selling frozen game. Most of the fruit and vegetable sellers are clustered in the middle aisle, and the selection is fresh and decent, but not monu- mental. There are few unusual or surprising products here. The formerly seedy Rákóczi tér, a few blocks from Blaha Lujza tér, is in a rapidly rehabilitating neighborhood. While you're here, be sure to visit the Chinese shop next door, which is a favorite among chefs at Budapest's Asian restaurants.

VIII. RÁKÓCZI TÉR 7-9 ✦ TEL: 476-3952 ✦ OPEN MONDAY *through* FRIDAY 6AM *to* 6PM, SATURDAY 6AM *to* 1PM M1 (*to Blaha Lujza tér*), TRAM 4, 6 (*to Rákóczi tér*)

HUNGARIAN HONEY

························

HONEY DOESN'T PLAY A MAJOR ROLE IN HUNGAR-IAN COOKING, BUT ABOUT 20,000 TONS OF IT are produced annually by 16,000 beekeepers. The most common varieties of Hungarian honey are *akácméz* (acacia), *hársméz* (lime blossom), and *vegyes virágméz* (mixed flower). Other types like *repceméz* (rape honey, or canola), *napraforgóméz* (sunflower), *gesztenyeméz* (chestnut), *facéliaméz* (phacelia), and *selyemfuméz* (milkweed) are collected in smaller amounts. Small-scale beekeepers often sell honey straight from their homes (look out for the *méz* sign) and at the markets. The best-known recipe starring honey is *mézeskalács*, or honey bread. Similar to ginger bread, *mézeskalács* is most often made as round golden-colored cookies glazed with white sugar, or in decorative shapes like hearts, which are plastered with red icing and colorful designs or messages. They're usually sold at fairs and markets and given as gifts.

PICKING YOUR PAPRIKA

· ·

HUNGARIAN PAPRIKA IS ONE OF THE MOST POPU-
LAR SOUVENIRS FROM HUNGARY. IT'S KNOWN FOR
its strong aroma and intense color, which varies from
deep reddish brown to bright orange. You're missing out if
you don't stock up, since the paprika sold abroad (even if it's
from Hungary) is often dull and flavorless from sitting
around too long. Skip the paprika in the touristy sacks at
the market and buy it at the grocery store instead for much
less. Better yet, if you can find it, buy a jar of homemade
paprika from a vendor at one of the markets. Like any spice,
store it tightly covered in a dry, dark, cool place and try to use
it within eight months. You can also make your own hot
paprika with a few dried red chili peppers and a coffee grinder.
There are four basic types of Hungarian paprika:

Különleges (Special) is the most finely ground, brightest red
paprika, with a strong aroma, and can be sweet or mild.

Csemege paprika (Gourmet) is a light red, slightly coarse
paprika, which can be hot or mild.

Édesnemes paprika (Noble) is a light red paprika, less finely
ground than Csemege, with just a little heat. It's mainly used
to flavor stews and meats.

Rózsa paprika (Rose) is a dark red, medium coarse paprika,
which tends to be very hot.

Paprika comes in varying degrees of heat. Often you won't
find the above labels, it will just be hot or sweet (not hot).

Édes: Sweet
Félédes: Mild or Semi-Sweet
Csípos or Eros: Hot

Paprika also comes other varieties:

Piros Arany ("Red Gold") is a smooth, creamy, red paprika
paste that comes in a red tube. It has a rich texture and flavor (it looks a bit like ketchup), and is good on sandwiches.
Hungarians often use a dab of it as a garnish. It comes mild
(*csemege*) or hot (*csípos*).

Eros Pista ("Strong Steve") is a much hotter and coarser paste
than Piros Arany and still contains seeds. It's often served with
soups and stews to add extra heat.

Édes Anna ("Sweet Anna") is a mild version of Eros Pista.

HUNYADI TÉR VÁSÁRCSARNOK

T HIS BELOVED NEIGHBORHOOD MARKET IS ALSO IN AN OLD-STYLE MARKET HALL, BUT IT'S STARTING TO show its age. Although the plaster is crumbling and the paint is peeling, it has a character that its regular shoppers adore. The selection here is quite small compared with the big ones like Lehel tér, the Central Market, and Fény utca. But for neighborhood residents, it's a nice place to do daily shopping. You can find all the basics here: there are two bakeries, two pickled vegetable shops, and one stall that sells a tiny selection of fish and game. There are several butchers and poultry specialists, and one small stall on the right aisle (Tamás Tumpek) sells particularly nice bacon, smoked meats, and *kolbász* (sausages). The fruit and vegetable selection is decent, but pretty homogenous. There's an open-air market on the street out front, which is at its best on Saturday mornings and when the sun is shining and can be hit-or-miss on other days. A highlight is the two cheesemakers who come to sell their handmade goat, cow, curd, and smoked cheeses. They also sell fresh milk and a few other dairy products. One comes only on Fridays and Saturdays, and the other only on Tuesdays, Thursdays, and Saturdays. There are plans to renovate this market, as well as the square in front of it, but it's still up in the air what that will mean for both the indoor market and the open-air market.

VI. HUNYADI TÉR ✦ WWW.HUNYADIPIAC.HU
OPEN MONDAY *through* FRIDAY 7AM *to* 6PM, SATURDAY
7AM *to* 2PM ✦ M1 (*to Vörösmarty utca*)

NAGYBANI PIAC
(Budapest Wholesale Market)

V ISIT BUDAPEST'S WHOLESALE MARKET FOR AN ALTOGETHER DIFFERENT KIND OF MARKET EXPERIENCE. SINCE 1991 this sprawling thirty-two-hectare market in the outskirts of southern Pest has been where most retailers get their produce. Seventy percent of fruits and vegetables imported to Hungary pass through the market annually as well as nearly 44,000 tons of domestic fruit and 167,000 tons of domestically grown vegetables. During the summer high season the place opens at midnight and closes down around the time the rest of the city's markets are just getting going. Everything here is big, from the loaded-down trucks heading out to make their early morning deliveries to the forklifts moving crates of cabbage and the sellers pushing handcarts full of watermelons and onions. Though the place is mainly for retailers to do their purchasing, individual buyers are also welcome to shop here as long as they don't mind buying in big quantities. The produce here comes from both industrial-sized farms and from small farmers who sell their stuff straight from the backs of their trucks. There are also a few eateries and shops here (like agricultural supply shops). It's really not easy to get out here by public transportation. But if you have no access to a car, you can take the bus. To enter by car, you'll have to pay a fee which varies depending on how much you buy.

XXIII. NAGYKŐRÖSI ÚT 353 ✦ TEL: 814-5300

WWW.NAGYBANI.HU ✦ OPEN MID MAY *to* MID SEPTEMBER

MONDAY *through* SATURDAY MIDNIGHT *to* 9AM, MID SEPTEMBER

to MID MAY MONDAY *through* FRIDAY 5AM *to* 1PM, SATURDAY 5AM

to 9AM ✦ BUS 54 (*to Zöldségpiac*)

MARKETS IN BUDA

FÉNY UTCA PIAC

BEHIND THE MAMMUT I SHOPPING CENTER, THE FÉNY UTCA MARKET IS A SPRAWLING PARTIALLY COVERED two-level market. The usual clusters of disheveled men hover around the cheap bars along the edges of the market, sipping beer, wine, and *pálinka* at any hour of the day. Near the Fény utca entrance, the left corner of the market is occupied by farmers selling their fresh chickens, slabs of bacon and lard, and stacks of dried sausages. Here you'll also find *házi* (homemade) sour cream, cream, and butter. There are round wheels of *házi gomolya* cheese, spiked with garlic, red onions, or chives. There's fresh *túró*, sheep cheese, and if you're lucky, goat cheese. The folding tables set up in the market's

central aisles (both upstairs and downstairs) are generally occupied by small-scale producers. Unlike the vendors who buy their stuff at the wholesale market every morning, most of the vendors at these tables actually grew or made whatever they sell. This is where you'll find more uncommon things like medlars, quinces, and Jerusalem artichokes. If it's strawberry season, you'll find some of the smallest, sweetest, freshest strawberries in town here.

One of the best things about the Fény utca market is that it's the best place in Budapest to buy Mangalica pork and Hungarian Grey beef. While there are three butchers here selling salami, fresh and dried sausages, and bacon made from these indigenous animals, there's just one butcher (upstairs on the right side) who regularly stocks unprocessed cuts like Grey beef tenderloin and Mangalica ribs and chops. Sautéeing onions in *szalonna* is the first step in many Hungarian dishes, and if you're going to use pork fat in your cooking it might as well be Mangalica *szalonna*, which is plentiful here and said to be healthier because it's higher in

polyunsaturated fat. The *savanyúság* stalls are upstairs, with their colorful displays of whole, stuffed, and shredded pickled vegetables. There's also a branch of the Szega Camembert Cheese Shop (see page 298) upstairs and a bakery that sells bread far superior to the supermarket loaves. You can't miss the row of florists along the front of the market, with their buckets of wild flowers, bouquets of tiny roses, and pretty potted plants. The Fény utca market is one of the best places in town to shop (or just browse), with a grocery store inside the mall for anything that can't be found at the market and the Ezerfuszer shop (see page 294) around the corner for specialty items.

II. LÖVOHÁZ UTCA 12 ✦ TEL: 345-4101

HTTP://FENYUTCAIPIAC.INTERNETTUDAKOZO.HU/CEGBEMUTATO.HTM

OPEN MONDAY *through* FRIDAY 6AM *to* 6PM, SATURDAY 6AM *to* 2PM

TRAM 4, 6 (*to Széna tér*), M2, BUS 5, 21, 22, 28, 39, 49, 56, 90, 128, 156,

TRAM 18, 56, 59, 61, 118 (*to Moszkva tér*)

KÓRHÁZ UTCA PIAC

ON A QUIET TREE-LINED STREET NESTLED BETWEEN NEIGHBORHOODS OF TALL 1960s PRE-FAB APARTMENT blocks, this doesn't look like much from the outside, but inside it's a bustling neighborhood market that's a lot bigger than it appears. Street vendors outside hawk inexpensive clothes, shoes, toys, and plants. One sells sewing supplies, and another sells cheap cooking utensils and equipment. Inside the low, covered building, the market has an excellent selection of produce and meat. A poultry butcher sells every bit of the chicken, goose, and duck—even a bin full of goose hearts, which are supposed to be good in stuffing. Several butchers sell *házi kolbász*, along with piles of *szalonna* and smoked duck, goose, and pork parts. One butcher sells Mangalica *teperto*, but you'll find few other Mangalica products at this working-class market where innards seem to be big sellers. The Sajt Sarok shop has a decent variety of cheese. Almost hidden away in a nearby side aisle, a woman sells fresh milk and homemade cheeses, including tasty paprika orange-tinted *korözött*. Across from her, the fishmonger has tanks full of live carp and catfish. Nearby, another *néni* has a table lined with big sacks of dried herbs like lavender, thyme, dried leeks and ramps, parsley, thyme, marjoram, oregano, and others that she sells cheaply by the cup. She's there from Wednesday to Saturday and also sells bunches of fresh herbs. There are several of the obligatory pickled-vegetable shops scattered throughout selling everything from pickled green tomatoes to pickled plums. Despite its bleak location, the selection of seasonal fruits and vegetables at this low-profile market is top-notch and can compete with any of the city's other markets. An added bonus: it's very far from the beaten tourist track. To get here, follow Kórház utca west from Flórián tér. The market is behind the Flórián tér shopping center, which is a few blocks west of Árpád híd.

III. KÓRHÁZ UTCA 37-41 ✦ TEL: 367-3847

OPEN MONDAY 7AM *to* 4PM, TUESDAY *through* FRIDAY 6AM *to* 6PM

SATURDAY 6AM *to* 2PM ✦ BUS 6, 86 (*to Flórián tér*)

MOM PARK ÖKOPIAC
(Organic Market)

WHILE IT SEEMS THAT THERE'S A BIO BOLT (ORGANIC SHOP) ON EVERY BLOCK IN BUDAPEST, THIS WEEKLY organic market is really the only place with an extensive selection of fresh organic produce, meat, dairy, and more. Located near the MOM Park shopping center in the backyard of a cultural center, the entrance is actually around the corner on Sirály utca. Follow the big Socialist-Realist figures on the side of the building and the shoppers with baskets overflowing with bright vegetables and two-liter soda bottles of milk. This open-air market is where Budapest's growing number of organic food enthusiasts flock on Saturday mornings, with their wicker baskets, canvas shopping bags, and stroller baskets ready to be filled with natural food brought straight from the countryside.

Everything here is guaranteed organic by the Hungarian Bio-kultúra Association (the group responsible for certifying nearly all of the country's organic food). Even if you don't insist on eating organic, come here for the selection and the top-notch products. Every Saturday between forty and sixty independent farmers, producers, and artisans are here selling whatever's in season, and reminding us of the benefits of seasonal eating. Fruits and veg-etables are the stars here, but dairy is a close second. The several dairy farmers have a great selection of creamy artisanal cheese and goat-milk products like raw milk, yogurt, whey, and kefir. There are homemade breads and desserts; fresh herbs; meats like Racka mutton, Mangalica, and Hungarian Grey beef; Mangalica sausage, salami, and cracklings; organic fish; juice; bottled pre-serves and sauces; plants and flowers; honey; and even bio wine from Lake Balaton. Tomatoes are normally best avoided until mid-summer, but even the May tomatoes here are quite tasty.

One vendor to check out is the Open Garden Foundation (Nyitott Kert Alapítvány), which runs a community-supported agriculture project based in Gödöllo (about twelve miles east of Budapest). While Budapest's other markets may be excellent places to shop, this is a true farmer's market, where growers and producers come with pride to sell their products. Vendors at the big markets often lack that individual touch that makes market-ing fun, but here they're friendly and usually eager to answer questions or offer samples. Sure, it's more expensive to shop here, but you get the satisfaction of directly supporting the farmers. Alas, it's only one morning a week.

XII. CSÖRSZ UTCA 18 ✦ TEL: 06-30/678-3772
WWW.BIOKULTURA.ORG ✦ OPEN SATURDAY 6:30AM *to* NOON
TRAM 61 (*to Csörsz utca*)

FEHÉRVÁRI ÚT PIAC

THIS FLUORESCENT-LIT BUILDING FITTED WITH A BIG GLASS WALL, GREY TILED FLOORS, CONCRETE BLOCKS, and bright white walls is fairly sterile for a market hall, but there's a fine selection to choose from. Just a block from the busy Móricz Zsigmond körtér transportation hub, the building was first put up in 1977 and restored in 2005. The atrium-like build-ing has an odd structure, with several graduated L-shaped levels. The basement holds a supermarket and some fruit and vegetable vendors. On the ground level there's a row of florists selling cut flowers, plants, and seedlings. The smoky top level is full of cheap food stands and the kind of drinking spots that do a brisk business in fröccs and beer early in the morning. Similar to the Central Market Hall, there's also a mushroom display on the top level (the mushroom-examination trailer is in the parking lot).

Most of the action is on the middle level. A good place to start is the dairy stand where you'll see a huge metal vat of fresh raw milk (*nyers tej*). Here there's also whey (*savó*), fresh sour cream, and butter. It's hard to pass up on the wonderful fresh cheeses—like *gomolya*, big rounds of mild goat cheese, sheep cheese, and curd cheese—which smell of fresh milk and cut grass. The fruit and vegetable selection is plentiful, and there are vendors selling small quantities of more uncommon things like potatoes the size of gumballs in the spring. It's a bit annoying that some of the smaller vendors (usually located around the edges) have no price labels, making it difficult to comparison shop. You can find excellent homemade products here occasionally, like home-smoked bacon and rosehip jams. The smell of vinegar and cabbage dominates in the corridors leading away from the main area, where the savanyúság (pickle) stalls are located. A *halbolt* sells live ponty (carp), *busa* (silver carp), and *kárász* (Crucian carp). Another shop sells nothing but dried fruit (*aszalt gyümölcs*), candies, and nuts. A near-Eastern shop towards the back has some basic condiments and a decent selection of olives, but little else. Butchers have the usual assortment of meat—everything from boxes full of chicken heads to beef tenderloin and goose liver.

XI. FEHÉRVÁRI ÚT 22 *or* KORÖSY JÓZSEF UTCA 7-9
TEL: 385-6563 ✦ OPEN MONDAY 6:30AM *to* 5PM, TUESDAY *through* FRIDAY 6:30AM *to* 6PM, SATURDAY 6:30AM *to* 1PM ✦ FLORISTS OPEN MONDAY *through* FRIDAY 6:30AM *to* 6PM, SATURDAY 6:30AM *to* 4PM, SUNDAY 7AM *to* 2PM ✦ TRAM 6, 18, 19, 41, 49, 61, 118, BUS 3, 7, 7A, 11, 27, 40, 53, 73, 153, 173 (*to Móricz Zsigmond körtér*)

ÁRPÁD FEJEDELEM ÚTJA PIAC

WALKING NORTH ON THE BUDA SIDE OF MARGIT HÍD, YOU'LL PASS THROUGH THE FRINGES OF THIS BUSTLING Saturday morning market before you reach its center. The open-air street market is in the parking lot in front of the Komjádi Béla *uszoda* (swimming pool) on Árpád fejedelem útja, with most of the action being on the two short blocks between Harcsa utca and Komjádi Béla utca. You'll spot it by the convoy of trucks, vans, and cars that set up shop, often selling their goods straight from the trunk. From afar, the hastily set-up market doesn't look promising, but tasty treasures can be found here. There are farm-fresh fruits and vegetables, dairy products, bread and baked goods, cheap clothes and shoes, questionable electronic equipment, cleaning supplies, Tupperware, baskets, and used junk. A man wearing a straw hat sometimes sets up a collection of handmade wool blankets, rugs, tablecloths, and painted ceramic plates and jugs from Transylvania. Someone sells fresh, still-dirty eggs from the back of a van. A battered old caravan proudly displays a dozen types of homemade cheeses, while folding tables hold displays of *kolbász* (sausages) and bags of cracklings. Farmers set up their produce on tables, in crates, in buckets, in the backs of cars, or wherever there's space. Tubs of pickled vegetables sit on long creaky wooden tables. Some vendors have just a few crates of a single product, like cherries, strawberries, or potatoes, elsewhere others have elaborate pyramids of fruits and vegetables. Plump old ladies wearing scarves on their heads and floral aprons around their waists sell little bunches of wildflowers, herbs, or bags of dried beans. "*Tessék drágám,*" they call out (Here you go, my dear) as they thrust the scraggly flowers towards you. The nice thing about this market is that all of the vendors sell their own home-grown produce and products, and it's considerably cheaper than other markets. There aren't any touristy bags of paprika or tins of goose liver here, and there aren't even any tourists. Come here to taste a little slice of Budapest—with some good food, a healthy dose of chaos, and some pushing, shoving, and haggling thrown in for good measure.

II. ÁRPÁD FEJEDELEM ÚTJA ✦ OPEN SATURDAY 6AM *to* 2PM
BUS 6, 60, 86 (*to Komjádi Béla uszoda*), TRAM 4, 6, 17 (*to Margit híd, Budai hídfo*), HÉV (*to Margit híd*)

SHOPPING TRANSLATOR

N OT SPEAKING HUNGARIAN IS NO REASON TO STAY AWAY FROM THE MARKETS. YOU DON'T NEED THE language to do your shopping, but these are some good words to know:

Mennyibe kerül? How much does it cost?

drága: expensive

olcsó: cheap

Kérek egy kiló... I would like one kilo...

darab (db.): piece

csomó (cs.): bunch

Pasztorözött? Is it pasteurized?

házi: homemade

aszalt gyümölcs: dried fruit

baromfi: poultry

bolt: shop

hal: fish

hús-hentesáru: butcher (also *hentes* or *húsbolt*)

savanyúság: pickled vegetables

tejbolt: dairy shop

vad: game

zöldség-gyümölcs: vegetables and fruit

öko or *bio:* organic

egy: one

két/ketto: two

három: three

négy: four

öt: five

hat: six

hét: seven

nyolc: eight

kilenc: nine

tíz: ten

CHAPTER 8:

SPECIALTY FOOD & WINE SHOPS

Az éhség a legjobb szakács.
Hunger is the best chef.

Jó bornak nem kell cégér.
Good wine needs no label.

—HUNGARIAN PROVERBS

THE PASTRY SHOP WAS SUCH THAT NOT A SINGLE TABLE LEG WAS HIDDEN FROM THE AUDIENCE, THEREFORE the proprietress could always follow what was happening under the tables.

—*The Last Cigar at the Arabs Szürke,* GYULA KRÚDY

SHOPPING

....

THE GENERAL HUNGARIAN WORD FOR SHOP IS *BOLT*. CONVENIENCE STORES CAN BE CALLED *ÉLELMISZER*, *csemege*, or *ABC*. See the Shopping Translator in Chapter 7 for more shopping terminology.

The fall of Communism brought the big European grocery store chains to the outskirts of Budapest. It's no longer necessary to shop at several different stores—one for meat, one for fruit, and one for bread—but many people still do their shopping that way, since shopping at the markets and the small specialty shops is a more personal experience. These days, shopping lists also might include a few ethnic food shops and maybe an organic shop. Compared to the 1990s, Budapest is now virtually a food lover's paradise. And there's a health food (*bio*) shop on practically every block (most of which only carry dry goods, grains, and teas). If you're used to shopping at America's gourmet emporiums, then Budapest's closet-sized shops will look downright quaint, with their sometimes non-existent window displays and small selections. Most markets have a few kiosks that sell cheap kitchen utensils, and it may be worth picking up a few things that are hard to find outside of Hungary (like a *szaggató*, which is a special tool used for making *galuska*).

GENERAL

....

ÁZSIA

Located in the lower level of the Central Market Hall, the crowded aisles at Ázsia attest that its Budapest's favorite international food specialty shop. It has the best selection of dried spices in town, a good variety of Asian ingredients, Mexican staples, oils, vinegars, pastas and grains, and harder-to-find vegetables and herbs. For bakers, there's a small but well-stocked baking supply section, with a wide selection of flour and decorations. They stock a few kitchen utensils like woks, mortars and pestles, and Chinese-style dishes. There's frozen seafood, lots of tea, and brands like Heinz and HP for homesick travelers.

IX. VÁMHÁZ KÖRÚT 1-3 (*Inside the Nagy Vásárcsarnok*)
TEL: 366-3452 ✦ CC ✦ OPEN MONDAY 10AM *to* 5PM

TUESDAY *through* FRIDAY 7AM *to* 6PM, SATURDAY 7AM *to* 2PM
M3 (*to Kálvin tér*), TRAM 2, 2A, 49 (*to Fovám tér*)

CULINARIS DELICATESSE

WHEN THE FIRST CULINARIS STORE OPENED ON HUNYADI TÉR IN NOVEMBER 2003, IT WAS LIKE a windfall for food-loving Budapesters who wanted to stock their pantries with non-Hungarian products, and for expats who missed their favorite brands from home. The tiny shop had a fantastic selection of sauces, condiments, chocolate, cheese, pasta, spices, herbs, bread, and more. In early 2006 Culinaris expanded, opening a significantly larger outlet in Buda where a sign lists more than eighty types of cheese, bread is baked daily, and the shelves are groaning with temptations and inspirations. They'll even make sandwiches for you from whatever they have in stock that day. There's a great wine and spirits selection and more chocolate than at most chocolate specialty stores. There's butter from France and Germany, sausage from Spain and Italy, paprika vinegar from Austria, a variety of olive oil, and a produce section that often stocks baby bananas, mangoes, chilis, kefir lime leaves, fresh herbs, ginseng, and galangal. The place also sells the simpler guilty pleasures that expats or travelers might miss from home like Doritos and Ben & Jerry's ice cream. Both shops have good cookbooks in English. Culinaris is constantly expanding its palette of purveyors and introducing new products from around the world. Culinaris also holds occasional discovery dinners at local restaurants and international cooking classes.

VI. HUNYADI TÉR 3 ✦ TEL: 341-7001 ✦ WWW.CULINARIS.HU
CC ✦ OPEN MONDAY NOON *to* 7PM, TUESDAY *through* SATURDAY
9AM *to* 7PM ✦ M1 (*to Vörösmarty utca*), TRAM 4, 6 (*to Oktogon*)

III. PERC UTCA 6-8 ✦ TEL: 345-0780 ✦ CC
OPEN MONDAY NOON *to* 8PM, TUESDAY *through* SATURDAY
9AM *to* 8PM ✦ BUS 86, 6 (*to Timár utca*)

DELIKÁT ÜZLET

THIS TINY GOURMET SHOP CARRIES FANTASTIC BREAD— AIRY CHALLAH BREAD, LONG BAGUETTES, WALNUT BREAD ideal for eating with cheese, and more—delivered every morning from a bakery in the countryside. There's also a decent selection of imported cheese and a small variety of different types of sliced ham. Regulars stand around sipping espresso, and pensioners sit outside in the courtyard chatting over their cappuccino and pastries.

XII. APOR VILMOS TÉR 9-11 (*Hegyvidék Bevásárlóközpont*)
TEL: 214-5073 ✦ CASH ONLY ✦ OPEN TUESDAY *through* FRIDAY
9AM *to* 6PM, SATURDAY 8AM *to* NOON ✦ TRAM 59, BUS 105, 112
(*to Apor Vilmos tér*)

EZERFUSZER

THERE AREN'T REALLY A THOUSAND SPICES AT THIS STORE, AS THE NAME IMPLIES. BUT WHILE PEST HAS several stores that have good selections of dried herbs and spices, specialty flours and dry goods, and international condiments and sauces, this is one of the few in Buda. Besides spices, the shop sells Asian sauces including several types of fish and oyster sauces; a good variety of green, yellow, and red curry sauces; a small selection of Mexican ingredients; and a few odd cans of Campbell's soup for homesick Americans. Get inspired by the appealing variety of oils (flax seed, walnut, sesame, mustard seed, and almond), pick up some fresh vegetables at the market, and throw together a salad. Ezerfuszer is behind the Mammut I mall, and conveniently located underneath the Fény utca piac.

II. LÖVÖHÁZ UTCA 12 ✦ TEL: 345-4170 ✦ CASH ONLY
OPEN MONDAY *through* THURSDAY 9AM *to* 6PM, FRIDAY 8AM *to*
6PM, SATURDAY 7:30AM *to* 2PM ✦ TRAM 4, 6 (*to Széna tér*), M2,
BUS 5, 21, 22, 28, 39, 49, 56, 90, 128, 156, TRAM 18, 56, 59, 61, 118
(*to Moszkva tér*)

NAGYMAMA GYÜMÖLCSKERTJE TEJ BOLT

HERE THERE ARE FRESH FRUITS AND VEGETABLES JUST AS GRANDMA (NAGYMAMA) WOULD HAVE LIKED. Bright murals of Hungarian village life cover the walls, and old kitchen utensils complete the picture. They also sell surprisingly good little mignon-type confections made with nuts, seeds, fruit, and chocolate that they call *reform konyha* ("health food") sweets. Adjacent (through a separate entrance) is the dairy and bread shop, which can barely hold two customers at any time, but is worth waiting for even if there's a line. Here you'll find one

HUNGARICUM

. . . .

W HAT DO UNICUM, PICK SALAMI, HEREND PORCE-
LAIN, AND HALAS LACE FROM KISKUNHALAS
have in common? They're each referred to as a
Hungaricum, a term used to describe something which is
supposed to be quintessentially Hungarian. If you spend
enough time talking to Hungarians, sooner or later someone will proudly describe something as a *Hungaricum*, as
if the term was known around the world. A *Hungaricum*
is a product so intricately linked with Hungarian culture,
tradition, and image that it can be produced nowhere
else. It's a loosely applied term—often overused—sometimes referring to products which don't bring Hungary
to mind at all. Some companies would like to make
Hungaricum into a more formal category and to limit
the amount of products, places, and services that use the
name. To this end, the Hungaricum Club was founded
in 2000 by Herend, Pick Szeged, Zwack Unicum, and
the Tokaj Kereskedoház with the goal of strengthening
both the country's image and the international reputation of their brands. The club plans on limiting new
members in order not to dilute the value of the term.
While it sounds like a noble goal, it may not prevent
every Zoli and Laci from calling his father's lethal
home-distilled *pálinka* a *Hungaricum*.

THE IRRESISTIBLE TÚRÓ RUDI

....

I F A BAR MADE OF CHOCOLATE-COVERED CURD CHEESE
DOESN'T SOUND APPEALING, THEN YOU HAVEN'T YET
tasted the irresistible *túró rudi*. It's one of the best-
known Hungarian brands, and probably the country's most
loved confection. Many sweet-toothed Hungarians living
abroad say this is what they miss most about Hungary.
Túró rudi translates roughly as "curd cheese stick" (it
sounds much better in Hungarian, as *rudi* is also the
diminutive form of the name Rudolf) and they're little
thirty-gram rounded bars made of a stick of slightly
sweetened, yet still tart, curd cheese dipped in dark chocolate (there's also an *óriás*, or large size). They now come in
different varieties with a strip of flavor like apricot, raspberry, hazelnut, or strawberry running through the center.
There are also *túró rudi* ice cream bars. Frankly, I'm a *túró
rudi* purist, and can't bring myself to stray from the perfect
original *natúr* variety. They're perishable and you'll find
them in the dairy case of practically every supermarket
and convenience store in Hungary. You won't miss them
with their distinctive red-spotted wrappers, and they're
even sold in their own dedicated vending machines at
schools. *Túró rudi* was born during the Communist era
after a group from the Hungarian dairy industry traveled
to the Soviet Union on a study tour and apparently came
up with the idea for this delicacy. It was only introduced in
Hungary in 1968, however, after twelve years of experi-
mentation. Perfection takes time, it seems. The delicious
and addictive *túró rudi* is hardly available anywhere outside of Hungary (although I have seen Russian versions of
it), making it very dangerous to fall in love with the things
only to leave the country and have your access cut off.

of the better selections of fresh bread in the city, fresh milk, homemade sour cream, lots of fresh cheese, *korözött*, homemade Mangalica sausage, and bins of marinated olives. The *pogácsa* and the strudel just might be the best in Budapest. Scrawled on the chalkboard outside is their long list of dairy products, and they also deliver. The shop is on the expensive side, but the quality makes it worth the price.

I. PAULER UTCA 5 ✦ TEL: 202-7393 ✦ CASH ONLY
OPEN MONDAY *through* FRIDAY 8AM *to* 7PM, SATURDAY 8AM *to* 1PM
TRAM 18, BUS 78 (*to Krisztina tér*), BUS 5 (*to Alagút utca*)

CHEESE

S & S SONKA ÉS SAJT KÜLÖNLEGESSÉGEK

SWISS AND GERMAN CHEESE AND HAM ARE THE SPECIALTY HERE—DOZENS OF VARIETIES OF YOUNG AND old cheeses sit in the refrigerator case, and a variety of ham and pork products behind the counter. There are also a few Italian and Austrian products. Although the selection is small, Swiss and German expats will surely appreciate the familiar cereal, chocolates, and sweets stocked here.

II. SZILÁGYI ERZSÉBET FASOR 121 (*Budagyöngye shopping center*)
TEL: 391-6583 ✦ CASH ONLY ✦ OPEN MONDAY *through* FRIDAY
9AM *to* 6PM, SATURDAY 8AM *to* 3PM
BUS 22, RED 56, TRAM 56 (*to Budagyöngye*)

SECTOR 69

SECTOR 69 IS ACTUALLY A CHEESE WHOLESALER, WHICH SELLS TO SHOPS AROUND THE COUNTRY. IT ALSO HAS its own shop at the Cédrus market where it sells imported Polish, Danish, French, Dutch, Slovak, and Italian cheese, as well as Hungarian cheese and other dairy products.

X. FEHÉR ÚT 1-3 (*Cédrus Piac*) ✦ TEL: 414-0921
WWW.SECTOR69.HU ✦ CASH ONLY ✦ OPEN MONDAY
through SATURDAY 7AM *to* 8PM ✦ M2 (*to Örs vezér tere*)

SZEGA CAMEMBERT SAJTSZAKÜZLET

THE CHEESE AVAILABLE IN MOST HUNGARIAN SUPER-MARKETS CAN LEAVE LOTS TO BE DESIRED, WHICH is why I go to the Szega cheese store when I want a pretty chunk of goat cheese decorated with a little leaf or a piece of French Camembert so ripe that it oozes when you cut into it. The knowledgeable staff can help you find the cheese you have in mind, and the selection is fantastic, although it is mostly French, and it isn't inexpensive. If you can't find the cheese you're craving here, then you probably won't find it anywhere else in Hungary. In addition, they have other products like goat milk, Italian pasta, and jams from England. There are three locations, but the Budagyöngye location listed here is the headquarters, where the selection is by far the best. The other shops are at the Fény utca piac and the Rózsakert shopping center.

II. SZILÁGYI ERZSÉBET FASOR 121 (*Budagyöngye shopping center*)
TEL: 200-6777 ✦ CASH ONLY ✦ OPEN MONDAY *through* FRIDAY
9AM *to* 7PM, SATURDAY 8AM *to* 3PM ✦ BUS 22, RED 56,
TRAM 56 (*to Budagyöngye*)

T. NAGY TAMÁS SAJTÜZLET

TAMÁS NAGY'S CHEESE SHOP NEAR DEÁK TÉR WAS ONE OF BUDAPEST'S FIRST QUALITY SPECIALTY FOOD shops, and a welcome destination for cheese lovers who wanted more than mild Hungarian cheese. Though the shop still does have an excellent selection of European cheese—and you can smell it before you open the door—it no longer has the monopoly on fine, stinky cheese in Budapest. Still, come here to

buy British Stilton or Cheddar, Swiss Appenzeller or Tête de Moine, or Italian Robiola or Taleggio. Without a doubt, the specialty here is French cheese. Try the Livarot, the P'tit Basque, the Comté, the Mimolette Jeune, or one of the dozens of others. There are disappointingly few Hungarian cheeses available, but there are good loaves of bread, like herb or walnut flavored, that are perfect for the cheese. The place stocks a few more gourmet-type items like ham, olives, Irish butter, and good chocolate. The staff is very knowledgeable about the cheese they sell. Tamás Nagy's cheeses can also be sampled down the street at the Gerlóczy Kávéház (see page 171), which he owns.

V. GERLÓCZY UTCA 3 ✦ TEL: 317-4268 ✦ WWW.SAJTKER.HU
CC ✦ OPEN MONDAY *through* FRIDAY 9AM *to* 6PM, SATURDAY
9AM *to* 1PM ✦ M1, M2, M3, TRAM 49 (*to Deák tér*)

MEAT

....

BAROMFI ÜZLET

A S THE NAME IMPLIES, ONLY POULTRY (BAROMFI) IS SOLD HERE. TRY ONE OF THE SMOKED DUCK BREASTS sitting on top of the counter. I like to thinly slice them, sauté for a few seconds, and drape the slices over a green salad.

II. SZILÁGYI ERZSÉBET FASOR 121 (*Budagyöngye shopping center*)
TEL: 275-0855 EXT. 220 ✦ CC ✦ OPEN MONDAY *through* FRIDAY
8AM *to* 7PM, SATURDAY 8AM *to* 3PM ✦ BUS 22, RED 56
TRAM 56 (*to Budagyöngye*)

CSIP-CSIP

D ESPITE BEING A BIT OUT OF THE WAY (FOR THOSE IN PEST, ANYWAY), THE SMALL BUT TOP-QUALITY MEAT selection at this little shop makes the trip worthwhile. There are tiny organic squab chickens, big cream-colored whole goose livers, Mangalica sausages, meaty ribs, whole pork tenderloins, and cherry-red steaks. You won't find the cheaper cuts of meat or the rough looking variety meats here, Csip-Csip only stocks the top cuts. There's also pasta, olive oil, canned truffles in oil, and a few other gourmet-type products that might go well with your meat.

XII. APOR VILMOS TÉR 9-11 (*Hegyvidék Bevásárlóközpont*)
TEL: 201-2901 ✦ CASH ONLY ✦ OPEN TUESDAY *through*
SATURDAY 8:30AM-6PM ✦ TRAM 59
BUS 105, 112 (*to Apor Vilmos tér*)

HÚS-BAROMFI ÜZLET

I N THE BASEMENT OF THE BUDAGYÖNGYE SHOPPING CEN-TER IS A CLUSTER OF FOOD SHOPS WHICH ARE GREAT for imported cheeses, as well as sausage and salami made from Mangalica pigs and Hungarian Grey cattle. The common cuts of meat sold at this butcher are complemented by several types of good Mangalica sausages, and packages of homemade dried egg pasta.

II. SZILÁGYI ERZSÉBET FASOR 121 (*Budagyöngye shopping center*)
TEL: 275-0877 ✦ CASH ONLY ✦ OPEN MONDAY *through*
FRIDAY 8AM-7PM, SATURDAY 8AM-3PM ✦ BUS 22, RED 56,
TRAM 56 (*to Budagyöngye*)

HÚS-DELICAT SZÜRKEMARHA MINTABOLT

I**T'S WORTH MAKING THE TREK TO THIS BUTCHER FOR ONE SINGLE PRODUCT: THE MONTE-NEVADO MANGALICA** ham, produced by a joint Hungarian-Spanish company which raises the pigs in Hungary and then sends the hams to Spain, where they're aged and cured for three years in the Serrano style. The finished products are sold in exclusive shops in Spain, and are rarely brought back to Hungary (this is the only place I've seen it sold here). The only problem was that the shopkeeper roughly chopped the ham into thick chunks, rather than slicing it into paper-thin slices like it's meant to be. They also have an excellent selection of Hungarian Grey cattle sausage and salami.

II. SZILÁGYI ERZSÉBET FASOR 121 (*Budagyöngye shopping center*)
TEL: 275-0877 ✦ CC ✦ OPEN MONDAY *through* FRIDAY 8AM-7PM
SATURDAY 8AM-3PM ✦ BUS 22, RED 56, TRAM 56 (*to Budagyöngye*)

PICK HÚS ÁRUHÁZ

D**ID YOU EVER WONDER WHAT HAPPENS TO THE ENDS OF SALAMIS AFTER THE REST HAS BEEN SLICED UP** and sold? At the Pick brand store they're all thrown together, vacuum packed, and sold at a discount. Pick, based in Szeged, has been making *szalámi*, *kolbász*, and the beloved winter salami (*téli szalámi*) since 1869. *Téli szalámi*—with its red, white, and green bands—might as well be called Hungary's national salami. Mild and distinctively spiced, it's smoked, then cured for three months. Pick also produces more than twenty other types of salami and dry sausage, and most of them are for sale at this shop next to the Parliament on Kossuth Lajos tér. The Városház utca location has a smaller selection, a more sullen staff, and is more like a little grocery store than a Pick brand outlet.

V. KOSSUTH LAJOS TÉR 9 ✦ TEL: 331-7783 ✦ WWW.PICK.HU
CASH ONLY ✦ OPEN MONDAY *through* THURSDAY
6AM *to* 7PM, FRIDAY 6AM *to* 6PM ✦ M2, TRAM 2 (*to Kossuth tér*)

V. VÁROSHÁZ UTCA 14 ✦ TEL: 337-8139 ✦ CASH ONLY

OPEN MONDAY *through* FRIDAY 7AM *to* 7PM

M1, M2, M3, TRAM 49 (*to Deák tér*)

SEZGIN TÖRÖK HÚS-HENTESÁRU

FOLLOW THE FRAGRANT SCENT OF EASTERN SPICES INTO THIS TURKISH-OWNED BUTCHER SHOP. ALONG WITH A small selection of standard meat cuts, you'll find pre-skewered kebabs and several types of Turkish sausages made from marinated minced meat and spices. There's also fresh pita bread and a selection of imported Turkish products, like cheese, hummus, olives, dips, and spices. It's a shame the shop doesn't sell any cooked kebabs to take away.

V. MAGYAR UTCA 52 ✦ TEL: 266-9900 ✦ CASH ONLY

OPEN MONDAY *through* FRIDAY 9AM *to* 6PM, SATURDAY 9AM *to* 2PM

M3 (*to Kálvin tér*)

SZALÁMI BOLT

OWNED BY CHEESE-GURU TAMÁS NAGY, THIS SMALL SHOP SITS PRACTICALLY NEXT TO NAGY'S GERLÓCZY Kávéház. The place opened at the very end of 2006 and specializes in cured ham and salami, mostly from Italy, but also from as far away as Virginia. There are also quite a few Hungarian-made salamis and sausages, such as the lesser-known *stifolder* (which is a paprika-flavored sausage made to a Swabian recipe). There are other epicurean treats here like olive oils, jars of black truffles, pâté, and lots of Normandy cider (which isn't commonly found in Hungary). The shop is simple and classy, with a shiny red meat slicer taking center stage and a side counter where you can order coffee and sandwiches.

V. VITKOVICS MIHÁLY UTCA 3-5 (*corner of Kammermayer tér*)

TEL: 06-20/443-5012 ✦ WWW.SAJTKER.HU ✦ CC

OPEN MONDAY *through* FRIDAY 9AM *to* 6PM, SATURDAY 9AM *to* 1PM

M1, M2, M3, TRAM 49 (*to Deák tér*)

SZEGA SONKASZAKÜZLET

A FEW METERS AWAY FROM THE CHEESE STORE AT BUDA-GYÖNGYE, THE SZEGA EMPIRE SELLS IMPORTED HAM on the bone like prosciutto, cured Iberian ham, Tuscan ham studded with red and green peppercorns, and Hungarian Mangalica at their separate ham shop. Pre-sliced mortadella, pancetta affumicata, and more are also available. While the meat is the main attraction here, there are also other imported specialty items like chocolate fondue mix, spice mixes, Italian pasta, and nearly a dozen types of gorgeous-looking pâté.

II. SZILÁGYI ERZSÉBET FASOR 121 (*Budagyöngye shopping center*)
TEL: 200-6777 ✦ CASH ONLY ✦ OPEN MONDAY *through* FRIDAY
9AM *to* 7PM, SATURDAY 8AM *to* 3PM ✦ BUS 22, RED 56,
TRAM 56 (*to Budagyöngye*)

See pages 186–187 for another list of butchers, who also serve meat cooked on the premises.

CHOCOLATE

AZTEK CHOXOLAT

A T BUDAPEST'S MOST CHOCOLATE-OBSESSED CAFÉ THE PROPRIETORS HAVE CREATED THEIR OWN DELICIOUSLY rich recipe for hot chocolate, which they offer in more than a dozen varieties (including one with chili pepper). The cozy café, which has just a few tables, also sells truffles, molded chocolates, bonbons, and big chunks of dark chocolate for those chocolate purists. Caffeine also comes in the form of coffee here, with more than twenty exotic varieties available.

V. KÁROLY KÖRÚT 22 - SEMMELWEIS UTCA 19 (*in the courtyard*)
TEL: 266-7113 ✦ OPEN MONDAY *through* FRIDAY 7AM *to* 7PM
SATURDAY 9AM *to* 2PM ✦ CASH ONLY ✦ M1, M2, M3, TRAM 49
(*to Astoria or Deák tér*)

BELGA PRALINE

THIS CHOCOLATIER, WHICH HAS OUTLETS IN A FEW BUDA-PEST MALLS, MAKES SEVENTY VARIETIES OF GOOD-quality artistic bonbons in flavors like lavender, caramel, Grand Marnier, pistachio, and strawberry. The colorful, creatively executed chocolates are made from Belgian chocolate, both white and dark. It also sells chocolate in bars, cookies, marzipan sweets, and sugar-free candies.

V. SZABADSÁGTÉR 7 (*Bankcenter*) ✦ TEL: 302-9038
WWW.BELGAPRALINE.HU ✦ CASH ONLY ✦ OPEN MONDAY
through FRIDAY 9:30AM *to* 5:30PM ✦ M2 (*to Kossuth tér*),
M3 (*to Arany János utca*)

II. LÖVOHÁZ UTCA 2-6 (*Mammut I shopping center*) ✦ TEL: 345-8161
CC ✦ OPEN MONDAY *through* SATURDAY 10AM *to* 9PM, SUNDAY
10AM *to* 6PM ✦ TRAM 4, 6 (*to Széna tér*), M2, BUS 5, 21, 22, 28, 39,
49, 56, 90, 128, 156, TRAM 18, 56, 59, 61, 118 (*to Moszkva tér*)

ÍZ-LELO CSOKOLÁDÉ ÉS BORSZAKÜZLET

CHOCOLATE AND WINE DON'T ALWAYS GO TOGETHER—EACH IS A RATHER PERFECT CREATION IN ITSELF—but this little shop specializes in both. There's chocolate from Domori, Côte d'Or, Valrhona, Amedei, Michel Cluizel, Hachez, and more than a dozen more. A better choice might be the refrigerator case full of stuffed handmade chocolates in all shades, including ones filled with Tokaji *aszú*. The wine selection isn't big, but the wines come from some of the country's best cellars including St. Andrea in Eger, János Árvay in Tokaj, and János Konyári in Balaton. There's a small selection of other fine foods—caviar, truffles, and canned goose and duck liver—to nibble on before devouring the chocolate.

V. ARANY JÁNOS UTCA 12 ✦ TEL: 269-0494 ✦ WWW.IZLELO.HU
CC ✦ OPEN MONDAY *through* FRIDAY 11AM *to* 7PM
M3 (*to Arany János utca*)

KOMKOM HOLLAND CSOKOLÁDÉZÓ

PROBABLY BUDAPEST'S MOST CREATIVE CHOCOLATIER, KOMKOM OFFERS LITTLE CHOCOLATES FILLED WITH flavors like wasabi, galangal, cardamom, star anise, Tokaji *aszú, törköly pálinka*, bay leaf, and spice combinations like Dutch and Moroccan. The pleasant chocolate café has three tables on the ground level—with a perfect view of the tempting chocolate case—and more upstairs in a gallery. As you'd expect, they do excellent hot chocolate as well. Several menu pages list flavor options—chili, ginger, rose, and banana, to name a few—and all can be prepared with either milk chocolate or white chocolate. The tea list is lengthy, but I can think of no good reason to order tea when you can have chocolate instead. There's a breakfast combination of cappuccino (or hot chocolate) plus a fresh baked muffin.

VII. WESSELÉNYI UTCA 19 ✦ TEL: 352-6026
WWW.KOMKOMCHOC.COM ✦ CASH ONLY ✦ OPEN MONDAY
through FRIDAY 8AM *to* 10PM, SATURDAY 10AM *to* 10PM, SUNDAY
10AM *to* 6PM ✦ M2 (*to Astoria or Blaha Lujza tér*)

WINE

....

AUREUM VINUM

AUREUM VINUM IS A SMALL WINERY IN MÁD, IN THE TOKAJ REGION, OWNED BY A GROUP OF FOREIGN INVESTORS. It's also a shop in Budapest where the winery sells its own high-quality wines, along with those of a few other select Tokaj wineries. The selection isn't big, and it isn't cheap, but the shop concentrates on quality wines (mostly sweet) from small Tokaj winemakers, some of which aren't easy to find outside of the Tokaj region. Located in a brick cellar, the shop can also organize tastings from its selection for groups (with at least a day's notice), and their winery in Tokaj can be visited with an appointment.

V. BELGRÁD RAKPART 19 ✦ TEL: 483-1456
WWW.AUREUMTOKAJI.HU ✦ CC ✦ OPEN MONDAY *through*
FRIDAY 10AM *to* 6PM, SATURDAY 10AM *to* 2PM
TRAM 2, 2A, 49 (*to Fovám tér*)

BELVÁROSI BORSZALON

LOCATED ON A ONE-BLOCK STREET, THIS FRIENDLY LITTLE SHOP STOCKS ONLY THE BEST WINES. WHILE THE SELECtion is small, every bottle here is a winner. The place follows the philosophy of the Guild of Pannonian Wines (*the Pannon*

Bormíves Céh), which aims to promote quality and ethics in winemaking. The shop only sells wines made by members of the guild—József Bock, Tamás Dúzsi, Ottó Légli, and István Szepsy to name a few—and it hosts occasional wine tastings lead by the guild's winemakers.

V. VÁRMEGYE UTCA 7 ✦ TEL: 317-9448 ✦ WWW.BORSZALON.HU
CC ✦ OPEN MONDAY *through* FRIDAY 10AM *to* 7PM, SATURDAY
10AM *to* 2PM ✦ M2, TRAM 49 (*to Astoria*), M3 (*to Ferenciek tere*)

BORÁSZOK BOLTJA

I F YOU DO MORE THAN DRINK WINE, THE "WINEMAKER'S STORE" CAN SUPPLY BOTH HOBBY WINEMAKERS AND professionals with the tools of the trade from equipment and machinery to bottles, labels, and corks. They have a few bottles of wine for sale, but head down the street to Karaffa Borszalüzlet (see page 315) for more of a selection.

III. BÉCSI ÚT 52 ✦ TEL: 240-6215 ✦ WWW.EUROTRADEKFT.HU
CASH ONLY ✦ OPEN MONDAY *through* FRIDAY 10AM *to* 5PM
TRAM 17, BUS 6, 29, 60, 65, 86 (*to Kolosy tér*)

BOR ÉS A TÁRSA BORSZAKÜZLET

D ESPITE BEING LOCATED IN THE BASEMENT OF THE MOM PARK MALL, THIS CLASSY PLACE DOESN'T FEEL like a typical mall shop. It's also more than just a wine shop. There's a deli, in addition to the fine selection of wine which comes mostly from Hungary, with a few bottles from Australia, Chile, France, and elsewhere. The fine cheese, cured ham, and marinated olives make an easy match for a bottle of wine, and there are bunches of herbs and fresh pasta if you're in the mood for cooking. All of the top Hungarian winemakers are represented, and so are many of the smaller lesser-known ones like Ede Herger in Villány, and Vay Pince in Tokaj.

XII. ALKOTÁS ÚT 53 (*MOM Park shopping center*) ✦ TEL: 202-0471
WWW.BORESATARSA.HU ✦ CC ✦ OPEN MONDAY *through*
SATURDAY 9AM *to* 8PM, SUNDAY 10AM *to* 6PM
TRAM 61 (*to Csörsz utca*)

BORKÁPOLNA

THERE'S NO WAY TO TELL HOW FAR THIS CELLAR WINE SHOP WINDS BACK UNTIL YOU GO INSIDE AND see it for yourself. The 800-square-meter shop claims to have an overwhelming 1,100 types of wine, mostly Hungarian, but one shelf stocks bottles from around the world. Other than this enormous underground stockpile, there are almost no options for buying decent wine in this neighborhood near Városliget. There are tastings here every Tuesday and Thursday at 7pm. The name of the shop means "wine chapel," and there actually is a chapel in the rear of the cellar (originally part of a church that was once located nearby and was destroyed during the Communist era).

VII. DAMJANICH UTCA 52 ✦ TEL: 343-5258
WWW.WINEFORYOU.HU ✦ CC ✦ OPEN MONDAY *through*
FRIDAY 9AM *to* 7PM, SATURDAY 10AM *to* 3PM
TROLLEY 70, 78 (*to Damjanich utca*)

BORTÁR BORSZAKÜZLET

THIS SMALL FAMILY-RUN WINE SHOP STOCKS VINTAGES MOSTLY FROM HUNGARY'S TOP WINEMAKERS, A FEW types of Italian wine, and some top-notch *pálinka*. Their selection of Tokaj, which includes a few hard-to-find bottles, might be their best feature.

XII. BÖSZÖRMÉNYI ÚT 34/A ✦ TEL: 355-1004 ✦ CC
OPEN MONDAY *through* FRIDAY 10AM *to* 6PM, SATURDAY
10AM *to* 1PM ✦ TRAM 59, BUS 102, 105, 112 (*to Apor Vilmos tér*)

BORTÁRSASÁG

THE "WINE SOCIETY" IS BUDAPEST'S PREMIER WINE SHOP, AND WAS REALLY THE FIRST GREAT WINE STORE to open in the city. It has expanded from its Batthyány utca flagship location to shops throughout the city and the country. The selection here is much smaller than you might expect from one of the country's best wine stores, but you can be assured that every bottle of it is good, as they carefully select each wine they carry. There is a small international selection, but the focus here is on Hungarian wine. The English-speaking staff never fails to make smart recommendations, and are able to thoroughly answer questions about Hungarian wine. The shop also sells wine books, glasses, accessories, and a house line of chocolate filled with Hungarian wine. There is a fine selection of *pálinka*, especially *törköly pálinka* made by winemakers. There are regular tastings hosted by winemakers in the shops, and winemaker dinners are organized at restaurants. All shops accept credit cards.

I. BATTHYÁNY UTCA 59 ✦ TEL: 212-2569
WWW.BORTARSASAG.HU ✦ OPEN MONDAY *through* FRIDAY
10AM *to* 8PM, SATURDAY 10AM *to* 6PM ✦ TRAM 4, 6 (*to Széna tér*),
M2, BUS 5, 21, 22, 28, 39, 49, 56, 90, 128, 156, TRAM 18, 56, 59, 61,
118 (*to Moszkva tér*)

II. GÁBOR ÁRON UTCA 74 (*Rózsakert shopping center*)
TEL: 200-5538 ✦ OPEN MONDAY *through* FRIDAY 10AM *to* 8PM
SATURDAY 10AM *to* 7PM, SUNDAY 10AM *to* 4PM
BUS 11 (*to Pusztaszeri út*), BUS 91 (*to Rózsakert*)

II. SZILÁGYI ERZSÉBET FASOR 121 (*Budagyöngye shopping center*)
TEL: 275-2194 ✦ OPEN MONDAY *through* FRIDAY 9:30AM *to* 7:30PM
SATURDAY 9AM *to* 3PM ✦ BUS 22, RED 56
TRAM 56 (*to Budagyöngye*)

V. SZENT ISTVÁN TÉR 3 ✦ TEL: 328-0341 ✦ OPEN MONDAY
through FRIDAY NOON-8PM, SATURDAY 10AM *to* 4PM
M3, BUS 15 (*to Arany János utca*)

IX. RÁDAY UTCA 7 ✦ TEL: 219-5647 ✦ OPEN MONDAY *through*
FRIDAY NOON *to* 8PM, SATURDAY 10AM *to* 3PM
M3, TRAM 4, 6 (*to Kálvin tér*)

BUDAI BORPATIKA

THIS BELOW-GROUND WINE SHOP NEAR THE BUDA END OF MARGIT BRIDGE HAS A SMALL SELECTION, BUT A loyal neighborhood clientele. The wine here comes from Villány, Sopron, Szekszárd, Badacsony, and Somló. About half is in standard bottles, while the rest comes in oversized 1.5-liter bottles. There's stuff from Bock and Polgár, as well as from other lesser-known and less reliable producers. Maybe the best buys here are the big bottles of Szeremley "house red" and "house white," especially if you're having a party.

II. TÖRÖK UTCA 10 ✦ TEL: 06-20/561-6017 ✦ CASH ONLY
OPEN TUESDAY-FRIDAY 10AM-6PM, SATURDAY 10AM-2PM
TRAM 4, 6 (*to Margit híd, Budai hídfo*)

BUDAI BORVÁR

WHILE THE SELECTION IS BETTER (AND MORE COMPETI-TIVELY PRICED) DOWN THE STREET AT BORTÁRSASÁG (see above), this place has the advantage of being open on Sundays. It is in a mall, after all, and it comes with all the atmosphere of a mall. But there is a decent selection of wine, from top producers throughout Hungary, as well as glasses and accessories. The other downside here is that there's barely room to squeeze through and look at the shelves when there are even just one or two other customers. Check the sale (*akció*) boxes on the floor for bargains.

II. LÖVOHÁZ UTCA 2-6 (*Mammut I shopping center*) ✦ TEL: 345-8098
WWW.BORARIUM.HU ✦ CC ✦ OPEN MONDAY *through*
SATURDAY 10AM *to* 9PM, SUNDAY 10AM *to* 6PM
TRAM 4, 6 (*to Széna tér*), M2, BUS 5, 21, 22, 28, 39, 49, 56, 90, 128,
156, TRAM 18, 56, 59, 61, 118 (*to Moszkva tér*)

DECANTER BORSZAKÜZLET

IT'S NOT HARD TO FIND A WINE SHOP THESE DAYS THAT STOCKS WINE MADE BY THE BIG NAMES IN HUNGARIAN wine, but it is more difficult to find one that has wine made by smaller up-and-coming Hungarian producers. In Hungary's case, those small producers might be extremely small, making just a few hundred bottles a year of what would be called boutique wine anywhere else. The nice thing about Decanter's selection is that even those who are already Hungarian wine aficionados will likely find something new and different here—the type of thing that's hard to find unless you know exactly what you're looking for. There's also, of course, wine from most of the big winemakers and a small selection of imported wine (including one from India). A selection of *pálinka* made by winemakers includes: Kopár marc *pálinka* (the Kopár cuvée is Attila Gere's flagship wine) and *pálinka* made by Tiffán and Légli. Hidden away on a residential street behind MOM Park, this classy little shop also holds regular wine tastings through its wine club.

XII. KLÉH ISTVÁN UTCA 3 ✦ TEL: 201-9029

WWW.WINEANDARTS.HU ✦ CC

OPEN MONDAY *through* FRIDAY 3 *to* 8PM, SATURDAY 10AM *to* 2PM

TRAM 61 (*to Csörsz utca*)

DIAMANT BORHÁZ

O WNED AND RUN BY THE FRIENDLY CSERES FAMILY, THIS WINE SHOP HAS A GOOD THOUGH SMALL SELECTION of Hungarian wine from most of the country's wine regions. Prices here are reasonable, and art or photography exhibitions are occasionally held in the empty upper level. I once saw a display of images from prolific photographer Tibor Dékány, who specializes in photographing winemakers and everything wine-related. There's also a musty, candle-lit, exposed brick cellar with a few rustic tables where wine tastings for groups of up to twenty can be held. The owners will help you choose the wine based on your preferences and provide a few snacks to munch on.

VI. JÓKAI UTCA 18 ✦ TEL: 269-1099

WWW.DIAMANTBORHAZ.HU ✦ CC ✦ OPEN MONDAY *through*
FRIDAY 10AM *to* 8PM ✦ M3, TRAM 4, 6 (*to Nyugati pályaudvar*)
M1 (*to Oktogon*)

DOMUS VINORUM BORHÁZ

A SHORT WALK FROM THE BASILICA, THIS SPACE IS IDEALLY SUITED TO BE A WINE SHOP. THE ENGLISH-speaking staff is helpful, and there's a decent selection. If you have a group of wine-loving friends, you can arrange for a tasting in the dimly lit basement, with its faded brick floors, vaulted ceilings, wrought-iron candle holders, and nooks stacked with bottles of wine.

V. BAJCSY-ZSILINSZKY ÚT 18 ✦ TEL: 225 8962

WWW.DOMUSVINORUM.HU ✦ CC ✦ OPEN MONDAY *through*

FRIDAY 10AM *to* 6PM, SATURDAY 10AM *to* 1PM

M3 (*Arany János utca*)

EL-HORDÓ BORBOLT

THIS MODEST WINE SHOP DOES MOST OF ITS BUSINESS IN *KANNÁS BOR*, BULK WINE THAT HASN'T BEEN BOTTLED and is sold by the liter. Most *kannás bor* is just labeled by the region and the variety, but this place also sells two pretty decent bulk wines by Szekszard winemaker Ferenc Takler—a red cuvée and an *olaszrizling* at bargain prices. They'll let you taste if you're not sure about buying your wine in a plastic bottle. If *kannás bor* isn't your thing, they also have a small but decent selection of bottled wine.

XIII. BALZAC UTCA 38 ✦ TEL: 349-4442 ✦ CASH ONLY

OPEN MONDAY *through* FRIDAY 10AM *to* 6PM, SATURDAY 9AM *to*

1PM ✦ BUS 15 (*Radnóti Miklós utca*), BUS 133 (*to Csanády utca*)

TROLLEY 76 (*to Hegedus Gyula or Csanády utca*), TROLLEY 79

(*to Radnóti Miklós utca*)

ELSO BUDAPESTI BORSZALON

THOUGH OFF THE BEATEN TRACK AND SMALL, THERE IS QUITE A GOOD SELECTION OF WINE FROM THE POLGÁR vineyard in Villány. It's also one of the handful of shops that stock Polgár's excellent sparkling wine, as well as the Polgár dessert wine called *Aranyhárs*.

XI. TAS VEZÉR UTCA 16 ✦ TEL: 209-4115

WWW.BUDAIBORSZALON.HU ✦ CC ✦ OPEN MONDAY *through*

SATURDAY 10AM *to* 8PM ✦ TRAM 18, 19, 49, 118, BUS 7, 12, 86, 73

(*to Kosztolányi Dezso tér*)

HEIDRICH PINCE MÁRKABOLT

THIS SMALL SHOP BEHIND THE CENTRAL MARKET HALL SELLS WINES MADE BY THE ENDRE HEIDRICH WINERY in Tokaj. Heidrich has vineyards in several parts of the Tokaj region and an old cellar in Sárospatak. It's a relatively new winery, which bottled its first dry wines in 2002, and began bottling sweet wines the following year. It now produces the full range of Tokaj wines, including uncommon types like *fordítás* and *máslás* and the prized Tokaji *aszú eszencia*.

IX. ERKEL UTCA 4 ✦ TEL: 476-0683 ✦ WWW.HEIDRICHPINCE.HU
CASH ONLY ✦ OPEN MONDAY *through* FRIDAY 10AM *to* 6PM
M3 (*to Kálvin tér*), TRAM 2, 2A, 49 (*to Fovám tér*).

HILLTOP BORBOLT

THE HILLTOP WINERY IN NESZMÉLY SELLS ITS OWN WIDE RANGE OF WINE (ALONG WITH A FEW BY OTHER winemakers) at this shop connected to its Budapest office in Újpest. The selection here ranges from Hilltop's wine in a box to its top *muzeális* wine. Even though Hilltop's wines are popular in Hungary, it's best known for being one of the biggest suppliers of inexpensive Hungarian wine to the UK. But it also produces more expensive bottles like Tokaji five *puttonyos aszú*. The Hilltop wines sold here—from the white pinot noir to the premium chardonnay—are sold at slightly lower prices than you'd find elsewhere, which would make the metro ride from the center worth your while if you're picking up a few bottles. (You'll see the window display from the street, but enter the shop through the alley.)

IV. ÁRPÁD ÚT 89 ✦ TEL: 272-0215 ✦ WWW.HILLTOP.HU
CASH ONLY ✦ OPEN MONDAY *through* FRIDAY 8AM *to* 4:30PM
M3 (*to Újpest-Központ*)

IN VINO VERITAS

ALONG WITH BORTÁRSASÁG, IN VINO VERITAS IS ONE OF THE COUNTRY'S MOST HIGH-PROFILE WINE DISTRIBUTORS/ shops. Wine lists at some of Hungary's best restaurants are

designed and supplied by In Vino Veritas. The classy shop with its dark wood furniture is a fantastic place to shop for wine. The staff is young and friendly, and always eager to make suggestions or answer questions. The mostly Hungarian selection is just the right size—big enough to tempt you with new things, but not so big as to overwhelm. You can be sure that there are no unworthy bottles here, and everything is fairly priced. Best of all, the shop organizes monthly (and free) meet-the-winemaker tastings at which they bring in Hungary's top vinters to answer questions and pour several types of wine. The tastings generally aren't publicized, as the shop usually fills up for them. You'll have to ask about upcoming tastings. Regular customers should consider joining the In Vino Veritas club, which gives a ten percent discount and access to special offers. The shop also organizes regular wine-tasting dinners. Rumo has it there are plans to transform the store next door into a wine café.

VII. DOHÁNY UTCA 58-62 ✦ TEL: 341-0646
WWW.BORKERESKEDES.HU ✦ CC ✦ OPEN MONDAY
through FRIDAY 9AM *to* 8PM, SATURDAY 10AM *to* 6PM
TRAM 4, 6 (*to Wesselényi utca*), TROLLEY 74 (*to Erzsébet körút*)

KARAFFA BORSZAKÜZLET

THERE'S HARDLY ROOM FOR MORE THAN ONE CUSTOMER IN THE TINY BRANCH OF THIS WINE STORE ON BÉCSI ÚT, and it can barely hold all of the wine stacked nearly ceiling high. Owner György Bauer, who speaks a little English, is eager to recommend something to complement your mood or your meal.

III. BÉCSI ÚT 57-61 ✦ TEL: 387-8083
WWW.KARAFFA.E-ADATBAZIS.HU ✦ CC
OPEN MONDAY *through* FRIDAY 10:30AM *to* 6:30PM, SATURDAY
10:30AM *to* 3:30PM ✦ TRAM 17, BUS 6, 29, 60, 65, 86 (*to Kolosy tér*)

XIII. TEVE UTCA 1/D/1 ✦ TEL: 688-1130 ✦ CASH ONLY
OPEN MONDAY *through* FRIDAY 10:30AM *to* 6:30PM
SATURDAY 10:30AM *to* 3:30PM ✦ M3 (*to Árpád híd*)

LA BOUTIQUE DES VINS

BEFORE OPENING WHAT HE CLAIMS TO BE BUDAPEST'S FIRST SPECIALTY WINE SHOP IN 1992, CSABA Malatinszky was a sommelier at Gundel. He's now one of Villány's top winemakers, so you can be sure that whatever you buy at his wine shop will be good. Obviously, Malatinszky's own wines, which are made under the label Malatinszky Kúria, are the stars of the shop. Here you can find his three wine lines: the top unfiltered Kúria reds, the Noblesse wines (the cabernoir blend—cabernet sauvignon and pinot noir—has been highly praised), and the reasonably priced Le Sommelier line. The shop also stocks other wines, particularly those from Tokaj and Bordeaux, where Malatinszky spent time learning the trade. If you're not looking for the shop, it can be easy to miss—the entrance is actually a few steps off of József Attila utca, facing a playground on Hild tér.

V. JÓZSEF ATTILA UTCA 12 ✦ TEL: 317-5919
WWW.MALATINSZKY.HU ✦ CC ✦ OPEN MONDAY *through*
FRIDAY 10AM *to* 6PM, SATURDAY 10AM *to* 3PM ✦ M1, M2, M3
TRAM 49 (*to Deák tér*), TRAM 2, 2A (*to Eötvös tér*)

MONARCHIA BORSZAKÜZLET

M ONARCHIA, WHICH IS RUN BY A FORMER TELECOM EXECUTIVE WITH A PASSION FOR HUNGARIAN WINE, has succeeded in exporting Hungarian wines to high-end New York restaurants and retailers. They bill the Hungarian wines in their portfolio as high-quality boutique wines. They know they will never compete with large-scale wine-producing countries like Spain and France, so they've turned Hungarian wine into a niche product. The company buys from a select list of producers including Ferenc Takler, Zoltán Demeter, and Nyakas Pince. The chief winemaker is Dr. Tamás Pók in Eger, who creates Monarchia's own label of wines which have easy-to-pronounce names like Evolution, Zen, and Rhapsody. Now known as Monarchia Matt International due to a merger, this shop mostly carries Monarchia's own wine, with smaller selections of other Hungarian wine and foreign wine. The shop usually hosts winemakers for tastings several times monthly, and often organizes wine-tasting dinners at restaurants.

IX. KINIZSI UTCA 30-36 ✦ TEL: 456-9800
WWW.MAGYARBOROK.HU, WWW.MONARCHIAMATT.COM
CC ✦ OPEN MONDAY *through* FRIDAY 10AM *to* 6PM, SATURDAY
NOON *to* 6PM ✦ M3 (*to Ferenc körút*)

PÁNTLIKA BORHÁZ

T HANKS TO THE UNWELCOMING BARS ON THE WINDOWS AND THE HOMELY WINDOW DRESSING, IT'S EASY TO PASS this place by—especially when In Vino Veritas is just a few blocks away. But it's worth checking Pántlika out for a few reasons. Firstly, the store is connected to the Pántlika Winery in the Dörgicse Valley of Balatonfelvidék, and most of their own (mainly white) wines are sold at the shop. Though the selection is small, there are also a few other gems mixed in, like three from the Polgár winery in Villány which aren't widely available: the Polgár Pearl Crémant Rosé 2004 and the Polgár Pearl Crémant Blanc 2004 (both sparkling wines), and the Villányi *Aranyhárs* (a late-harvest dessert wine).

VII. DOHÁNY UTCA 30/A ✦ TEL: 328-0115

WWW.PANTLIKAPINCESZET.HU ✦ CASH ONLY

OPEN MONDAY *through* FRIDAY 10AM *to* 6PM ✦ M2 (*to Astoria or Blaha Lujza tér*), TROLLEY 74 (*to Nyár utca or Nagydiófa utca*)

RADOVIN PESTHIDEGKÚTI BORKERESKEDÉS

D EEP IN THE BUDA HILLS, IN THE PESTHIDEGKÚT NEIGHBORHOOD, THIS WINE SHOP HAS A GREAT SELECTION of fine Hungarian wines, including some from small, lesser-known producers. Since it is located so far from the center of town (at least two bus rides), however, it's really not convenient unless you're already in the neighborhood. Wine tastings are occasionally held here.

II. HIDEGKÚTI ÚT 71 ✦ TEL: 274-6129 ✦ WWW.RADOVIN.HU

CC ✦ OPEN MONDAY *through* FRIDAY 11AM *to* 7PM, SATURDAY 9AM *to* 3PM ✦ BUS 57 (*to Széchenyi utca*), 64, 257 (*to Galóca utca*)

SZENT ISTVÁN BORSZAKÜZLET

S ZENT ISTVÁN BORSZAKÜZLET AND PARLAMENT BORSZAKÜZLET ARE OWNED BY THE SAME TEAM AND stock lots of pretty bottles, wine glasses, and accessories that would make welcome gifts for wine lovers. They even etch wine bottles for gifts or special occasions. But they also have a serious selection of wine, particularly ones from Tokaj. Owner István Vitkóczi, who is a winemaker himself, offers a supply of his own Tokaj wine. Stacks of brochures from wineries abound, and the staff can arrange wine tastings or tours if any of them appeal to you.

SZENT ISTVÁN BORSZAKÜZLET, XIII. POZSONYI ÚT 49

TEL: 339-6854 ✦ WWW.BROTHERBT.INI.HU ✦ CC

OPEN MONDAY *through* FRIDAY 10AM *to* 6PM, SATURDAY 10AM

to 2PM ✦ TROLLEY 76, 79 (*to Szent István park or Csanády utca*)

PARLAMENT BORSZAKÜZLET, V. FALK MIKSA UTCA 6

TEL: 269-1537 ✦ CC ✦ OPEN MONDAY *through* FRIDAY

11AM *to* 7PM, SATURDAY 10AM *to* 2PM ✦ M2 (*to Kossuth Lajos tér*)

SZÍVBOR

THIS TINY SHOP, WHICH TRANSLATES AS "HEART WINE" (AS IN HEALTHY FOR THE HEART), SPECIALIZES IN WINE from Montenegro. Montenegro makes big red wines and Szívbor is one of the few places where they're sold in Hungary. The wine comes from the Plantaze Estate, 2,300 hectares near the capital of Podgorica, and the shop stocks just half a dozen reds. The flagship wine, Vranac ("black stallion" in Serbian) is an award-winning blend of the vranac grape, the kratosija grape, and cabernet sauvignon. Szívbor opened at the end of 2006 and will likely expand its selection and opening hours.

II. KELETI KÁROLY UTCA 20/A ✦ TEL: 06-30/228-4322

WWW.SZIVBOR.HU ✦ CC ✦ OPEN MONDAY *and* WEDNESDAY 2

to 6PM ✦ TRAM 4, 6 (*to Széna tér or Mechwart liget*)

VÍG-VINO BORKIMÉRÉS

THE WORD UNPRETENTIOUS IS OFTEN USED TO DESCRIBE WINES, BUT IT WOULD BE AN UNDERSTATEMENT TO SAY that about this little family-run wine shop. Owner János Víg has been in this shop since 1980. Half of his selection is from top Hungarian winemakers like Bock, Malatinszky, Tiffán, and Vylyan. The other half is *kannás bor* (bulk wine) sold inexpensively in two-liter bottles. Regulars stream in and out carrying their own containers for *kannás bor*. Mr. Víg is exceedingly friendly, loves to engage his customers in conversation (even if they don't speak Hungarian), and may proudly pull out a pile of old newspaper clippings featuring his shop.

XIII. POZSONYI ÚT 5 ✦ TEL: 340-4915 ✦ CASH ONLY

OPEN MONDAY *through* FRIDAY 10AM *to* 6PM, SATURDAY

10AM *to* 1PM ✦ TRAM 4, 6, TROLLEY 76, 79 (*to Jászai Mari tér*)

VINCZE BÉLA BORSZERTÁR

A SHORT WALK FROM THE CENTRAL MARKET HALL, THIS TINY SHOP FOCUSES ON THE WINES OF TOP EGER winemaker Béla Vincze, which are primarily reds. Vincze was Hungary's winemaker of the year in 2005, and is known for making great *Egri Bikavér*. There are very few other wines available here, and the place holds occasional wine tastings.

V. KIRÁLYI PÁL UTCA 9 ✦ TEL: 266-8944 ✦ WWW.VINCZEBOR.HU
CC ✦ OPEN MONDAY *through* FRIDAY 11AM *to* 7PM, SATURDAY
10AM *to* 1PM ✦ M3, TRAM 49 (*to Kálvin tér*)

PÁLINKA

BÉKÉSI PÁLINKÁRIUM

T HE BÉKÉSI FAMILY MAKES *PÁLINKA* IN, COINCIDENTALLY, THE TOWN ALSO NAMED BÉKÉS NEAR THE ROMANIAN border. In recent years the distillery has been picking up more and more awards at Hungary's most prestigious *pálinka* competition, the Kisüsti Pálinkaverseny in Gyula. In the spring of 2006 the family expanded their business and opened a spacious brand store in Budapest which stocks nothing but their own pálinka. There are dozens of flavors to choose from, most highly esteemed according to the judges are: *cigánymeggy* (cherry), *kökény* (sloe), *szilva* (plum), *ágyas Vilmoskörte* (Poire William, with whole fruit in the bottle), *birs* (quince), *kajszi ágyas* (apricot, with whole fruit in the bottle), *barack* (apricot), *bodza* (elderberry). If you're in the area of Békés, the distillery is open for visits and tastings.

VII. NAGYDIÓFA UTCA 7 ✦ TEL: 786-0172
WWW.PALINKARIUM.HU ✦ CC ✦ OPEN MONDAY *through* FRIDAY
10AM *to* 7PM, SATURDAY 10AM *to* 1PM ✦ M2 (*to Astoria or Blaha Lujza tér*), TROLLEY 74 (*to Nyár utca or Nagydiófa utca*)

MESTER PÁLINKÁK

J ÓZSEF JÓNÁS, A JOURNALIST AND AUTHOR, WROTE A BOOK DETAILING THE NEW *PÁLINKA* CULTURE AND THE increase in quality distilleries throughout Hungary, and opened this shop at the end of 2006. The book, *Mesterpálinkák pálinkamesterek*, is only available in Hungarian, but the shop is for everyone. Jónás is, obviously, thoroughly knowledgeable on the subject of *pálinka* (but doesn't speak much English). That's alright, because everything in his shop is good, and it is probably the best selection of fine *pálinka* you'll find in one place. An added plus is that it's located just a few steps from the basilica. There's a list of translations into English for the exotic *pálinka* flavors he stocks, many of which are from small producers who make exceptionally small quantities. There's a big variety of *törköly pálinka*, some of which comes in charming 150-ml bottles (perfect for sampling to find your favorite). This innovative shop is part of this new Hungarian *pálinka* culture, and it is also the first in Budapest to hold regular *pálinka* tastings (every odd Tuesday 4 to 6:30pm at the time this book went to press).

V. ZRÍNYI UTCA 18 ✦ TEL: 301-8736

WWW.MESTERPALINKAK.HU ✦ CC ✦ OPEN MONDAY *through*

FRIDAY 10AM *to* 6PM, SATURDAY 10AM *to* 2PM

M3 (*to Arany János utca*)

PANYOLAI PÁLINKÁK

THIS *PÁLINKA* DISTILLERY, WHICH IS BASED IN PANYOLA NOT FAR FROM THE UKRAINIAN BORDER, OPENED ITS own-brand shop near Váci utca in early 2006. The distillery is located in Szabolcs-Szatmár-Bereg county, a region known for its top-notch plum orchards and the *pálinka* and jam that's made from them. But Panyolai makes more than *szilva pálinka*. Its handmade *pálinka* selection includes wild strawberry, redcurrant, apple, apricot, poire William, and more unusual flavors like blackcurrant and black cherry. Additionally, there is a nice selection of "Fruit de Bereg" all-natural fruit jam, which is also made in Szabolcs-Szatmár-Bereg county. The mainstay is the plum *lekvár* which is made the traditional way (without any added sugar), said to use 500 grams of plums to make 100 grams of jam.

V. IRÁNI UTCA 10 ✦ TEL: 06-30/383-67-63 ✦ WWW.PANYOLAI.HU

CASH ONLY ✦ OPEN MONDAY *through* FRIDAY 10AM *to* 6PM

SATURDAY 10AM *to* 2PM ✦ M3, BUS 5, 7, 15, 78 (*to Ferenciek tere*)

A MAGYAR PÁLINKA HÁZA

"THE HUNGARIAN HOUSE OF PÁLINKA" WAS THE FIRST DEDICATED *PÁLINKA* SHOP TO OPEN IN BUDAPEST, before the trend for small-batch high-quality *pálinka* really started. The staff here is generally knowledgeable and can guide you through the shelves to that perfect bottle. The place is owned by the Szicsek Distillery (based in Szolnok), but it carries hundreds of types of *pálinka* from more than two dozen producers, in all price ranges.

VIII. RÁKÓCZI ÚT 17 ✦ TEL: 338-4219

WWW.MAGYARPALINKAHAZA.HU ✦ CC ✦ OPEN MONDAY

through SATURDAY 9AM *to* 7PM ✦ M2 (*to Astoria or Blaha Lujza tér*)

BUS 7, 78 (*to Kazinczy utca*)

ZSINDELYES PÁLINKA

JUST BECAUSE THIS TINY SHOP SELLS NOTHING BUT *PÁLINKA* MADE BY THE ZSINDELYES DISTILLERY DOESN'T mean there's not much to choose from. The distillery has been making *pálinka* since 1984 in Érpatak and there are several lines to choose from. Its line of fruit *pálinka* (in tall black bottles) comes in twelve different varieties. The *Vadócok* line comes in clear 200-ml bottles in flavors like sloe, dogberry, and wild cherry. There's also mixed-fruit *pálinka*, *marc pálinka* aged in wooden barrels, and bright red cherry *pálinka*. The company has picked up awards from *pálinka* competitions around the country over the years for its high-end *pálinka*. The shop opened in 2006, and the distillery can also be visited.

V. RÉGIPOSTA UTCA 14 ✦ TEL: (42) 290-325
WWW.ZSINDELYES.HU ✦ CC ✦ OPEN MONDAY *through* FRIDAY
10AM *to* 6PM, SATURDAY 9AM *to* 1PM ✦ M1, M2, M3 (*to Deák tér*)
TRAM 2 (*to Március 15 tér*), BUS 15 (*to Szervita tér or Petofi tér*)

RÉZÜSTI PÁLINKA

THIS CLASSY LITTLE SHOP IS DOING ITS BEST TO CHANGE THE IMAGE OF *PÁLINKA* FROM A CRUDE GUT-BURNING drink to something fine enough to sip after dinner. The shop sells a variety of top brands like Brill, Zsindelyes, Csalló, Panyolai Szilvórium, and Tarpa. The English-speaking staff can help explain the intricacies of the language of the bottle labels and the different varieties. Several types of fruit jams and dried fruit from the *pálinka*-producing regions are sold here. *Pálinka* drinking accessories like glasses in several shapes, carafes, and bottle stoppers are also available.

V. MOLNÁR UTCA 3 ✦ TEL: 06-20/487-8668 ✦ WWW.REZUSTI.HU
CC ✦ OPEN MONDAY *through* SATURDAY 10AM *to* 6PM
M3, BUS 5, 7, 15, 78 (*to Ferenciek tere*)

JAM

ELSO HAZAI LEKVÁRIUM

IF YOU'VE EVER HAD HOMEMADE HUNGARIAN *LEKVÁR* (JAM), YOU'LL HAVE A HARD TIME GOING BACK TO THE mass-produced supermarket varieties. I've gotten used to the homemade type, and have found that most commercially available jams suffer from a few problems: they're overly sweet, they have an unpleasant gelatinous texture, and the essence and the flavor of the fruit is lost. Not so with the jams sold here. They have that perfect home-style texture (and no preservatives), which makes them more like sauce compared to commercially made jam. Jam is an important ingredient in Hungarian dessert recipes, and this store sells almost nothing else. For help with the dozens of flavors available, there's a list of the Hungarian names translated into several languages.

VII. DOHÁNY UTCA 39 ✦ TEL: 321-6543 ✦ WWW.VILLA.HU
OPEN MONDAY *through* FRIDAY 10AM *to* 6PM, SATURDAY 10AM *to* 2PM ✦ M2, TRAM 4, 6 (*to Blaha Lujza tér*)
TROLLEY 74 (*to Nyár utca of Nagy Diófa utca*)

HONEY BREAD

MÉZES KUCKÓ

N O HUNGARIAN FAIR OR FESTIVAL WOULD BE COMPLETE WITHOUT THE BRIGHTLY COLORED PIECES OF HONEY bread (*mézeskalács*) shaped like hearts, animals, houses, and anything else that a baker fancies. They're topped with red and white sugar glazes, decorated with names, and sometimes pieces of mirrored glass. The fancy ones are meant to be souvenirs or tokens of love, while the simpler ones are meant to be eaten. *Mézeskalács* looks like gingerbread, and even tastes a bit similar, but it's made by kneading together flour, sugar, and eggs with lots of honey. This shop—which is the size of a milk carton—specializes in honey cake, from fancy decorated ones, to different types of flavored cookies. There are also several types of honey available.

XIII. JÁSZAI MARI TÉR 4/B ✦ TEL: 06-20/344-5778 ✦ CASH ONLY
OPEN MONDAY *through* FRIDAY 10AM-6PM, SATURDAY 9AM *to* 1PM
TRAM 4, 6, TROLLEY 76, 79 (*to Jászai Mari tér*)

STRUDEL (RÉTES)

FANTASTIC STRUDEL CAN ALSO BE FOUND AT THE CENTRAL MARKET HALL AND AT THE NAGYMAMA GYÜMÖLCSKERTJE/ TEJ BOLT (SEE PAGE 294).

BATTHYÁNY RÉTESBOLT

THIS SHOP OFFERS A CHANGING VARIETY OF FRESHLY MADE *RÉTES*, POSTED ON A SIGN OUTSIDE.

I. BATTHYÁNY UTCA 14 ✦ TEL: 06-30/970-1795 ✦ CASH ONLY
OPEN MONDAY *through* FRIDAY 8:30AM *to* 5PM ✦ M2, TRAM 19,
HÉV, BUS 11, 39, 60, 86 (*to Batthyány tér*)

RÉTESBOLT

THE DELICIOUSLY THIN-CRUSTED STRUDEL HERE IS SOME OF THE BEST IN BUDAPEST; THE ONLY DOWNSIDE IS THE long metro ride from central Pest. The strudel comes in the full variety of usual flavors—curd cheese, cherry, poppy seed, cabbage, and more—and it's baked in the ovens behind the counter. Try to get it while it's hot and eat it standing up at one of the tables.

IV. LEBSTÜCK MÁRIA UTCA 40 ✦ TEL: 06-20/886-0155 ✦ CASH ONLY
OPEN MONDAY *through* FRIDAY 8AM *to* 6PM, SATURDAY 8AM *to* 2PM
M3 (*to Újpest-Központ*)

RÉTESBOLT

THOUGH IT'S NOT CENTRAL, THIS HOLE-IN-THE-WALL STRU-DEL SHOP HAS LOTS OF ADMIRERS WHO COME FOR ITS variety of house-made strudel and *pogácsa*.

XIII. LEHEL UTCA 38 ✦ CASH ONLY ✦ OPEN MONDAY *through*
FRIDAY 10AM *to* 7PM ✦ TRAM 1 (*to Lehel utca*), 14 (*to Róbert Károly körút*)

RÉTES FAJTÁK

THERE'S NOTHING BUT SLICES OF *RÉTES* AT THIS BRIGHT SHOP ON THE CORNER OF BUDAFOKI ÚT AND KRUSPÉR utca. Served warm, the crispy paper-thin shells are filled with curd cheese, cherries, poppy seeds, apples, apricots, plums, walnuts, or savory cabbage. There are even sugar-free varieties.

XI. BUDAFOKI ÚT 16 ✦ TEL: 361-9326 ✦ CASH ONLY
OPEN MONDAY *through* FRIDAY 10AM *to* 7PM, SATURDAY
10AM *to* 4PM ✦ TRAM 18, 19, 49 (*to Bertalan Lajos utca*)

ROZI NÉNI FRISS HÁZI RÉTESE

THE STRUDEL HERE COMES IN MYRIAD FLAVORS, LISTED ON THE DOOR. NOT ALL ARE ALWAYS AVAILABLE, BUT they sometimes have the very delicious combination of curd cheese and dill.

VIII. NÉPSZÍNHÁZ UTCA 42 ✦ CASH ONLY ✦ OPEN MONDAY
through FRIDAY 10AM *to* 6PM ✦ TRAM 28, 37 (*to Teleki László tér*)

ROZI NÉNI RÉTES BOLT

THIS STRUDEL SHOP IS NOTHING MORE THAN A WINDOW AND A FEW TRAYS OF WARM *RÉTES*. IN THE SAME COMPLEX as the Déli train station (around the corner on a small street), there's no better place to pick up a snack while you're waiting for a train.

I. KOSCIUSZKÓ TÁDÉ UTCA 1 ✦ CASH ONLY ✦ OPEN MONDAY
through FRIDAY 9AM *to* 5PM ✦ M2, TRAM 59, 61 (*to Déli pályaudvar*)

KOSHER

KOVÁRI DEZSO MÉSZÁROS

THIS KOSHER BUTCHER SEEMS TO KEEP ERRATIC OPENING HOURS. SINCE THE KOSHER WINE CELLAR ON Klauzál tér closed in early 2007, the butcher also stocks kosher wine from Eger by the bottle and by the liter.

VII. DOB UTCA 35 ✦ TEL: 342-1639 ✦ CASH ONLY
OPEN TUESDAY *through* THURSDAY 8AM *to* 3:30PM, FRIDAY
8AM *to* 11AM ✦ M1, M2, M3, TRAM 49 (*to Deák tér*), M2 (*to Astoria*)

KÓSER BOLT

THERE'S NOT MUCH TO CHOOSE FROM IN THIS SMALL KOSHER SHOP RUN BY THE ROTHSCHILD SUPERmarket chain, mostly just canned foods, dry goods, packaged snacks, and baby food, but there is a refrigerator stocked with meat and several types of kosher wine and *pálinka*.

VII. DOB UTCA 12 ✦ TEL: 267-5691 ✦ WWW.ROTHSCHILD.HU
CC ✦ OPEN MONDAY *through* THURSDAY 10AM *to* 7PM, FRIDAY
10AM *to* 3PM ✦ M1, M2, M3, TRAM 49 (*to Deák tér*), M2 (*to Astoria*)

ROTHSCHILD

WHILE NOT ENTIRELY KOSHER, OTHER BRANCHES OF THE ROTHSCHILD SUPERMARKET CHAIN HAVE DEDICATED kosher aisles with Hungarian, French, and Israeli wine, *pálinka*, French chocolate bars, coffee, pasta, cereal, and more.

XIII. SZENT ISTVÁN KÖRÚT 4 ✦ TEL: 320-4147 ✦ CC
OPEN MONDAY *through* FRIDAY 6AM *to* 9PM, SATURDAY 7AM *to*
7PM, SUNDAY 9AM-6PM ✦ TRAM 4, 6, TROLLEY 76, 79
(*to Jászai Mari tér*)

V. ARANY JÁNOS UTCA 27-29 ✦ TEL: 332-3345 ✦ CC
OPEN MONDAY *through* FRIDAY 7AM *to* 8PM, SATURDAY
7AM *to* 4PM, SUNDAY 9AM *to* 2PM ✦ M3 (*to Arany János utca*)

HEALTH FOOD & ORGANIC

BIO ABC

THE MOST ESTABLISHED AND BEST-STOCKED *BIO* SHOP IN CENTRAL BUDAPEST, THIS PLACE IS WHERE EVERY organic/health food eater ends up at some point. There is a decent selection of fruits, vegetables, and herbs; cheese, eggs, and dairy; meats; and frozen food. The shop also has freshly baked goods and snacks, as well as freshly squeezed juice and even a mineral water tap. In addition to the plentiful selection of cereals, seeds, and flours, there's also a fine selection of oils and vinegars, jams, and other condiments. Check the bulletin boards for information on new products, *bio* events, classes, and news.

V. MÚZEUM KÖRÚT 19 ✦ TEL: 317-3043 ✦ CC ✦ OPEN MONDAY
through FRIDAY 10AM *to* 7PM, SATURDAY 10AM *to* 2PM
M2, TRAM 49 (*to Astoria*), *or* M3 (*to Kálvin tér*)

BIOHÁLÓ

MOST HEALTH FOOD STORES IN BUDAPEST ARE NO BIGGER THAN WALK-IN CLOSETS AND HAVE frustratingly small selections of the same merchandise. While Biohálló is also modestly sized, it carries a nicer than average selection of fresh products like goat cheese, meat, tofu burgers, and baked goods. Its specialty is sprouts—wheat, radish, broccoli, onion, and red cabbage to name a few—and it usually has more than a dozen types at any given time. Like wine cuvées, there are even sprout mixtures with whimsical names. There's a nice selection of toiletries made from natural ingredients, and some interesting condiments. The family who runs the place speaks English, and are knowledgeable about the products they sell.

II. FRANKEL LEÓ ÚT 36 ✦ TEL: 326-1189
WWW.BIOHALO.COM ✦ CASH ONLY ✦ OPEN MONDAY
through FRIDAY 9AM *to* 6PM, SATURDAY 9AM *to* 1PM
TRAM 4, 6 (*to Margit híd, Budai hídfo*)

BIORITMUS CSARNOK

COMPARED TO THE PLETHORA OF TINY *BIO BOLTOK* (BIO SHOPS) IN BUDAPEST, THIS ONE IS PRACTICALLY A warehouse. The place stocks a bigger variety of both Hungarian and imported organic products than you'll find anywhere else. The aisles are wide and spacious, just like a supermarket. There's a big variety of flours, grains, cereals, and seeds, as well as sauces, condiments, juice, tea, and coffee. There's also a small dairy aisle with cheese, milk, and a few meat products. For fresh fruits and vegetables head next door to the Gödör Biokertészet. Though there are a few types of bakery products here, there's a better selection next door at the Ambrózia Pékség-Cukrászat.

X. FEHÉR ÚT 1-3 (*Cédrus Piac*) ✦ TEL: 431-6873 ✦ CC
OPEN MONDAY *through* SATURDAY 7AM *to* 8PM
M2 (*to Örs vezér tere*)

TÁPLÁLÉK ALLERGIA CENTRUM

O N THE UPPER LEVEL OF THE LEHEL TÉR CSARNOK, THIS SHOP SPECIALIZES IN GLUTEN-FREE PRODUCTS.

XIII. LEHEL TÉR ✦ TEL: 288-6833 ✦ CASH ONLY
OPEN MONDAY *through* FRIDAY 7:30AM *to* 6PM, SATURDAY 7:30 *to*
1PM ✦ M3, TRAM 1, 14, BUS 4, 15, 133, TROLLEY 76, 79 (*to Lehel tér*)

BOOKS

GASZTROFILM KÖNYVKERESKEDÉS

T HIS PLACE IS A COOKBOOK LOVER'S DREAM. IT'S A LITTLE *ANTIKVÁRIUM* (USED BOOK STORE) DEVOTED TO books about gastronomy and film (it's located next to an art house cinema). Best of all, a good chunk of the cookbooks are in English, and I've snatched up some great finds here like several out-of-print Hungarian cookbooks in English. There are old café menus hanging on the walls, and a display case with old silver-ware, ashtrays, and restaurant memorabilia.

XIII. HOLLÁN ERNO UTCA 9 ✦ TEL: 789-2401 ✦ CASH ONLY
OPEN MONDAY *through* FRIDAY 10AM *to* 6PM ✦ TRAM 4, 6,
TROLLEY 76, 79 (*to Jászai Mari tér*)

KITCHEN SUPPLIES

MESTER PORTA

D ESPITE THE FACT THAT HUNGARY IS WELL KNOWN FOR ITS HANDMADE FOLK ARTS, AUTHENTIC ITEMS ARE hard to find in Budapest. While it may be tempting to stock up on red-and-white woven tablecloths and colorfully painted plates on Váci utca or on the upper level of the Nagyvásárcsarnok, don't do it. The stuff may be pretty, but most likely it's not the

real thing. Instead, head to this shop connected with the Association of Hungarian Folk Artists. Everything here is a genuine handmade piece by a Hungarian craftsman, and there are items that come from all parts of the country. If you ask, the staff will even tell you about the artists. You'll find textiles, clothing, painted eggs, baskets, jewelry, furniture, lace, folk instruments, candles, pottery, and wood carvings here. While the dishes may look too pretty to actually use, they're affordable enough to be your everyday coffee cups and cereal bowls. The music selection holds a fantastic selection of Hungarian folk music, jazz, and world music.

I. CORVIN TÉR 7 ✦ TEL: 486-1189 ✦ WWW.MESTERPORTA.HU

CASH ONLY ✦ OPEN MONDAY *through* FRIDAY 10AM *to* 6PM

M2, BUS 60 (*to Batthyány tér*), BUS 86 (*to Corvin tér*)

TRAM 19 (*to Halász utca*)

BOGRÁCS:

THE ULTIMATE KITCHEN UTENSIL

....

THE WAYS OF THE WANDERING MAGYARS HAVE LEFT MARKS ON HUNGARY'S COOKING STYLE which have lasted to this day. "Our nomadic ancestors have also handed down kitchen utensils," wrote Károly Gundel in the *Hungarian Cookery Book*. "One of which is still with us after more than a thousand years." It's thought that the *bogrács* was used by the ancient Magyars, hung from their saddles as they migrated from the Asian steppe to what is now Hungary. The *bogrács* essentially gave them freedom and independence, since they could bring their "kitchen" with them anywhere. "This is a copper cauldron with a rounded bottom and handle so that it could be hung over an open fire," continued Gundel. Today, the *bogrács* is still used, and you can see the contraptions—which are hung over a fire on a chain hung from the middle of a three-legged stand—displayed in kitchen supply stores throughout the country. Heading to the country (or just to the backyard), gathering wood, building a fire, and setting up the *bogrács* to cook a *gulyás* or *halászlé* is a much-anticipated activity. But today, the *bogrács* is made more frequently from steel than copper or cast iron, and it's the romance of it that attracts enthusiastic cooks, rather than the necessity of cooking food with minimal effort. A bowl of *bográcsgulyás* is the ultimate one-pot meal, but is it worth the effort? Hungarians will tell you yes. Just like when you grill steaks over charcoal, the flavor from the smoke gets into the soup simmering away in the uncovered kettle, giving it an unmistakably outdoorsy, homemade taste. Setting up the *bogrács* and making a primitive stew is a cherished ritual, no matter how long it takes to get the fire started.

CHAPTER 9:

....

ESSENTIALS

BUDAPEST ORIENTATION

....

THE FIRST THING TO KNOW IS THAT THE DANUBE (*DUNA*) SPLITS THE CITY, WITH BUDA ON THE WEST side and Pest on the east. Óbuda (Old Buda) is also on the west side of the Danube, north of Buda. With the exception of the pretty Fo tér—where there are a few good restaurants, a baroque town hall, and a museum inside a former palace—it's hard to tell that Óbuda is the oldest section of the city. It's now mostly tall blocky Communist-era apartment buildings, but it was once a haunt for Hungary's nineteenth-century writers and artists, who were also big eaters and drinkers. Getting oriented isn't as easy as knowing which side is Buda and which is Pest. Budapest spreads over twenty-three districts (a district is called a *kerület*, abbreviated as *ker*), and has a population of about 1.7 million people. To get the most of a visit here you'll need to get familiar with the public transportation system, or you'll have to love walking.

Buda is mostly hilly. Castle Hill, which rises up from the narrow streets in the Víziváros neighborhood, is one of the city's most visible landmarks and is also a UNESCO world heritage site. Nearby, Moszkva tér is an important transportation hub, and the more attractive Batthyány tér sits directly opposite Parliament across the Danube. Gellért Hill is to the south, and is topped by the citadel and the Communist-era Liberation Monument. Leafy neighborhoods like Rózsadomb and Svábhegy are full of pricey villas, walking trails, bicycle trails, and viewing towers. There are also caves, conservation areas, and a few museums scattered around the Buda hills. The main method of transportation into the hills is the bus, but there's also a chairlift (*libego*) in János hegy, a children's railway (*gyermekvasút*), and a funicular railway (*fogaskereku vasút*), which are nice alternative transportation options when exploring the area.

One of Budapest's best features is its stunningly beautiful Danube panorama (also a UNESCO world heritage site) and the bridges (*híd* in Hungarian) linking Buda and Pest. Margit Sziget is an island park that sits between Margit híd and Árpád híd, and is a haven for bicyclers, joggers, swimmers, walkers, and anyone else who wants to see green and breathe fresh air.

Compared to Buda, Pest is flat. The enormous Parliament building dominates this side of the Danube. The downtown business and banking centers are south of Parliament. Deák tér is considered to be the heart of the city, and is where all three metro lines meet. Tree-lined Andrássy út—which is lined with stately old villas and mansions—runs from Deák Ferenc tér (usually just referred to as Deák tér, and in this book too) to Hosök tere (Heroes Square), and is yet another world heritage site. This is where the 300-acre Városliget (City Park) begins and where the Museum of Fine Arts and the Palace of Arts are located.

Most of the major sights in Pest (except for those around Városliget) are between the Danube and a ring road (actually, it's more like an arc road) called the *Nagykörút*, which changes names every ten blocks or so. Starting in Pest on a south-to-north progression, it's called Ferenc körút, József körút, Erzsébet körút, Teréz körút, and then Szent István körút. On the Buda side of the Margit híd, the ring road turns into Margit körút and ends with Krisztina körút and the Déli (Southern) railway station. Also in Pest, there's a smaller *körút* (called the *Kiskörút*) that contains the inner city, or the Belváros. This small ring road begins at Deák tér and ends at Szabadság híd (Freedom Bridge). Its name also changes from Vámház körút (where the Central Market is located) to Múzeum körút and then to Károly körút. To make things more confusing, there's a third *körút* that runs farther out in Pest (past the City Park).

Budapest is divided into twenty-three numbered districts. Districts 1 to 3, 11, 12, and 22 are on the Buda side (Castle Hill is in the first district). Districts 4 to 10, 13 to 21, and 23 are on the Pest side. The city center is the fifth district, and districts 6 to 9 encircle it to the east and southeast. Budapest's neighborhoods also have names. Some of the central ones include Erzsébetváros ("Elizabeth town," district 7), Józsefváros ("Joseph town," district 8), Víziváros ("Water town," parts of districts 1 and 2), Belváros ("downtown," district 5), and Ferencváros ("Frank town," district 9). In this book, most of the restaurants, cafés, and shops are in these central districts, although there are also a few destinations in the outer districts.

ADDRESSES AND MAPS

For the sake of simplicity, I have not used postal codes in the addresses in this book. Postal codes are also used to indicate the district number of an address: the two digits in the middle of the four-digit code identify the district (eg. the postal code 1015 indicates a building in district one). In this book, the district number is in Roman numerals before the street address (e.g. VII. Dohány utca 37 means that this address is in the seventh district). When you're looking for a specific address it's important to know the district number since a street of the same name may be located in several districts. In Hungary, like much of the rest of Europe, floors are not numbered from the ground floor, which is the *földszint*. The floor above it is considered the first floor (I. *emelet*). Some buildings have a mezzanine level, called a *félemelet*, between the ground floor and the first floor.

The free maps that you can pick up at tourist offices and hotels aren't great, but should be suitable for short visits. For more serious explorations of the city, save the frustration and buy a more thorough map. Cartographia's *Budapest Atlasz*, a spiral bound map with a street index, is the one I prefer. Maps can be bought at bookstores such as the Libri chain found throughout the city and the specialized map shop, Földgömb és Térképbolt [VI. Bajcsy-Zsilinszky út 37; Tel: 312-6001; Open Monday through Friday 9am to 5pm; M3 (to Arany János utca)].

PUBLIC TRANSPORTATION

Budapest is a city made for walking. But the extensive public transportation system goes nearly everywhere and is preferable to navigating the city's congested streets by car. The network consists of three metro lines (*metró*), trams (*villamos*), buses (*busz*), trolley buses (*trolibusz*), suburban trains (*HÉV*), and the cogwheel railway (*fogaskereku vasút*) that heads up Széchenyi Hill. There are also riverboats that go from central Budapest to Rómaifürdo. Check www.bkv.hu for detailed fare, route, and schedule information.

The ticketing system can be confusing to newcomers. Purchasing a daily or weekly pass is highly recommended, as using the ticket system can be a hassle to the uninitiated. Tickets must be purchased before boarding and then validated by punching them in the ticket machines onboard buses, metros, trams, and trolleys. Ticket inspectors regularly check tickets, and they are notoriously unfriendly to anyone without valid tickets. Tickets can be bought at cashiers (*pénztár*) at metro stations, from some newspaper kiosks, and from automated ticket machines (which are few and only sometimes work). The same tickets are valid for all forms of public transport within the city limits, but if you transfer (including changing metro lines), you'll have to validate a new ticket. There are a few different types of tickets available for use on the metro: the more expensive metro transfer tickets can be used when transferring metro lines, and cheaper section tickets can be used when you're just traveling three stops. Books of tickets, day passes, multiple-day passes, weekly passes, and monthly passes are also sold at a discount.

The quick and efficient metro is the preferred way to travel in Budapest. There are currently three lines, with a fourth on the way. The yellow line (M1), also called the *földalatti*, is the oldest metro line in continental Europe. It was built in 1896 to celebrate the country's millennium and runs from Vörösmarty tér, along Andrássy út, through Városliget, and ends at Mexikói út. The red line (M2) runs east-west from the Déli railway station in Buda, stopping at the transportation hubs of Moszkva tér and Batthyány tér, to the Keleti station in Pest and then farther east, ending up at Örs Vezér tere. The blue line (M3) runs from northern Pest to southern Pest, and passes the Nyugati railway station. All three lines intersect at Deák tér. The metro runs daily from 4:30am to around 11:30pm.

Trams are the next best way to get around since they don't get stuck in traffic like the buses and trolleys. The most useful tram routes to know are the numbers 4 and 6, which circle most of the inner city along the *Nagykörút*. Some routes are also good for sightseeing and for getting oriented. The number 2 route runs along the Pest side of the Danube from Margit híd, next to the Parliament building, and then past the National Theater and Concert Hall. Ride this tram for a good view of the Danube and Castle Hill. On the Buda side, trams 19 and 41 run from Batthyány tér to Gellért tér (and beyond), with nice views of the Pest side and Gellért Hill above. Most routes operate daily from 4:30am to around midnight.

Buses and trolley buses cover all of the territory that metros and trams don't. They can be slow and crowded, even when it's not rush hour. The *várbusz* ("castle bus") leaves from the top of Moszkva tér, and runs the length of the Buda Castle, before returning to Moszkva tér (it has a picture of the castle instead of a number). The night bus network is an option for night owls (night buses are numbered in the 900s).

The suburban railway (*HÉV*) has faster trains that run on four lines, with just a few stops in the city. The most useful *HÉV* line for travelers (and the only one mentioned in this book) runs from Batthyány tér to the center of Szentendre, passing Aquincum in Óbuda and Rómaifürdo along the way. The same tickets can be used on the *HÉV* until the Budapest city limits (which is the Békásmegyer stop), and from there the fare is based on which stop you get off at. Buy a ticket before you board at the ticket office if it's open, or from the ticket inspectors onboard the train.

The BKV operates a boat service (*hajójárat*) which docks at Boráros tér, Petofi tér, Batthyány tér, Margitsziget, and Jászai Mari tér and goes to Rómaifürdo. Boats run between late April and early September. From Batthyány tér to Rómaifürdo, the trip is approximately an hour and a half.

Mahart Passnave runs another boat service (Tel: 484-4013; www.mahartpassnave.hu), which begins at Budapest's Vigadó tér (and also stops at Batthyány tér) and ends in Szentendre. The trip is about an hour and a half.

TAXIS

The best way to get a taxi is to order one by phone from one of the city's reliable companies. In fact, it isn't easy to hail a taxi on the street, and it's not recommended as there are lots of dodgy taxi drivers out there. Most companies have English-speaking operators and there are also designated taxi stands scattered throughout the city. Never enter an unofficial or unmarked taxi, and always make sure the meter is running. Reliable companies include: City Taxi (Tel: 211-1111), FoTaxi (Tel: 222-2222), BudaTaxi (Tel: 233-3333), and Tele5Taxi (555-5555).

Hungary has a zero-alcohol-tolerance policy and if you've been drinking and don't want to leave your car behind there are several drink and drive taxi services (*soforsegély*) in Budapest. They will send a driver to pick you up—usually it takes at least thirty minutes to arrive—and then drive you home in your own car. Some companies include: After (Tel: 06-30/600-6003), Alkony (Tel: 06-20/940-4040), Argo (Tel: 06-20/961-4675), AWD (Tel: 06-30/331-3310), Ittasofor (Tel: 06-30/250-2000), Korona (Tel: 06-20/999-3978), Soforsegély (Tel: 06-20/950-5505), and Vénusz noi soforszolgálat (Tel: 06-20/253-9899).

WEB SITES

www.chew.hu
An English-language food blog which chronicles the eating and dining scene

www.pestiside.hu
An irreverent take on Hungary, plus the latest on Budapest's bar scene

www.budapestinfo.hu
Budapest Tourism Office

www.gotohungary.com
The Hungarian National Tourist Office in New York

www.caboodle.hu
Hungary's best English-language web portal

www.budapesttimes.hu
A weekly English-language general interest newspaper)

www.budapestsun.com
A weekly English-language general interest newspaper

www.bbj.hu
A weekly English-language business newspaper

www.spasbudapest.com
Budapest's bathhouses

www.biokultura.org
The Hungarian Bioculture Federation offers a list of organic farms that can be visited

www.bkv.hu
Budapest's public transportation routes, schedules, and prices

HUNGARIAN NAMES

In Hungary the last name precedes the first name. In this book, however, I have used the English form of given names first and family names second. Many Hungarian streets are named after historical figures, and I have left these as they are written in Hungarian to avoid confusion.

TRAVELING WITH CHILDREN

Hungarians love children. But getting around with a stroller can be challenging. Most metro stations don't have elevators, and some don't even have escalators. It's also necessary to cross many busy streets using underpasses, which means lots of going up and down stairs. Waiters and restaurateurs are usually accommodating towards children, but often the facilities are not very child-friendly (there are few dedicated changing areas, and not all restaurants have highchairs). The main problem is that places can be quite smoky. Even if there's a separate non-smoking section (and there isn't always), it's often just a table or two right next to the smoking section.

DISABLED ACCESS

Access to much of Budapest can be difficult for physically disabled travelers. Even the sidewalks can be too narrow (or filled with parked cars) for wheelchairs to pass. More museums and public places have become accessible recently, but public transport can still be a problem and few restaurants have special accommodation for the disabled. Some bus lines and a few metro stations have been configured for the disabled, but it's necessary to arrange service in advance. Call the National Federation of Disabled Persons (MEOSZ) (III. San Marco utca 76; Tel: 388–5529; www.meosz.hu) for information on accessibility. The website has a continuously updated list of hotel options, sightseeing possibilities, and public transport accessibility.

FURTHER READING

I F YOU BROWSE BUDAPEST'S MANY *ANTIKVÁRIUMS* (USED BOOKSTORES), WITH LUCK YOU MIGHT COME ACROSS an out-of-print English-language Hungarian cookbook. Otherwise, these are some of the best readily available cookbooks, reference books, and travel books about Hungary:

THE CUISINE OF HUNGARY
by George Lang

Half food history and half recipes, this is the most thorough history of Hungarian cuisine that exists. It's highly recommended for anyone interested in Hungarian history or its cuisine.

NOBODY KNOWS THE TRUFFLES I'VE SEEN
by George Lang

Lang's life story reads like a fast-paced screenplay. In 1946 he escaped from a labor camp and learned that his parents died in Auschwitz. He arrived in New York with dreams of becoming a concert violinist. Instead, he became the man who "creates restaurants."

CULINARIA HUNGARY
by Anikó Gergely

As part of a series of photo-heavy world food books, this comprehensive guide to Hungarian food covers nearly every aspect of Hungarian cuisine from onions and lard to descriptions of holiday celebrations and regional specialties. There are also recipes.

THE HUNGARIAN COOKBOOK
by Susan Derecskey

One of the few good Hungarian cookbooks available on the American market, the recipes in this collection are reliable, but slightly Americanized.

THE WINES OF HUNGARY
by Alex Liddell

This is the most thorough book in English about the Hungarian wine industry's current condition, but it's already slightly outdated. The first part covers Hungary's winemaking history and the second profiles individual wineries. It's a bit technical for the casual reader.

KAFFEEHAUS
by Rick Rodgers

*Rodgers—an award-winning chef and author—*collected these recipes from pastry chefs at coffeehouses in Budapest, Prague, and Vienna. The recipes are labor intensive and complex, but the results are worth the effort. It's illustrated with gorgeous photos.

A TASTE OF THE PAST: THE DAILY LIFE AND COOKING OF A NINETEENTH-CENTURY HUNGARIAN JEWISH HOMEMAKER
by Andras Koerner

Koerner tells the story of his great-grandmother and the tastes of old Hungarian Jewish traditions through her recipes. Part cookbook and part history, he recreates the details of her life and has reconstructed the recipes for modern tastes.

BUDAPEST: A CRITICAL GUIDE
by András Török

The most personal guidebook to Budapest, this guide is full of fascinating facts about the city, as well as Hungarian culture and history. This book reveals the real soul of Budapest with Török as your personal guide.

HUNGARY: THE BRADT TRAVEL GUIDE
by Adrian Phillips and Jo Scotchmer

This comprehensive and reliable guidebook about Hungary is one of the best there is. There's also a pocket-sized guide to Budapest by the same authors.

TOKAJ: THE WINE OF FREEDOM
by Laszló Alkonyi

This book, full of gorgeous photographs, is one of the best there is on the complex topic of Tokaj wine. It's easy to find at most of Budapest's bigger bookstores.

BUDAPEST 1900: A HISTORICAL PORTRAIT OF A CITY AND ITS CULTURE
by John Lukacs

Lukacs, a Budapest native and renowned historian, tells the story of the city's golden age around the year 1900, when it was one of the great metropolitan centers in the world.

CULINARY DICTIONARY

....

HUNGARIAN IS A NOTORIOUSLY DIFFICULT LANGUAGE FOR FOREIGNERS TO LEARN, AND Hungarians are usually thrilled—and often amused—when they make an effort to communicate in Magyar. Waiters in Budapest should speak enough English to get you through your meal, but some may not be able to satisfactorily explain the contents or preparation of menu items. Bad menu translations are common, and it can be useful to compare the English and Hungarian versions if you are really concerned about getting what you want. Even for Hungarians, the dozens of different styles of meat preparations on menus can be confusing. When you get out into the countryside—particularly in regions like Villány where the second language is German and few speak English—these glossaries will be more helpful. But even in Budapest, being able to decipher a few words of Hungarian will be particularly helpful at the smaller restaurants, at the markets, and in the shops.

But it's not easy for beginners (and even for people who have been living in Hungary for years). Unlike most European languages, which are Indo-European, Hungarian is a Finno-Ugric language, which is related only to Finnish, Estonian, and a few languages spoken by small groups of people around the Urals. One thing that takes some getting used to in Hungarian is that words can have several different endings tacked onto them (for example, *étterem* means restaurant and *étteremben* means "in the restaurant"). In English we have prepositions, and in Hungary there are postpositions, and there are many, many endings that can be connected to words. Plural nouns are formed with the "k" ending (added straight to the vowel if it's a vowel ending, or added to an additional vowel if it's a consonant ending). So, remember that the Hungarian words in these glossaries can have suffixes and postpositions added to them. Of course, that's just a simplified explanation, but it should get you started. The lists include the dishes and words you're most likely to see on Hungarian restaurant menus, the items you might see in the grocery stores and markets, and the terms you should know when exploring

Hungarian wine. Also included are some more uncommon words that might make your eating and drinking better. The terminology here does not include words that appear elsewhere in the book. See the separate meat translator (page 44), wine translator (page 68), *pálinka* translator (page 87), restaurant translator (page 110), coffee translator (page 192), and shopping translator (page 289) for more.

HUNGARIAN-ENGLISH

....

A

....

abált szalonna: boiled bacon topped with a mixture of garlic, paprika, and salt; served cold

áfonya: blueberry/bilberry; also called *feketeáfonya*

akácméz: acacia honey

alkalmi sörkülönlegesség: seasonal beer

alkoholmentes: alcohol-free

alma: apple

almapaprika: pale yellow "apple peppers," named for their round shape, and often pickled; they are usually hot

almás pite: "apple pie": two layers of crust stuffed with an apple (and often walnut) filling, served in squares rather than wedges

ánizs: anise, aniseed

apró: small

apróhús: bite-sized chunks of meat

aprópecsenye: small pieces of roasted or fried meat

aranygaluska: "golden dumplings": yeast-raised buns, brushed with melted butter, flavored with apricot jam and ground walnuts, and sprinkled with vanilla sugar

árpa: barley

articsóka: artichoke

ásványi anyaggal dúsított víz: water with added minerals

ásványvíz: mineral water

aszalt gyümölcs: dried fruit

aszalt szilva: prune

ászok: lager

avokádó: avocado

B

....

bab: bean

babgulyás: bean gulyás

bácsi: "uncle"; also a polite way to refer to an older man

Bajai halászlé: this version of *halászlé* has pasta added

bajor kenyér: Bavarian bread

bak: bock beer; a strong lager which can be dark, amber, or pale in color

Bakonyi módra: meat served with mushrooms in sour-cream sauce

banán: banana

bár: bar; also *kocsma* (pub), *sörözo* (beer hall), *borozó* (grungy wine bar), or *kert*

barack: apricot; also *sárgabarack* or *kajszibarack*

báránycomb: leg of lamb

barna sör: dark German-style beer

baromfi: poultry; also called *szárnyas*

bazsalikom: basil

Bécsi szelet: Wiener schnitzel; traditionally breaded and fried veal cutlet, but in Hungary often made with pork

bejgli: long roulade cakes stuffed with walnuts or poppy seeds

bélszín: beef tenderloin or fillet

Bikavér: Bull's Blood cuvée

birkagulyás: *gulyás* made from mutton

birs: quince; often called *birsalma* when shaped like an apple, or *birskörte* when shaped like a pear

birsalmasajt: a paste-like block of quince jelly

bivaly: buffalo

bodza: elderberry

bodzavirág: elderflower

bogrács: cauldron

bográcsgulyás: *gulyás* cooked in a cauldron

bor: wine

borjúborda: veal cutlet

borjúmirigy: veal sweetbreads

borkorcsolya: snacks to eat with wine

borkóstoló: wine tasting

borleves: wine soup

borozó: wine bar

borravaló: tip

bors: black pepper; also *fekete bors*

borsikafu: savory, an herb related to the mint family; also called *csombor*

borsó: peas

borvidék: wine region

Brassói aprópecsenye: cubes of sautéed pork and deep-fried potatoes seasoned with paprika, garlic, and marjoram

bryndza: sheep-milk cheese, similar to *juhtúró*; *bryndza* sold in Hungary is usually Slovakian

buborékos: carbonated water

budai zöld: indigenous white grape variety

Budapest bélszin: steak with sauce made of chopped peppers, peas, tomatoes, mushrooms, and chunks of goose liver

büfé: snack counter

burgonya: potato; also called *krumpli*

burgonyafánk: potato croquette; also called *burgonyakrokett*

burgonyakrokett: potato croquette; also called *burgonyafánk*

busa: silver carp

búza: wheat

búzasör: wheat beer

búzakenyér: wholewheat bread

C

cékla: beetroot

cérnametélt: thin, delicate pasta; commonly added to soups

chilipaprika: chili pepper

cigánymeggy: the collective name for any type of small cherries

cigánypecsenye: "gypsy roast" is a pork cutlet sprinkled with paprika and topped with raw crushed garlic and a chunk of roasted *szalonna*

cirfandli: acclimatized white grape variety

citrom: lemon

cl: centiliter, the metric unit of measurement used for liquor, also used for measuring tasting portions of wine; equivalent to about one third of an ounce

Classicus: second highest category in the Villány appellation

cordon bleu: breaded and fried chicken breast that has been stuffed with ham and cheese;

didn't originate in Hungary but is widely served here

Csabai kolbász: named for the town of Békéscsaba, these are firm, dried, smoked pork sausages seasoned with hot and sweet paprika, and a little garlic

Csáky rostélyos: created in honor of Sándor Csáky, a famous twentieth-century chef, this dish is a sirloin steak cooked with *lecsó*, eggs, and sour cream

családi: family-run

csalamádé: mixed pickled vegetables, most often cabbage, peppers, carrots, and onions

csapolt: on tap

csapolt sör: draft beer

csapvíz: tap water

csárda: restaurant; traditionally a folksy roadside inn

csarnok: (market) hall; see also *ivócsarnok*

császármorzsa: "emperor's crumbs": a homemade cake-like dessert broken up into crumbs, flavored with raisins and served with jam

császárszalonna: boneless, meaty back bacon slab that can be fried or boiled

csemege: small grocery store, also can be called *élelmiszer* or *ABC;* also means delicacy

csemegepaprika: "gourmet" paprika: slightly coarse and can be hot or mild

csemegeuborka: pickle

cseresznye: cherry

cseresznyepaprika: cherry pepper or chili pepper (sometimes called Hungarian cherry pepper abroad); they're small, round, and usually very hot

cserszegi fuszeres: a white hybrid grape variety

csészében: in a cup

csiga: snail; also refers to a round pastry with a swirl of poppy seeds or walnuts

csigatészta: tiny pieces of pasta, curled with a stick into the shape of snails

csiperke: mushrooms from the champignon family, like button mushroom and white mushroom

csipetke: tiny pinched pasta made from flour and eggs

csipkebogyó: rosehip

csípős: hot (as in spicy)

csípős kolbász: hot sausage seasoned with hot paprika

csíra: sprouts (various kinds)

csirkecomb: chicken leg

csokoládé: chocolate

csombor: savory, an herb related to the mint family; also called *borsikafu*

csomó: bunch

csont: bone

csontleves: "bone soup": broth made from bones and root vegetables, can also be used as stock

csontvelo: bone marrow; also called *velo* or *velocsont*

csuka: pike

csülök: knuckle

csülök pékné módra: pork knuckle cooked "baker's-wife" style, roasted with chunks of potatoes and onions

csúsztatott palacsinta: "slipped pancakes": a dessert made from layers of *palacsinta* alternated with jam or chocolate and topped with meringue

cukkini: zucchini

cukor: sugar

cukordinnye: honeydew melon or cantaloupe; also called *mézdinnye*

cukorka: candy

cukormentes: sugar-free

cukrász: confectioner

cukrászda: pastry shop

cukros: sweetened

cuvée: blend

D

dara: semolina/grits; also called *gríz*

darab: piece

daragaluska: semolina dumplings

derelye: stuffed pasta similar to ravioli, often filled with jam or curd cheese

desszert: dessert

dinnye: melon

dió: walnut, or nut

diós bejgli: walnut roulade cake

diós kenyér: walnut bread

diós kifli: walnut-filled crescent rolls

diótorta: walnut cake

disznósajt: head cheese/brawn

disznótor: pig killing

disznótoros: pork charcuterie; "pig killing" platter is a platter piled with pork sausages, bacon, and other types of pork

dl: deciliter, the metric measurement used for measuring wine and other beverages; equivalent to 3.4 ounces or 100 ml

Dobos torta: layered vanilla sponge cake smothered with chocolate butter cream, and topped with thin wedges of caramel-glazed cake

Dorozsmai módra: carp larded with smoked bacon cooked in sauce made from sautéed onions, mushrooms, peppers, tomatoes, paprika, and sour cream; served with irregularly shaped flat pasta

Dunai halászlé: fisherman's soup in which the ingredients aren't puréed

dzsem: jam; also called *lekvár* or *íz*

E

ecet: vinegar

ecetes: pickled

ecetes paprika: pickled green pepper

édes: sweet

Édes Anna: mild paprika paste

édeskömény: fennel

édesnemes paprika: "noble" paprika: mainly used to flavor stews and meats

édesség: dessert

egész: whole

egres: gooseberry

élelmiszer: small grocery store, also can be called *csemege* or *ABC*

előételek: appetizers

Ementáli sajt: Emmenthal cheese

endívia: endive

eper: strawberry

eperlevél: square-shaped pasta with ribbed edges

erdei: wild; also *vad*

erdei meggy: wild cherry

erdei vadmálna: wild raspberry

Erdélyi szalonna: bacon slab cut from the belly, with a thin layer of meat

erőleves: "strength soup": consommé usually served with quail eggs or matzo balls

erős: hot (as in spicy)

Erős Pista: hot paprika paste; usually added to soups

Esterházy rostélyos: named for Prince Pál Antal Esterházy, who was known as an extravagant gourmet, this steak is served with a puréed sauce made from carrots, parsnips, white wine, cream, and capers

Esterházy torta: layers of walnut cake, spread with

layers of whipped cream, and topped with a thin layer of fondant

étcsokoládé: dark chocolate

ételbár: snack bar

étkezde: simple restaurant, usually open only for lunch; also called *kifozde*

étterem: restaurant

ezerjó: indigenous white grape variety

F

fácán: pheasant

facéliaméz: phacelia honey

fagylalt: ice cream

fahéj: cinnamon

fánk: doughnut

farok: tail

farsang: carnival season

farsangi fánk: carnival doughnuts

fatányér: "wooden plate" with a mix of grilled and fried meats; could also be called *Erdélyi fatányéros* (Transylvanian mixed grill)

fehér: white

fehérbor: white wine

fehérbors: white pepper

fehércsokoládé: white chocolate

fehér eper: mulberry

fehér kenyér: white bread

fehérrépa: turnip

fejessaláta: lettuce

feketeáfonya: blueberry/bilberry

feketecseresznye: black cherry

fekete-erdo torta: "Black Forest cake": chocolate layer cake with sour cherries, whipped cream, and chocolate shavings

feketegyökér: black or Spanish salsify

feketeretek: black radish

feketeribizli: blackcurrant

fekete tokehal: black cod

félbarna kenyér: bread made with half white and half rye flour

félbarna sör: semi-dark beer

félédes: semi-sweet (in terms of wine); mild (in terms of paprika)

felfújt: soufflé

félszáraz: semi-dry

fiatal: young

finom: delicious; *fincsi* is the informal form

finomliszt: all-purpose

flekken: barbecued meat, usually pork

flódni: traditional Jewish dessert, three layers of pastry filled with ground walnuts, poppy seeds, and apples

fokhagyma: garlic

fokhagymás szalonna: bacon flavored with garlic

fogas: pike perch from Lake Balaton and its tributaries; from the *Sander lucioperca* family; also sometimes called *zander* (the German name); young pike perch is called *süllo* or *fogas süllo*

fogoly: partridge

foltos tokehal: haddock

forralt bor: mulled wine

fordítás: this wine from Tokaj, which literally means "turning over," is made by macerating the residue left after pressing the first *aszú* berries and then soaking it in fresh must

forró csokoládé: hot chocolate

fott: boiled

fott marhahús: boiled beef, usually served with horseradish

fott sonka: boiled ham, usually served with horseradish; a traditional Easter dish *fott szalonna:* boiled bacon

fozelék: boiled vegetables mixed with sour cream and roux, eaten as a main course

francia krémes: two crisp layers of puff pastry filled with a thick layer of cream and topped with a thin layer of coffee-flavored icing

francia saláta: "French salad" (commonly referred to as "Russian salad" elsewhere)

friss: fresh

friss kolbász: sausage containing only meat and seasonings, no innards or fillers

frissensültek: prepared-to-order dishes

fröccs: wine spritzer; a mix of wine and soda water

füge: fig

fül: ear

fürj: quail

fürjtojás: quail egg

furmint: indigenous white grape variety

füstölt: smoked

füstöltsajt: smoked cheese

füstölt szalonna: smoked bacon

fuszer: spice

fuszernövény: herb

fuszerpaprika: paprika powder

G

galamb: pigeon

galuska: flour dumplings eaten with stew (better known as spaetzle); also called *nokedli*

Gerbeaud szelet: invented by Swiss pastry chef Emile Gerbeaud, this cake (sliced into rectangles) is cake layers alternated with apricot jam and ground walnuts and topped with chocolate glaze; sometimes spelled *Zserbó szelet*

gesztenye: chestnut

gesztenyeméz: chestnut honey

gesztenyepüré: sweet chestnut purée, served with whipped cream

gesztenyetorta: "chestnut cake": cake layers alternated with chestnut purée

göcsej csemegesajt: a semi-firm, smooth cow's milk cheese

gomba: mushroom

gombafej: mushroom head

gombavizsgálat: mushroom examination

gombóc: dumpling; can be sweet (see *túrós gombóc*) or savory

gomolya: a traditional type of cheese—made from either cow or sheep milk—which is firm, round, and dotted with small holes

görögdinnye: watermelon

gozölt: steamed

gránátoskocka: potatoes and pasta seasoned with paprika

grillázs: caramel

grillezett: grilled

gríz: semolina; also called *dara*

gulyás: goulash, also called *gulyásleves* (goulash soup); originally the word *gulyás* referred to a shepherd

Gundel palacsinta: walnut-stuffed pancakes topped with chocolate sauce

gyökér: root

gyömbér: ginger

gyöngyöző bor: lightly sparkling or frizzante wine

gyöngytyúk: guinea fowl

gyors büfé: fast-food joint

gyors étterem: fast-food restaurant

Gyulai kolbász: firm, medium-spicy sausage made from pork and bacon, stuffed into a natural casing, and smoked;

has a distinctive paprika
and garlic taste

gyümölcs: fruit

gyümölcskenyér: fruit cake

gyümölcsleves: fruit soup, served
chilled

H

....

hab: foam

habtejszín: whipped cream

hagyma: onion

hagymás rostélyos: a thin
sautéed steak topped with
onions that have been dredged
in flour and deep-fried; served
with mustard

hal: fish

halászlé: fisherman's soup;
heavily seasoned with paprika
and prepared differently in
different regions

harcsa: scaleless fresh water
catfish; also called European
catfish, sheatfish, wels, or wels
catfish (*Silurus glanis*)

harcsa halászlé: catfish
fisherman's soup

harcsa pörkölt: catfish stew

hárslevelő: indigenous white
grape variety

hársméz: lime-blossom honey;
also called linden or basswood

hasábburgonya: fried potatoes;
also called *sült burgonya*

házi: homemade

Hédervári szalonna: a type
of *császárszalonna*; usually
smoked and spiced

hentes: butcher

hentesáru: meats; refers to a
butcher shop

hentes módra: "butcher's style"
signifies meat that's cooked
with sausage or bacon

here: testicles

hering: herring

heti ajánlat: weekly specials;
heti ajánlatunk is "our
weekly specials"

hideg: cold

hideg gyümölcsleves: cold fruit
soup

hidegtál: cold plate, an assortment
of sliced meats, cheeses,
peppers, and tomatoes

homár: lobster

hordó: barrel

Hortobágyi palacsinta: meat-
stuffed pancake with paprika
sour-cream sauce

hurka: sausage, made of blood
or liver (black or white
pudding)

hús: meat

hús-hentesáru: butcher shop

húsleves: "meat soup": essentially
a consommé, made by slowly
simmering beef, bones, and
vegetables

húsvét: Easter

hütött: chilled

I

....

ilmici: a semi-soft *óvár*-style
cheese, holey with a moist
orange rind

indiáner: chocolate-covered
pastry filled with whipped
cream

író: buttermilk

irsai olivér: white hybrid grape
variety

ischler: chocolate-glazed cookie
filled with jam

ivócsarnok: "drinking hall"
where spring water is sold
by the glass or by the liter

ivóvíz: drinking water

íz: jam; also means flavor

J

....

jégkocka: ice cube

jégretek: white radish/daikon

jérce: pullet

jóasszony módra: meat prepared in the style of the "good wife": braised and served with a mixture of bacon, potatoes, and mushrooms

joghurt: yogurt

Jókai bableves: named for writer Mór Jókai; a hearty soup made with fresh or dried shell beans, smoked pork knuckle, vegetables, *csipetke*, and flavored with vinegar and sour cream

juhfark: indigenous white grape variety

juhsajt: sheep-milk cheese

juhtúró: sheep-milk curd cheese

juhtúrós galuska: dumplings with sheep cheese

K

kacsamáj: foie gras (fattened duck liver)

kacsasült: roasted duck, typically served with red cabbage and potatoes

kadarka: acclimatized red grape variety

kajszibarack: apricot; also called *sárgabarack* or *barack*

kakaó: cocoa

kakas: rooster

kakukkfu: thyme

kalács: challah bread

kannás bor: bulk wine; wine that hasn't been bottled and is sold by the liter

kapor: dill

káposzta: cabbage

káposztás kocka: pasta with shredded cabbage sautéed in a bit of bacon fat

káposztás pogácsa: pogácsa flavored with cabbage

kappan: capon

kapribogyó: caper

kapros: seasoned with dill

kapros túrós lepény: curd cheese flavored with dill and very little sugar, sandwiched between two layers of short crust

karácsony: Christmas

karalábé: kohlrabi

karamell: caramel

karaván: a processed smoked cheese

kardamon: cardamom

kardinális szelet: the "cardinal" slice is sponge cake and a thick layer of meringue, with jam or fruit sometimes sandwiched between

karfiol: cauliflower

kaszinótojás: devilled eggs

kávé: coffee; refers to espresso

kávéház: coffeehouse or café

kávézó: an inexpensive place to drink coffee

kaviár: caviar

kecsege: sterlet; related to the sturgeon, and found in the Danube and Tisza rivers

kecske: goat

kecskesajt: goat cheese

Kedvessy bélszin: created by nineteenth-century chef Nándor Kedvessy, this dish consists of a piece of butter-fried bread topped with sautéed mushrooms, a piece of steak, and a slice of goose liver, served with a sauce of onions, paprika, tomatoes, peppers, cream, and dill

kefír: kefir: a fermented milk drink that originated in the Caucasus; most commercially made *kefir* is like a more sour, thinner version of yogurt

kékfrankos: acclimatized red grape variety; known as *blaufränkisch* or *lemberger* in other countries

kéknyelu: indigenous white

grape variety, primarily grown in Badacsony

kékoportó: the traditional name for the acclimatized red grape variety now called *portugieser* (also known as *blauer portugieser*)

kék tokehal: blue whiting

kel: kale; also *marhakáposzta*

kelbimbó: Brussels sprouts

kelkáposzta: Savoy cabbage

kemence: traditional brick or earthenware oven; *kemencés* means cooked in the oven

kenyér: bread

kenyérszalonna: thin slab of smoked bacon, similar to fatback, which is almost purely fat

képviselofánk: choux puffs filled with vanilla cream and whipped cream

kert: open-air bar

kerti csiperke: horse mushroom

keseru: bitter

keszeg: rudd, a small boney fish

készételek: ready-made dishes

kifli: typical crescent-shaped bread roll

kifozde: simple restaurant, usually open only for lunch; also called *étkezde*

kígyóuborka: long, smooth-skinned cucumber

kínai kel: the type of cabbage with long pale green leaves known as Chinese leaves, Napa cabbage, or Peking cabbage

királyleányka: indigenous white grape variety

kisburgundi: the rarely used Hungarian name for pinot noir

kisvendéglo: "small restaurant"

kocka tészta: small square-shaped pasta

kocsma: pub

kocsonya: pork jelly with a mix of pig parts like feet, ears, and snouts, and extras like hard-boiled eggs, set into gelatinous aspic made from rich meat consommé that congeals when chilled

kökény: sloe (a small, wild European fruit that comes from the blackthorn)

kolbász: sausage, either fresh or dried

Kolozsvári káposzta: a dish consisting of layers of sauerkraut, rice, sausage, bacon, and sour cream, baked and served with fried pork chops; also called *rakott káposzta*

Kolozsvári szalonna: slightly smoked slab bacon with some bones

kömény: caraway

köménymag: caraway seed

köret: garnish; usually potatoes or rice

korhely halászlé: "hangover fish soup," flavored with lemon juice and sour cream

korhelyleves: "hangover soup," made from sauerkraut, smoked sausage, paprika, and sour cream

koriander: cilantro

köröm: hock

körözött: curd cheese spread seasoned with paprika, garlic, onions, salt, and caraway seeds; known as *Liptauer* in some countries

korpás kenyér: bread made with graham or wholewheat flour, wheat bran, and oat bran

korsó: 500 ml (16.9 ounces) mug of beer

körte: pear

kóser: kosher

kovászos uborka: cucumbers preserved by the process of lactic acid fermentation *kövérszolo:* indigenous white grape variety

kövidinka: indigenous white grape variety

krém: cream (the filling for pastries)

krémes: similar to the *francia krémes*, minus the whipped cream, and a dusting of confectioner's sugar replaces the coffee icing

krémsajt: cream cheese

krokett: croquette

krumpli: potato (also called *burgonya*); *krumpli* is also a dessert of marzipan balls dusted with cocoa

krumplipüré: mashed potatoes

krumplis kenyér: bread made with a small amount of potato added to the dough

krumplis pogácsa: pogácsa made with potato dough

kucsmagomba: morel mushroom

Kugler csokoládés máktortája: dense, flourless two layer chocolate and poppy seed cake with a thin layer of jam in the middle and chocolate glaze on top

kuglóf: coffee cake baked in a Bundt pan

kukorica: corn

kukorcás kenyér: bread made with wheat flour and a small amount of corn flour

különleges minoségu bor: finest quality wine

különleges paprika: the most finely ground paprika; can be sweet or mild

különlegességek: specialties

kürtoskalács: long thin strips of dough wrapped around a metal spit, glazed with sugar, and rotated until it's cooked and the glaze has caramelized

L

lajta sajt: a semi-soft *óvár*-style cheese, holey with a moist orange rind

lángolt kolbász: a collective name for dried *kolbász* that has been smoked a certain way

lángos: a fried piece of dough (often with potatoes added), commonly topped with sour cream and grated cheese

laskagomba: oyster mushroom

lazac: salmon

lé: juice, or broth

leányka: indigenous white grape variety

lebbencs: irregularly shaped flat pasta

lecsó: tomato and pepper stew cooked in a small amount of lard

lekvár: jam, also called *dzsem* or *íz*

lencse: lentil

lepény: tart or pie

lépesméz: honeycomb

leves: soup

libamáj: foie gras (fattened goose liver)

libasült: roasted goose; typically served with red cabbage and potatoes

likor: liqueur

lilahagyma: red onion

Linzertorta: a crust made from ground almonds, grated lemon rind, and butter, topped with jam and a lattice crust

liszt: flour

lúdláb torta: lúdláb means "goose leg," and when this cake is made at home it is often cut into tiny triangles resembling goose feet; the thin chocolate sponge cake is topped with chocolate mousse, brandy-soaked cherries, and chocolate glaze

M

macesz: matzo; also called *pászka*

madársaláta: mâche/lamb's lettuce

madártej: floating islands: cold dessert consisting of an egg custard topped with chunks of meringue

mag: seed

magos kenyér: bread with added seeds

magyarosan: "Hungarian"-style meat: served with a tomato, pepper, and onion sauce spiced with paprika

májashurka: sausage that contains liver, as well as some innards and fillers

májgombóc: liver dumpling, often added to *húsleves*

majonéz: mayonnaise

majoránna: marjoram

mák: poppy seed

mákos bejgli: poppy-seed roulade cake

mákos guba: poppy-seed bread pudding

mákos kifli: poppy-seed-filled crescent rolls

mákos tészta: pasta mixed with poppy seeds, powdered sugar, and melted butter

makréla: mackerel

málna: raspberry

mandula: almond

mangalica: an indigenous Hungarian pig, prized for its tasty meat

mángold: Swiss chard

marcipán: marzipan (sweetened almond paste)

margarin: margarine

marhanyelv: ox tongue

marhasült: roast beef

mártás: sauce

márványsajt: "marble cheese": blue cheese; can also be called *kéksajt*

máslás: "copy": a type of Tokaj wine made by pouring must on the *aszú* and fermenting it again

Mátrai borzaska: breaded pork cutlet topped with sour cream, cheese, and garlic

mazsola: raisin

medvehagyma: these green leaves have many names in English—ramson, ramp, wood garlic, or bear's garlic—and are sold in bio stores in the spring; best used in salads, soups, and sandwiches

meggy: sour cherry

meggyes piskóta: sponge cake baked with a layer of cherries on the bottom and dusted with powdered sugar

meleg: hot or warm

mell: breast

menta: mint

metélőhagyma: chives, also called *snidling*

méz: honey

mézdinnye: honeydew melon or cantaloupe—they go by the same name; also called *cukordinnye*

mézes: honey-flavored

mézeskalács: honey bread (similar to ginger bread)

mignon: petit four

minőségi bor: "quality wine"

módra: style

mogyoró: hazelnut

mogyorótorta: hazelnut cake

muskotály: the Hungarian name for the muscat ottonel grape

mustár: mustard

müzli: muesli cereal

N

napi ajánlat: daily specials; *napi ajánlatunk* is "our daily specials"

napi étlap: daily menu

napraforgóméz: sunflower honey

napraforgóolaj: sunflower oil

narancs: orange

natúr: plain; in terms of meat it refers to meat simply dredged in flour and fried

nélkül: without

néni: "aunt"; also a polite term used to refer to an older woman

nyers: raw

nyers tej: raw (unpasteurized) milk

nyúl: rabbit

O

öko: organic

olaj: oil

olívaolaj: olive oil

olaszrizling: the most widely planted grape in Hungary; also called *Welschriesling* or Italian riesling

olívabogyó: olive; also called *olíva* or *olajbogyó*

omlett: omelet

orda: whey cheese; similar to ricotta

oregáno: oregano

orjaleves: soup traditionally made on pig-butchering day with the pig's backbone

Orly: the cooking method of frying fish in beer batter

örölt: ground

Orosz krém torta: "Russian cream cake": a light sponge cake topped with a thick layer of creamy filling flavored with rum and candied fruits and raisins, and topped with whipped cream

oszibarack: peach

óvári: a mild, medium-firm cheese with dense irregular holes

ozgerinc: saddle of venison (or a type of chocolate cake)

P

pácolt: marinated

padlizsán: eggplant/aubergine

palacsinta: thin pancakes

pálmalevél: palmier

palócleves: soup made with lamb and green beans, and finished with sour cream

pálpusztai: soft ripened, pungent cheese with an orange-colored rind and a creamy interior; similar to Limburger

Pannónia: similar to Swiss Emmental and Gruyère; a semi-hard cow's milk cheese matured for six to eight weeks

panzió: small family-run guest house

paprika: either the red spice powder or any fresh or dried pepper; the most common fresh pepper is long, pale green, and sweet (called the Hungarian wax pepper or banana pepper abroad); it's called *tölteni való paprika*, or *TV paprika* for short ("pepper for stuffing")

paprikás: meat or stew slowly braised in paprika sauce, thickened with sour cream

paradicsom: tomato

Párizsi borjúszelet: veal scallops dredged in flour and eggs and fried

párlat: any kind of distilled drink

párna: "pillow": a filled pastry

párolt: steamed or braised

parasztsonka: dried "peasant sausage"

pászka: matzo; also called *macesz*

pástétom: pâté

patisszon: pattypan squash (or custard marrow or summer crookneck)

pék: baker

pékség: bakery

péksütemény: baked goods

perec: pretzel

petrezselyem: parsley; flat-leaf (or Italian) parsley is the most common in Hungary

petrezselyemgyökér: parsley root (also called Hamburg parsley or parsnip-rooted parsley); common in Central Europe, but slightly different than the parsnip

pezsgo: sparkling wine

piac: market

Pick Szalámi: a company founded in 1869 in Szeged that still makes *téli szalámi* from the original secret recipe

pikoló: 200 ml (6.7 ounces) glass of beer

pilzeni: pilsner; also called *pils*

pincepörkölt: *pörkölt* cooked in red wine

pirítós: toast

pirított: sautéed

piros: red

piros arany: mild red paprika paste

piskóta: sponge cake

pisztácia: pistachio

pisztráng: trout

pite: pie

pogácsa: savory, buttery scones/biscuits in a variety of flavors

pohár: glass; in terms of beer *pohár* refers to a 300 ml (10.1 ounces) glass of beer

pónty: a variety of carp native to the Danube river system

pónty halászlé: carp fisherman's soup

porcukor: powdered sugar

póréhagyma: leek

pörkölt: stew; the word also means roasted

portugieser: acclimatized red grape variety, formerly called *kékoportó*, and also known as *blauer portugieser*

Pozsonyi kifli: small crescents filled with walnuts or poppy seeds

puliszka: cornmeal porridge (polenta)

puncstorta: "punch cake": a bright pink sponge cake studded with rum-soaked dried fruits and topped with pink frosting

püré: purée

püspökkenyér: "bishop's bread": a fruitcake-like loaf

puttony: a wooden tub that holds macerated botrytized grapes. The number of *puttonyos* a bottle of Tokaj wine has refers to the number of tubs of grapes added to the wine: the higher the number, the sweeter the wine

R

rablóhús: "robber's meat": meat cooked on a skewer; also called *saslik*

Racka juh: a Hungarian indigenous breed of sheep; also called the *Hortobágyi Racka*

rácponty: Serbian-style carp; a dish with layers of sliced potatoes, carp larded with smoked bacon, *lecsó*, and sour cream

Rajnai rizling: The Hungarian name for the Rhine riesling grape

rák: any type of crustacean

Rákóczi túrós: *Rákóczi* cheese-cake, a layer of short crust topped with a curd-cheese mixture and a lattice of meringue and apricot jam

rakott: layered

rakott káposzta: see *Kolozsvári káposzta*

rántott: fried

rántotta: scrambled eggs

rántott borjúláb: breaded calf foot, served with tartar sauce and lemon

rántott csirke: fried chicken

rántott sajt: fried cheese

rántva: fried

rebarbara: rhubarb

reform konyha: healthy food

reggeli: breakfast

repceméz: rape honey (also known as canola in English)

reszelt: grated

retek: radish

rétes: strudel

réti csiperke: meadow mushroom or field mushroom

ribizke: currant; also called *ribizli*

Rigó Jancsi: cake named for a Gypsy violinist who ran away with a Belgian baroness: squares of chocolate mousse sandwiched between layers of chocolate cake and glazed with chocolate

ringló: greengage; a type of sweet plum with light-green-colored flesh and red or greenish-yellow skin

rizibizi: rice with green peas

rizlingszilváni: Hungarian name for the *müller-thurgau* grape

rízs: rice

rizottó: risotto

ropogós: crispy

ropogós malacsült: crispy roasted suckling pig

rostélyos: braised steak

röszti: potatoes grated then fried

or browned in the oven

roston: grilled

rostonsült: grilled

rostos üdítő: fruit juice

rövid: a "short": a shot of liquor

rozé: rosé

rozmaring: rosemary

rózsa paprika: "rose" paprika is medium coarse and tends to be very hot

rozskenyér: rye bread

rozs sör: rye beer

rukkola: arugula

ruszli: pickled fish

S

Sacher torta: created in Vienna by Franz Sacher, this firm two-layered chocolate cake is spread with apricot glaze, topped with chocolate glaze, and served with fresh whipped cream

sáfrány: saffron

sajt: cheese

sajtos pogácsa: pogácsa flavored with cheese

sajtos roló: a long round piece of pastry filled with cheese cream, with ends dipped in grated cheese

sajtos rúd: a savory cheese pastry

saláta: salad or lettuce

sárgabarack: apricot; also called *barack* or *kajszibarack*

sárgaborsó: yellow pea

sárgadinnye: honeydew melon or cantaloupe; also called *cukordinnye*

sárgamuskotály: Hungarian name for the yellow muscat/ muscat lunel grape

sárgarépa: carrot

sárgarépatorta: carrot cake

sárga rókagomba: chanterelle mushroom

sárga tokehal: whiting

saslik: meat cooked on skewers; also called *rablóhús*

savanyú: sour

savanyú káposzta: sauerkraut; often called *Vecsési káposzta*

savanyúság: pickled vegetables

savó: whey

selyemfuméz: milkweed honey (or silkweed honey)

serpenyos: serpenyo means skillet/frying pan, and *serpenyos* refers to a skillet-cooked/pan-fried dish

sertés: pork; also *disznó or disznóhús*

sertésborda: pork chop

shiitake gomba: shiitake mushroom

Sissi kávé: espresso with Sissi apricot cream liquor

snidling: chive; also called *metélohagyma*

só: salt

sólet: cholent (a traditionally Jewish bean stew with additions like different types of smoked meats or boiled eggs)

som: European cornel (a species of dogwood that produces fruit); used to flavor *pálinka*

Somlói galuska: chocolate and vanilla sponge cake with vanilla custard, raisins, walnuts, chocolate syrup, and whipped cream

sonka: ham

sör: beer

sörfozde: brewery; also called *sörgyár* or *serfozde*

sörozo: beer hall or a pub

sós: savory or salty

sóska: sorrel

spárga: asparagus

spenót: spinach

sprotni: European sprat (similar to herring)

Stefánia torta: sponge layers alternated with chocolate butter cream and dusted with cocoa powder

süllo: young pike perch (*fogas*), which weighs between half a pound and two pounds; also called *fogas süllo*

sült: typically means roasted; can mean fried, as in *sült burgonya* (fried potatoes)

sült csülök: roasted knuckle of pork

sült szalonna: cooked bacon

sütemény: cakes, pastries, and cookies

sütötök: squash or pumpkin, similar to butternut squash; also called *tök*

szalámi: salami

szalonna: bacon

számla: the bill

szamóca: wild strawberry

száraz: dry

szárazbab: dried bean

száraz kolbász: dried sausage (doesn't have to be cooked)

szardella: anchovy

szardínia: sardines

szárnyas: poultry

szarvas: venison; also called *szarvashús*

szarvasgomba: truffle

szeder: blackberry

Szegedi halászlé: a variation of *Tiszai halászlé*

szegfuszeg: clove

székelykáposzta: beef and sauerkraut stew seasoned with paprika and flavored with sour cream; also called *székelygulyás*

szelet: slice

szendvics: sandwich

szénsavas: sparkling water (with gas)

szénsavmentes: still water (without gas)

szerecsendió: nutmeg

szezámmag: sesame seed

szilva: plum

szilvás gombóc: dumplings made from potato dough, stuffed with plums, and coated in bread crumbs

szív: heart

szódavíz: soda water; traditionally called *szikvíz*

szolo: grape

szörp: concentrated fruit syrup to mix with soda or water

sztrapacska: potato dumplings tossed in bacon drippings with sheep-curd cheese and bacon

szürkebarát: Hungarian name for the pinot gris grape

szürkemarha: Hungarian grey cattle, an indigenous breed that nearly died out

szurt: filtered

szuz: tenderloin; also means "virgin"

T

tarhonya: dried pasta (which looks like barley) made from a kneaded flour and egg dough

tarkabab: speckled, colorful shell beans known as cranberry or borlotti beans

tárkony: tarragon

tartármártás: tartar sauce; in Hungary it is mayonnaise with added sour cream

táska: "bag": a filled pastry

tatár beefsztek: steak tartare

tea: tea

teasütemény: small savory pastry

tehén: cow

tehéntej: cow milk

tehéntúró: cow-milk curd cheese

tej: milk; often sold in plastic bags in Hungary

tejberízs: rice pudding

tejföl: sour cream

tejszín: cream

tekercs: a roll that looks something like a croissant, but is made with yeasty dough

téli szalámi: "winter salami": a firm, mildly spiced salami made from finely chopped pork; it's a vibrant pinkish-red color, and the skin is coated with a grayish white mold

tengeri csuka: hake

tengeri hal: saltwater fish

teperto: cracklings, which are usually eaten with bread and red onions; also called *töpörtyo*

tepertos pogácsa: *pogácsa* flavored with cracklings

természetes ásványvíz: natural mineral water

tészta: pasta; can also refer to dough or pastry

Tiszai halászlé: the main characteristic of this *halászlé* recipe is that all ingredients are put in the pot at once, but there are many versions

tojás: egg

tök: squash or pumpkin, also called *sütotök*

Tokaji aszú: wine made from select late-harvested botrytized grapes with concentrated levels of sugar; it's measured in terms of sweetness from three to six *puttonyos* depending on how many tubs of *aszú* berries were used

Tokaji aszú eszencia: wine made by adding *eszencia* syrup to Tokaji *aszú*

Tokaji eszencia: the thick syrup that results from the pressure of *aszú* berries pushing down on each other; has such a high sugar content that it ferments too slowly to achieve an alcohol level of more than a few percent

Tokaji szamorodni: Wine made from a mixture of partly botrytized grapes; can be dry or sweet; similar to Spanish sherry

tokány: meat stew cooked in its own juices; vegetables can be added, and it can be thickened with sour cream

tokehal: cod

tokhal: sturgeon

töki pompos: a thick piece of bread, spread with sour cream, cheese, onions, and chunks of bacon

tökmagolaj: pumpkin-seed oil

tölgy: oak

töltött: stuffed

töltött káposzta: stuffed cabbage; cooked with sauerkraut

töltött karalábé: stuffed kohlrabi

töltött paprika: stuffed peppers cooked in tomato sauce

tonhal: tuna

töpörtyu: cracklings; also called *teperto*

töppedt szolobol készült: produced with botrytized grapes

torma: horseradish

torta: cake, usually refers to a layer cake

tramini: the Hungarian name for the gewürztraminer grape

trappista: a semi-soft neutral-tasting cheese made from pasteurized cow milk

traubisoda: Hungarian white grape soda

trombitagomba: black chanterelle or black trumpet mushroom

tükörtojás: sunny-side-up eggs

tükörtojás sonkával: ham and eggs

túró: farmer's cheese or curd cheese; often translated as cottage cheese, but bears no relation to the more liquidy cottage cheese found elsewhere

túrógombóc: curd-cheese dumplings coated with bread crumbs

túró rudi: a bar of sweetened curd cheese coated in chocolate

túróscsusza: pasta with curd cheese, sour cream, and bacon

túrós lepény: "cheese pie": curd cheese filling sandwiched between two layers of short crust

túrós pogácsa: pogácsa flavored with curd cheese

túrótorta: cheesecake made with curd cheese, often thickened with gelatin, and usually with a cake-like crust

tyúkhúsleves: chicken soup

U

uborka: cucumber

üdíto: non-alcoholic beverage

UHT tej: milk that has been partially sterilized by ultra-high temperature (UHT) processing

újburgonya: new potato

újfokhagyma: new garlic

újhagyma: spring onions

Újházy tyúkhúsleves: hearty chicken and vegetable soup with pasta added

Unicum: bitter liquor made from more than forty herbs and spices, distilled, and aged in oak casks for six months

üveges sör: bottled beer

V

vad: two meanings: game or wild

vadas módra: "hunter's style" meat is served with game

sauce or brown sauce; often with bread dumplings

vadhús: game

vadkacsa: wild duck

vadnyúl: wild rabbit

vadszárnyas: wild fowl

vaj: butter

vajas burgonya: buttered potatoes

vajas pogácsa: *pogácsa* made with rich butter dough

vanília: vanilla

vargabéles: a cake made from a noodle and curd cheese filling cooked between layers of strudel dough

vargánya: porcini mushroom; sometimes called by its Latin name, boletus, or its French name, cèpe

vásárcsarnok: covered market hall

vasi pecsenye: pork cutlets soaked in milk and garlic before being dredged in paprika-laced flour and sautéed

vastag kolbász: thick sausage

vegetáriánus: vegetarian

vegyes: mixed

vegyes halászlé: "mixed fisherman's soup" made from several types of fish

vegyes saláta: mixed salad

vegyes virágméz: mixed flower honey

velo: marrow or brains

veloscsont: bone marrow

velo rántva: fried brains

velorózsa: brains

vendéglo: restaurant

véreshurka: blood sausage/black pudding

vese: kidney

világos sör: pale ale

vilmoskörte: William's or Bartlett pear

virsli: hot dog or frankfurter

víz: water

vörös: red

vörös áfonya: cranberry

vörös bor: red wine

vöröshagyma: onion

vöröskáposzta: red cabbage

W

wels: wels catfish (*Silurus glanis*); a scaleless fresh water catfish, also called European catfish; in Hungarian catfish is called *harcsa*

Z

zabpehely: oatmeal

zeller: celery

zellergyökér: celeriac/celery root

zengo: white hybrid grape variety

zenit: white hybrid grape variety

zéta: white hybrid grape variety; formerly called oremus

zeusz: white hybrid grape variety

zöldbab: green bean

zöldborsó: green pea

zöldcitrom: lime

zöldhagyma: scallion

zöldség: vegetables

zöldszilváni: Hungarian name for the sylvaner grape

zöldveltelini: Hungarian name for *grüner veltliner*; the white-wine grape grown principally in Austria

zsálya: sage

zsemle: typical Hungarian round bread roll

zsemlegombóc: bread dumplings

zserbó szelet: see *Gerbeaud szelet*

zsír: lard (or grease)

zsíros kenyér: bread spread with lard and sprinkled with paprika and sliced onions

zsírszalonna: unprocessed fatback, which is bright white (no meat streaks); used for cooking, baking, and making cracklings

zsírszegény: low fat

zweigelt: a cross between the *kékfrankos* and St. Laurent grape

ENGLISH-HUNGARIAN

A

acacia honey: akácméz; also called Black Locust in America

alcohol-free: alkoholmentes

almond: mandula

anchovy: szardella

anise: ánizs

appetizers: eloételek

apple: alma

apple pie: almás pite; two layers of crust stuffed with apple (and often walnut) filling, served in squares rather than wedges

apricot: barack, kajszibarack, and sárgabarack

artichoke: articsóka

arugula: rukkola

asparagus: spárga

avocado: avokádó

B

bacon: szalonna

baked goods: péksütemény

bakery: pékség

banana: banán

bar: kocsma (pub), sörözo (beer hall), bár (bar), borozó (grungy wine bar), or kert

barbecued meat: flekken; usually pork

barley: árpagyöngy or árpa

Bartlett pear: vilmoskörte

basil: bazsalikom

Bavarian bread: bajor kenyér

bean: bab; see also zöldbab (green bean), szárazbab (dried bean) or tarkabab

bean gulyás: babgulyás

bean soup: Jókai bableves is the most common variety; it's named for writer Mór Jókai; a hearty soup made with fresh or dried shell beans, smoked pork knuckle, vegetables, csipetke, and flavored with vinegar and sour cream

beef tartare: Tatár beefsztek

beef tenderloin: bélszín

beer: sör

beetroot: cékla

bitter: keseru

blackberry: szeder

black chanterelle: trombitagomba

black cod: fekete tokehal

Black Forest cake: fekete-erdo torta

Black Locust honey: akácméz; also known as acacia honey

black pudding: véreshurka

blood sausage: véreshurka

black trumpet mushroom: trombitagomba

blueberry: áfonya or feketeáfonya

blue cheese: márványsajt or kéksajt

bluefin tuna: nagy tonhal

blue whiting: kék tokehal

bock beer: bak

boiled: fott

bone: csont

bone marrow: csontvelo, velo, or *veloscsont*

bone soup: csontleves; a broth made from bones and root vegetables (can also be used as stock)

borlotti beans: tarkabab

bottle: üveg

bottled beer: üveges sör

bread: kenyér

bread dumplings: zsemlegombóc

bread roll: zsemle (round) or *kifli* (crescent shaped)

breakfast: reggeli

breast: mell

brewery: sörfozde, sörgyár, or less frequently *serfozde*

brick oven: kemence; kemencés means cooked in the oven

broth: lé

Brussels sprouts: kelbimbó

buffalo: bivaly

bulk wine: kannás bor

Bull's Blood: Bikavér

bunch: csomó

butcher: hentes

butcher shop: hús-hentesáru (bolt)

butter: vaj

buttermilk: író

buttered potatoes: vajas burgonya

C

cabbage: káposzta; see also *kelkáposzta, vöröskáposzta,* and *kínai kel*

café: kávéház; also *kávézó* and *eszpresszó*

cake: torta (usually refers to a layer cake)

candy: cukorka

cantaloupe: sárgadinnye or *cukordinnye*; also refers to honeydew melon

caper: kapribogyó

capon: kappan

caramel: karamell or *grillázs*

caraway: kömény

caraway seed: köménymag

cardamom: kardamon

carnival season: farsang

carp: ponty; a species native to the Danube river system

carrot: sárgarépa

carrot cake: sárgarépatorta

catfish: harcsa; a scaleless fresh water which is also called European catfish, sheatfish, wels, or wels catfish

catfish stew: harcsa pörkölt

cauldron: bogrács

cauliflower: karfiol

caviar: kaviár

celeriac/celery root: zellergyökér

celery: zeller

cereal: müzli

challah bread: kalács

champignon mushrooms: csiperke; such as button mushrooms and white mushrooms

chanterelle mushroom: sárga rókagomba

cheese: sajt

cheesecake: túrótorta; made with curd cheese, often thickened with gelatin, and usually with a cake-like crust

cherry: cseresznye; also *erdei meggy* (wild cherry), *meggy* (sour cherry), *feketecseresznye* (black cherry), and *cigánymeggy* (small cherries)

cherry pepper: cseresznyepaprika

chestnut: gesztenye

chestnut cake: gesztenyetorta; cake layers alternated with chestnut puree *chestnut honey: gesztenyeméz*

chestnut purée: gesztenyepüré

chicken leg: csirkecomb

*chicken paprikás: csirke
   paprikás*

chili pepper: chilipaprika

chilled: h tött

*chive: snidling or
   metélohagyma*

chocolate: csokoládé

cholent: sólet; a traditionally
   Jewish bean stew with additions like different types of
   smoked meats or boiled eggs

Christmas: karácsony

cilantro: koriander

cinnamon: fahéj

clove: szegfuszeg

cocoa: kakaó

cod: tokehal

coffee cake: kuglóf; baked in a
   Bundt pan

coffeehouse: kávéház

cold: hideg

cold plate: hidegtál; an assortment of sliced meats, cheeses,
   peppers, and tomatoes

chicken soup: tyúkhúsleves; see
   also *Újházy tyúkhúsleves*

cilantro: koriander

condensed milk: sőrített tej

coriander: koriander

corn: kukorica

cornmeal: puliszka; polenta or
   cornmeal porridge

cow: tehén

cow's milk: tehéntej

cracklings: töpörtyu or teperto

cranberry: vörös áfonya

cranberry beans: tarkabab

cream: tejszín (as in cream for
   coffee or whipping cream) or
   krém (as in fillings for pastries
   and cakes)

cream cheese: krémsajt

crispy: ropogós

*croquette (potato): krokett, bur-
   gonyakrokett, or burgonyafánk*

crustacean: rák

*cucumber: uborka or
   kígyóuborka*

curd cheese: túró; tehéntúró
   (cow's milk) or *juhtúró*
   (sheep's milk); often
   translated as cottage cheese,
   but different than the cottage
   cheese found elsewhere; see
   also *bryndza* and *túró rudi*

currant: ribizke or ribizli;
   feketeribizli (black currant)

D

daikon: jégretek

daily menu: napi étlap

daily specials: napi ajánlat;
   napi ajánlatunk is "our daily
   specials"

dark beer: barna sör

dark chocolate: étcsokoládé

delicious: finom; fincsi is
   informal

devilled eggs: kaszinótojás

dill: kapor; kapros means
   flavored with dill

doughnut: fánk or farsangi fánk

draft beer: csapolt sör

dried: aszalt (as in dried fruit)

dried bean: szárazbab

dried fruit: aszalt gyümölcs

drinking hall: ivócsarnok;
   where spring water is sold by
   the glass or by the liter

drinking water: ivóvíz

dry: száraz

dumpling: gombóc can be sweet
   (see *túrós gombóc*) or savory;
   galuska or *nokedli* (better
   known as spaetzle) are flour
   dumplings eaten with stew;
   daragaluska are semolina
   dumplings; *juhtúrós galuska*

is a dish of dumplings served with sheep cheese; *sztrapacska* is a dish consisting of potato dumplings tossed in bacon drippings with sheep-milk curd cheese and bacon; *szilvás gombóc* (plum dumplings) are made from potato dough and stuffed with plums and coated in bread crumbs

E

ear: *fül*

earthenware oven: *kemence*; *kemencés* means cooked in the oven

Easter: *húsvét*

egg: *tojás*

eggplant: *padlizsán*

elderberry: *bodza*

elderflower: *bodzavirág*

Emmenthal cheese: *Ementáli sajt*

endive: *endívia*

F

family-run: *családi*

farmer's cheese: *túró*; *tehéntúró* (cow's milk) or *juhtúró* (sheep's milk); often translated as cottage cheese, but different than the cottage cheese found elsewhere; see also *bryndza* and *túró rudi*

fast-food restaurant: *gyors étterem* or *gyors büfé*

fennel: *édeskömény*

fermented cucumbers: *kovászos uborka*

field mushroom: *réti csiperke*; also known as meadow mushroom

fig: *füge*

fillet: *filé*

fish: *hal*

fisherman's soup: *halászlé*; see also *Bajai halászlé, Dunai halászlé, harcsa halászlé,* *korhely halászlé, ponty halászlé, Szegedi halászlé, Tiszai halászlé, vegyes halászlé*

floating islands: *madártej*; cold dessert consisting of an egg custard topped with chunks of meringue

flour: *liszt* or *finomliszt*; all-purpose flour

foie gras: *kacsamáj* (fattened duck liver) or *libamáj* (fattened goose liver)

foot (veal): *borjúláb*

frankfurter: *virsli*

fresh: *friss*

fried: *rántva* or *rántott*

fried cheese: *rántott sajt*

fried chicken: *rántott csirke*

fried potatoes: *hasábburgonya* or *sült burgonya*

fruit: *gyümölcs*

fruit cake: *gyümölcskenyér* or *püspökkenyér* ("bishop's bread")

fruit soup: *gyümölcsleves*

frying pan: *serpenyo*; *serpenyos* refers to a pan-fried dish

G

garbanzo bean: *csicseriborsó*

garlic: *fokhagyma*

garnish: *köret*

gewürztraminer: *tramini*

ginger: *gyömbér*

gizzard: *zúza*

glass: *pohár*; in terms of beer, *pohár* refers to a 300 ml (10.1 ounces) glass of beer; see also *korsó* and *pikoló* goat: *kecske*

goat cheese: *kecskesajt*

gooseberry: *egres*

goose liver: *libamáj*

goulash: *gulyás*; see also *babgulyás, birkagulyás, bográcsgulyás,* and *gulyásleves*

grape: *szolo*

grated: *reszelt*

grease: *zsír*

greengage: *ringló*; a type of sweet plum with light-green flesh and red or greenish-yellow skin

grilled: *rostonsült* or *roston*

ground: *orölt* (refers to spices), *darált* (refers to meat)

ground meat: *darálthús* or *vagdalt hús*

grüner veltliner: *zöldveltelini*

guinea fowl: *gyöngytyúk*

H

haddock: *foltos tokehal*

hake: *tengeri csuka*

ham: *sonka*

ham and eggs: *tükörtojás sonkával*

hangover soup: *korhelyleves*; made from sauerkraut, smoked sausage, paprika, and sour cream

hazelnut: *mogyoró*

hazelnut cake: *mogyorótorta*

head cheese: *disznósajt*

health food: *reform konyha*

heart: *szív*

herb: *fuszernövény*

herring: *hering*

hill: *hegy*

hock: *köröm*

homemade: *házi*

honey: *méz*; *mézes* is honey flavored

honey bread: *mézeskalács*; similar to ginger bread

honeycomb: *lépesméz*

honeydew melon: *sárgadinnye*; also refers to cantaloupe and can also be called *cukordinnye* or *mézdinnye*

horseradish: *torma*

hot: *eros* or *csípos* (as in spicy) or *forró* (as in warm)

hot chocolate: *forró csokoládé*

hot dog: *virsli*

Hungarian Grey cattle: *szürkemarha*; an indigenous cattle breed that nearly died out

I

ice cream: *fagylalt*

ice cube: *jégkocka*

J

jam: *íz, lekvár,* or *dzsem*

juice (fruit): *rostos üdíto* or *lé*

K

kale: *kel* or *marhakáposzta*

kebab: *saslik* or *rablóhús*

kefir: *kefir*; a fermented milk drink which originated in the Caucasus; most commercially made kefir is like a more sour, thinner version of yogurt

kidney: *vese*

kohlrabi: *karalábé*

kosher: *kóser*

L

lager: *ászok*

lard: *zsír*

layered: *rakott*

leek: *póréhagyma*

leg cuts (of meat): *comb*

leg of lamb: *báránycomb*

lemon: *citrom*

lentil: lencse

lettuce: saláta or fejessaláta

lime: zöldcitrom

lime blossom honey: hársméz;
also known as linden or
basswood honey

Liptauer: a spread made with
curd cheese, paprika, and
other spices; called *körözött* in
Hungary

liqueur: likor

liver dumpling: májgombóc;
often added to *húsleves*

lobster: homár

low fat: zsírszegény

M

mackerel: makréla

mâche: madársaláta

made-to-order dishes:
frissensültek

malt: maláta

Mangalica pig: an indigenous
Hungarian pig, prized for its
tasty meat

margarine: margarin

marinated: pácolt

marjoram: majoránna

market: piac, csarnok (hall), or
vásárcsarnok

marzipan: marcipán; sweetened
almond paste

mashed potatoes: krumplipüré

matzo: pászka or macesz

mayonnaise: majonéz

meat soup: húsleves; a
consommé, made by slowly
simmering beef, bones, and
vegetables

melon: dinnye

milk: tej

milk chocolate: tejcsokoládé

milkweed honey: selyemfuméz;
also known as silkweed honey

mineral water: ásványvíz

mint: menta

mixed: vegyes

mixed flower honey: vegyes
virágméz

mixed salad: vegyes saláta

morel mushroom: kucsmagomba

muesli: müzli

mulberry: fehér eper

mulled wine: forralt bor

müller-thurgau: rizlingszilváni

muscat lunel: sárgamuskotály

muscat ottonel: muskotály

mushroom: gomba; also csiperke,
gombafej, kucsmagomba,
laskagomba, szegfu gomba,
ozlábgomba, réti csiperke,
sárga rókagomba, Shiitake
gomba, téli fülokekerti
csiperke, trombitagomba,
vargánya

mushroom examination:
gombavizsgálat

mustard: mustár

N

Napa cabbage: kínai kel;
cabbage with long pale green
leaves, also known as Chinese
leaves or Peking cabbage

new garlic: újfokhagyma

new onion: újhagyma

new potato: újburgonya

non-alcoholic beverage: üdíto

nut: dió

nutmeg: szerecsendió

O

oak: tölgy

oatmeal: zabpehely

oil: olaj

olive: olajbogyó, olívabogyó
or olíva

olive oil: olívaolaj

omelet: omlett

onion: hagyma or *vöröshagyma*; see also *lilahagyma, újhagyma,* and *zöldhagyma*

oregano: oregáno

organic: bio or *öko*

orange: narancs

ox tongue: marhanyelv

oyster mushroom: laskagomba

P

pale ale: világos sör

pancakes: palacsinta; also *csúsztatott palacsinta* (a layered *palacsinta* dessert), *Gundel palacsinta* (walnut stuffed pancakes topped with chocolate sauce), and *Hortobágyi palacsinta* (savory meat stuffed pancakes with paprika sour cream sauce)

paprika: paprika: either the red spice powder or any type of fresh or dried pepper (but not black pepper)

parfait: parfé

parsley: petrezselyem; in Hungary flat-leaf or Italian is most commonly used

parsley root: petrezselyem-gyökér; also called Hamburg parsley or parsnip rooted parsley, which is common in Central Europe, but slightly different than the parsnip

partridge: fogoly

pasta: tészta (can also refer to dough or pastry)

pastries (savory): teasütemény

pastries (sweet): See dessert

pastry shop: cukrászda

pâte: pástétom

pattypan squash: patisszon

peach: oszibarack

pear: körte

peas: borsó; also *cukorborsó* (sugar pea, sugar snap pea), *zöldborsó* (green pea), or *sárgaborsó* (yellow pea)

pepper: bors or *fekete bors* (the black pepper spice); *fehérbors* (white pepper); *paprika* (any variety of bell pepper); see also *paprika*

petit four: mignon

phacelia honey: facéliaméz

pheasant: fácán

pickled: ecetes

pickled cucumber: csemegeuborka

pickled fish: ruszli

pickled vegetables (or fruit): savanyúság; see also *csalamádé*

pie: pite; see also *lepény*

piece: darab

pig slaughter: disznótor

pigeon: galamb

pike: csuka

pike perch: fogas; from Lake Balaton and its tributaries; from the *sander lucioperca* family; also sometimes called *zander* (the German name); young pike perch is called *süllo* or *fogas süllo* (when it weighs between half a pound and two pounds)

pilsner: pilzeni or *pils*

pinot gris: szürkebarát

pinot noir: kisburgundi is the Hungarian name, but is rarely used

pistachio: pisztácia

plain: natúr; in terms of meat it means simply dredged in flour and fried

plum: szilva

plum dumplings: szilvás gombóc; potato dough dumplings stuffed with plums and coated in bread crumbs

poached: bevert

poppy seed: mák

porcini mushroom: vargánya, sometimes called boletus or cèpe *pork: sertés* or *disznóhús*

pork chop: sertésborda

pork jelly: kocsonya; a mix of pig parts like feet, ears, and snouts, and extras like hard-boiled eggs, which are set into gelatinous aspic made from rich meat consommé that congeals when chilled

portugieser: acclimatized red grape variety, formerly called *kékoportó*, and also known as *blauer portugieser*

potato: krumpli or *burgonya*

poultry: baromfi or *szárnyas*

powdered sugar: porcukor

pretzel: perec

prune: aszalt szilva

pub: kocsma, sörözö (beer hall), *bár* (bar), *borozó* (wine bar), or *kert*

puff pastry: leveles tészta

pumpkin: tök (or *sütotök*); see also *patisszon*

pumpkin-seed oil: tökmagolaj

purée: püré

Q

quail: fürj

quail egg: fürjtojás

quality wine: minöségi bor

quince: birs; often called *birsalma* when it's shaped like an apple and *birskörte* when it's shaped like a pear

quince jelly: birsalmasajt

R

rabbit: nyúl

Racka sheep: Racka juh; a Hungarian indigenous breed of sheep, also called the *Hortobágyi Racka*

radish: retek

raisin: mazsola

ramp/ramson: medvehagyma

rape honey: repceméz; more commonly known as canola in English

raspberry: málna or *erdei vadmálna* (wild raspberry)

raw: nyers

raw milk (unpasteurized): nyers tej

ready-made dishes: készételek

red: piros or *vörös*

red cabbage: vöröskáposzta

red onion: lilahagyma

red wine: vörös bor

restaurant: csárda, étkezde, étterem, kifozde, kisvendéglo, or *vendéglo*

Rhine riesling: Rajnai rizling

rhubarb: rebarbara

rice: rízs; see also *barna rízs* and *rizibizi*

rice pudding: tejberízs

risotto: rizottó

roast beef: marhasült

roasted: roston or *sült*

rooster: kakas

root: gyökér

rosé: rozé; see also *siller*

rosehip: csipkebogyó

rosemary: rozmaring

röszti potatoes: potatoes grated then fried or browned in the oven

roulade cake: bejgli; they're long and stuffed with walnuts (*diós bejgli*) or poppy seeds (*mákos bejgli*)

rudd: keszeg

Russian salad: francia saláta; called "French salad" in Hungary, it's a cold salad made of diced carrots, potatoes, corn, and peas, saturated in mayonnaise dressing

rye beer: rozs sör

rye bread: rozskenyér

S

saddle: *gerinc*

saddle of venison: *ozgerinc*

saffron: *sáfrány*

sage: *zsálya*

salad: *saláta*; see also *csalamádé*

salami: *szalámi*; see also *téli szalámi*, *Pick szalámi*

salmon: *lazac*

salsify: *feketegyökér*; also known as Spanish salsify

salt: *só*; *sós* (salty)

saltwater fish: *tengeri hal*

sandwich: *szendvics*

sardine: *szardínia*

sauce: *mártás*

sauerkraut: *savanyú káposzta* or *Vecsési káposzta*

sausage: *kolbász*

sautéed: *pirított*

savory: *csombor* or *borsikafu* (an herb related to the mint family)

savory: *sós*; as in not sweet

Savoy cabbage: *kelkáposzta*

scallion: *zöldhagyma*

scone: *pogácsa*; savory, buttery biscuits in a variety of flavors

scrambled eggs: *rántotta*

seasonal beer: *alkalmi sörkülönlegesség*

seed: *mag*

semi-dark beer: *félbarna sör*

semolina: *gríz* or *dara*

semolina dumplings: *daragaluska*

sesame seed: *szezámmag*

sheep's milk cheese: *juhsajt* or *juhtúró* (curd cheese)

shell beans: *tarkabab*

shiitake mushroom: *shiitake gomba*

shop: *bolt*; small grocery store

are also called *élelmiszer*, *csemege*, or *ABC*

shot (of liquor): *rövid*

silkweed honey: *selyemfuméz*; also known as milkweed honey

silver carp: *busa*

skillet: *serpenyo*; *serpenyos* refers to a skillet-cooked dish

slice: *szelet*

sloe: *kökény*; a wild European plum-like fruit that comes from the blackthorn

small: *apró*; see also *apróhús* and *aprópecsenye*

smoked: *füstölt*

smoked bacon: *füstölt szalonna*

smoked cheese: *füstöltsajt*

smoking section: *dohányzó*

snack: *falatok* (or bite)

snack bar: *ételbár* or *büfé*

snail: *csiga*; also refers to a round pastry with a swirl of poppy seeds or walnuts

soda water: *szódavíz*

sorrel: *sóska*

soufflé: *felfújt*

soup: *leves*

sour: *savanyú*

sour cherry: *meggy*

sour cream: *tejföl*

sparkling (water): *szénsavas* or *buborékos*

sparkling wine: *pezsgo*

specialties: *különlegességek*

spice: *fuszer*

spinach: *spenót* or *paraj*

sponge cake: *piskóta*

spring onion: *zöldhagyma*

sprouts: *csíra*

squash: *tök* or *sütotök*; see also *patisszon*

steamed: *párolt* (or braised) or *gozölt*

sterlet: kecsege; related to the sturgeon, and found in the Danube and Tisza rivers

stew: pörkölt; see also *lecsó, paprikás, pincepörkölt, sólet, tokány*

still (water): szénsavmentes

strawberry: eper or *szamóca* (wild)

strudel: rétes

stuffed: töltött

stuffed cabbage: töltött káposzta

stuffed kohlrabi: töltött karalábé

stuffed peppers: töltött paprika

sturgeon: tokhal

style: módra

sugar: cukor

sugar-free: cukormentes

sunflower honey: napraforgóméz

sunflower oil: napraforgóolaj

sunny-side-up eggs: tükörtojás

sweet: édes

sweetened: cukros

Swiss chard: mángold

sylvaner: zöldszilváni

syrup: szörp; concentrated fruit syrup to mix with soda or water

T

tail: farok

tap: csapolt

tap water: csapvíz

tarragon: tárkony

tart: lepény

tartar sauce: tartármártás; in Hungary it is mayonnaise with added sour cream

tea: tea

tenderloin: szuz

testicles: here

thyme: kakukkfu

tip: borravaló

toast: pirítós

Tokaji: wine from the Tokaj region; also *fordítás, furmint, máslás, puttony, Tokaji aszú, Tokaji aszú eszencia, Tokaji eszencia,* and *Tokaji szamorodni*

tomato: paradicsom

tongue: nyelv

trout: pisztráng

truffle: szarvasgomba

tuna: tonhal

turnip: fehérrépa

U

Unicum: bitter liquor made from more than forty herbs and spices, distilled, and aged in oak casks for six months

V

vanilla: vanília

veal cutlet: borjúborda

veal sweetbreads: borjúmirigy

vegetables: zöldség; see also *fozelék*

vegetarian: vegetáriánus

vinegar: ecet

W

walnut: dió

walnut bread: diós kenyér

walnut cake: diótorta

warm: meleg

water: víz

watermelon: görögdinnye

weekly specials: heti ajánlat; heti ajánlatunk is "our weekly specials"

wels: wels catfish (Silurus glanis); a scaleless fresh water catfish, also called European catfish. In Hungarian catfish is called *harcsa.*

Welschriesling: olaszrizling

("Italian riesling"); the most widely planted grape in Hungary

wheat: búza

wheat beer: búzasör

whey: savó

whey cheese: orda; similar to ricotta

whipped cream: habtejszín

white: fehér

white bread: fehér kenyér

white chocolate: fehércsokoládé

white radish: jégretek

white wine: fehér bor

whiting: sárga tokehal

whole: egész

wholewheat bread: búzakenyér

Wiener schnitzel: Bécsi szelet; traditionally breaded and fried veal cutlet, but in Hungary it's often made with pork

wild: erdei or *vad*

wild boar: vaddisznó

wild duck: vadkacsa

wild fowl: vadszárnyas

wild rabbit: vadnyúl

William's pear: vilmoskörte

wine: bor

winery: borászat

wine snacks: borkorcsolya

wine soup: borleves

wine spritzer: fröccs

wine tasting: borkóstoló

without: nélkül

Y

yeast: éleszto

yellow muscat: sárgamuskotály

yellow pea: sárgaborsó

yogurt: joghurt

young: fiatal

Z

zucchini: cukkini

zweigelt: a cross between the *kékfrankos* (portugieser) and St. Laurent grapes.

INDEX BY NEIGHBORHOOD

RESTAURANTS, CAFÉS, BARS and
MARKETS by NEIGHBORHOOD

....

INDEX BY NAME

RESTAURANTS, CAFÉS, BARS, SHOPS,
PASTRY SHOPS, *and* MARKETS

....

ACKNOWLEDGEMENTS

NO AMOUNT OF THANKS WOULD BE ENOUGH FOR GÁBOR BÁNFALVI, WHO HELPED WITH TRANSLATING, research, ideas, my terrible Hungarian spelling, and all around encouragement. Gábor and Anna also deserve a thank you for accompanying me to restaurants even when they didn't feel like it. I'm grateful to Charles, Louise, and Danny Chapman for so enthusiastically helping with the "research" when they were in town, for reading my manuscript, and for not complaining because I live so far away. Thanks to Katalin Bánfalvi for giving me the best education in Hungarian food and cooking that there is. Her dishes have been the standards to which I have compared all others. Thanks to Dr. Tamás Török for his help in the pre-book phase. Thanks to András Török for putting me in touch with Park Könyvkiadó, my Hungarian publisher, and for later commenting on my manuscript. Thanks to Erik D'Amato for offering comments on my manuscript and for writing the bar listings. Many thanks to Mari Roberts in London for editing my manuscript for the version of the book that was published in Hungary. A huge thank you to Park Könyvkiadó, especially Marianne Szalay and András Rochlitz, who agreed that a book like this was needed and made it happen. I am grateful also to all of the winemakers who spent time showing me around, letting me taste their wines, and patiently explaining all about winemaking in Hungary. I interviewed many people for this book, who deserve thanks, as well as everyone who supplied me with information, tips, and suggestions. Finally, I am very grateful to The Little Bookroom for bringing this book to an American audience, especially Angela Hederman, who shared my enthusiasm for this book right from the beginning, and Eugenia Bell, who did a fantastic job adapting the book to create this American version. George Konkoly-Thege's gorgeous photos brought the book to life. And the design team at Louise Fili Ltd, especially Louise Fili and Jessica Hische, made the book look more beautiful than I imagined it would.

ABOUT THE AUTHOR

....

Carolyn Bánfalvi, a native of Washington D.C., has lived in Hungary since 1999 except for a period during which she attended culinary school in the United States. She has contributed to various travel guides to Hungary, as well as to *Gastronomica, The Wall Street Journal, Four Seasons,* and other publications. Her web site, www.carolynbanfalvi.com, will post book updates and reviews of additional restaurants and shops.

ABOUT THE PHOTOGRAPHER

....

George Konkoly-Thege was born in Hungary. His photographs have appeared in many publications, including *Cosmopolitan,* Malév Airlines' *Horizon* magazine, and *Playboy.*